The Jews of Eastern Europe

Studies in Jewish Civilization

Volume 16

Proceedings of the
Sixteenth Annual Symposium
of the Klutznick Chair
in Jewish Civilization-
Harris Center for Judaic Studies

September 14-15, 2003

The Jews of Eastern Europe

Studies in Jewish Civilization
Volume 16

Editors

Leonard J. Greenspoon
Ronald A. Simkins
Brian J. Horowitz

The Klutznick Chair in Jewish Civilization-
Harris Center for Judaic Studies
The Kripke Center for the Study of Religion and Society

Creighton
UNIVERSITY PRESS

Distributed by the University of Nebraska Press

Copyright 2005, by Creighton University Press
All rights reserved

No part of this book may be reproduced or transmitted in any form or by any means, electronic or mechanical, including photocopying, recording, or any information storage and retrieval system, without permission in writing from the Publisher, except in the case of brief quotations embodied in critical articles and reviews.

Library of Congress Cataloguing-in-Publication Data

The Jews of Eastern Europe/Studies in Jewish Civilization, Volume 16/
    Leonard J. Greenspoon, Ronald A. Simkins, and Brian J. Horowitz, editors.
    p. c.m—(Studies in Jewish Civilization, ISSN 1070-8510; 16)
    "Proceedings of the Sixteenth Annual Symposium of the Klutznick Chair in Jewish Civilization-Harris Center for Judaic Studies, September 14-15, 2003"
    Half t.p.
    ISBN 1-881871-47-9 (paper)
    1. Jews—Europe, Eastern—Civilization—Congresses. 2. Jews—Europe, Eastern—Intellectual life—Congresses. 3. Jews—Europe, Eastern History—Congresses. I. Greenspoon, Leonard J. (Leonard Jay), Simkins, Ronald A., Horowitz, Brian J.
    II. Klutznick Chair in Jewish Civilization-Harris Center for Judaic Studies (16th : 2005: Creighton University)
    III. Series

EDITORIAL
Creighton University Press
2500 California Plaza
Omaha, NE 68178

MARKETING & DISTRIBUTION
University of Nebraska Press
1111 Lincoln Mall
Lincoln, NE 68588-0630

Printed in the United States of America

Dedicated to

Dorothy and Henry
Riekes

Table of Contents

Acknowledgments xi

Editors' Introduction xv

Contributors xix

The Russian Rabbinate under the Czars 1
Avraham Greenbaum

The Image of Russian Jews in Russian-Jewish
    Historiography, 1860-1914 9
Brian Horowitz

The Ashkenazic Gaze: Creating the Jewish Art Book 29
Seth L. Wolitz

Beyond "Jewish Luck": The Institutional Context
    of Early Russian-Jewish Art 61
Alina Orlov

Karl Emil Franzos and Bertha Papenheim's Portraits
    of the (Eastern European Jewish) Artist 79
Elizabeth Loentz

The Politics and Priorities of Jewish Music
    Publishing in Eastern Europe 101
Susan M. Filler

The Radical Assimilated: Hungarian "Urbanists"
    and Jewish Identity in the 1930s 117
Richard S. Esbenshade

The Transformation of Jewish Vilna, 1881-1939 143
Theodore R. Weeks

Russian Literature and Jewish Death 165
Gary Rosenshield

"…even beyond Pinsk": *Yizke Bikher* [Memorial Books]
 and Jewish Cultural Life in the Shtetl 175
Jeffrey Veidlinger

New Jews: David Bergelson and Birobidzhan 191
Harriet Murav

Nokhem-Meyer Shaykevitsch: Another Classic
 of Yiddish Theater 203
Andrey Bredstein

From "Little Man" to "Milkman": Does Jewish
 Art Reflect Jewish Life? 217
John D. Klier

The Politics of Philanthropy: Migration, Emigration,
 and the Transformation of Jewish Communal
 Governance in Bialystok, 1885-1939 233
Rebecca Kobrin

Enlightened Self-Interest: The Men and Women
 Who Opened Schools for Jewish Girls in
 Late Imperial Russia 265
Eliyana R. Adler

The Transformation of Zionist Religious Rhetoric
 as Seen Through Its Yiddish-Language Propaganda:
 The Case of Galicia 285
Joshua Shanes

Aristotle & the Ostjuden: Philosophical
     Thought Among the first Generations
     of Eastern European *Maskilim* 297
Abraham P. Socher

Searching for "Catholic Israel" in Focsani:
     Solomon Schechter's Childhood in Romania 313
Howard Lupovitch

Language Violence: Auschwitz Convent Controversy 329
Zev Garber

Coming into Their Inheritance: Jewish-American
     Autobiographers Encounter Eastern Europe 339
Steven Weiland

Previously Published Books in Series 352

Acknowledgments

Anyone who plans activities for/in the Jewish community—especially when universities are also involved—knows how difficult it is to schedule events in the fall. Thus, it is not surprising that the annual Klutznick-Harris Symposia and the annual conferences of the Midwest Jewish Studies Association (MJSA) have often been scheduled on the same dates. Through the cooperation and generosity of Dean Bell (Spertus College), then MJSA president, we arranged to have these two fall events—the Sixteenth annual Klutznick-Harris Symposium and the Fifteenth Annual Conference of the MJSA—at the same time, September 14 and 15, 2003, and in the same location, Omaha, Nebraska. On the whole, this collaboration turned out well, bringing together more than twice the number of scholars we usually have and providing several additional papers for this volume. I am deeply grateful for the extra efforts made by Dean and his MJSA colleagues.

The choice of topics—"The Jews of Eastern Europe"—was, as has often been the case with our Symposia, the result of the confluence of several factors. In the spring of 2002 and of 2003, I had spent several weeks as visiting lecturer at the Goldstein-Goren Center of Hebrew Studies of the University of Bucharest, Romania. This experience rekindled the interest in Eastern European Jews I had been nurturing because of my father's background: as a boy of thirteen, he came to the United States from Kreminitz, Ukraine, along with mother and older brother, arriving at Ellis Island on the ship Rotterdam, July 12, 1920. Because my father died when I was young, I never knew as much as I wanted to about him or his background. At the same time, members of the Nebraska Jewish community were expressing an interest in individuals and families who had emigrated from these lands. Moreover, a colleague, Brian Horowitz, then at the University of Nebraska-Lincoln, expressed his interest in working with us on this topic, which represents his field of expertise. Brian's service as an organizer of the Symposium and as a co-editor of this volume has been invaluable; I offer him sincere thanks.

In addition to providing a series of marvelous presentations on Sunday, September 14, and Monday, September 15, we were privileged to be able to sponsor two photographic exhibits. One, at the Lied Art Gallery at Creighton University, featured Laurence Salzmann's "The Last Jews of Radauti (Romania)." The other, at the gallery of the Omaha Jewish

Community Center, was titled "My Grandparents' Belarus: Journey Through a World Abandoned"; the photographs were by Joshua Eli Plaut. These two exhibits, which each ran for a month and thereby expanded considerably the audience for our Symposium, were made possible by the Dr. Bruce S. Bloom Memorial Endowment and the Creighton Department of Fine and Performing Arts. Special thanks also go to Ted Bohr, S.J., curator of Creighton's Lied Gallery, for his extraordinary efforts to make these exhibits the success they were.

The joint meetings of the Klutznick-Harris Symposium and the MJSA necessitated even greater precision in organizing than usual. We were fortunate to have the support of dedicated individuals at the Jewish Federation of Omaha and the Omaha Jewish Community Center, especially Guy Matalon, Mary Sue Grossman, Gary Katz, Pat Morgan, and Leigh Carlson. What would we do without each of you!

On the "academic" side, we continue to enjoy the full support and cooperation of the Norman & Bernice Harris Center for Judaic Studies at the University of Nebraska-Lincoln and its then director, Gerald Shapiro, and his support staff. At Creighton, Ronald A. Simkins, director of the Creighton Center (now Kripke Center) for the Study of Religion and Society, continued in his role as co-organizer of the Symposium, co-editor of this volume, and selfless purveyor of sagacity and sanity. Adrian Koesters, who worked with both the Chair and the Center, was responsible for insuring that everyone and everything were where they should be for the Symposium. As in previous years, she worked her magic to perfection. Illness led Adrian to resign between the time of the Symposium and the preparation of this volume. To her successor Fran Minear, we owe the success of this volume. Without her extraordinary dedication and sense of professionalism, this volume would not have been published. We also thank the ever helpful and patient staff at the University of Nebraska Press, who are responsible for the production and distribution of our volumes.

The best of intentions and careful planning are clearly prerequisites for the success of any significant endeavor. But they are not sufficient. We also depend on the kindness and generosity of a number of organizations and individuals, without whom the Symposium and this volume would not have come to fruition.

I offer my sincere thanks to the following for making the Symposium possible:

> Dorothy and Henry Riekes
> The Ike and Roz Friedman Foundation
> The Jewish Federation of Omaha
> The Creighton College of Arts and Sciences
> The Midwest Jewish Studies Association
> The Henry Monsky Lodge of B'nai B'rith
> The Dr. Bruce S. Bloom Memorial Endowment
> The Creighton Department of Fine and Performing Arts
> Soul Desires Book Store.

It is a pleasure to dedicate this volume to Dorothy and Henry Riekes, whose generous support has been a mainstay of our annual Symposia. Henry, who passed away last year, was a brother of Ethel Riekes Klutznick, Phil Klutznick's wife.

Leonard Greenspoon
Omaha, Nebraska
July 2005
ljgrn@creighton.edu

Editors' Introduction

The Sixteenth Annual Klutznick-Harris Symposium, devoted to the theme of Jews in Eastern Europe, harvested a rich crop of ripe papers (in Nebraska an agricultural metaphor feels appropriate), which we are sharing with the public. A number of acute problems in the field of Eastern European Jewish history are broached in the volume, and I will treat them individually below.

Several of the articles touch on the tension between the identity of Jews in their "host countries" and the single identity of all Eastern European Jewry, Ashkenaz. At a panel devoted to this theme at the 2003 conference of the Association of Jewish Studies, Israel Bartal concluded that at certain times Eastern European Jews orientated themselves toward a larger pan-Eastern European Jewish unity, while at other times they attempted to integrate, considering themselves citizens of their host countries. Ashkenaz was conceptually alive before Jews began to integrate into their host countries in the middle of the nineteenth century and became alive again with the rise of Jewish nationalism at the end of the nineteenth century. Nevertheless, in modern times Ashkenaz identity has had to compete with the ideology of integration, which offered economic and cultural benefits.

Avraham Greenbaum views the rabbinate in czarist Russia as pulled in two directions. "State rabbis" were supposed to fulfill bureaucratic functions; but, especially at the end of the nineteenth century, some of these rabbis took their leadership role seriously, desiring to enhance the political power of their Jewish communities. Unconsciously, they viewed themselves as Jewish representatives rather than advocates of Russification. Additionally, my own paper [**B.H.**] specifies how Russia's Jewish historians, imbued with the Haskalah ideology, perceived the masses as morally deficient and in need of change. Education and social conditioning were supposed to reform them. The rise of Jewish nationalism permitted Jewish historians to rethink their preconceptions and discover ideal qualities in the masses. Historians such as S. Dubnov, S. Ginzburg, and I. Zinberg were clearly influenced by the idea of "Ashkenaz."

The theme of integration occupies many of the scholars. Several authors describe the benefits of integration, especially in the making of visual art. In his article, "The Ashkenazic Gaze: Creating the Jewish Art

Book," **Seth L. Wolitz** points to the ways Chagall and El Lizitzky both contributed to and borrowed from the Russian avant-garde to create their unique amalgams. Wolitz, who was the Symposium keynoter, is the Gale Professor of Jewish Studies at the University of Texas at Austin. Three other scholars also deal with the Jewish arts and arrive at very similar conclusions: **Alina Orlov** examines the institutional contexts, especially those provided by S. An-Sky's expeditions and by the Jewish Society for the Encouragement of Jewish Arts, in which Jewish artists made the transition from traditional to modern cultural modes; **Elizabeth Loentz** provides finely nuanced portraits of two Eastern European Jewish artists, Karl Emil Franzos and Bertha Pappenheim; and **Susan M. Filler** painstakingly chronicles Jewish music publishing in central and Eastern Europe prior to the Holocaust. In contrast, **Richard S. Esbenshade** invokes the dangers of assimilation in his paper on Hungarian Jews of the 1930s, in which he describes the denial by many Jews of their heritage in a frantic, but unsuccessful effort to blend in.

The comparative approach to the study of Eastern European Jewry has an exemplary model in the work of **Theodore R. Weeks**, who studies the city of Vilna (also Wilno orVilnius) from the viewpoint of all its inhabitants--Poles, Lithuanians, and Jews in equal parts--while recalling that the city was ruled by Russians. **Gary Rosenshield** describes a vision of the Jew as "other," writing about the way Russian authors depicted Jewish death. Jews died loudly, gesticulating wildly, and without inner peace, in contrast presumably to the quiet and dignified death of Christians.

The two articles on the Soviet period treat how the denationalization of Jewish identity, apparently the goal of Soviet ideology, was never fully completed. **Jeffrey Veidlinger's** article on Yizkor Books shows how postwar memoirs clashed with Soviet ideology—World War II represented the victory of all the Soviet peoples; Yizkor Books served as a means to write Jewish national history in a country where it was dangerous to do so. **Harriet Murav** wonders whether Socialist Realism in its Yiddish rendition is really able to reduce Jewish content to zero or whether the language itself carries an element of Jewishness.

Murav's article, perhaps unexpectedly, dovetails with **Andrey Bredstein's** piece on N. Shaykevich, a mid-nineteenth century Yiddish author who was very famous in his time, but who received endless criticism later as an author of *shun* or worthless literature. Bredstein asks questions concerning literature's function, whether it is to provide aesthetic merit, to entertain, to teach about Judaism, or to give political instruction. **John D. Klier** runs along the same road, asking pertinently whether Jewish art reflects Jewish life. His conclusion, as might be expected, is intentionally inconclusive. Art, because it has access to the imagination, inevitably surpasses life, but in part does reflect reality. Moreover, life has an uncanny way of reproducing literature in real events. That insight raises new possibilities for understanding literature's role in Eastern European Jewish life.

Two scholars directly raise the theme of Jewish communal institutions. This theme, while seemingly new, throws light upon a time in the 1920s and 30s when there were communities with powerful Jewish institutions. Perhaps, the reappearance of this theme now reflects the new visibility of Jewish-American philanthropic and political committees. **Rebecca Kobrin** writes about Jewish communal self-governance in Bialystok (including the vital role played by émigrés who settled in New York City) in the decades preceding the Holocaust; **Eliyana R. Adler** depicts Jewish girls' schools, revisiting the debates that inspired select *maskilim* to devote their lives to modern education.

Many of the articles do not belong to any category, but appear thematically sui generis. **Joshua Shanes'** article about Zionist propaganda in Yiddish is especially interesting in this regard because elsewhere, outside of Galicia, Zionists, denouncing Yiddish, had long campaigned for Hebrew. **Abraham Socher** tackles issues centering on the nature of philosophical thought among early Eastern European maskilim, in particular the influence of Aristotle on Solomon Maimon. For **Howard Lupovitch**, the key to understanding scholar and educator Solomon Schechter's use of the term "Catholic Israel" lies in the city of Focsani, Romania, where Schechter grew up at the crossroads of Ashkenazic and Sephardic traditions. **Zev Garber** deals with a perennial issue—the importance of language and of symbols, especially when religious traditions and values are concerned—within the context of a contemporary controversy, involving the placement of a convent and other Christian institutions, at or near the site of the Auschwitz concentration camp. And **Steven Weiland** treats the Eastern European Jewish theme in several Jewish-American autobiographies, whose authors had uniformly intense, but distinctly different experiences when they returned to their own or their family's hometowns.

Fundamentally these papers raise the question of identity: Did Jews feel close to their brethren throughout Eastern Europe—that is, see themselves as Ashkenazim—or was their primary mode of self-identification as Jews of Russia, Poland, Romania, and Hungary? How did the Jewish and non-Jewish communities interact? How did Jews govern themselves? What kind of art did they create? What language choices did they make? The articles here answer these and many other questions, elucidating the dynamic world of Eastern European Jewry in the last three centuries.

Brian Horowitz
Tulane University
horowitz@tulane.edu

Contributors

Eliyana R. Adler

University of Maryland
Joseph and Rebecca Meyerhoff
Center for Jewish Studies
College Park, MD 20742
adler@umd.edu

Andrey Bredstein

University of Texas at Austin
Department of Germanic Studies
Austin, TX 78712
bredstein@mail.utexas.edu

Richard S. Esbenshade

University of California, Santa Cruz
rikesben@ucsc.edu

Susan M. Filler

Chicago, IL
sfiller2@juno.com

Zev Garber

Los Angeles Valley College
Program in Jewish Studies
Valley Glen, CA 91401-4096
zevgarber@juno.com

Avraham Greenbaum

Hebrew University of Jerusalem
Dinur Center for the Study
of Jewish History
Givat Ram 91904 ISRAEL
agreenbaum@bezeqint.net

Brian Horowitz

Tulane University
Jewish Studies
New Orleans, LA 70118
bhorowtiz@tulane.edu

John D. Klier   University College London
                                 London ENGLAND
                                 j.klier@ucl.ac.uk

Rebecca Kobrin   New York University
                                 Skirball Department of Hebraic and
                                 Judaic Studies
                                 New York, NY 10012-1075
                                 rkobrin@aya.yale.edu

Elizabeth Loentz   University of Illinois at Chicago
                                 Department of Germanic Studies
                                 Chicago, IL 60607-7115
                                 loentz@uic.edu

Howard Lupovitch   Colby College
                                 History Department
                                 Waterville, ME 04901
                                 h_lupovi@colby.edu

Harriet Murav   Univ. of Illinois at Champaign-Urbana
                                 Urbana, IL 61801
                                 hlmurav@uiuc.edu

Alina Orlov   San Diego State University
                                 Department of History
                                 Department of European Studies
                                 San Diego, CA 92108
                                 alinaorlov@hotmail.com

Gary Rosenshield   Univ. of Wisconsin-Madison
                                 Department of Slavic Languages
                                 Madison, WI 53706
                                 grosen@slavic.wisc.edu

Abraham P. Socher	Oberlin College Department of Religion & Program in Jewish Studies Oberlin, OH 44074 Abe.Socher@oberlin.edu
Joshua Shanes	Spertus Institute of Jewish Studies Chicago, IL 60605 jmshanes@hotmail.com
Jeffrey Veidlinger	Indiana University Department of History Bloomington, IN 47405 jveidlin@indiana.edu
Theodore R. Weeks	Southern Illinois University Department of History Carbondale, IL 62901-4519 tadeusz@siu.edu
Steven Weiland	Michigan State University College of Education East Lansing, MI 48824-1044 weiland@pilot.msu.edu
Seth L. Wolitz	University of Texas at Austin Department of French and Italian Austin, TX 78712 slwolitz@earthlink.net

The Jews of Eastern Europe

Studies in Jewish Civilization
Volume 16

Proceedings of the
Sixteenth Annual Symposium
of the Klutznick Chair
in Jewish Civilization-
Harris Center for Judaic Studies

September 14-15, 2003

The Russian Rabbinate under the Czars

Avraham Greenbaum

The Russian rabbinate in the second quarter of the nineteenth century became split between the official or crown rabbi—in Russian usually called *kazennyi ravvin*—and the so-called spiritual rabbi [*dukhovnyi ravvin* in Russian]. In Yiddish the official rabbi was usually referred to by the German term *rabiner* as distinct from *rov*. This dual rabbinate was the result of the Czarist government's insistence that rabbis, in order to fulfill their role properly, had to be literate in a modern language; in the original decree it was Russian, Polish, or German.[1] At that time most of the Jewish public looked at a person with a modern education as a likely heretic and about the least likely candidate for a rabbinical position. As a result, the crown rabbi was frequently no more than a communal clerk, whose main duty was to record births, deaths, and marriages, while the spiritual rabbi, employed by the local *kehila* [religious community] under various guises, fulfilled the rabbi's traditional functions.

Crown rabbis were in existence in some towns in the 1820s, according to the 1828 book *Te'udah be-Yisrael* [Custom of Israel] by the pioneer of the *Haskalah* [Jewish enlightenment movement], Isaac Baer Levinsohn (1788-1860).[2] In 1835, the old regulation was reconfirmed by Czar Nicolas I[3] and was apparently henceforth much more rigidly enforced, so that the number of crown rabbis grew apace. Many attempts were made over the years by Jews of various political persuasions to abolish the dual rabbinate,[4] but they all failed, and the system lasted until the nascent Communist government, which had as little use for one type of rabbi as for the other, separated religion and state in 1918.

The crown rabbi, then, needed no training beyond literacy in Russian, necessary both for satisfying government requirements and maintaining the metrical books. It seems that as time went on the doctor's degree, no longer rare among Jews by the end of the nineteenth century, was a requirement in practice,[5] in line with what was happening in neighboring Germany. One would think that some Jewish learning was necessary, but it was not; we find complaints that persons without elementary Hebrew literacy and not religiously observant were able to obtain positions.⁶

We should not assume, however, that all Russian crown rabbis were nonentities in search of a livelihood. Some Hebrew and Yiddish writers obtained such positions, including the outstanding Yiddish writer Sholem Aleikhem.⁷ More influential was the Hebrew-Yiddish writer and journalist Judah Loeb Kantor (1849-1915), who in the later part of his life served as crown rabbi in the important communities of Vilna and Riga.⁸ In the twentieth century, some leading Zionists became rabbis, probably in response to the demand of the founder of Zionism, Theodor Herzl, to "conquer the communities." One such was the crown rabbi of Vitebsk, Zvi Bruk.⁹ In Ekaterinoslav (today Dnepropetrovsk) the rabbinate was held for a time by the Zionist politician and journalist Shmarya Levin (1867-1935).¹⁰ An outstanding crown rabbi who was also an active Zionist was the Moscow rabbi Jacob Mazeh (1859-1924), whose prestige and Jewish knowledge made people forget that he was not ordained.¹¹ Some spiritual rabbis—not many—with at least a minimal knowledge of Russian managed to get appointed as crown rabbis. In Poland, which operated under a different set of laws, the *tsenz* [government license] was easier to obtain and the number of crown rabbis with a traditional Talmudic education correspondingly larger. At the 1910 rabbinical conference, the Czarist government was urged by a participant to extend the Polish model to Russia.¹²

The crown rabbinate and the attending government activity show how closely the authorities involved themselves in Jewish affairs. They were guided by the conviction that the Jews were a people corrupted by false doctrines and in need of moral reform, which rabbis of a new type were expected to give. To this end, the government founded rabbinical seminaries and set up a rabbinical commission that was supposed to have regular meetings. The rabbinical seminaries, which were opened in Vilna and Zhitomir, were despised by the people, with the exception of a small group of Haskalah adherents; their equally despised graduates had great difficulty getting positions even as crown rabbis. Having failed of their purpose, the rabbinical seminaries were closed in 1873.¹³

The rabbinical commission was slightly more successful, especially so since there was some participation by Orthodox rabbis. It functioned as both a supervising body and an appeals court against decision by local rabbis, especially in the area of marriage and divorce. The meetings of the rabbinical commission, which were few and irregular, have recently been documented by ChaeRan Freeze, who sees the institution as an unsuccessful attempt to imitate the French *consistoire* system of supervising religious life. The Czarist regime was by its nature too centralistic to delegate the necessary amount of authority.[14]

After the government allowed freedom of association in 1905, we find a number of rabbinical conferences. Some government supervision existed, but a conference of rabbis could not readily be dominated by outside forces. It gave the spiritual leaders a chance to come out of hiding, so to speak, and to have a say. They clashed with the more reform-minded elements, but by the time of the last conference, which took place in the capital in 1910,[15] the regime had changed course and supported anything that gave some promise of stemming the revolutionary tide, a tide that had engulfed much of Jewish youth. This meant supporting the much-derided *heder* [elementary religious school][16] and the yeshiva rather than the road to the gymnasium and the university. The government now openly supported the spiritual rabbis, though it did not abolish the crown rabbinate, a step for which even the Orthodox-dominated meeting did not dare to ask. The fact that the concurrent session of the rabbinical commission was chaired by Judah Leib Zirelson, the spiritual and crown rabbi of Kishinev,[17] was probably considered a sign of things to come, but the slow working of the bureaucracy and the outbreak of war in 1914 left things pretty much as they were until the Czarist regime and all it stood for came to an end in 1917.

One of the leading spiritual rabbis in Russia in the nineteenth century, and an outstanding rabbinic scholar, was Rabbi Isaac Elhanan Spektor of Kovno (1817-1896). In a letter from the year 1889 to a communal leader residing in the capital, Spektor asked Jews who had the ear of the authorities to persuade the government that a rabbi had to know what were permitted and forbidden foods, forbidden labors on Sabbaths and holidays, the rules of unleavened bread on Passover, the *sukkah* and the "four species" on the Sukkot holiday, laws of marriage and divorce, rules of proper business behavior, and much more. These would not be taught in any rabbinical seminary.[18] We should add that rabbis in Eastern Europe and many of their descendants objected even to Orthodox seminaries, since, according to their point of view, Torah knowledge is without limit and cannot be contained in a prescribed course of study.

Among other prominent spiritual rabbis who functioned as communal rabbis were Joseph Baer Soloveichik (1820-1892), founder of a rabbinic dynasty and during the last period of his life rabbi in Brest-Litovsk; his son and successor Hayim Soloveichik (1853-1918), a leading participant at the 1910 conferences, who was said to have enjoyed great popularity; David Tebele Katzenelenbogen (1847?-1930), rabbi in Suvalk and from 1907 in St. Petersburg-Leningrad, whose influence lasted until his death in the Soviet period; Meir Simhah Katz (Kagan) of Dvinsk (1843-1926), who became Latvia's outstanding rabbi; and a number of others whose names and cities are noted in the old Russian-Jewish encyclopedia.[19]

The age-old communal rabbinate, for which the crown rabbinate was a nuisance rather than a competitor, faced competition from other quarters as the nineteenth century progressed. In the first place, there were rabbinic scholars without rabbinic posts, whose reputation rested on their learning and writing. One such was Hayim Ozer Grodzenski of Vilna (1863-1940), who never had more than a minor post in a city where for various reasons no communal rabbi had been appointed for many years. Another category consisted of the heads of those yeshivot that in the nineteenth century gained a nationwide reputation and drew thousands of boys and young men who otherwise might have studied with their local rabbis. Among the most notable were Naphtali Zevi Judah Berlin of Volozhin (1817-1893), Eliezer Gordon of Telz (1841-1910), and Nathan Zevi Finkel of Slobodka (1849-1927).[20]

But the greatest competitor to the old-style rabbi was the charismatic Chasidic leader, or rebbe. It is generally thought that the relative isolation of the rabbi, and his being uninvolved in the day-to-day concerns of his community's members, led to the quick spread of the Chasidic movement. It began around 1740, before the divisions of Poland brought the Jews into the Russian empire, but extended its influence until it became dominant in Poland and in the Russian empire's Southern provinces. But even in the North, in White Russia and Lithuania, Chasidim formed a sizable minority.

The Chasidic-dominated communities did have rabbis; only rarely was the office of rabbi and rebbe combined in one person. But the spiritual life of the Chasid revolved around the rebbe, and some rebbes had a huge following. The most influential rebbe at the beginning of the twentieth century was the head of the Lubavich (Habad) movement, Shalom Dov Ber Schneersohn (1860-1920). He was a leading figure at the 1910 conferences, even though he was unable to speak Russian and had to communicate through an interpreter.[21]

A final point we should discuss is the relationship on the local level between the crown and spiritual rabbis. It is clear that the crown rabbi, usually ignorant at least of the fine points of Jewish law, was dependent, especially in problematic marital situations, on the local experts: the old-style rabbi and the *dayanim* [rabbinical court judges]. From the cases adduced in Freeze's book the picture is mixed—sometimes there was cooperation and sometimes antagonism.[22] But much more research is needed before a clearer picture emerges.

The Russian rabbinate in the period we are dealing with was beset by many problems, the most notable of which were the efforts of the regime to force a secularly educated rabbinate on its Jewish subjects as part of its drive to modernize them. These efforts proved unsuccessful in the long run after doing much damage. But the changes that affected Jewish society caused many who had no use for the crown rabbinate to look for alternatives to the traditional type of communal rabbi.

NOTES

[1] The requirement is first found in the règlement of 1804—the initial attempt to regulate the status of Russia's newly acquired Jews—with a totally unenforceable target date of 1812. See Azriel Shohat, *The Crown Rabbinate in Russia* (Hebrew, with English summary; Haifa: The University of Haifa, 1975), 149 n. 3.

[2] I. B. Levinsohn, *Te'udah be-Yisrael* (Vilna, 1828), as cited by Shohat, *Crown Rabbinate*, 9. Levinsohn has contempt for both types of rabbis and speaks of "mounting the lame on the blind."

[3] Shohat, *Crown Rabbinate*, and see Michael Stanislawski, *Tsar Nicholas II and the Jews* (Philadelphia: The Jewish Publication Society of America, 1983), 134.

[4] They have been extensively documented in Shohat's work. A brief English summary can be found in ChaeRan Y. Freeze, *Jewish Marriage and Divorce in Imperial Russia* (Hanover: University Press of New England for Brandeis University Press, 2002), 256-59. At the moment a student at the University of Pennsylvania, Tamar Kaplan Appel, is writing a doctoral dissertation on the crown rabbis from 1905 to 1917. I thank Mrs. Appel for sharing some information with me.

[5] So it seems from a report in the Hebrew newspaper *Hamelits*, April 18, 1901, on the election of Zvi Hirsh Bruk as crown rabbi of Vitebsk, cited in the Vitebsk memorial volume: Baruch Karu, ed., *Vitebsk* (Tel Aviv: Association of former

Vitebsk Area Residents in Israel, 1957), 24. On Bruk, active in the Zionist movement, see also ibid., 109-12, and *Evreiskaia entsiklopediia* (St. Petersburg: Brokgaus-Efron, 1908-1913), 5:38.

[6] This is a frequent complaint in the literature; see, for example, Karu, *Vitebsk*, 24. Vladimir Temkin, the crown rabbi of Elizavetgrad in 1910, is described in the memoirs of a communal leader as unable to read Hebrew; see Henry Sliozberg, *Dela minuvshikh dnei* (Paris: Izd. Komiteta po chestvovanie 70-ti letnogo iubeileia G. B. Sliozberga, 1933-1934), 3:271.

[7] Charles A. Madison, *Yiddish Literature: Its Scope and Major Writers* (New York: Schocken Books, 1971), 63. Sholem Aleichem, then only 20 years old, was a crown rabbi in Lubni, Poltava province, from 1880 to 1883.

[8] *Leksikon fun der nayer Yidisher literatur* (New York: Congress for Jewish Culture, 1956-1981), 8:70-71.

[9] See above, note 4. Appel wrote me that her sample to date does not permit a conclusion as to whether the majority of crown rabbis in the new century were Zionists. But all those I found in the larger cities were.

[10] Levin was also an outstanding memoirist, and his voluminous memoirs appeared in several languages including English. An abridged edition appeared under the title: *Forward from Exile* (Philadelphia: Jewish Publication Society of America, 1967).

[11] Mazeh also left extensive memoirs (*Zikhronot* [Tel Aviv: Yalkut, 1936],) but in English there seems to be little on him besides the entry in *Encyclopedia Judaica*.

[12] Sliozberg, *Dela*, 265.

[13] Shohat, *Crown Rabbinate*, 38; Freeze, *Jewish Marriage*, 103.

[14] Ibid., 86.

[15] The most extensive description of the two concurrent 1910 meetings is by a participant, Shimshon Dov Yerushalmi (Yerusalimski), "Commissions and Conferences of Rabbis in Russia" [Hebrew], *Heavar* 3 (1955):86-94. The above-mentioned communal leader Sliozberg, one of the few representatives of the non-Orthodox laity, described them in his memoirs with character sketches of some participants: *Dela*, 3:265-80.

[16] See, for example, Isaac Levitats, *The Jewish Community in Russia, 1844-1917* (Jerusalem: Posner, 1981), 120-21; and especially the entry "*kheder*" in *Evreiskaia entsiklopediia*, 15:586-89. On the change in official attitudes towards traditional Judaism, see Freeze, *Jewish Marriage*, 255.

[17] Zirelson (1860-1941) became one of the most important rabbis of interwar Romania after Kishinev changed hands.

[18] Jacob Lipschitz, *Zikhron Yaakov* [The Memorial of Jacob], (Israel: n. p., 1968),

3:139-42. Some of Spektor's religious decisions are noted by Freeze, *Jewish Marriage* (see index). Spektor as a *posek* [decider of religious questions] tended toward leniency. In English, see Ephraim Shimoff, *Rabbi Isaac Elchanan Spektor: Life and Letters* (Jerusalem: Sura, 1961).

[19] *Evreiskaia entsiklopediia*, 13:231-33. On Hayim Soloveichik, see also Sliozberg, *Dela*, 3:270; on Katzenelenbogen, the present writer's bio-bibliographical lexicon *Rabbis of the Soviet Union during the Interwar Period, 1917-1939* [Hebrew] (Jerusalem: Centre for Research and Documentation of East European Jewry, 1994), 51-52.

[20] A pioneering study of the three yeshivot is Shaul Stampfer, *The Lithuanian Yeshiva* [Hebrew] (Jerusalem: The Zalman Shazar Center for Jewish History, 1995). Stampfer informs me that an English edition is in the offing.

[21] Sliozberg, *Dela*, 3:270. There is a considerable literature on Chasidism in general and Lubavich in particular.

[22] Freeze, *Jewish Marriage*, 106-07.

The Image of Russian Jews in Russian-Jewish Historiography, 1860-1914

Brian Horowitz

At the Russian government's Rabbinical Commission of 1861, so-called "enlightened" Jews advocated prohibiting the publication of Yiddish books in Russia.[1] Although the Russian official who himself bore the ill-deserved title, Minister of Enlightenment, rejected this proposition, maintaining that such a "forced prohibition...would be a futile and even harmful measure," the suggestion itself deserves examination. The fact, surprising to us today, is that during the 1860s the modern emancipated Jewish intelligentsia held Yiddish in absolute contempt. They considered the "jargon," as they called Yiddish, a distorted dialect of German and blamed it for the backwardness and isolation of the Jewish people. Nearly without exception, the vast majority of these intellectuals placed their hopes in Russian as the means for realizing the modernization and integration of the Jews. If the Jews were to become fully integrated citizens of the Russian Empire, it behooved them to adopt and use the national language.

Forty-seven years later, at the Czernowitz Language Conference of 1908, the majority of participants recognized Yiddish as a national language of the Jewish people. Although Czernowitz symbolizes a realignment of attitudes, official recognition was really the last step in acknowledging broader changes in perspective that had formed much earlier. At Czernowitz the Jewish intelligentsia recorded its unqualified respect for the speakers of Yiddish, the Jewish people.

What had happened in the years from 1861 to World War I that caused the Jewish intelligentsia to change so drastically its view of the Jewish masses? Historians point to four main developments. First, the pogroms of 1881-82 evoked widespread sympathy among the intelligentsia for its victims. Second, the repressive May laws of 1882, denying the Jews access to Russian society, led to a push toward Jewish "self-sufficiency." Third, the popularity of the Bund in the 1890s showed that the Jewish masses could be a major political force; and fourth, the creative awakening of Yiddish literature won over the intelligentsia's sympathies for the "language of the masses."

I do not deny the importance of these factors. Each contributed to the identification of the Jewish intelligentsia with the Jewish people and to the national awakening of Russia's Jews. Nevertheless, I contend that a positive image of the Jewish people had to be developed; the intelligentsia had to be educated, encouraged to shed old axioms. Significantly, at least until the late 1880s, secular Jewish intellectuals found it hard to surrender the view that the Jewish people were on a lower cultural level than other Western peoples and that their language, Yiddish, reflected this lower stage of development. Although one could successfully trace the development of attitudes toward the Jewish people by examining Yiddish or Hebrew literature or by studying the process of "nationalization" in political life, in this paper I fix my attention primarily on Jewish historians and issues of Jewish historiography.

Russian-Jewish historiography was inextricably connected with and followed the zigzags of the government's policies. This is true not only because the experiences of the individual historians became embodied in their work, but more importantly because Jewish historians purposely hitched up their historical views to political concerns.[2] In fact, without exception, Jewish historians played important roles in the struggle for Jewish emancipation in a country that permitted no legal political parties until after 1905. In this regard, it is important to recognize that the best historians of Russia had no training in history: Mikhail Morgulis and Ilya Orshanskii were trained as lawyers, and Semyon Dubnov and Iulii Gessen had no university training at all. Employed as journalists, editors, lawyers, and teachers, Russian-Jewish historians never adopted a purely objective, academic approach similar to the one we recognize in our own universities. Rather, the events of Jewish political life influenced to an acute degree the evolution of Russian-Jewish historiography.

One may view the gradual improvement in the attitude of the intelligentsia toward the Jewish masses beginning from the 1860s until the late 1890s, when it finally became unambiguously positive. During the first stage in the 1860s, the intelligentsia felt close to the government and distant from its own people, while in the final stage the reverse was true. In between the two poles, however, we find various degrees of identification and repulsion that do not reflect a smooth development, but show leaps and skids, progress and regress in viewpoint.

I begin in 1860 not because historical writing started at that time—Shmuel Feiner has done a superb job showing us the kind of historical genres that *maskilim* [enlightened Jews] cultivated before 1860—but because, with the crowning of Alexander II and the implementation of his reforms, the Haskalah [Jewish Enlightenment movement] entered a completely new phase.[3] The primary language of the Jewish intelligentsia switched to Russian, although Hebrew continued to be written. The intelligentsia became a social class with a credible size, as opposed to mere potential. Jewish newspapers in Russian and soon after in Hebrew and Yiddish were issued, the Society for the Promotion of Enlightenment among the Jews of Russia was opened in 1863 in St. Petersburg, and a branch was opened in Odessa in 1867. This organization, especially the Odessa branch, was devoted to disseminating secular literature in Russian, and one of its central goals was to cultivate a historical literature about Jews in Russia.[4]

Historical works in the 1860s, the enlighteners hoped, would be of a higher standard than previously. In the historical writings of the previous generation authors did not care to ascertain whether their sources were historically truthful. Instead, the most colorful and exotic sources were included. The authors chose far away subjects and themes, such as the ancient world or the heroes of the Bible for their topics.[5] They avoided studying the Jews of Russia or touching upon times closer to their own.

The attitude toward Jews of their own time was unabashedly negative. Lev Levanda's article, "A Few Words about the Jews of the Western Territories of Russia," which appeared in the first issue of the Russian-Jewish newspaper, *Rassvet*, in 1860, can serve as a typical example.[6] Levanda writes:

> One has to see for oneself, one has to enter a crowded, half-dilapidated hut, which always houses no less than three families, which compete among themselves for the prize of poverty. One has to see how the half-naked children of all three families crowd around the unheated oven and fight over a piece of animal skin, which each child wants to wrap around himself to warm his body, freezing from the cold. One has to be there when the father of one family arrives at the door with a loaf of bread and his children jump off the oven with shouts of joy, singing and clapping their hands together. The children of the other families, whose fathers have not brought food, turn away their eyes so as not to see their

comrades' happiness, which was not to be theirs.[7]

Although Levanda's searing description of poor Jews may have been elicited by a scene the author witnessed, it also displays a conventional perception. Jewish intelligentsia coopted the views of Russian government officials: the Jewish masses were religious fanatics and woefully ignorant of Western knowledge. They needed to become transformed, educated, secularized, and civilized.

The Jewish intellectuals deemed the transformation of the Jews a worthy aim, since the acquisition of civil rights hinged on this change. According to the wisdom of the time, the government was supposedly prepared to lighten Jewish liabilities if Jews would transform themselves, leave their isolation, and acquire Western knowledge, including knowledge of the Russian language. Since changing the masses was their goal, when the intelligentsia did describe the Jewish people, they criticized them, displayed their flaws, pointing out what qualities Jews should strive to acquire. Admittedly, sometimes the writers of newspapers like *Rassvet* or *Sion* praised a Jewish institution or the longevity of the religion, but the object of appreciation was always something abstract—an institution or concept (the people's will)—and not the masses living then.[8] The actual Jews living in Russia were in need of radical transformation.

When it started to become clear during the 1870s that the transformation of the Jews would not necessarily lead to an expansion of rights, Jewish historians began to examine the causes for the breakdown of the "emancipation contract." Particularly at this time, "in their reconstruction of the Russian-Jewish past, their strategies for emancipation in the future, and their search for self-definition as Jews in post-Reform Russia, educated Jewish elites relied to a remarkable degree on juridical categories and modes of thought," correctly observes Benjamin Nathans.[9] Not surprisingly, having lost faith in the political efficacy of self-criticism, Jewish historians began to notice much that was positive about the Jews themselves.[10]

A more positive image of the Russian Jew occurred in the 1870s in large part as a result of the Odessa pogroms of 1871.[11] Even worse than the physical destruction of the city was the psychological crisis experienced by Odessa's Jewish intellectuals. Although, due to censorship restrictions, the Odessa intellectuals were unable immediately to speak about the pogrom in the Jewish newspaper *Den'*, the violence against Jews caused a crisis of belief. The two editors of *Den'*, Morgulis and Orshanskii, had fought for over a decade to convince their brethren to integrate, to trust the non-Jew. While they had always understood that such violence was possible in the countryside, where the Jews had not modernized, they were certain it could not happen in Odessa, where Jews were the most progressive in all Russia. Their experience forced them to re-examine the premises upon which their views were constructed.

In articles collected in the volume *Questions of Jewish Life* [*Voprosy evreiskoi zhizni*] (1886), Morgulis departed from the previous ideas that Jews themselves were guilty of their fate. Choosing to focus on the government-sponsored schools established in the 1840s—because they served as the linchpin in the government's rhetoric that emancipation was impossible, since Jews were incapable of being educated—Morgulis argued that it was not the Jews but the schools themselves that were the problem. Morgulis demonstrated the coercive aspect of the schools, arguing that Jewish communities were forced to pay for them, although parents tended to boycott the schools. Furthermore, while the textbooks—translations into German of Jewish religious texts—never found use in the classroom, they must have been costly for the destitute Jewish communities of the time (admittedly, Morgulis's estimation of 200,000 rubles has never been independently verified).[12]

Margulis pointed out that, although intellectuals were deeply critical of the traditional *heder*, government-sponsored Jewish schools had not enjoyed any popularity among the Jewish people. Instead of reiterating the viewpoint that the people kept clear of the schools because they feared their children would be pressured to convert to Christianity, Morgulis persuasively argued that the schools simply did not meet the needs of the community.[13] In particular, the *heder* provided cheap child-care. Children arrived at the *heder* early and stayed until late in the evening, thereby allowing the mother, often the sole bread-winner in the family, to spend her days in her shop or market stall, while the father was out studying Talmud. By contrast, the schools let the pupils out in the early afternoon. Furthermore, the schools were very costly, and often the education received there offended the parents' religious principles.[14]

Instead of viewing Jews as ignorant and regressive, Morgulis held that they understood their own interests. If they refused to modernize, it was not because they were backward, but because they had more to gain by remaining unchanged. What was needed, Morgulis believed, was to tailor knowledge to real conditions in order to make it useful and beneficial.

Margulis' assertions struck a blow at the Haskalah ideology because, instead of seeing the people as benighted, he levied his criticisms at the government and Jewish intelligentsia, which had arrogantly supported the modern schools without considering the needs and desires of the people. But Morgulis was himself still an enlightener. He criticized the way the Jews were asked to change, but not the idea of change itself. In articles written at the same time, Morgulis called for Jews "to engage in productive work, [to have] the chance to move from those places where their hands are inactive and move to those places where there is a pressing need for them."[15] By productive work, Margulis understood farming and crafts.

From his side, Orshanskii also re-examined the Jewish question and found the Jews innocent of misconduct.[16] The guilty party every time was the government, which used the institutions of the state, its police, church, and legal statutes to keep Jews from successfully integrating. For example, in his study, "Russian Legislation on the Jews" [*Russkoe zakonodatel'stvo o evreiakh*], Orshanskii discovered that, instead of applying any consistent principles in treating Jews, Russian lawmakers over many decades had created a confusing labyrinth of decrees, many of which were inspired by medieval attitudes of intolerance or were themselves self-contradictory.[17] What was needed, he declared, was a cleansing and simplification of the legal code: a cleansing to remove those pre-modern laws that offered negative precedents for future legislation and a simplification to remove all the contradictions and repetitions. With a streamlined set of laws freed of discriminatory legislation against the Jews, there would be no reason to have any special regulation for Jews at all.

In his political program, Orshanskii argued that discrimination interfered with the goal of integration and Russification.[18] If the government wanted the Jews to become Russian citizens and contribute to the wellbeing of the state, it needed to expand their rights and make them equal to non-Jews. Because the government concentrated on "negative" legislation that prohibited the Jews from activities, rather than positive laws that encouraged certain actions, Russification "is purely mechanical, external, and not only does not coincide with the interests and conditions of life of both the Christian and Jewish populations, but is often antagonistic to them. Russification, therefore, can lead to results that are directly opposed to those that they want to achieve."[19]

Aware that his indictment of the state only showed the Jew as victim, Orshanskii portrayed Jews as a sympathetic people who express their misfortune creatively. In his article, "Folksongs of the Russian Jews" [*Prostonorodnye pesni russkikh evreev*], Orshanskii recognized that simple Jews had their own unique culture, admittedly unknown to non-Jews: "A Christian knows [the Jew] only as the exploitative trader, the money lender, tavern keeper; is it astounding that he has a rotten view of the Jew?"[20] According to Orshanskii, the songs of any people reflect their culture, way of life, and worldview, and the Jews are no exception. Foremost, the songs of Russia's Jews mirror their unhappy reality. Jews sing of their sadness, poverty, and misery, of the conditions particular to their society—abandoned wives left by men who have emigrated, recruitment into the czar's army, and conflicts between the rich and poor.[21]

Orshanskii shaped a positive image of the Jews by adding new categories to the former ideas of religious fanaticism and wretched poverty. He sketched a human portrait of the Jews that entirely contradicted the anti-Semitic images printed in the Russian press. Nevertheless, as an intellectual in tune with Russian trends of Populism and neo-Romanticism, Orshanskii felt that Russian and Ukrainian peasants were closer to nature and in this sense superior. He criticized the Jews' lack of a feeling for nature, attributing this flaw to their largely urban habitat, and characterized their folk culture as subjective rather than objective, idealistic rather than realistic.[22]

It is revealing that neither Orshanskii nor Morgulis positively regarded Yiddish. They refused to relinquish their belief that Russian was the key to a positive future and the sooner the people accepted it as their native language the better. In *Den'* Morgulis wrote a series of articles condemning the position of Judah Leib Gordon that Hebrew could serve the Jews as a means of Enlightenment.[23] The negative attitude toward Yiddish was so obvious that it did not even warrant such a response, although Morgulis did admit that if any language besides Russian should be used pragmatically, Yiddish at least was understood by all of Russia's Jews. But he refused to acknowledge that Yiddish could offer a positive means of bringing enlightenment to Russia's Jews.

Noting Orshanskii and Morgulis' ambivalence toward the Jewish masses, one can conclude that the 1870s were not as distant from the 1860s as one might think. While defending Jews against unfair accusations, they nevertheless encouraged their transformation into modern citizens. Just as *maskilim* before them, Orshanskii and Morgulis were contradictory. They were unable to find a way to reconcile their feelings of profound pride in the Jewish heritage and undiminished demands for change.

Dominating the next generation, Semyon Dubnov rejected the juridical approach of the 1870s, preferring at least in the first period of his work an approach that applied ideal concepts—reason, freedom, and universalism—to the historical experience of the Jews. In his works Dubnov focused his attention on the people as the central agent of history. In his later writings the history of the Jewish people acquired a messianic dimension. The study of history enabled the Jews to take justifiable pride in their remarkable survival despite centuries of tribulations and persecution, But it was more than that. Dubnov believed the Jewish people attained a collective immortality through history. These ideas, however, came into play at the start of the 1890s. During the 1880s, Dubnov's image of the Jewish people contained the ambivalence of his predecessors. He was still reluctant to question the earlier practice of measuring Jewish against Western culture and finding the Jews wanting.[24]

For example, in his article on Sabbatai Zvi, published just after the pogroms of 1882, Dubnov compares Zvi with his contemporary, Spinoza, writing: "The Jewish people stood at a crossroads. The Amsterdam philosopher called them to enlightenment, showed them the glowing dawn of a new life, new civilization. The kabbalist from Smyrna tempted them toward ignorance and darkness, the thick gloom of the past....A Judaism reborn cursed the former and followed the latter. It was a decisive, fatal step."[25] Dubnov's desire for the Jewish people to follow Spinoza reflects his commitment to progress, freedom, and rationality, ideals he imbibed from the idols of his youth, John Stewart Mill, Hippolyte Taine, and Ernest Renan.

Refusing to surrender his ideals, Dubnov also rejected writing a history of ideas; that was exactly what he objected to in Heinrich Graetz's work, the domination of the Jewish idea over the Jewish people.[26] Dubnov's solution was to valorize the Jewish people by discovering what he called the "universal in the particular," i.e., he portrayed the Jews' endless quest for survival as a revelation of universal virtues. By universal, Dubnov understood the ideals of European humanism.

In his long article of 1888, "The Emergence of Chasidism" [*Vosniknovenie Khasidizma*], the people become the undisputed hero of Jewish history. Instead of debunking the myth of the Baal Shem Tov, Dubnov accepted the people's legend as an indisputable historical fact.[27] Moreover, in his research Dubnov valorized sources based on oral genres, folktales, stories, and poems, the product of the people's creative energy. About Zalman Shneerson's *Eulogy for Besht*, Dubnov writes, "The Besht biography that has come down to us is a collective work and entirely by the folk. It was not created by a single person, but compiled from a mass of oral legends disseminated among the people. In this book everything essential that the people's memory has preserved, everything that the people's imagination has created about the life and works of the founder of Chasidism finds a place."[28]

In recounting the life and teaching of *Besht* (that is, the Baal Shem Tov), Dubnov certainly writes with great sympathy, refraining from criticizing Besht's fondness for mysticism and indifference to rationality. Moreover, Dubnov sympathizes with the causes that contributed to the popularity of Chasidism. As opposed to the formalism, intellectualism, and elitism of the Orthodox *mitnagdim* [opponents of Chasidism], which had alienated the simple people from the Jewish leadership, Besht promoted a Jewish faith based on feeling, mystical knowledge, and joy. Dubnov writes, "Besht's genuine optimism, expressed in the bright, optimistic picture he painted, his views on the meaning of prayer and communication with God as the essence of faith, his consciousness of the great task of his teaching—all this was embodied in the form of a magical vision."[29] This religious orientation, based on natural feeling instead of actual faith (Dubnov did not believe in God), could bring about equality by reducing the hold of the rabbinical hierarchy. Furthermore, by underpinning Judaism in feeling, the Besht was really a spokesman for individual freedom and tolerance, since no one had the right to deny one the right to one's personal experience. Although it might seem strange to us, Dubnov depicted the founder of Chasidism—usually considered the most exclusive and fanatic wing of Judaism—as the embodiment of Europe's highest values.

Dubnov's praise for the Besht contrasted with his disdain for the institution of the *tsaddikim* [dynastic Chasidic leaders], which formed after Besht's death. He strongly disliked their materialism and their manipulations. Moreover, in forcing the people to communicate with God through them, the tsaddikim contradicted Besht and ruined his greatest achievement, that of enabling all Jews to attain direct contact with God through feeling.[30]

Having valorized the emotional appreciation of religion, Dubnov took the next step of applying the same principles to historiography. He attributed to historiography the same functions of religion. He believed that history can bring immortality and salvation. This view can best be seen in his 1891 book, *On the Study of the History of Russia's Jews and the Establishment of a Russian-Jewish Historical Society*.[31] According to Dubnov, Russia's Jews must take the initiative by beginning to collect documents, artifacts, communal chronicles, anything that provides evidence of a Jewish past in Russia. Once that is done the process of national resurrection may take place. Alluding to the prophet Ezekiel's gathering of the Jewish armies, Dubnov writes:

> Dry bones, the remains of past generations are strewn in a valley. *Will these bones come alive?*—the prophet asks. And suddenly the bones begin to come together, veins and flesh appear, they tighten up with skin, only there is no spirit in them....And I began to prophesy; and suddenly spirit arrives and the bones live and stood up, an exceeding great army. And the Lord said to me: "Son of Man! These bones are the entire house of Israel."

Here Dubnov interjects, bringing the story up to date: "Yes, we will soon witness and even participate in the great act of resurrection."[32]

Just how this secular messianism would work is not entirely clear, but if we understand him correctly, resurrection refers to an attitude toward history. By integrating the past into the present and carrying it into the future, the Jewish people rise from the dead and make themselves immortal. Resurrection here combines material and mystical aspects: material, in that the Jewish nation really awakens to its national purpose; mystical, in that this purpose is linked somehow with the ultimate prophecy of Jewish messianism. Moreover, the Jewish historian, as the interpreter of the purpose of the Jewish people, would become the leader of the entire Jewish people. As Amos Funkenstein has noted in this regard, "While it is true that during the nineteenth century historiography became professionalized and, therefore, less accessible to the reading public, it is likewise true that at the same time the historian was given a special position as a high priest of culture, responsible for the legitimation of the nation-state."[33]

These ideas, it seems to me, reflect a real change in Dubnov's focus. Instead of seeing the Jewish people as embodying universal values, Dubnov views Jewish history as having its own path and meaning for the Jews alone. Moreover, the immortality he has in view is not the possession of an individual, but of the collective. But Dubnov's rationalism did not abandon him. Nowhere is God visible. Rather, by surviving in history, the Jewish people attain a secular, collective immortality.

In this way, Dubnov helps invent a modern idea of the Jewish people that is joined to the idea of nation. The Jews have political goals, just like other modern nations, but the Jews' goals also include the ancient prophecy of collective salvation. Although clearly Dubnov's image of the Jewish people is entirely positive, nonetheless one may accuse him of abstract thinking. Whereas earlier the Jew was considered backward and morally flawed, Dubnov now sees the embodiment of ideas, such as historical essence, religious meaning, and spiritual accomplishment. In addition, the Jews have turned from being a people inferior to others because of their separateness to one that is superior. For Dubnov, the lack of a state makes them preeminently historical because it is only their historical experience and not geography that keeps them together.

In this period, when Jewish nationalism came to dominate the thinking of many Jewish intellectuals, it is interesting to note Dubnov's views about Yiddish. In many places, and at the first meeting of the Jewish Literary Society in St. Petersburg in 1908, Dubnov spoke out in favor of "tri-lingualism," the view that Hebrew, Russian, and Yiddish should all be considered national languages of Russia's Jews.[34] Similarly, in his 1909 article, "The Affirmation of the Diaspora," written in response to Ahad Ha'am's polemical article of the same year, "Negation of the Diaspora" [*Shelilat ha-galut*], Dubnov explained that Yiddish could serve as a national language.[35] Published a year after the Czernowitz Language Conference, this statement of the use of Yiddish as a tool of nationalization reflects departures from Dubnov's earlier treatment. It can be remembered that, as the literary critic of *Voskhod* during the 1880s, Dubnov had spearheaded positive attitudes toward Yiddish literature.[36]

By 1908, the positive attitude of the Jewish intelligentsia toward the folk was entirely unexceptional. In fact, the reappraisal of the people would turn into a cult, with all the trappings typical of romantic idealization. An example of this treatment can be found in the work of Semyon An-Sky (1863-1920), the creative writer, journalist, ethnographer, and political activist. In his 1908 article, "Jewish Folk Art" [*Evreiskoe narodnoe tvorchestvo*], An-Sky claimed that, as opposed to Christian nations having their origins in paganism, "such motifs as the idealization of military strength, enthusiasm for battle, praise of the glory and the victories of knights, have been entirely foreign to Jewish national and folk poetry. Similarly foreign is any admiration for triumphant physical strength."[37]

He continued, "Jewish creativity is entirely imbued with the idea of monotheism, which in its foundation is hostile to any struggle, and does not permit the cult of the individual, and places spiritual perfection above material and, in particular, above physical perfection."[38]

Many Jewish writers attacked An-Sky, pointing out the depictions of Joshua and Samson in the Bible and Bar Kochba and the Roman Wars as examples of Jewish militarism.[39] Nevertheless, An-Sky's attribution of the Jewish people as exclusively characterized by spiritual aims epitomizes a fundamental change in attitude of part of the Jewish intelligentsia. From entirely negative in the 1860s, the image of the Jewish people was now an object of idealization.

This new view of the people propelled An-Sky to organize the Jewish Ethnographic Expedition in 1912. Seeking the help of an assistant, two ethnographers, a composer, a musicologist, and photographer, An-Sky decided to travel through the Pale of Settlement with the goal of collecting the tangible evidence of the Jewish past.[40] He and his assistants visited sixty-six sites in Volynia and Podolia. Over a two year period, An-Sky collected 2,000 photographs, 1,800 folktales and legends, 1,500 folk songs, 500 cylinders of Jewish folk music, 1,000 melodies to songs and niggunim without words, countless proverbs and folk beliefs, 100 historical documents, 500 manuscripts, and 700 sacred objects acquired for the sum of 6,000 rubles.[41]

The object of the expedition was to document the soul of the Jewish shtetl. Although the aim was praiseworthy, the relationship of scholar to material was unique. After all, the Jews there were still alive. Nevertheless, An-Sky insisted that the end was close, already viewing traditional Jewish life as a graveyard even before the outbreak of World War I. He writes:

> Jewish life has undergone an enormous upheaval during the last fifty to sixty years and the losses in our folk creations are among the most unfortunate victims of this change. With every old man who dies, with every fire that breaks out, with every exile we endure, we lost a piece of our past. The finest examples of our traditional lives, our customs and beliefs, are disappearing; the old poetic legends and the songs and melodies will soon be forgotten; the ancient, beautiful synagogues are falling to ruin or are laid waste by fire and there the most precious religious ornaments are either lost or sold, often to non-Jews; the gravestones of our great and pious ancestors have sunk into the ground, their inscriptions

all but rubbed out. In short, our past, sanctified by the blood and tears of so many innocent martyrs, is vanishing and will soon be forgotten.[42]

But capturing the experience of the Jewish people was not an end in itself for An-Sky. Rather, folklore had a deeper meaning. Convinced that modern Jews were alienated from religion and community, An-Sky believed folk culture could have the same anthropological function as the Torah had had in earlier times. That is, folklore could serve as the spiritual source, the glue—so to speak—keeping the Jewish people together and giving them a vision of the ideal that Judaism can be.[43] Although such an idea was blasphemy, An-Sky was convinced of its certitude. Moreover, since folklore was not exclusive to one nation, An-Sky was convinced that it could draw other nations closer to the Jews. The *Dybbuk* provides a good example of An-Sky's idea of the uses of folklore, since it was meant both to entertain and revitalize Jewish national identity.

One can clearly acknowledge Dubnov's influence on An-Sky's view that the Jews' folk stories represented the height of Jewish creativity and were sacred and capable of providing religious salvation. An-Sky's image of the Jews is ecstatic. The Jews have theurgy; with their folktales they can channel divine force. At the same time a dark premonition feeds An-Sky's anxiety that Eastern European Jewish life will soon end. In this sense, collecting artifacts is not the same as putting them in a museum, but rather the bridge that will help surviving Jews to come into contact with the original theurgic power of the Jewish people.

It seems obvious that An-Sky's influences emerge from Russia's Silver Age. He was a close friend of Fyodor Sologub and was familiar with the ideas of Russian Symbolism that attributed "God-building" powers to extraordinary men, heroes, poets, mystical seers. What makes An-Sky unique, however, is his attribution of such powers to the Jewish people. By making the entire people the hero, An-Sky reveals his long affiliation with Russian Populism.

Although the majority of his writings were in Russian, An-Sky viewed Yiddish positively. Although, like Dubnov, he defended the use of Hebrew, Russian, and Yiddish at the first meeting of the Jewish Literary Society in 1908, An-Sky apparently came to understand the exclusive value of Yiddish at key historical moments, when one needed to make particular allusion to the Eastern European national tradition.[44] Therefore, An-Sky used Yiddish to write his three-volume chronicle of the destruction of the

Jewish communities during World War I: *The Destruction of the Jews of Poland, Galicia and Bukovina* [*Der yidisher hurbn fun Poylen, Galitsiye un Bukovine von togbuch, 1914-1917*].[45]

In conclusion, for the Jewish intelligentsia to take a positive view of the masses, the intelligentsia had to be taught to see, understand, and value the folk. Works of history played an essential role in that formation. Certainly, once the Jewish intelligentsia began to regard the people favorably, it was not long before it would valorize Yiddish and see in it another sign of the unique and praiseworthy quality of the Jewish people. The process of change took over thirty years and ultimately led to the symbiosis of the people and the intelligentsia in the first decade of the twentieth century, a symbiosis that brought brilliant results in Jewish cultural life of the time. The image of the Jewish masses in Russian historiography evolved in connection with political conditions in Russia. When it seemed likely that the government would increase rights, the Jewish intelligentsia was inclined to see the world from the government's viewpoint. As that possibility diminished, the view of the intelligentsia departed from the government, leading to criticism of the government's behavior vis-à-vis the Jews and to reevaluations of the Jewish masses. When Jewish nationalism took hold among a broad segment of the Jewish intelligentsia in the 1890s, the attitude turned overwhelmingly positive. The intelligentsia began to view the people as the embodiment of the best qualities and values—ones that should not only be preserved, but also developed.

After the war, the conditions in Soviet Russia created an entirely new situation, in which the problem of intelligent/people disappeared and commissar/people came to the fore. New communist institutions devoted to weeding out religion and making the Jew a Soviet citizen appeared, but already the model was no longer one of bottom-up—the people changing the intelligentsia—but the other way around; the commissars were intent on changing the people. In this strange return to the 1860s, communist Jewish representatives in the 1920s saw the Jewish people as deficient and in need of transformation. As if entirely ignorant of history, they viewed themselves as the force that had to and could do it.

ACKNOWLEDGMENTS

This research was made possible by a generous grant from the Alexander Von Humboldt Foundation.

NOTES

[1] E. Cherikover, *Istoriia Obshchestva dlia rasprostraneniia prosveshcheniia sredi evreev v Rossii*, (St. Petersburg, 1913), 71.

[2] Benjamin Nathans makes this point clearly: "From its inception in the era of the Great Reforms, the historiography of Jews in the Russian Empire took as its central concern the Jews' legal standing, in other words, the development of official legislation regarding the Jewish population." See his "Jews, Law, and the Legal Profession in Late Imperial Russia," *Evrei v Rossii, istoriia i kul'tura* 5 (St. Petersburg Jewish University, 1998), 104.

[3] See Shmuel Feiner, *Haskalah and History: the Emergence of a Modern Jewish Historical Consciousness*, (trans. C. Naor and S. Silverston; Portland: Littman Library of Jewish Civilization, 2002).

[4] Leon Rosenthal, *Toledot hevrat marbei haskalah beyisr'el be'erets rusiyah*, two vols. (St. Petersburg, 1886-90), 1:23-28.

[5] The first volumes of historical research by Russian Jews appeared in 1866-67 under the auspices of the Society for the Promotion of Enlightenment among the Jews of Russia: *Sbornik statei po evreiskoi istorii i literature, izdavaemyi obshchestvom dlia rasprostraneniia prosveshcheniia mezhdu evreiami v Rossii* (St. Petersburg, 1866-67), two volumes. Interestingly, nearly all the articles in the volume deal with either earlier periods in Jewish life, especially ancient history and biblical philology, or with foreign Jews. Contemporary Russian Jewry does not appear to have interested these scholars. For a discussion of the earliest historical research on the Jews of Russia, see Isaiah Trunk, "Istoriki russkogo evreistva," in *Kniga o evreisktve ot 1860-kh godov do revoliutsii 1917 g.: sbornik statei* (New York: Soiz russkikh evreev, 1960), 12-35; see also Feiner, *Haskalah*,157-203.

[6] L. Levanda, "Neskol'ko slov o evreiakh zapadnogo kraia Rossii. Pis'mo v redaktsiiu (Iz goroda Igumena, Minsk[oi] guber[nii])," *Rassvet* 1, 27 May (1860): 7-9.

[7] Ibid., 8. This and all following translations are by the author.

[8] No matter how critical *Rassvet* got, one should recall the insight of Saul Ginzburg that "the lofty ideals and principles of Judaism, everything great and noble, which were brought down to us from the many centuries of our historical existence and composed the true basis of our singular way of life, remained for them no less sacred than for their enemies." S. M. Ginzburg, *Minuvshee: istoricheskie ocherki, stat'i i kharistaristiki* (Petrograd, 1923), 80.

[9] Nathans, "Jews, Law," 103.

[10] In the next section I do not treat Nikolai Bershadsky, since he was ethnically and culturally Russian. I acknowledge that an examination of Bershadsky would

likely elicit similar conclusions to those I make about the Jewish intellectuals M. Morgulis and I. Orshanskii.

[11] See I. Sosis, "Period 'obruseniia': natsional'nyi vopros v literature kontsa 60-kh i nachala 70-x godov," *Evreiskaia starina*, 129-42.

[12] This fact is unproved. Morgulis accuses the *maskil* L. Mandel'shtam of having earned a high salary for his work in translating the textbooks, but Mandel'shtam's biographer, Saul Ginzburg, argues that Morgulis was not well paid at all. M. Morgulis, *Voprosy evreiskoi zhizni: sbornik statei* (2nd ed.; St. Petersburg: Tip. A. N. Mikhailova, 1903), 167; for S. Ginzburg's view, see "Iz zapisok pervogo evreia-studenta v Rossii," *Perezhitoe*, 4 vols. (St. Petersburg, 1908-1913), 1: 8.

[13] M. Morgulis, *Voprosy evreiskoi zhizni*, 200.

[14] In his review of Morgulis' book, published in 1889, Semyon Dubnov took issue with Morgulis' idea that the *heder* served primarily to watch over children and for that reason enjoyed popularity. Dubnov points to the religious aims and traditional attitudes of the *heder*, explaining that parents wanted to send their children to *heder* even when they didn't need baby-sitting. See his review of *Voprosy evreiskoi zhizn'* by Kritikus in *Voskhod* 1 (1890): 27.

[15] M. Morgulis, *Vosprosy evreiskoi zhizni*, 294.

[16] In his short life, Orshanskii published a large body of writings that appeared in such volumes as *Jews in Russia: Sketches on the Economic and Social Life of Russian Jews* (1872) [*Evrei v Rossii-ocherki ekonomicheskogo i obshchestvennogo byta russkikh evreev*], and *Russian Legislation on the Jews* (1877) [*Russkoe zakonodatel'stvo o evreiakh*].

[17] I. Orshanskii, "Russkoe zakonodatel'stvo o evreiakh" *Evreiskaia biblioteka* 5 (1874): 5-68.

[18] For more on *Den'*, especially on polemics with the Russian press, see J. Klier, "The Jewish *Den'* and the Literary Mice, 1869-1871," *Russian History* 1 (1983): 31-49; see also Y. Shutsky, "*Den'*" (Chapters in the History of the Russian-Jewish Press)" [Hebrew], *He-avar* 3 (1960): 38-49.

[19] I. Orshanskii, "K voprosu ob obrusenii evreev," *Den'* 13, March 28 (1870): 219.

[20] I. Orshanskii, *Evrei v Rossii: ocherki ekonomicheskogo i obshchestvennogo byta russkikh evreev* (St. Petersburg: Tip. Sh. I. Bakst, 1877), 391-92.

[21] Ibid., 400.

[22] Ibid.

[23] M. Morgulis, "Natsional'nyi i prakticheskii vzgliady na znahenie drevne-evreiskogo iazyka," *Den'*, issues 3 and 6 (1869). In "National and Practical Views on the Purpose of the Hebrew Language," M. Morgulis condemned the view that

Hebrew could serve as the vehicle for enlightening Russia's Jews. According to this passionate advocate of Russification, there was no Hebrew reader among the masses and absolutely no book market. Furthermore, the absence of publishers for anything other than religious books in Hebrew left authors with one option, to turn to a rich notable for a subvention. Thus, modern Hebrew books are just a kind of vanity without any purpose.

[24] In his memoir, Semyon Dubnov offered a paradigm for understanding his own intellectual evolution. In his view he went through three phases: thesis, antithesis, and synthesis. His period of thesis was during the 1870s, when he rejected Jewish history and advocated radical cosmopolitanism. In the 1880s, he applied Western reason to the study of Jewish history; while in the period of synthesis after 1890, Dubnov overcame the first two phases, analyzing Jewish history as having its own unique, exclusive course, distinct from, although in places contiguous with, European history. In this last period he created his idea of "Jewish hegemonic centers." See *Kniga zhizni, vospominaniia i razmyshleniia: materialy dlia istorii moego vremeni* (Riga, 1934), 2:145.

[25] S. Dubnov, "Sabbatai Tsevi i psevdomessianism v 17 veke," *Voskhod* (1882):137.

[26] S. Dubnov, "Istoriograf evreistva. Geinrikh Grets, ego zhizn' i trudy," *Voskhod* (1892): 68.

[27] S. Dubnov, "Vozniknovenie Khasidizma," in *Evrei v Rossiiskoi Imperii XVIII-XIX vekov: sbornik trudov evreiskikh istorikov* (ed. A. Lokshin; Moscow: Jewish University in Moscow Press, 1995), 86.

[28] Ibid., 83.

[29] Ibid., 144.

[30] Ibid., 137-38.

[31] S. Dubnov, *Ob izuchenii istorii russkikh evreev i ob uchrezhdenii russko-evreiskogo istoricheskogo obshchestva* (St. Petersburg, 1891).

[32] Ibid., 88.

[33] Amos Funkenstein, *Perceptions of Jewish History* (Berkeley: University of California Press, 1973), 19.

[34] See Dubnov's own discussion of that meeting in *Kniga zhizni*, quoted in 3rd edition (St. Petersburg: Evreiskii universitet v Moskve & Rossiiskaia natsional'naia biblioteka, 1998), 297.

[35] S. Dubnov, "Utverzhdenie golosa (Po povodu 'Otritsaniia golosa' Akhad Gaama)," *Evreiskii mir* 5 (1909): 58. Dubnov writes, "When in our literature the question of language will be posed in its entire breadth, when it will be discussed not from the viewpoint of one or another party or literary group, but from the

general national viewpoint, then there will be no room among nationalists who do not negate the Diaspora for such a misunderstanding [toward Yiddish]. Inasmuch as we 'acknowledge' the Diaspora, we must also acknowledge 'the jargon,' as one of the instruments in the struggle for autonomy, equal to Hebrew and other factors of our national culture."

[36] For a description of the evolution of Dubnov's attitude toward Yiddish, see Samuel Niger-Charney, "Simon Dubnow as a Literary Critic," *YIVO Annual of Jewish Social Science* 1 (1946): 305-17. This article was originally published in *YIVO Bleter* 23 (1944). The paper was read at a memorial meeting for Dubnow arranged by the Yiddish Scientific Institute on October 17, 1943. See also Dubnov's own work, *Fun Zhargon tsu Yiddish* (Vilna: Kletzkin, 1929).

[37] S. An-Sky, "Evreiskoe narodnoe tvorchestvo," in *Evrei v Rossiiskoi Imperii XVIII-XIX vekov* (Moscow: Evreiskii universitet v Moskve, 1995), 644.

[38] Ibid.

[39] Among those who rejected An-Sky's claims were S. Shternberg and S. Ginzburg. For more, see V. Lukin, "Ot narodnichestva k narodu (S. A. An-Sky etnograf vostochno-evreopeiskogo evreistva)," in *Istoriia i kul'tura: Evrei v Rossi: Trudy po iudaike, istoriiia i etnografiia* 3 (St. Petersburg: Peterburgskii evreiskii universitet, 1995).

[40] Abraham Rechtman describes the expedition, "An-Sky organized an ethnographical expedition with colleagues including Joel Engel, a famous composer from Moscow; J. Kiselgaf, an expert on Jewish folk music from St. Petersburg: Shlomo Yudovin, a painter and photographer, An-Sky's cousin; J. Pikangor and S. Shrier, both students from the Jewish Acadmy in St. Petersburg, and of course, myself." A. Rechtman, "The Jewish Ethnographical Expedition," *Tracing An-Sky, Jewish Collections from the State Ethnographical Museum in St. Petersburg* (New York: Jewish Museum, 1992), 13.

[41] S. An-Sky, "Ot evreiskoi etnograficheskoi ekspeditsii," *Evreiskaia zhizn'* 17, April 30, (1917): 33-34.

[42] S. An-Sky, "Dos yidishe etnografishe program," L. I. Shternberg, ed., in *Man* (Petrograd, 1914), vol. 1, 11-11. Translation by Golda Werman; quoted in *S. An-Sky, The Dybbuk and Other Writings,* (ed. David G. Roskies; New York: Schocken Books, 1992), xxiv.

[43] D. Roskies "Introduction," *The Dybbuk and Other Writings by S. An-Sky* (New York: Schocken Books, 1992), xxiv.

[44] An-Sky's speech was titled, "Equality of Languages in Jewish Literature" [Ravnopravnost' iazykov v evreiskoi literature]. For more on this, see Ilya Serman, "Spory 1908 goda o russko-evreiskoi literature i posleoktiabrskoe desiatiletie,"

Cahiers du Monde Russe et Soviétique 36:2 Avril-Juin (1985): 167-74.

[45] *The Destruction of the Jews of Poland, Galicia and Bukovina* appeared in volumes 4-6 of An-Sky's *Gazamlte Shriftn* [*Collected Works*], 15 vols (Vilna, Warsaw, New York, 1920-1925).

The Ashkenazic Gaze: Creating the Jewish Art Book

Seth L. Wolitz

"They [books] are to our time what cathedrals with their frescoes and stain glass were to ages past. Books have become the monuments of modernity" (El Lissitzky [1919]).

The Jewish art book or the Jewish book with illustrations represents an essential contribution to the Jewish secular cultural renaissance that emerged among Ashkenazic Jewry, particularly the Jews of Eastern Europe, at the beginning of the twentieth century. Multiple social, economic, and political factors affected this subaltern people, both internally and externally, which triggered a sudden upsurge of Jewish creativity. The increasing contacts with Western secular life encouraged a cultural revolution that moved a traditionalist people to espouse Western modernity more and more. Some Jews would seek political and social emancipation, others economic or religious freedom, but all modernizing Jews were seeking to define and create a new Jewish secular culture.

As new comers to esthetic concerns and their privileged space, the Jews discovered in art a mirrored world in which to witness themselves, not as others saw them but as they saw their own gaze for the first time. Art offered a new territory, an almost substitute homeland, in which the new Jewish creator could experiment, question, redefine, or reinterpret himself and his own culture. Art proved as well a new weapon for political, social, or ethical satire, if not subversion. The arts provided a means to be full participants in, and even on the cutting edge of, esthetic expression in Western civilization. Breaking the religious taboos of representation and reveling in the newness of esthetic possibilities, the Jewish plastic artists who emerged sought both national and personal fulfillment, but they oscillated between social commitments and personal esthetic considerations, wanting to celebrate the ethnological realities of the people and aspiring to create a new and even universal worldview.[1]

Before 1900, there was no real consciousness of a Jewish art. One could even state that the concept of aesthetics had no significance to the Jewish intellectual world of that time. Only in the West were there stirrings of artists who were of Jewish origin, the most famous of whom was Camille Pissarro. In Russia, the first Jew to achieve any artistic fame was Mark Antokolsky, a Jewish sculptor who created mainly Russian historical figures. For the Jews and Gentiles alike, the concept of a Jewish art seemed an oxymoron.

By 1920, however, Marc Chagall (1887-1985) was recognized as a Russian and Jewish artist, appreciated from Paris to Moscow both by the Western avant-garde and by a select number of Jews, particularly in Eastern Europe [fig.1]. By 1920, there were a sufficient number of active Jewish artists in the Soviet Union, Poland, Paris, Jerusalem, and New York City to constitute an actual Jewish art presence. What its parameters were remains open to question and discussion to this day. But there existed Jewish artists who were active in their pursuit of Jewish art and who wanted to believe and create a Jewish art. At the same time, a growing Jewish audience developed that expected and demanded a Jewish art presence. Whether under the suasion of Zionism or Bundism, nationalism or consciousness raising Jews, a Jewish art needed to exist.

Jewish art would ultimately have to be a hybrid expression—as was the creation of modern secular Jewish culture in general—but Eastern European Jewish art was the felicitous fusion of Russian modernism and Jewish culture.[2]

Vitebsk in northeast White Russia would be the art center of the Russian Jewish expression and its gathering point beginning in 1897, when Yehudah Pen opened the first Jewish art school in the world. (Pen [1854-1937] was one of those early precursors who obtained artistic training in St. Petersburg and was friendly with the head of the Wanderers, Ilya Repin, who happened to have an estate in the area of Vitebsk.) This Jewish art school headed by a liberal Orthodox figure, who closed the school on the Sabbath, permitted young Jews to have their first professional artistic experience, which for the most part was denied to them in the Russian capital and elsewhere.[3] 1897 was also the year for the formation of Zionism and of Bundism.

Pen remained the head of his art school into the Revolution until 1918 [fig. 2]. During this period of twenty years, Pen saw most of the

Jewish artists and sculptors pass through his school who would go on to national and international fame. Chagall was one of his first and most appreciated students. With the Revolution, Chagall became the newly named Commissar of Art of Vitebsk and in 1919 drew his old teacher Pen and his students into the newly established Vitebsk Art School. Pen was made a teacher of art, Salomon Yudovin became a professor of graphics and wood cuts, and El Lissitsky, the protégé of Chagall, became a professor of architecture and graphics. Most of the students were Jewish and, with the arrival of Malevich by late 1919[4], would rapidly pass from being involved with Jewish figurative representations into Suprematist abstractions.

On his return to Russia, in 1914, Chagall's fame in Western art circles established him as one of the leading avant-garde artists, who brought Jewish subject matter to the fore dressed in Cubist lozenges, fragmentations, and multiperspectives with dramatic, highly saturated colors. By 1918, Abram Efros and Ya. Tugendkhold underscored his importance by publishing in Russian the first critical study of Chagall and his work. They invited Chagall to design the cover, which is an important moment in Jewish art history.[5]

This cover [fig. 3] not only reveals Chagall's originality as an artist, but also sets forth a Jewish mode of expression in the plastic arts and a distinct quality found in many later Jewish art books. The cover's image is really made of three circles, one inside the other. The outer one contains the name of Efros on the top; at the bottom, inversed, is the word *Iskusstva* [art]. All of this is in Cyrillic letters. The next circle inside has Tugendkhold at the top and the name Chagall at the bottom of the circle, again inversed. In the central and innermost circle, we have the artist and his universe, which deserve our attention because what we see is a figure drawn in Cubist black and white lozenges with the head inverted. This inverted head leads us into the sharpest display of the emergent Jewish plastic art culture, for it is a representation of the Yiddish idiom *fardreyter kop* [upside-down head], which idiomatically translates as a strange one, an eccentric, and by extension an artist. The head is in fact a caricature of Chagall's face. And to the right is a magic ball he seems to be holding on the tips of his fingers, which is actually in the shape of a sunflower. The sunflower can also be recognized as an Eastern European Jewish symbol of fertility with its thousands of seeds that Jews joyously chewed for centuries. The panorama inside this sunflower is none other than that of Vitebsk, his "home town," which he had already painted many times, with the Russian church and city buildings.

This remarkable cover, a work of art in itself, presents Chagall's avant-garde page design with a totally new concept of the art book as not just linear, but circular. One had to turn the book in a full circle in order to recognize, comprehend, and understand what its contents would be, and the upside-down head of the artist was an indication that as an artist he has turned art upside-down by his originality. To further appreciate this piece, we see how Chagall recycled these same images, which brought him fame in Paris and St. Petersburg, and created through *bricolage* a new work of art.

By 1920, the Jewish art world in Vitebsk reflected the tensions that the Revolution opened up to all the cultures inside the old Empire. One group wished to pursue a Jewish national art expression that would define itself in terms of style in addition to subject matter.[6] The younger artists were attracted to the newly emerging abstract art and its universalism represented by Malevich's Suprematism. By late 1919, El Lissitzsky (1890-1941), reflecting a certain trend, would pass from Chagallian Jewish matter and cubist/futurist figurative representations to Suprematism with its pure abstractions in the examples of his *Prouns*. Salomon Yudovin (1892-1954), however, with his *Yidisher Folks Ornament* (Vitebsk, 1920) sought to develop patterns and motifs that could help develop a Jewish style of painting [fig. 4]. These designs were drawn from gravestones, Torah ornaments, Simkhes Torah flags, designs from religious texts, and even old wall paintings in synagogues. Yudovin, Issachar Ber Ribak (1897-1935), Natan Altman (1889-1970), and Boris Aronson (1898-1980), were representative young artists determined to establish a stylistic that expressed the authenticity and uniqueness of Ashkenazic Jewry, the Jewry of Eastern Europe.

Their perspective drew on contemporary modernist thinking of the pre-World War I period, in which it was believed that the *Volksgeist* preserved the authentic core of the nation. In the West it was allied to Primitivism, the return to the earliest native traditions. Their cultural nationalism drew its intellectual roots from Herderian thinking about tapping into the folk genius as the source of new creativity and, without taxing the point, from Gobineau's theories of race. The Jews of Eastern Europe needed only observe the efforts of Mamontov on his estate at Abramstevo to reinterpret traditional elements of Russian Slavic forms and expression so as to see the direction in which they too were interested.

fig. 1 Pen, *Portrait of Chagall*

fig. 2 Pen, *Self Portrait*

fig. 3 Cover of *The Art of Marc Chagall*

fig. 4 Yudovin, cover of *Yidishe Folks Ornament*

The title of Yudovin's art publication, *Yidisher Folks Ornament*, must be understood as a serious statement underlining a new orientation that eschewed earlier Jewish expressive traditions with a biblical and religious orientation in order to present core plastic ornamental motifs of the Jewish folk of the *shtetlakh* on Slavic soil. This served to underline their authentic, legitimate, and constituent peoplehood with their own distinctive esthetic qualities and artistic expression. The title also implied an ideological positioning for the depiction of the Eastern European folk ornaments that affirmed, and was aligned to, the shared cultural ideologies of the Folkist party of Shimon Dubnov, Bundism, and socialism. This effort to define a Yiddish (here meaning Jewish) folk motif or pattern leading to a Jewish stylistic expresses a determined perspective that Jewish art emerged from the folk experience of everyday life [in Russian, *byt*] and not from past political and religious leadership.

The very cover of the volume uses square Hebrew letters copied from gravestones, from which the majority of the designs in the volume are based. The stone carvers of these seventeenth to early nineteenth century gravesstones were religious men who did not think they were doing art. Still they had an elaborated symbolism rich in motifs and patterns that reflected their Slavic environment. They stylized nature. Deer or gazelle, almost always two dimensional, implied family names like Hirsch or Zevi and symbolized goodness [fig. 5]. A dove represented goodness too and the fleeting soul. A lion represented nobility and the Lion of Judah. A tree symbolized fruitfulness as did vines of grapes. A broken tree implied an early death. Split hands established the family as Kohanic [fig. 6]. Crowns alluded to *Pirke Abot* 4.3 and stressed "the crown of a good name" as the highest quality of the buried figure.

These motivic designs were chosen to provide a possibility of developing a more uniquely Jewish style. In 1923 and 1924, Altman and Aronson, would continue this effort of trying to provide "pure Jewish Ashkenazic" stylized designs in their own art books called *Jewish Graphics*, in either Russian or German.

By chosing to call his volume *Yidisher folks ornament*, Yudovin was consciously drawing the line of demarcation between the sources of his esthetic worldview, the Eastern European world, and that of the earlier volume, *L'Ornement Hébreu* (Berlin, 1905), put out by Baron David Guenzburg and Vladimir Stassov [fig. 7]. *L'Ornement Hébreu*, already planned and in part published in 1886, reflects the work of the Russian nationalist theorist Stassov, whose influence upon Russian music and architecture of the second half of the nineteenth century was preponderant. Stassov was a Russian liberal thinker who believed in the multicultural realities of the Russian Empire. He encouraged the collecting and publishing of Jewish sources of Jewish art, as he had done with *Slavic Ornaments* earlier. Baron Guenzburg, an extremely rich, well-educated, and religious Jew, underwrote this limited edition publication and made the selection of the illuminated manuscripts and elements of "Hebrew style" gathered in this elephantine volume [fig. 8].

The volume had as its intended goal to prove that Jews too had an artistic inheritance that could be re-used just as contemporary Russians were using their medieval artistic inheritance to create new art objects. But these abstract ornaments and alphabetic shapes came from Sephardic sources. In fact, the provenance of all these texts was the Middle East and North Africa. The intention of this giant Russo-Judaic art book was to inspire a new Jewish art in Russia based on these motifs and zoomorphic designs on the serifs as well as the micrography. Russian Jewish artists, it was hoped, would rework these given patterns and motifs in order to construct a new art just as their Slavic counterparts were doing.

This book did not succeed in forging a new Jewish art based on those materials. Ashkenazic artists wanted to express their own patterns and motifs and not those borrowed from a thousand years ago. These Hebrew ornaments were foreign. Indeed the term "Hebrew" underscored that Hebrew harkened back to biblical material and its Near Eastern and Western European art expression. Eastern European Jewish artists drawn to biblical material and "oriental" motifs were those affected by the emergent Zionist movement and the new Hebrew culture being constructed in the resurgent Hebrew language, in opposition to the adoption of Yiddish by the Folkists and Bundists with their own ideological suasion. The "Hebrew" ornament, therefore, marked the emergence of a desired new Jewish plastic art, but one oriented Janus-like: toward the past, the elite rabbinic culture, and ultimately toward creating a Zionist state.

Thus, this massive volume did not constitute in itself the immediate revelation desired by Stassov and Guenzburg. But it did precipitate a polar reaction fifteen years later by Yudovin, who proffered entirely Ashkenazic folkic designs from anonymous sources. Chagall would be influenced by *L'Ornement Hébreu* in his zoomorphic designs on the serifs of later works in the twenties [fig. 9]. *L'Ornement Hébreu* serves as the starting point of a

fig. 5 Tombstone drawing of deer

fig. 6 Tombstone drawing of hands, etc.

fig. 7 Cover of *L'Ornement Hébreu*

fig. 8 Chagall, page from *L'Ornement Hébreu*

Kulturkampf between those who allied their art to Zionism and those who sought a Jewish folk expression on Slavic domains.[7]

The Betzalel School in Jerusalem, founded by Boris Shatz in 1906, proffered the proto-Zionist alternative perspective to creating a Jewish art for a new Hebrew culture. Shatz sculpted *Matiyahu the Maccabee,* which reenforced the biblical and post-biblical inheritance [fig. 10]. He also offered wooden plaques of celebrated rabbinic figures and encouraged the representation of the Middle Eastern landscape marked with ancient Jewish monuments. E. M. Lilien produced such landscapes and created Zionist postcards in *Jungenstil* that perfectly expressed ideological intentions far distant from Vitebsk Askenazic contemporary realities in the art, for example, of Pen.[8]

But the Betzalel school did fire the imagination of young Russian Jews, among whom was Yosef Tchaikov (1888-1986). Tchaikov provides a good example of the changing positions of artists toward the creation of Jewish modernist art and its illustrations from 1910 to 1922. Tchaikov, Y. Likhtensteyn, and others, including Marek Shvarts, met up in Paris at La Ruche in 1912, where they published the first Jewish art journal, titled *Makhmedim* [The Precious Ones]. This handmade series of volumes, based on the Jewish holidays in pure *Jungenstil,* expressed their vision of the Betzalel school with its emphasis on religious inheritance as the source of modern Jewish artistic expression. In 1912, Tchaikov published in this journal his pathetic drawing of *Adam and Eve* [fig. 11].

Chagall, who happened to live next door, mocked this vision of a new Jewish art and produced in parody one of his first biblical works, *Adam and Eve*, rich in color and cubist design. The figures—seemingly in the nude, with a phallus protruding, and his own added fantasies—reveal how completely Chagall had absorbed the latest French techniques. At the same time, Chagall projected his new sense of a contemporary Jewish presence in art by fusing a Jewish subject with a neo-primitivist quality alloyed to soft cubism [fig.12]. This confrontation permits us to recognize how far ahead Chagall really was of other Eastern European Jewish artists. But this *Adam and Eve* further underscores the triumph of the Vitebsk school for Chagall's main works in this pre-World War I period: it treats as subject matter his own contemporary Russian Jewish landscape, shtetl dwellers, and Slavic peasant life. His work reflects furthermore not only the physical world of Russian Jewry, but its psychology as well. Dreams and fantasies, fears and terrors abound in his paintings, which provide

fig. 9 Chagall, cover of *Shtrom*

fig. 10 Shatz, *Matiyahu the Maccabee*

fig. 11 Tchaikov, *Adam and Eve*

fig. 12 Chagall, *Adam and Eve*

the first real Jewish gaze, the first real Ashkenazic Jewish vision of the contemporary world.

Chagall never partook in the ethnological expeditions that Sh. An-Sky, the first significant Jewish folklorist, spearheaded between 1911 and 1914 into the Pale of Settlement. An-Sky's efforts were revolutionary in recognizing the legitimacy of a Jewish folk that had not been considered legitimate earlier. An-Sky's sweep to collect artifacts of Jewish folklore, Purim *shpils*, Torah covers, photographs of gravestones, recording of folk songs and cantorials, etc., was part of academic anthropological activities in Russian culture and throughout Western Europe. Yudovin, a relative of An-Sky, served as a photographer-recorder and eventually used these photographs when he became a graphic artist and especially a fine woodcut master [fig. 13]. Ribak and El Lissitzsky went on their own expedition and made drawings of wall paintings and of old wooden synagogues. And so did Altman and Aronson, who published stylizations of gravestones.[9] These artists and others spent their summers visiting out-of-the-way *shtetlekh* to record the Ashkenazic environment, as they considered the means to create a distinct Jewish art style on a formal level drawn from Ashkenazic folk roots. If their efforts yielded mainly ethnographic recordings of Jewish material life, that alone has proved most worthwhile. That they incorporated cubo-futurist designs and expressionist perspectives from Russia and the West only points to the reality of hybridization that is at the heart of Jewish secular culture.

With the end of the War years and the beginnings of the Revolution, young Jewish artists, having few material resources, sought to earn a living without the support of rich families as patrons. The collapse of the Tsarist Regime in 1917 and the end of the Ukase against the use of Yiddish during the War created a need to develop rapidly school books in Yiddish, as Yiddish emerged as the major language for instruction of the Jewish folk. Chagall, El Lissitzsky, Ribak, Tchaikov, and others were commissioned to illustrate children's texts, many by new Yiddish poets, such as Moshe Broderzon, Leyb Kvitko, and Perets Markish. Suddenly the needs of cultural nationalism and their esthetic concerns were joined in a practical application, making children books attractive and instructive while also reenforcing Jewish national cultural identity. The role of Jewish children's art books in the growth of Jewish art cannot be underestimated. Thousands of copies of these works were distributed throughout the Ukraine, White Russia, Russia, and even Poland, providing young Jews with their first encounters with both secular Jewish art and Westernized Jewish modernism.

Tchaikov was one of the most prolific illustrators of children's books. Having returned to Russia from France just before the War, his style evolved rapidly from *Jungenstil* to Russian cubo-futurism. His first cover after the Revolution in 1917 was for Broderzon's text, *Temerl*, with its transitional flavor [fig. 14]. By 1922, Tchaikov, in Markish's *Der Galaganer Hon* [The Arrogant Rooster], integrates the Hebrew letters of the title into the general composition, giving the letters the shape of further flourishes of tail feathers [fig. 15]. The new style reveals a stripped-down, almost cartoonish quality and approaches two dimensions, a trait common to most Jewish artists of the period.

Ribak's handling of a peacock motif, the Eastern European Jewish symbol of art and music, depicts the image as flat, folkloric, and stylized with an exaggerated extended feather [fig. 16]. This type of image did not originate with Ribak, but derived from the wall paintings of eighteenth century synagogues, which the artist copied in expeditions before and during the War. The belief was that these folk motifs would appeal to the eye of Jewish children and initiate them into their folk national inheritance. El Lissitzky's cover to the *Ukrainian Folktales,* translated into Yiddish by Kvitko (1922), sought by its design to create a modernist frame bordered by folk primitive and Ukrainian patternings that were derived from dress embroidery, but hatched with suprematist chevrons [fig. 17]. The lettering too has a folkic pattern. The Constructivist diagonal of El Lissitzky, already developed by 1918, streaks across the page with the title. The *aleph*, or silent letter in Hebrew, becomes indeed the creative letter—set off in black—to initiate the vocalized title. Archaizing and the abstract are joined here to reveal the modernist intent of the artist.

Introducing neighboring cultures and their folk texts was a major educational intent of the Bolsheviks at this early stage, along with the desire to make it attractive, appealing, and not yet excessively exotic. These labors by all the plastic artists for children's books have an esthetic value in themselves, not unlike a simple Mozart sonata for beginners. The artists permitted themselves a freedom and daring, stylizations and gameplaying to reach children, adhering to simple images and symbols that could capture the imagination of children and hold their attention.[10]

The Yiddish book became a major generic form of secular Jewish modernist expression after the Revolution. The Jewish book was already

fig. 13 Yudovin, woodcut of *Synagogue*

fig. 14 Tchaikov, cover of *Temerl*

fig. 15 Tchaikov, cover of *Der Galaganer Hon*

fig. 16 Ribak, "The Peacock"

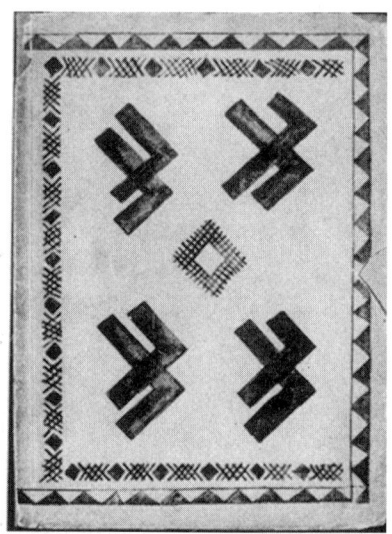

fig. 17 El Lissittzky, cover of *Ukraynishe Folkmayses*

familiar in Eastern Europe. Whether for children or adults, the traditional Jewish book represented something special, a sacral space. A worn-out book in Eastern Europe was never burned, but buried. The print itself, the Hebrew letter, was Israel incarnate. For the older religious generation, the very whiteness of the page carried signification. Kabbalists saw in the blanks between the letters the presence of God. The secularists sought to use the book as a means to create art in a familiar setting by defamilarization; that is, by subverting and reworking the religious inheritance. In 1917, a group of artists, Chagall, El Lissitzky, Moshe Altman, Tchaikov, and Ribak, joined a few poets and, with the economic support of A. F. Kagan-Shabshay, created a Jewish Society for the Arts and a publishing house, *Nasha iskusstvo [New Art] Shamir*, to publish art books and bring to the Jewish public contemporary secular Yiddish culture.

The first volume to emerge was *Sikhes Kholin* [Small talk] by Broderzon, a tongue-in-cheek erotic verse tale mocking a poor married Chasid, who, while daydreaming, is carried off by the *yetser hore* [evil inclination] to a seductive princess who makes him her captive and sex slave. But after a while he yearns for his family and obtains permission to return home for one year. He stays longer, and the demonic princess arrives and demands his return, going so far as to take him to a rabbinical court, where she loses the bigamy case. In despair, she asks for one last kiss and receives permission, at which point the Chasid experiences the kiss of death. This lighthearted tale teases the traditional Chasidic world, a favorite activity of early modern Yiddish literature. Its comic modern eroticism set in a folktale format also mocks the early Yiddish narrative poems and certainly *Monish* of Y. L. Peretz. This volume was for sale in two formats. As a book, it was made of fifteen pages with illustrations, but to intensify the intent of creating a Jewish book, the fifteen pages were also bound as a scroll, in imitation of the Scroll of Esther and boxed in a splendid container made to look like a big mezuzah.

El Lissitzky projected each page as an artistic whole. The imagery and text all jointly play their semiotic roles. The design of each page gives an archaizing flavor with modern secular allusions. Each page of the scroll unrolls or the page is turned, presenting a single unit. The unity of the work is maintained by the traditional two columns of script, with each new paragraph beginning with an elaborated first letter in pure medieval tradition, foliated, and hiding a small animal or sly hint of a female seductress. This large illustration, carefully placed on the page, either centered or decentered but harmoniously integrated, underscored the key event in the narrative on that page.

The title page projects the shape of traditional books. The framing is made of key symbolic images surrounding the title of the work. The Hebraic letters use the Prague style [fig.18]. The title page fuses the traditional "gate" or entrance way with the *Jugenstil* framing. The calligraphic strokes in sharply defined black ink integrated the imagery with the Hebrew lettering. This title page of *Sikhes Kholin* marks the real beginning of serious Yiddish book art. It is a masterful effort that stands on its own as a work of art.

The bird hovering above the title, its wide flat decorative wings given the fullest fluttering of scribal strokes, is the peacock, the symbol for Eastern European Jewry of its artistic muse; gloriously sweeping upward, it clutches a downcast Chasid being lifted off to new esthetic realms beyond his pinched imagination. Below, the title mocks him with the idiom in Yiddish of "Idle Chatter," and further below is the new scribe at his desk with the candle lit—enlightenment illuminating the secular poet, Broderzon, as he composes the verses and tale of the Chasid being carried away by his imagination.

The figures on the left and right are based on Eccelsia and Synagoga at the Reims Cathedral. The stone upon which they stand is a classic medieval Gothic base copied from the statues' socles. The Synagoga figure has been transformed into an old Jewish scribe, who wears a square Litvak skull cap. A goose quill rests in his head as if struck by an arrow. The scroll in his hand hangs down limp and useless. He is downcast like Synagoga, for he represents the past. The left figure, based on Ecclesia, looks upward and represents the new, the artist; the goose quill in his hand has become a brush, mixing paint on the palette, while his head and eyes face toward the peacock, his muse. In this remarkable title page we have an icon of the massive transition in Eastern European Jewish life: the passage from a religious civilization to an esthetic secular vision. The absorption of the gothic Christian religious civilization, appropriated by El Lissitzsky from the Reims cathedral, becomes a Judaized, secularizing event that subverts both religious traditions. All in all, a virtuoso performance.

The next page, which begins the written tale, is surrounded by a frame, at the top of which are sleepy rabbinic figures seemingly studying their texts [fig. 19]. On the right hand side is a young scholar, the protagonist, dreaming of other realms with erotic desire, for at his feet is the goat, symbol

The Ashkenazic Gaze

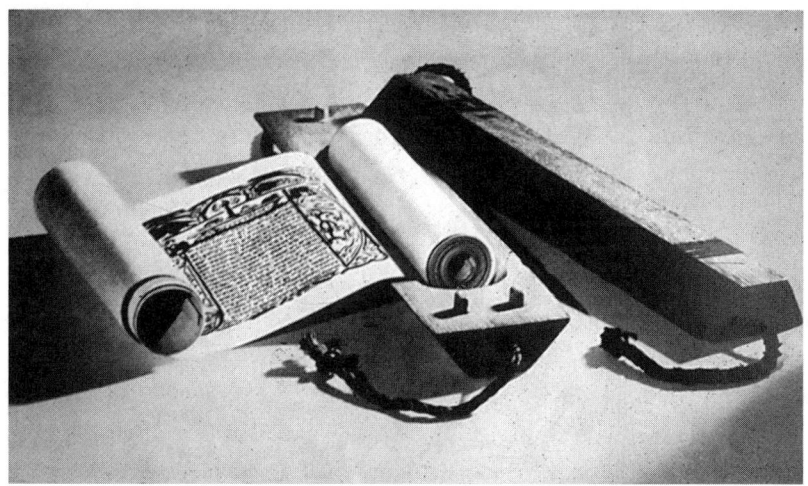

fig. 18 El Lissitzky, title page of *Sikhes Kholin*

fig. 19 First page of text from *Sikhes Kholin*

of Israel in exile but also of erotic power. The written text begins with a zoomorphic *aleph*, typical of traditional illuminated manuscripts. Here El Lissitzky has fused hebraic scribal play of micrography and zoomorphic design with modernist stylized archaizing figure and line still affected by *Jungenstil* practice.

This remarkable 1917 work is his first masterpiece. Unfortunately, few people can appreciate the full achievement of this work because the witty Broderzon text has not yet been translated and so the drawings are appreciated only as plastic illustrative efforts and not as a brilliant integration of imagery and text. El Lissitzky brought his own interpretative hand, which hints at his knowledge of the Psyche and Eros tale that I believe he integrates into his illustrations. This work, made entirely of strong quill strokes and scroll work, remains unique in his oeuvre, and art scholars have generally cast its into his juvenalia. This is a mistake. This work established El Lissitzky as the finest artist in book art design, and he would be invited to participate in many other Yiddish art book ventures.

The *Khad Gad ya* Series of 1919, published in Kiev by the Kultur Lige as colored lithographs, has excited most scholars of El Lissitzky because the text is the well-known Passover Aramaic poem built on the "Old King Cole" motif of addition and therefore the integration of text and imagery becomes easier to interpret. The Kultur Lige was the cultural ideological movement that used Yiddish language as the basis of the new Jewish secular culture. The Kultur Lige established schools and created a book publishing house of central importance to Yiddish literature and the arts. It organized an arts section, and El Lissitzky and most Russian Jewish artists became members. The Kiev branch was the most active in the period between 1917 and 1920. Here El Lissitzsky first did the water colors of the *Khad Gad ya* series, but, reworked them into ten illustrations with pro-Revolutionary sentiments. The text therefore is traditional, but the flavor of the illustrations is both Jewish and with hints of Bolshevism. It is clearly a hybrid Russian-Jewish illustration.[11]

Many consider this series the high point of his "Jewish" period. The atmosphere of the entire group of illustrations follows the fate of the little goat, who will be seemingly consumed by all the other animals as the song grows—but in the end it is the little goat who emerges safely: Israel in exile. If we look at the fifth lithograph, "Then came a fire and burnt the stick," we see that page design is divided into three parts, a tripart structure maintained throughout the illustrations with the domed frame containing strong cubo-futurist elements animated on suprematist diagonals (which El Lissitzky was already developing in his *Prouns*) [fig.20]. The Hebrew letter *Hay* is also the number five shaped like a goat. The *Jugenstil* dome, framed with the key passage in Yiddish, translates the above title from the Aramaic. The illustration depicts a swirling vortex consuming the church, if not the village.

Here we immediately sense the break of the text from the imagery. Where does the church come from and the village? This is the revolutionary reading of El Lissitzky. The red fire blazing away is the Red Revolution, which is burning away the Tsarist stick. The flames are the feathers of the fire and fuse well with the Russian folk image of the Fire Bird, who helps destroy evil Kashay the Immortal. The burning church is the passing away of superstition and religion. The *Khad Gad ya* song is not only the song of Jewish liberation at the end of Passover, but also the new liberation of all the peoples brought on by the Revolution. The third part of the composition is the quote at the bottom and outside of the frame (meaning of no consequence now), the original Aramaic opening of the stanza. It is cast out with the past.

The illustration of the *Khad Gad ya* series do introduce cubist elements, but still remain affected by the *Jugenstil.* Critical appreciation has emphasized the fresh handling of his colors, but a comparison of the hand-tinted pages of *Sikhes Kholin* with El Lissitzky's hand reveals no necessarily greater advance artistically, and indeed one can note the loss of the intense *Yiddishkeyt* quality of the earlier *Sikhes Kholin*. El Lissitzky would produce further art books in Yiddish, especially *Yingl, Tsingl Khvat* of Mani Leyb, but his intense search for a new Jewish art style would founder.[12] His change of political suasion would redirect his esthetics, leading to his embrace of pure abstraction and his full *gradus ad Parnassum*.

The period of 1919-20 was one of civil war and the murder of over 500,000 Jews by the Whites, local war lords, and Cossacks. In reaction to the Revolutionary romanticism that had seized the Jewish artists and poets from 1917 forward, there was shock and despair facing the contemporary pogroms and wanton butality. The new major poets, Kvitko, Markish, and Dovid Hofshteyn, wrote powerful, painful dirges, none of which have yet been translated. The plastic artists also wished to participate in protest and lamentation. Markish wrote *Di Kupe* [The Mound or The Pile] in violent expressionistic verse, with cinematic close-up intensity, to underscore the horror of it all. The first edition, in Warsaw (1921), had a cover by Henryk Berlewi in pure expressionist style, but entirely Polish Jewish in the use of expressionism, which also made use of Hebrew letters to the most esthetic effect.[13] The mounds of the slaughtered are depicted as triangles, pyramids of the dead that build upward into Hebrew letters of *Di Kupe,* with the poet's name at the top [fig. 21]. There was an important group of Polish Jewish art books, but I use this excellent example by the leading Polish Jewish artist of the period, Berlewi, who became a follower of El Lissitzky and ultimately became the second most important interwar Jewish abstract artist. This volume of *Di Kupe* and its cover brought fame to both artist and poet.

The following year, in 1922, Tchaikov in Kiev produced the cover of *Di Kupe* in the Soviet version, which had changes in the text [fig. 22]. This work marks the high point of Tchaikov's entrance into abstraction fused with his cubo-futurism and influenced by Chagall. The inverted lettering of *Di Kupe* describes the buried dead and reveals his knowledge of Chagall's inverted lettering in a circular page design, as seen earlier in the Efros-Tugenhold volume on Chagall. The Jewish survivors carry the corpses to the mound. The simplified cubistic letterings use flat black and white play to emphasize the darkness of the event. The black pyramid mound—obviously borrowed from Berlewi—sends up a cry to heaven, reminding one of El Lissitzky's *Beat the Whites* poster that used the triangle in this aggressive manner. The powerful diagonal of the rising pyramid piercing the circle of the earth and attacking the obscuring sun and clouds, symbols of lamentations, protests the destruction and the silent response above.

Both Berlewi's and Tchaikov's covers prepare the reader for the verbal violence and lamentations that are delivered on turning the page. Indeed, the use of the pyramid or the triangle serves symbolically as the tombstone for the victims who lack any. The poet and artist have joined to give them a proper burial in verse and art, which the violence denied them, while traditional religion failed to explain or serve them. We see how far the Jewish art book has moved from a child's introduction and experience of modern esthetics to the collective voice of a ruined people. In the case of *Di Kupe,* Jewish art books serve as the catafalque, repository, and *matseveh* of the slaughtered.

Chagall, who had produced many volumes of children's art books, was so disturbed by these events that he helped run a Jewish orphanage near Moscow at Malakhovka for the surviving children. There he decided, with his colleague and poet Hofshteyn, to publish a volume of verse and print drawings illustrating a dirge by Hofshteyn and to use the proceeds to help the orphanage. The title of the work was *Troyer* [Grief], a volume of twenty-nine pages with six illustrations providing a plastic ekphrasis of the verse [fig. 23]. This would be Chagall's last work in the Soviet Union, and it expressed his despair at the pogroms and his general fury with his own situation, which he integrated into the illustrations. The text is a modernist piece of poetry in harsh fragments, depicting a sort of pilgrimage through the Ukraine and its post-pogrom scenes with introspective musings veined with a clear indictment of the ethnic hatred. The drawings of Chagall protest far more strongly than Hofshteyn's verse, which is more guarded.

This art book reveals Chagall's most advanced artistic stylistics. He employed suprematist principles of construction to decry the inhuman destruction. His enemy was Kazimir Malevich, whose pure abstraction Chagall now uses and mocks for its lack of human figures, thereby implying that abstraction is inhuman and mechanical. The drawings all have tilted axes and use the diagonal as a knife blade of destruction. Chagall integrated verse lines and Hebrew letters as plastic shapes and phonetic symbols. This is Chagall's most superb integration of verse, graphics, typography, and page design. From the front cover to the last cover page, the text and art are fully integrated and echo each other. The dirge theme intensifies continually and suffering dominates, drawn in black with red letters representing blood letting.

Chagall organized the page composition along the diagonal to decenter the work and reveal psychological and physical destabilization. All the lines rush off to the peripheries. The letters of the title on the diagonal are an integral part of the composition. They serve as a knife thrust into the body, the scream and woe for the victim: *Troyer* or grief. The body is transgressed by the title, which dominates the page with zoomorphic letters. The doubling function of the Hebrew letters, on both the visual as well as the phonic/morphic levels, emits the primal scream. We also notice that the body itself is crippled. The feet are chopped off, the limbs are missing, and the two heads are superimposed. One is faceless as if effaced; the letters identify the faceless head as Chagall. As for the head above, chopped off, it is the head and face of Hofshteyn, whose name appears in letters shaped of modern guns and bullets. The implication is that now the Hebrew letters are turned into weapons. Art is a weapon of response, and this Yiddish art book is not just a lamentation, but also, an aggressive act. Both artists appear victimized. They are integrated as human victims within the dirge of the other murdered Jews inside the text.

The letters and cover provide the synchronic panorama of the entire work. The letters are written not in formal Hebrew block script, but in distinctive Ashkenazic "written" script. This choice of script intensified the folk identity of this Eastern European Jewry that the Yiddishists sought to distinguish as unique from the other Jewries in the world. Each letter as a visual icon used zoomorphically refers to a poem in the dirge sequence. Chagall built his iconography by using what he learned from the two volumes, *L'Ornement hébreu,* where he discovered the medieval play with Hebrew letters and animal forms, and from Yudovin's *Yidisher Folks-ornement.*

The *Tet* as shaped by Chagall fuses an ax, allusion to the pogroms, a shofar, the call of danger and repentance [*tikiah],* and a phylactery, the call of religious faith that constitutes the first poem. The *Resh* continues the image of the shofar, which becomes the scythe that cuts off the arm. The white fox entrapped inside the scythe alludes to Poem 6 and the pogrom poem. In the poem the white fox becomes the symbol of the frightened, hunted Jews. This appears to be an allusion to Ezekiel 13:4 about the foxes who inhabit the ruins; here, the ruined *shtetlakh*. *Resh* alludes too to Rasha, the evil person, the brute who cuts off the arm. The *Vov* becomes the ax striking the heart of the body and the weapon of choice among the peasants in the pogroms. The *Yud* is the smallest letter of the hebrew alphabet and traditionally represents in Eastern Europe the Jewish people, *Yidlekh*, the little Jews. It serves here as a drop of all the blood shed in the pogroms. The phonics are important here for the *Vov* and the *Yud* joined in yiddish become *oy*, the sound of despair and woe: *Troyer*, grief. The *Ayin* takes the shape of the goat, the *Khad Gad ya* figure, symbol of the Jewish people theatened but with the ability to survive. The final *Resh*, a clear shofar, calls for a return, a redemption. Inside the image we see the little Jew returning in his wagon to his shtetl home. The *Resh* at the beginning is blood red, the life-taker, while the last one is white for redemption. Are we to read into the text the passage from Isaiah, they shall beat swords into plowshares?

The cover turns Chagall and Hofshteyn into modern Christ figures on the cross of Christian Ukrainian peasant violence. The diagonal is the suffering blow. We also note that the christological motif is reenforced by the Suprematist doubling device of line and cross beneath the letters of

Troyer—and all in red! Jews are assimilated into being victims as Christ the Jew was. (The Russian Orthodox cross is always on a diagonal.) This cover design reveals the synchronic tour de force that Chagall has performed. The entire collection of verse has been given its essential representation.

Chagall's talent in page design is at its most sophisticated in the first poem, which is perhaps the single finest performance in page design in all of the Yiddish art books [fig. 24]. The page is split in half by the diagonal knife already revealed in the cover. But the page in fact reveals itself as a giant *Aleph*. The poem begins in hope, which will be crushed by violent death. The epigraph, "*Sivan* (Spring), then *Shvat* (January) misery." The epigraph is the dating and *mise-en-abyme* of the poem as well as marking the 1919 pogroms. The poem is binary, hope and destruction. The *Aleph* of the opening page means unity and beginning, the symbol of life. But suddenly it is split in half. The diagonal bar becomes a weapon and wounds the spoken voice, the poem. Simultaneous perspective of Cubism is grafted to the Suprematist diagonal. The slow motion as the blade swings—the different angles changing as our eyes move along the blade—divides life from death. The page design refuses total death. The *Aleph* being the life force, stands firm, but the blade takes human life. The diagonal of Suprematism represents the inhumane, whereas the *Aleph* of the Hebrew is the life-giving force. This page is a masterful performance of Chagall's integration of Hofshteyn's words and his art, creating this painful but remarkable art book. This art form is hybrid and modern and fuses Russian modernism with Jewish tradition. This art book, *Troyer*, was the most advanced art book produced in the Soviet Union or Eastern Europe. Other art books would still be produced in Yiddish, but none ever reached this level of sophistication and mastery.

The Yiddish art book reflects the tragic history of the Jews in the Revolutionary period, 1917-23. Jewish artists burst forth with incredible creativity and caught up to the cutting edge of the European avant-garde. These Eastern European Jewish artists captured for the first time how Jews saw themselves in their own gaze and illustrated themselves in their own art books, capturing their tragic Ashkenazic environment. Their art books are now recognized as worthy artistic accomplishments equal to the best in Western Europe and in Russia.

fig. 20 #5 from El Lissitzky, *Khad Gad ya*

fig. 21 Berlewi, cover of *Di Kupe*

fig. 22 Tchaikov, cover of *Di Kupe*

fig. 23 Chagall, cover of *Troyer*

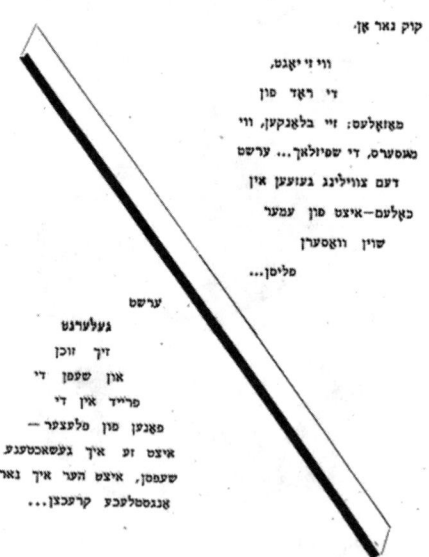

fig. 24 Chagall, page one from *Troyer*

NOTES

[1] There is a school of thought, starting with Richard Cohen, *Jewish Icons* (Berkeley: University of California Press, 1998); Kalman Bland, *The Artless Jew* (Princeton: Princeton University Press, 2001); Catherine Soussloff, ed., *Jewish Identity in Modern Art History* (Berkeley: University of California Press, 1999); and Maragaret Olin, *The Nation without Art* (Lincoln: University of Nebraska Press, 2001), that tries to attenuate the intense distain, scorn, hostility—and even violence at times—of Eastern European Jewry c. 1900 to the practice of the plastic arts among Jews. This traditional negative attitude draws its strength from the commandment against making graven images. Around 1900, with the initial renewal of cultural activities in Eastern Europe, this commandment was still meaningful to most traditional Jews. The above authors argue that the adherence to the commandment was spotty both in Jewish history (witness Dura Europos, etc.) and even in Eastern Europe. Did not Chagall consider himself a descendant of a certain Segal who painted the eighteenth century Mohiliev synagogue? I consider the latter position one of obfuscation. Chagall and El Lissitzky were as astonished as An-Sky, who organized expeditions in 1912-15 to find and collect Jewish art, to discover a few painted synagogues by what seemed to be Jewish journeymen folk artists. Such undertakings had been forgotten. The dominant anti-pictoral attitudes of Eastern European Jewry always reasserted themselves, and certainly throughout the nineteenth century, where there were no known painted synagogues. The Jews of Eastern Europe were the only people in 1900 in all of Europe who could even consider art as a negative. Chaim Soutine was beaten brutally by his *shtetl* for holding a paint brush and had to flee. Chagall's mother "secretly" took her son to meet Yehuda Pen, the first Jewish painter to open an art school, to have him tell her if her son had any talent—much against the scorn of the father. Sholem Aleichem, the classic writer, in his masterpiece *Motl, the Cantor's Son*, planned to have Motl in America become an artist! His mother wails throughout the book that it is a *shande* [a great shame] that a cantor's son could think of such a career. It was for her traditional mind a sinful activity! Sholem Aleichem was mocking her and felt he would have his readers on his side, but the very fact that he would bring out this anti-pictorial bias reveals how potent and widespread it was in Eastern Europe and fully known by his "enlightened" readership. To choose the life of a plastic artist was a true rebellion from Jewish tradition in 1900.

[2] Seth Wolitz, "The Jewish National Art Renaissance in Russia," in *Tradition & Revolution: The Jewish Renaissance in Russian Avant-Garde Art, 1912-1928* (ed.

Ruth Apter-Gabriel), 21-44.

[3] Benjamin Harshav, *Marc Chagall and his Times: A Documentary Narrative* (Stanford: Stanford University Press, 2004), 171.

[4] Alexandra S. Shatskikh, *Vitebsk: zhizn iskusstva, 1917-1922* (Moskva: Azyky russkoi kulturny, 2001).

[5] Benjamin Harshav, ed., *Marc Chagall: On Art and Culture* (Stanford: Stanford University Press, 2003); [Translation of A. Efros and Ya. Tugendhold; Moscow: Helicon, 1918].

[6] Seth Wolitz, "Vitebsk versus Bezalel: A Jewish Kulturkampf in the Plastic Arts," in *The Emergence of Modern Jewish Politics: Bundism and Zionism in Eastern Europe* (ed. Zvi Gitelman; Pittsburgh: University of Pittsburgh Press, 2003), 171.

[7] Ibid.

[8] Michael Berkowitz, *Zionist Culture and Western European Jewry before the First World War* (Cambridge: Cambridge University Press, 1993), 129.

[9] *Evreiskaia grafika Natana Altmana*, 1923 tekst maksa Osborna (Berlin: Petropolis, 1923); *Sovremennaia evreiskaia grafika* (Berlin: Petropolis, 1924).

[10] Yeheskiel Dobrushin, "Yidisher Kunst-primitiv un dos kunst-bukh far kinder," *Bikher-Velt* (Kiev) no. 4-5, August, 1919, 16-23.

[11] Hillel (Gregory) Kazovsky, *The Artists of the Kultur-Lige* (Jerusalem: Gesharim, 5763 [2003]), 34-40. (The text and illustrations are bilingual, Russian and English.)

[12] *Juedische Illustratoren des 20. Jahrhunderts*, catalogue edited with an introduction, "Jiddische Literatur und ihre Illustratoren im 20. Jahrhundert" (pp. 6-27), by Andrea von Huelsen-Esch and Marion Aptroot (Duesseldorf, Heinrich-Heine-Universitaet Duesseldorf, Seminar fuer Kunstgeschichte und Institut fuer Juedische Studien, 2004).

[13] Jerzy Malinowski, *Malarstwo I rzezba Zydow Polskich w XIX I XX wieku* (Warzawa: Wydawnictwo Naukowe PWN, 2000), 182-202.

Beyond "Jewish Luck": The Institutional Context of Early Russian-Jewish Art

Alina Orlov

Russia in the 1910s produced great Jewish artists, including Marc Chagall, El Lissitzky, and Natan Altman. At the same time, the idea of "Jewish art" gained prominence among critics.[1] There emerged an unprecedented number of less famous Jewish artists, including Abram Manevich, Mané-Katz, Isaak Ryback, Robert Falk, and Isaak Rabinovich.[2] These developments are usually discussed in the context of the heady days of World War I and the 1917 Revolution. In this topsy-turvy atmosphere, as it is seen, Jews, like other non-Russian parvenus from the Ukraine, Georgia, and Byelorussia, suddenly took center stage in painting and print-making, in particular, and to a minor extent in art criticism.[3] The appearance of Jewish artists is explained in broad strokes by pointing to increasing urbanization, the rise of nationalism, greater acculturation, and the dissolution of the Pale of Settlement. While we have biographies of individual artists, on the one hand, and histories of the larger processes, on the other, the two are somewhat disconnected. One way to link them is to examine the immediate institutional context in which the artists were able to make the transition from traditional to modern cultural modes.

In becoming professional artists, young Jews managed to find patrons, travel to cosmopolitan centers, attend art schools, rent studios, and exhibit their work.[4] While acknowledging that growing movements like Zionism and Jewish labor created an atmosphere of Jewish self-assertion at the turn of the twentieth century, the typical historic narrative has us marvel at the drive of individual artists. They persevered more or less on their own to only occasionally hit on a lucky break, and the resources available to them were scant. As a typical scenario, this certainly has merit. In comparison to a student in the Imperial Academy of Arts in St. Petersburg in the early 1900s, for example, a fledgling Jewish artist, whose chances of attending such a prestigious school were miniscule, was indeed at a disadvantage.[5] Without diminishing the power of his personal ambition, this essay suggests that a budding Jewish artist had more than "Jewish luck" to navigate the sometimes inimical world of fine art. He also had at his disposal the support of nascent organizations designed to promote Jewish artistic expression.

The importance of Jewish institutions that advocated visual creativity was first indicated by Hillel Kazovksy in his research on Yehuda Pen's art school in Vitebsk. At the close of the nineteenth century Chagall, Lissitzky, and Osip Zadkine received their education here.[6] Historians have also studied the *Kulturlige*, a group established in Kiev in 1919 to fuel the Jewish cultural renaissance.[7] Meanwhile, the role of organizations in St. Petersburg, a central hub of Jewish artistic life in the pre-revolutionary period, has not been adequately examined. We still know next to nothing about Mikhail Bernshtein's school, for example, established here in 1912, one of the few open to Jews. We know little about galleries, like Nadezhda Dobychina's, that sold art made by Jews.[8] Filling in this sparse history will help illuminate the circumstances under which Jews first became artists in Russia.

Two instances of St. Petersburg's institutional history were especially relevant for creating a generation of Jewish artists: the An-Sky Expeditions (sponsored by the Jewish Ethnographic Society) and the Jewish Society for the Encouragement of the Arts (henceforward JSEA). They offered guidance, community, and at times financial support to young Jewish artists. Natan Altman's (1889-1970) early career was particularly influenced by the two projects in ways that will be mentioned below. The An-Sky Expeditions and JSEA reinforced Altman's interest in Jewish folk art, inspired him to develop a formula for modern Jewish art, and helped connect him to a network of patrons.

THE AN-SKY EXPEDITIONS (1912-1914)

Solomon An-Sky's (Shlome Rappoport, 1863-1920) interest in salvaging the dying culture of the Pale of Settlement shtetl was a natural outgrowth of his earlier dedication to Russian Populism, which combined primitive aesthetics with political lobbying for peasant-worker rights. With an awakened sense of Jewish nationalism, An-Sky turned his attention from the Russian to the Jewish folk, a change that expressed itself vividly in 1910, when his correspondence with the political activist Khaim Zhitlovskii

(1882-1953) switched from Russian to Yiddish.[9] A great admirer of the Yiddish writer Leib Peretz (1851-1915), who affectionately portrayed shetl life, An-ski prized the Jewish village for the vibrant raw material it offered to contemporary artists. As a Populist turned Bundist, An-Sky was trained to foresee crises for the working poor and anticipated that the shtetl, as a socio-economic entity, was on the verge of disintegration. His fears were not unfounded; in the years from 1900 to 1904 alone, 4,500,000 people left this region for the United States. Others fled to nearby towns: Minsk, Kiev, Khar'kov, and, when they could accomplish the bureaucratic feat, to Moscow and St. Petersburg. As An-Sky figured, if the shtetl was doomed for extinction because of massive migrations, pogroms, and poverty, he could try to save its cultural artifacts, placing them "out of harm's way." [10]

In the summers from 1912 to 1914, An-Sky led a team of explorers into Pale of Settlement regions of Galicia, Podolia, and in the Kiev province.[11] Here they gathered Jewish folk prints [*lubki*], illustrated manuscripts, Torah ark covers, silversmith work, and other objects. An-Sky recorded legends and tales (one of which he memorialized in his play *Ha Dybbuk*), the artist Solomon Yudovin photographed people and places, and the musicologist Solomon Engel recorded song melodies on wax phonographic cylinders. Officially called "The Ethnographic Expedition named after Baron Horace [Goratsii] O. Ginzburg," the St. Petersburg philanthropist who provided an initial grant of 10,000 rubles, the enterprise eventually came to be known as "An-Sky's." Its total budget of 23,000 rubles was supplied by benefactors of the Jewish Ethnographic Society. The resulting collection consisted of 2,000 photographs, 1,800 folk tales and legends, 1,500 songs and mystery plays, 1,000 melodies, 100 historical documents, 500 manuscripts, and 700 antiques.[12] This formed the basis of the Jewish Museum, the first of its kind in Russia, which enjoyed only a brief existence in the year before the 1917 Revolution, at which point some of the treasures were scattered among various institutions in Kiev, Vilna, and St. Petersburg, while others were lost. As of now, the An-Sky collection in its original entirety has not been accounted for.[13] In 2000, I was fortunate enough to discover 300 of the lost "ethnographic" photographs taken during the expedition, which had been safeguarded by Altman from 1917 to his death in 1970.[14]

An-Sky inspired other Jewish artists to appreciate old forms of art found in the Pale. Several of them followed suit by making pilgrimages of their own to sites of Jewish art making. In 1913, for example, Altman traveled to Gritsev's Jewish cemetery, where he traced tombstone designs onto paper. His series of linoleum cut "Jewish Prints" of the same year re-interpreted the gravestone ornaments in the language of nascent Cubo-Futurism.[15] Two years later Isaak Ryback and El Lissitkzy traveled to Worms, Germany, to study the oldest surviving synagogue in Europe.[16] Around the same time Ryback and Lissitzky visited Mogilev, on the Dnieper River, which was also visited by the artist and art historian Rachel Wischnizer, who would later write about the extravagant ceiling and wall decorations of its eighteenth century wooden synagogue.[17] Like An-Sky, these artists were awed by the artistic expressiveness of traditional Jewish culture. Lissitzky described his impressions of Mogilev: "It was quite a different feeling from the one I had when I first entered a Roman basilica, a Gothic chapel, a Baroque mosque in Germany, France or Italy. I felt like a child enveloped by a screen, opening his eyes upon awakening."[18]

An-Sky's journey also provided the template for expeditions JSEA would plan to make to areas south of Russia in 1916, but its plans for further exploring were foiled by political upheaval. Still, as late as 1919, the leadership of the JSEA did not give up on the idea of collecting more folk art and solicited help from its members.[19] Later, in 1927, Yudovin hoped to travel in the Zhitomirskaia and Khmel'nitskaia regions.[20] And in the 1940s, Jewish artist David Goberman traced An-Sky's original journey and witnessed the remains of shtetl culture.[21]

An-Sky's collection was not exhibited in the Jewish Museum long enough to exert any direct influence on contemporary artists.[22] We know of only two instances when artists relied directly on its materials in their work. Yudovin's exquisite woodcuts of the Jewish shtetl of the 1920s closely approximated his own photographs from the trip.[23] And Altman's 1957 illustrations of the first Soviet publication of Sholem Aleichem relied on two of Yudovin's photographs, a portrait of a woman in a headscarf and a distinctive composition of a synagogue exterior and street lamp.[24]

Still, An-Sky's impact was to instill a high esteem for Jewish visual culture, adding momentum to burgeoning Jewish book illustration and Jewish theater. For Altman specifically, An-Sky's expedition served to demonstrate the value of ethnography in relation to art. For later book illustrations and stage designs for the State Jewish Theater (GOSET), Altman carried out studies of the customs and dress of various ethnic groups.[25] Later, while designing stages for Kiev's GOSET in 1940, he consulted Isai M. Pul'ner, the director of the Ethnographic Museum in St. Petersburg, so as to ensure the accuracy of his representations.[26] Altman's journals from the 1940s contain notations of books on Bessarabia of the nineteenth century, presumably for similar productions. Further, Altman studied the dress of South American Indians in preparation for his drawings on the subject.[27]

Altman developed a lifelong habit of noting ethnographic details in his travels. The photo postcards he sent from France depicted local ethnic costumes and rows of dressed up folk dancers in various regions of France.[28] His letters to his wife in 1940, from his tour to the Soviet south with GOSET, discussed ethnographic rarities and remains from the past. From Lvov, for example, he wrote: "Here there are splendid Baroque churches and an ancient synagogue, which is called 'The Golden Rose.' There are Jews here as you have never seen, such that even I have seen only in pictures."[29]

It is mainly through this ethnographic principle, then, that An-Sky's imprint on Altman's work manifested itself. The collection's effect on other Jewish artists, and for that matter on other Russian artists, was probably even less. As a group of objects to preserve, study, and display, which was An-Sky's intention, the collection failed to the extent that the Museum failed to survive. We can only wonder about its influence on artists, especially those associated with JSEA, which housed the Museum, had the collection survived longer. Still, An-Sky's expedition served several important functions: it indicated a new direction in visual art toward the folk, the primitive, and the "ethnographic" elements of the Jewish Pale. It spawned several similar albeit smaller expeditions, which were carried out by Altman, Lissitsky, Ryback, and Wischnitzer. Finally, An-Sky's expedition set a general tone in which Jewish art making was deemed precious and its appreciation—in an institutional context—worthwhile.

THE JEWISH SOCIETY FOR THE ENCOURAGEMENT OF JEWISH ART (1915-1919)

If An-Sky's expedition found evidence of Jewish visual creativity in the past, JSEA helped bring it about in the present by hosting lectures, holding contests and competitions, securing commissions, and finagling residential permits for its members, many of whom, including Chagall and Altman, had no legal basis for living in the capital. Like Icarus, An-Sky had suggested the limits of what was possible, and JSEA, like the Wright brothers, worked out the mechanics that would actualize this idea. Modeled on social labor unions, JSEA provided community, infrastructure, schools, exhibition halls, and money to its members, aiming thereby to advance them as a group.

JSEA came into being on September 20, 1915, when it registered with the city of St. Petersburg. Its mission statement quoted almost verbatim from that of the Imperial Society for the Encouragement of the Arts, which had been established in 1821 to aid the poorer of the students of the Imperial Academy.[30] JSEA diverged from its forerunner in a novel way, by including in its goal "the expansion of the plastic arts (painting, sculpture, architecture, etc.) among the Jews, artistic education of the Jewish masses, and the development of a national creative art."[31] Its Jewish orientation made explicit, JSEA was the first and probably only such group in Russia's history, devoted to promoting art among the Jews, that was granted rights to gather, exhibit, publish, organize museums, libraries, and schools, and conduct research.[32] Ilya Gintsburg assumed its directorship, and on November 29, 1915, seventy-five people came to its first meeting. In December, JSEA opened a branch in Moscow.[33] In 1916, JSEA also opened branches in Kiev, where An-Sky served as director, and Khar'kov, bringing the total number of members to 239 and the annual budget to 4,500 rubles.

The founders of JSEA included Maxim Vinaver, a wealthy businessman, active in politics, who had supported Jewish talent privately for years. Baron Osip G. Ginzburg and his mother Baroness Matilda Ginzburg were active JSEA members from 1915 to 1918. In this respect, Ginzburg was continuing the tradition of his father Baron David G. Ginzburg (1857-1910), the philanthropist and Orientologist who, three decades earlier, had famously published ancient Hebrew manuscripts with Vladimir Stasov, another initial champion of Jewish art.[34] JSEA's most active leader was Gintsburg, the onetime student of Mark Antokol'skii and now professor of sculpture at the Academy of Arts, who discussed the topic of Jewish art in his courses. The sculptor's circle of acquaintances included Ilya Repin, Lev Tolstoy, Vladimir Stasov, Maxim Gorkii, and Fedor Chaliapin. Thus he was able to connect artist to benefactor.[35] Whatever guidance, tutelage, and social connections these men could provide on an individual basis, they hoped to systematize and expand by banding together in an official capacity.

The institutors of JSEA, while diverging in their political and aesthetics leanings, shared a common belief that the main impediments to Jewish involvement in the arts were Jewish poverty and Russian prejudice. They could only chisel away at problems like limited educational opportunities, insufficient access to scholarship money, and scarce exhibiting venues. They did manage, however, to help young Jews from provinces with the more immediate and ubiquitous problem of obtaining residency in the capital.[36] Even established artists like Isaac Levitan, despite his position as professor at the Moscow School of Painting, was forced to leave that city, which had similar residency laws, because of lack of proper paperwork. Chagall was once jailed for not having necessary permits.[37]

In its first years, JSEA held its meetings at the Jewish Convalescent Home named after M. A. Gintsburg on Vasilievskii Island, Line 5-50.[38] In a chapter dedicated to the Home, Mikhail Beizer describes it as a nexus of Jewish cultural activity, although its primary purpose was to house the sick and elderly.[39] In its halls, Simon Dubnow delivered lectures on a regular basis for what was informally known as the "Jewish University." Emblazoned on the façade of the Home was the name of its founder, Gintsburg, related neither to Baron Ginzburg nor to the sculptor and JSEA director Gintsburg. One can make out the letters on the front of the building in one of the An-Sky collection photographs that Altman had owned. Presumably, the photo was taken by Yudovin after the expedition, when the collection made up the Jewish Museum and was housed in the Home.[40]

JSEA took on a great variety of tasks. It supported scholarship investigating Jewish artistic expression and sponsored various lectures, including, in 1916, Gintsburg's "Sculpture among the Jews" and Maxim Syrkin's "Jews and Art" and "Jewish Art and Our Times."[41] In 1918, JSEA invited historian Rachel Wischnitzer to carry out a systematic study of Jewish ornamentation. According to JSEA's records, in August 1919, Wischnizer was "collecting materials in the Asiatic Museum and the Public Library [and] photographing illustrations in different *hagades* for the purposes of slide-demonstrations."[42]

In 1916, JSEA put on several exhibitions and auctions in St. Petersburg and Moscow, the benefits from which went to the victims of the war. It held competitions for commissioned ex-libris designs and postcards. The Society planned the construction of a technical and crafts school in Ekaterinoslav, for which it received a grant. It discussed the possible reconstruction of the St. Petersburg Choral Synagogue. It also received and distributed among its members various orders for book illustrations and festivity decorations. Together with the Jewish Ethnographic Society,

JSEA maintained a small library and the aforementioned Jewish Museum.[43] JSEA made itself sufficiently well known to elicit numerous letters from around the country from places like Simferopol', Novo-Vorontsovka of Kherson province, Chernigov, Nevel in Vitebsk province, Genichesk in Tavricheskaia province, Mestechko Podobrianka of Mogilev province, and Trostianets of Khar'kovskaia province.[44] In these letters, young men sought advice and funding, asking if they could send samples of their work.[45]

Another of JSEA's achievements was to provide a venue for discussing the theory of Jewish art. In the beginning of 1916, Altman first raised the issue at a meeting, saying that "no one has an opinion as to what kind of art Jewish artists should produce."[46] A year later in Kiev, JSEA leader Iakob Tugendhol'd delivered a lecture on this topic, arguing that while Jewish national art exists only in theory and in practice is usually "cosmopolitan," art made by Jews is linked perhaps only in "spiritual" ways.[47] In 1918, JSEA discussed whether or not to drop "national art" from its mission statement. Some argued that without this clause, JSEA had no raison d'être.[48] Others insisted that JSEA should support all artists of Jewish descent, regardless of the content or style of their work.[49] The latter non-exclusionary position held sway within JSEA, prioritizing the making of good art above that of national art. The show the Society organized in 1916, for example, included the work of Leon Bakst, who was not a member of JSEA or interested in making "Jewish" art. The accompanying catalogue bragged about the "limitless range" of art produced by Jewish artists.[50]

Despite a yearlong paralysis in 1917, JSEA continued its activities starting in April 1918, when it reviewed its statutes and even expanded some of its goals. It established contact with magazines such as *Art of the Commune, Art and the Worker,* and *Art*, which were organs of the Department of Fine Arts (IZO) established under the leadership of Anatoly Lunachrasky.[51] While Gintsburg stayed on, the burden of directorship shifted to Isaac Brodskii, A. M. Bramson, and A. B. Lakhovskii.[52] A budget of 380,000 rubles was estimated for the year 1919.[53] But the leadership now became beholden to the government, which doled out money and adjudicated questions of artistic merit.

As an attempt to retain a degree of autonomy within this new structure, in March 1918, several members made a motion to form a Jewish Artistic Club called "Mneiro." Bramson envisioned it as an independent body that would "realize, on a practical level, those activities that educated the artistic side of the general mass and facilitated the development of national art."

But little seems to have come out of this plan.⁵⁴ JSEA remained active under state governance until May 1919. During its last year, the Society's scope of activities dwindled to one project, a publication of textbook illustrations and posters on Jewish themes. After a lengthy review process of artists' submissions, over a dozen commissions were offered, including ones to Altman, Pasternak, and Chagall. Because JSEA's funds were soon cut off, these designs were never published.⁵⁵ It is worth noting that Altman, as a JSEA artist submitting his work for selection, would have benefited from his post in the Department of Fine Arts, which he had taken in 1918, in effect judging his own work.⁵⁶

JSEA played an important role in launching the career of Altman, one of its most active members. If An-Sky inspired Altman to turn to shtetl ethnography, the JSEA encouraged him to develop and championed his shtetl aesthetics. When JSEA held a competition for the design of its insignia in 1916, Altman won the first prize. The competition rules demanded a "Jewish style." After a discussion of what this would entail, JSEA surrendered to the ambiguity of the situation. "We know full well," announced the committee, "that a Jewish style as such does not exist."⁵⁷ In requesting submissions from a broad pool of artists, including non-members, by placing adds in a range of magazines, such as *Zodchii*, an organ of the Imperial Society of Architecture, JSEA refused to specify its criteria for "Jewish style" in any detail. Internally, however, it cultivated certain expectations, such as "Eastern ornamentation," as the meeting notes make clear.⁵⁸

The selection of the winner by a jury of artists, including Boris Anisfeld, B. F. Blokh, and Abram Manevich, resolved the vagueness around "Jewish style" and ended JSEA's ostensible naïveté in this regard. Now there was a reference point for what JSEA meant by a Jewish style.⁵⁹ Executed in a manner that grew out of his *Jewish Prints*, Altman's black and white emblem featured Hebrew characters arranged symmetrically across the margins. It was Primitivist in concept, lacking figuration and compositional complexity.

In return for providing JSEA with an example of a modern Jewish style, the organization made Altman its darling. It awarded him prizes and commissions, mentioned him along with Chagall in lectures and publications, and showcased his work in JSEA exhibits. JSEA's spotlight on Altman helped buoy him to high status in related spheres. Providing the momentum for Altman's innate ambitions, JSEA helped launch Altman into a career in the Jewish theater, administrative positions, teaching, and book illustration, all of which were the more profitable career paths for artists in the 1920s.

This essay suggests the need to consider institutions in our studies of the genesis of modern Jewish art. It underscores the importance of self-organized groups, which replaced traditional synagogue-based Jewish communities. Led by motivated individuals like An-Sky and Gintsburg, these groups rallied around modern secular culture as a cause. Their activities served to support—both morally and financially—emerging Jewish artists. In the case of some, like Solomon Yudovin, a young artist who collaborated most closely with both An-Sky and the JSEA in the mid-1910s, the role of these groups was intensely formative. Yudovin stayed exceptionally committed to An-Sky's idea of folk-derived Jewish iconography in his work of the 1920s and 30s and tried to pass on this legacy to the next generation. For many others, such as Abram Manevich and Leonid Pasternak, who only briefly interacted with the JSEA and at a time when their artistic directions had already been set, the group's effect on their work was less than negligible. For Altman, their influence can be characterized as palpable albeit brief, with JSEA, especially, propelling him to a new level of prominence.

Overall, the An-Sky Expedition and JSEA served to create a favorable climate for early efforts by Jews to produce fine art. In generating research and publications and establishing initial patronage and exhibition systems, these organizations lent credibility to the notion of Jewish artistic talent and created public forums for its appreciation.

NOTES

[1] A notable example is Nikolai Lavrskii, *Iskusstvo i evrei* [Art and the Jews] (Moscow: Iskusstvo i zhizn', 1915).

[2] Surveys of this period include Avram Kampf, "The Quest for a Jewish Style in the Era of the Russian Revolution," Chapter 1 in his *Jewish Experience in the Art of the 20th Century* (South Hadley: Bergin and Garvey, 1984), 15-47; and Ruth Apter-Gabriel, ed., *Tradition and Revolution: The Jewish Renaissance in Russian Avant-Garde Art, 1912-1928* (2nd ed.; Jerusalem: Israel Museum, 1991).

[3] Nicoletta Misler, "The Future in Search of Its Past: Nation, Ethos, Tradition and the Avant-Garde in Russian Jewish Art Criticism," in Apter-Gabriel, *Tradition and*

Revolution, 143-54.

[4] The biographical approach is best exemplified by Waldemar George, "The School of Paris," in *Jewish Art: An Illustrated History* (rev. ed; ed. C. Roth; Greenwich: New York Graphic Society, 1971), 229-60.

[5] The Imperial Academy of Arts in St. Petersburg continued its long-standing quota of three new Jewish students per year well into the twentieth century. This was despite the outstanding successes of its Jewish pupils like Mark Antokol'skii, Ilya Gintsburg, Moisei Maimon (1860-1924), and Isaac Brodskii.

[6] Gillel' Kazovski, *Ieguda Pen i ego ucheniki* (Shedevry evreiskogo iskusstva; Moscow: Image, 1993).

[7] Victor Margolin, *The Struggle for Utopia. Rodchenko, Lissitzky, Moholy-Nagy* (Chicago: University of Chicago Press, 1997).

[8] John E. Bowlt, "The Moscow Art Market," in *Between Tsar and People: Educated Society and the Quest for Public Identity in Late Imperial Russia.* (ed. E. W. Clowes, et al.; Princeton: Princeton University Press, 1991), 108-30.

[9] YIVO. Chaim Zhitlovsky papers, 1895-1920. See reference in Fruma Mohrer and Marek Webb, eds., *Guide to the YIVO archives* (Armork: M. E. Sharpe, 1998). Zhitlovky's early political transformation is indexed by the two parties he helped found: first the Russian Socialist Revolutionary Party and later the Jewish Socialist Labor Party; this trajectory shaped An-Sky's own political evolution.

[10] Chagall wrote in his memoirs that in painting the inhabitants of Vitebsk in 1914, he had wanted to put them "out of harm's way." *My Life* (trans. Elizabeth Abbott; New York: Orion Press, 1960), 134.

On the collapse of the Pale, see Mark Levitats, *The Jewish Community in Russia, 1844-1917* (Jerusalem: Posner, 1981); and Ezra Mendelsohn, *The Jews of East-Central Europe Between the World War* (Bloomington: Indiana University Press, 1983).

[11] An-Sky's team included Iu. Engel', Z. Kissel'gof, and Solomon Yudovin.

[12] S. An-Sky, "Pis'mo v redaktsiiu: O rabotakh Etnograficheskoi Ekspeditsii," *Evreiskaia starina.* 2 (Apr-June 1915): 239-40. Recently, some of the melodies have been restored on a CD that was produced in Kiev.

[13] Upon returning to St. Petersburg in the early 1920s, Yudovin reopened the Museum and took on the task of safeguarding it. At one point, he even moved into its quarters. He tried expanding its collection of Jewish art by purchasing pieces by Altman, Yudovin, Yehuda Pen, and Aleksandr Tyshler. In 1929, the Museum reportedly owned 1,500 photographs, 350 sound cylinder recordings, and 350 ceremonial objects. The Museum was closed and reopened several times in the late 1920s and early 1930s until its final closing in 1934.

[14] Aleksander Pasternak, Altman's friend and colleague, after preserving the photographs from 1970 to 2000, entrusted them to the Jewish Museum in St. Petersburg, newly re-founded by Valerii Dymshitz and Victor Kel'ner. The publications of the photos are forthcoming in *East European Jewish Affairs*.

[15] These were later reproduced in *Evreiskaia grafika Natan Al'tmana* (introd. Max Osborn; Berlin: Petropolis, 1923).

[16] Lissitzky's own notes about the date of these travels were ambiguous. Margolin, *The Struggle*, 24 fn. 40.

[17] Rachel Wischnitzer, "The Ornaments of the Mohilev Synagogue," *Heavar* 15 (1968): 251-53 [in Hebrew]. According to Kampf, Wischnizer went to Mogilev in 1912. Kampf, "The Quest," 17. For an example of her art, see the inside cover design in M. Balaban, et al., ed., *Istoriia evreiskogo naroda*, vol. 1 (Moscow: Mir, 1914).

[18] Quoted in Kampf, "The Quest," 17-18; El Lissitzky, "Al bet hakneset bemogilev," *Rimmon* 3 (1923): 9-12. Also appears in Yiddish in *Milgroim* 3 (1923): 9-13.

[19] A JSEA member named O. G. Breitbart, who was traveling south for health reasons, was asked to see what he could gather on behalf of JSEA. Another member, M. G. Serebrenyi, who was traveling to Vilna for separate reasons, was requested to do the same. And a certain member named Gutmanovich was sent to the south on a special assignment [*komandirovka*] for this reason. See Letters to O. G. Breitbart and M. G. Serebrenyi in Central State Historical Archive in St. Petersburg f. 1722 n. 5, pp. 173, 183, 185.

[20] Although outside the historical parameters that concern us here, two final mentions should be made with regards to the reverberations of An-Sky's original expedition. His path through Galicia and the Ukraine was retraced in the 1940s by Yudovin's disciple and artist David Goberman. See his *Evreiskie nadgrobiia na Ukraine i v Moldavii. Vystavka fotografii* (St. Petersburg: Iskusstvo Rossii, 1999). The founding of the Jewish Museum in St. Petersburg in recent years and the attempt to document surviving synagogues in the regions of the former Pale, an effort of St. Petersburg-based historians led by Valerii Dymshitz, also continue An-Sky's legacy.

[21] David Goberman, *Carved Memories: Heritage in Stone from the Russian Jewish Pale* (New York: Rizzoli, 2000).

[22] John E. Bowlt has made this argument in his conference paper, "Ethnic Loyalty and International Modernism: The Ansky Expeditions and the Russian Avant-Garde," *Between Two Worlds: S. Ansky at the Turn of the Century* (Conference at Stanford University, March 2001).

[23] I. Ioffe and E. Gollerbakh, *S. Yudovin: graviury na dereve* (Leningrad: Akademiia

Kudozhestv, 1928).

[24] Sholem Aleichem, *Siarmarki: Rasskazy* (trans. R. Rubina; illust. Natan Altman; Moscow: Gosudarsvennoe Izdatel'stvo, 1957).

[25] Altman outfitted Indians, Alaskans, and ancient Romans in Berta Lask, *À travers les âges: voyages d'un elephant sur un cheval ailè* (illust. Natan Altman; Paris: Éditions sociales internationales, 1933).

[26] I kindly thank Liudmila Uritskaia, the current Deputy Director of the Archives at the Ethnographic Museum, for conveying this information in a personal conversation.

[27] E. Zibert, *Legendy i skazki indeitsev latinskoi ameriki* (illust. N. Altman; Moscow: Gosudarstvennoe izdatel'stvo khudozhestevennoi literatury, 1962). Around the same time, Altman painted a portrait of his wife, Irina Shchegoleva, in Indian headwear, a work that now hangs in his family's private collection in St. Petersburg.

[28] In September 1930, Altman sent two posters to his wife in Paris from Bretagne: "Fete des Drapeaux Bretons. Costumes" featured a group of dancers in embroidered clothes; "Une Pont-Avenaise" showed a woman in traditional costume.

[29] Archive of the Russian Museum f. 199 op.1 n. 7 p. 9.

[30] For a history of this society, see P. N. Stolpianskii, *Staryi Peterburg i Obshchestvo Pooshchreniia Khudozhestv* (Leningrad: Komitet populiarizatsii khudozhestvennykh izdannii, 1928).

[31] *Ochet evreiskogo obshchestva pooshreniia khudozhestv za 1916 g.* (1917). In writing the proposal for JSEA, the founders relied on the model provided by the Greater Russian Society for the Encouragement of the Arts, an organization of long-standing repute that provided stipends to the needier of students at the Imperial Academy. Isaac Brodskii, for example, had received a stipend from this organization when he studied there in 1903. Central State Historical Archives f. 448 n. 1283.

[32] *Vestnik evreiskogo prosveshennia* 35 (1915): 23.

[33] The appointed directors of the Moscow branch were little-known artists L. M. Antokol'skii (unrelated to the sculptor); M. I. Gabovich, an engineer; an amateur collector named Ia. F. Kagan-Shabshai; and government barrister, A. L. Fuksf. Central State Historical Archive 1722 n. 4. 3, 5.

[34] D. Gunzbourg and Vladimir Stassof, *Ornementation des anciens manuscript hébreux de la Bibliothèque Impériale Publique de Saint Pétersbourg* (St. Petersburg: Gunzbourg, 1886).

[35] Gintsburg introduced Chagall to his first benefactor, Baron David Ginzburg, who provided him with a stipend of ten rubles a month. Chagall, *My Life*, 82.

[36] JSEA helped Altman, for example, list his official address with the Baron Ginzburg family, at Vasilevsky Island Line 1, 44. His real residence, as it appeared in the JSEA directory of members, was in an apartment one block away from the Society, at Vasilveskii Island, Line 4, 66. *Ves' Peterburg na 1914 god: Adresnaia i spravochnaia kniga g. S. Peterburga* (St. Petersburg, Izdatel'stvo Tov-va A. S. Suvorina "Novoe vremia," 1914); JSEA's Members Directory, 1916, Central State Historical Archive f. 1722 n. 5.

[37] Larry Silver, "Diaspora, Nostalgia, and the Universal Conditions of Modern Jewish Artists," in *Transformation: Jews and Modernity* (ed. Larry Silver, et al.; Philadelphia: Arthur Ross Gallery at University of Pensilvania, 2001), 13-34.

[38] Central State Historical Archives f. 1722 n. 2 p. 1.

[39] Mikhail Beizer, *Evrei v Peterburge*. (Jerusalem: Biblioteka Aliia, 1989), 131-53.

[40] The photograph pictures several rows of frail aged people, tidily dressed in pressed uniforms and well groomed, lined up neatly in front of the building.

[41] Ilya Gintsburg, "Skul'ptura i kul'turnye zadachi evreev," *Evreiskii mir* 1 (Jan 1909): 123-8; and M. Syrkin, "Evrei i iskusstvo," *Evreiskaia nedelia* 25 (19 June 1916): 38-40. See also notes from Syrkin's unpublished lecture, "Evreiskoe iskusstvo i novye vremena," in the Central State Historical Archive f. 1722, n. 5 p. 148; f. 1722 n. 1 p. 71.

[42] f. 1722 n. 2. p. 19.

[43] Chagall's claim that the JSEA ran a school cannot be confirmed by archival evidence. Chagall wrote that he was allowed to enter the school at the third-year level, but we have yet to ascertain what exact institution he had in mind. Chagall, *My Life*, 82.

[44] Central State Historical Archives f. 1722, n.1 pp. 1-35

[45] For ten such letters, see Alina Orlov, "K istorii Evreiskogo Obshchestva Pooshchreniia Khudozhestv, 1915-1919," *Ezhegodnik Evreiskogo Muzeia* [Jewish Museum Annual, St. Petersburg], edited by Viktor Kel'ner. Forthcoming.

[46] January 2, 1916, f. 1722 n. 3 p. 2 back.

[47] Central State Historical Archives f. 1722 n. 1 p. 51 C78

[48] A. M. Bramson, M. F. Blok, D. L. Ziv, and I. Ia. Gintsburg favored maintaining the "national art" phrasing; Central State Historical Archives f. 1722 n. 2 p. 9.

[49] A. Lakhovskii and M. Siniaver wanted to do away with the clause. f. 1722 n. 2 p. 10.

[50] Evreiskoe obshchestvo pooshchreniia khudozhestv, *Katalog vystavki kartin i skul'ptury khudozhnikov evreev* (Moscow, 1917). Some artists shunned the organization for ideological reasons. Leonid Pasternak, for example, declined an

Beyond "Jewish Luck"   75

invitation to join JSEA because he was averse to the idea of a national art. Mané-Katz and Abram Manevich, both of whom came to St. Petersburg from Kiev via Paris, were JSEA members for only a brief period in 1916.

[51] Central State Historical Archives f. 1722 n. 5 p. 26.

[52] Others to join the director's board were M. F. Blockh, M. I. Solomonov, D. K. Ziv, and O. G. Breitbart; Central State Historical Archives f. 1722 n. 6 p. 42.

[53] Ibid.

[54] Central State Historical Archives f. 1722 n. 5 pp. 2-7; Bramson's quote is from April 13, 1918: f. 1722 n. 2 p. 8.

[55] The following theme assignments were offered on January 3, 1919: to Pasternak — "Father Returns Home from Work"; Chagall — "Children with Family" and "Wedding"; A. Lakhovskii — "The Taylor and the Shoemaker"; S. Simkhovich— "Passover"; P. I. Geller— "The Carpenter"; I. Brodskii — "Mother and Child"; N. Altman— "Celebrating the Sabbath" and "The Alphabet"; M. Blokh and I. A. Greenman — "The Locksmith"; A. Ia. Piatigorskii — "The Fairy-Tale" and "The Teacher"; M. Maimon — "Chanukah"; M. L. Shafran — "Sukkoth"; M. G. Slepian— "The Watchmaker"; S. M. Zaidenberg — "Grandpa and Grandma"; M. G. Shatan — "Purim"; and S. N. Gruzenberg — "The Carriage Driver." M. I. Solomonov received an offer to produce the poster for the fight against tuberculosis for the Society of the Protection of Health among the Jewish Population.

[56] See reports on IZO's activities *in Iskusstvo kommuny* 19 (13 Apr 1919), 4. JSEA made a request to IZO to fund the poster project for children, showing ten posters as samples; the members of the board, including Altman, Gruzenberg, Lakhovskii, and Simkhovich, considered the petition and affirmed six of the posters. f. 1722 n. 6 pp. 93-109, 119.

[57] Central State Historical Archives f. 1722 n.1 p. 59, back.

[58] Ibid., f., 1722 n. 1 p. 36.

[59] Ibid., f., 1722 n. 3 p. 2.

Yudovin, "Gravestone"

Yudovin, "Jewish Cemetery"

Beyond "Jewish Luck"

Yudovin, "Jewish Tailor"

Yudovin, "Shtetl Jews"

Yudovin, "*Shtetl* Shop"

An-Sky Collection, St. Petersburg Jewish Museum

Karl Emil Franzos and Bertha Pappenheim's Portraits of the (Eastern European Jewish) Artist

Elizabeth Loentz

Karl Emil Franzos (1848-1904) was a journalist for the Viennese *Neue Freie Presse* and other major German-language newspapers. His fame was founded on a trilogy of travelogues on Eastern Europe, *Aus Halb-Asien* [From Half-Asia], and a collection of novellas, *Die Juden von Barnow* [The Jews of Barnow], which were translated into 16 languages.[1] In addition to his own prolific literary and essayistic production, Franzos published an anthology of Austrian literature and a biweekly literary journal, *Deutsche Dichtung* [German Literature], and edited the collected works of German author Georg Büchner (who wrote *Woyzeck*, the basis of Alban Berg's opera *Wozzeck*).[2] Bertha Pappenheim (1859-1936), who is now better known as Anna O., the first case study in Sigmund Freud and Josef Breuer's *Studien über Hysterie* [Studies on Hysteria][3] and the (co)inventor of the talking cure, was well known during her lifetime as a social worker (focusing on aid for Eastern European Jewish refugees and immigrants, and women's and children's issues, including the *agunoth* and unwed mothers). She was also a leading activist in the campaign against white slavery, the founder of the Jewish Women's League of Germany and co-founder of the International Jewish Women's League, and a literary author and translator of Glückel of Hameln's memoirs and other early modern Yiddish works.[4] Both authors were born and raised in Austria (Franzos in Czortkow, the Barnow of his stories; and Pappenheim in Vienna), and both relocated to Germany as adults (Pappenheim in 1888 to Frankfurt, her mother's home; and Franzos in 1887 to Berlin).

In her review in the Viennese Jewish periodical *Dr. Bloch's Wochenschrift* [Dr. Bloch's Weekly], Regina Neißer compared, with good reason, Pappenheim's *Kämpfe: Sechs Erzählungen* [Struggles: Six Stories (1916)] to the stories of Franzos.[5] Of the numerous similarities in the two authors' writings, the most striking are their fictional portrayals of the dilemma of young, would-be Jewish artists in Chasidic and ultra-Orthodox Jewish communities in the Eastern regions of the Austro-Hungarian Empire. The affinity is most evident in Franzos's posthumously published novel *Der Pojaz* [The Clown (written 1873, published 1905)][6] and Pappenheim's story *Der Wunderrabbi* [The Tzaddik or The Miracle Rabbi]. *Der Pojaz* is the story of Sender Glatteis, a gifted Chasidic Jewish orphan who surreptitiously learns German and studies the German classics in the vain attempt to become an actor. His adoptive mother Rosel promised his dying father Mendele, a *schnorrer* [an itinerant multi-talented entertainer], that she would prevent Sender from following in his footsteps; Sender has no idea that acting is in his blood. Sender's education is guided by a cadre of mentors: Adolf Nadler, the German-speaking Jewish director of a traveling theater; Heinrich Wild, a Viennese soldier re-stationed to the provinces as punishment for his revolutionary activities; Father Marian Poczubut, a monk banished to the local monastery for writing a heretical book; and Malke, an educated and acculturated female *maskil* who narrowly escapes an engagement to a Chasid. Just when it appears that Sender is about to reach his goal, his adoptive mother begs that he abandon his acting. Unwilling to repay her selflessness with defiance, he returns home, where he succumbs to the tuberculosis-like respiratory disease that developed from years of study in the unheated monastery library and from reading through the night.

Arjeh, the protagonist of Pappenheim's "The Tzaddik,"[7] likewise secretly reads the German classics at night. Unlike Rosel, Arjeh's mother supports her son's artistic pursuits. She persuades her husband to release Arjeh (who like the "Pojaz" suffers from tuberculosis, which is aggravated by his nocturnal studies) from his obligation to follow in his father and grandfather's footsteps as the next miracle-working *tzaddik* and instead send him to Vienna to study German literature. Notably, the spiritual gift of the *tzaddik*, which is traditionally passed from father to son, is destroyed (from the traditional perspective) or rationalized (from the enlightened one) by the gift of Western (especially German) literature. Instead of the gift of the *tzaddik*, Arjeh inherits his father and grandfather's secret obsession with German books.

While "The Tzaddik" is clearly in dialogue with Franzos's novel, it is also a companion piece to Pappenheim's story *Ein Schwächling* [A Weakling], which was first published in 1902 (that is, before the publication of *The

Pojaz).[8] Gabriel, the protagonist of "A Weakling" (who is based loosely on the historical figure Philipp Veit, a grandson of Moses Mendelssohn, who converted to Catholicism and became an artist in the Nazarene school),[9] is introduced to secular culture (music and the visual arts) by his new Christian neighbors, a violinist and his daughter. His neighbors discover and help him to develop his natural gift for drawing. When his father, a teacher at a Talmud school, discovers his drawings and that he has been consorting with his neighbors, he sends him to another city to begin a business apprenticeship. Gabriel abandons his apprenticeship and runs away to Vienna to become a painter. Burdened by poverty and anti-Semitism, Gabriel contemplates suicide but is "rescued" by a priest. He converts, studies art in Rome, and becomes a famous painter of biblical scenes. Later regretting his betrayal of his father and his faith and people, he commits suicide.

The Jewish artist (visual artist, musician, composer, writer, or actor) was a contested figure in late nineteenth and early twentieth century Central and Eastern Europe. Germanophone anti-Semitic critics, including Jews, charged that Jews possessed neither aesthetic sensibilities nor creative powers. Among others, these critics included Richard Wagner, Otto Weininger, Karl Kraus, and Heinrich von Treitschke. Jewish artists whose work was traditional or conventional, or in line with current trends, were dismissed by these critics as imitators lacking originality. Avant-garde innovators were accused of creating degenerate art that was a corruption of the (German) national/cultural body.

Zionists and other Jewish nationalists, as well as their assimilationist opponents, on the other hand, debated the existence and/or desirability of a Jewish national art. Important figures in the inter-Jewish discussion of Jewish national art included Cultural Zionist Martin Buber, David Kaufmann and other proponents of the *Wissenschaft des Judentums* [Science of Judaism], and Boris Schatz, the founder of Bezalel,[10] the first institutional effort at promoting Jewish national art.[11]

Franzos and Pappenheim, however, were not chiefly concerned with debunking anti-Semites' rejection of the Jewish artist or carving a place for him (their artists are all male) within German culture, nor did they share the Cultural Zionist project of defining and promoting Jewish art as an integral part of the Jewish national project.[12] Rather, their texts were intent on furthering the Haskalah ideal of dual and compatible German national/cultural and Jewish religious identities among as yet unacculturated Central and Eastern European Jews. In the Chasidic communities (and *mitnaggedim* and other Orthodox communities that were opposed to Haskalah ideals) targeted by Franzos and Pappenheim, secular artistic pursuits were discouraged. They were viewed, at best, as a waste of time and a distraction from more worthy pursuits; at worst, as immoral and anathema to the Jewish religion. The development of Yiddish into a literary vernacular distracted from the study of religious texts. Overexposure to the dominant language, especially German, was a corrupting influence that promoted apostasy.

Professional musical performance was largely restricted to religious practice, the art of the cantor, or communal celebrations, such as weddings.[13] The visual arts suffered under presumed Jewish aniconism or the fear of idolatry. Critical of Chasidism, but equally opposed to the newer rival ideologies that might supplant it (in particular, Zionism and other Jewish nationalisms, Bundism, and Socialism), as well as conversion, Pappenheim and Franzos employed the figure of the Eastern European artist to illustrate alternatives to these movements. Their texts seek to demonstrate that tolerating or even promoting the younger generation's interests in German secular culture would not speed the erosion of tradition, but actually serve to preserve it by preventing defection and apostasy.

JEWISH AUTHORS CROSSING THE EAST-WEST DIVIDE

Franzos and Pappenheim were not natives or insiders, neither were they complete strangers or outsiders to the Eastern European Jewish communities portrayed in their works. Franzos grew up in Eastern Galicia, but his father was an imperial government official and an ardent German nationalist. His family was not religiously observant, but they considered themselves nominally Jewish by religion and condemned conversion. In his preface to *Der Pojaz*, Franzos describes his childhood as follows:

> My schoolmates and playmates were Christians.[14] I seldom entered a Jewish house and never a synagogue. My parents did not observe rituals or dietary laws. I grew up as if on an island. Language and culture separated me from my classmates and from the Jewish boys. I was a Jew, but a different kind of Jew, and I didn't completely understand their language. I was very enthusiastic about Judaism, but had only scant knowledge of the real life of the Jews around me.[15]

Despite his admittedly superficial knowledge of Eastern European Jewry, Franzos's travelogue trilogy, *Aus Halb-Asien,* earned him the reputation of an expert on the subject. In the preface to the 1901 edition, Franzos attributes his expertise to his dual East-West identity or insider-outsider status:

> My work is as different in content and bias from the travelogues of Western tourists as it is from Eastern European authors' own portrayals of their homeland. To native patriots, even Rumania and Bessarabia seem splendid, and tourists are so shocked and disgusted by the enormous strangeness/exoticism, that everything appears submerged in the deepest darkness....I was born in the East but as the son of German parents. I grew up in a Galician town but in a German house. My precocious national consciousness instinctively sharpened my perception and gave me a certain objectivity towards the conditions in the East. I had the opportunity to become acquainted with these conditions in every detail....But I was also able to become acquainted with the cultured peoples of the West. I know the East, but not only the East. Completely free from both inner prejudice and external pressures, I am in the enviable position of being able to say openly what I think.[16]

Although Pappenheim was born in Vienna and grew up there, she was well acquainted with the milieu of Eastern European Orthodox Jewry. Her father, who came from Pressburg (Bratislava, Slovakia), was a founder of the Viennese Orthodox *Schiffschul,* whose members were predominantly Hungarian and Galician Jews. Based on her mission work in Eastern Europe, her social work with Eastern European Jewish immigrants in Germany, her extensive *Studienreisen* [investigative travels] in Eastern Europe, and her essays on the Eastern European Jewish question, Pappenheim was also considered an expert on Eastern European Jewry.

Pappenheim was initiated into the world of Jewish social work in Frankfurt in the early 1890s, working in a soup kitchen for needy Jewish immigrants from Eastern Europe. In 1900, she published her first pamphlet on the Eastern European Jewish question, *Zur Judenfrage in Galizien* [On the Eastern European Jewish Question in Galicia].[17] In the early 1900s, she belonged to the *Komitee für die ost-europäischen Juden* [Committee for the East European Jews] in Frankfurt; in 1901, she founded the Frankfurt women's organization *Weibliche Fürsorge* [Care by Women], whose projects included aid for Eastern European immigrants. In addition to aiding Eastern Jewish immigrants, Pappenheim and the *Weibliche Fürsorge* founded nursery schools in Galicia and sent numerous female "cultural missionaries" to work there.

In 1903, under the auspices of the Frankfurt *Israelitischen Hilfsverein* [Jewish Aid Association] and the *Jüdischen Zweigkomitee zur Bekämpfung des Mädchenhandels* [Jewish Branch Committee for the Battle Against the Trafficking of Women], Pappenheim undertook with Dr. Sara Rabinowitsch the first of several *Studienreisen* to Galicia. Her report on this trip, *Zur Lage der jüdischen Bevölkerung in Galizien: Reise-Eindrücke und Vorschläge zur Besserung der Verhältnisse* [On the Situation of the Jewish Population in Galicia: Impressions from a Tour and Recommendations for Improving the Conditions],[18] established her reputation as an expert on the social welfare of Eastern European Jewry. In the spring of 1906, Pappenheim traveled to Russia to assess damage to pogrom-stricken Jewish communities and to organize local relief efforts. After the trip she arranged for the adoption of 120 Jewish orphans by Western European Jewish families. In 1908, she embarked on a further *Agitationsreise* [Agitation Trip] to Galicia. In 1909, Pappenheim traveled throughout the Balkans, where she petitioned Queen Carmen Sylva of Rumania to join in the crusade against white slavery. In 1917, she served as *Fabrikpflegerin* [factory social worker/workers' guardian] for the 300 Eastern European Jewish females forced to labor in munitions factories in Frankfurt-Griesheim and Höchst. In 1918, she organized aid for 80,000 Russian Jewish and 50,000 Polish Jewish orphans. In 1926, she journeyed to the Soviet Union, where she toured the Jewish Agro-Joint colonies. In November 1935, (just six months before her death), she traveled to Krakow to inspect the Beth Jacob Seminary.

Like Franzos's preface to *Aus Halb-Asien*, Pappenheim's preface to her report *Zur Lage der jüdischen Bevölkerung in Galizien* likewise extols the unique aptitude of the insider-outsider to objectively assess the situation of Galician Jews and offer recommendations for reform:

> Above all, I must refrain from wanting to be regarded as an expert on Galicia after a mere five-week visit.
>
> My Austrian citizenship/heritage, my Orthodox Jewish upbringing, and especially my occupation, which lets me look back on ten years of experience in caring for the poor, are my excuses for

volunteering to take this journey, which I hope will not remain without practical results.

Because not everything about the Galician Jews that seems foreign or disconcerting to a non-Austrian or non-Orthodox Jew can simply be put on the list of things that should be smoothed out by the carpenter's plane of West European Culture....Demands for reform should be made only in instances, where there is an ignorance or degeneration of cultural norms recognized as universal and indispensable....To have a thorough knowledge of a land and its people, one must have lived there for years. On the other hand, when one has lived in a country for years and has immersed oneself in the customs and practices of a people, one can easily lose the ability to observe and judge impartially, and what is gained in depth is lost in clarity.[19]

Although both authors position themselves as insider-outsider, there is a qualitative difference in their insider knowledge of Chasidic and traditional Orthodox Eastern European Jewry. Pappenheim's upbringing in the very traditional Eastern-Western *Schiffschul*, her social work in Eastern Europe and with Eastern European immigrants to Germany, not to mention her knowledge of Yiddish, allowed a greater intimacy than either Franzos's insular secular upbringing in Eastern Europe or his later tourism. Especially Pappenheim's involvement shortly before her death with the Beth Jacob Seminary in Krakow attests to her willingness to cooperate with traditional Orthodox and Chasidic Jews in Eastern Europe.[20] Sara Schnirer, the founder of the Beth Jacob movement, grew up in an Chasidic family, and the school was generally tolerated by even the most traditional communities. A number of Chasidic leaders, including the exceedingly strict Belzer Rebbe, spoke favorably of the school, and the Ger and Lubavitcher Rebbe even allowed Chasidic girls to attend. The schools were funded in part by Agudat Israel, an international Orthodox organization, which had been founded largely in opposition to the advancement of Zionism, Bundist socialism, and Reform Judaism, and had united in this cause three relatively disparate factions: German (Neo-)Orthodoxy, Hungarian Orthodoxy, and Polish and Lithuanian Orthodoxy (including Chasidic Jews). Although the German Neo-Orthodox Agudat Israel was open to secular culture and favored the integration of Orthodox Jews into general European society, the more conservative Polish and Lithuanian branch did not.

Although it is not possible here, a comparison of Pappenheim's, Franzos's, and other German and Austrian Jewish writers' texts to those by Eastern European Jewish writers (including Americans of Eastern descent), especially those raised within Chasidic or Orthodox traditions, would be worthwhile. These could include Yiddish author and amateur musician Sholem Aleichem's (1859-1916) trilogy of novels, *Stempenyu* (1888), *Yosele Solovey* [The Nightingale, or, The Saga of Yosele Solovey the Cantor](1889), and *Blonzhende shtern* [Wandering Stars](1909-1910); and American novelist and painter Chaim Potok's (1929-2002) novels, *My Name is Asher Lev* (1972) and *The Gift of Asher Lev* (1990).[21]

JEWISH SELF-CRITIQUE

Jewish self-critique was a hallmark of Pappenheim's social work and activism, and it caused her to be a much-maligned public figure. For example, her public remarks that the majority of white slave traders were Jews prompted fearful accusations that she was inciting anti-Semitism;[22] a 1907 speech that suggested that Jewish women's lack of religious education had reduced them to the status of sexual objects or breeders prompted a barrage of attacks from the men in the audience.[23] Pappenheim, who once signed a later "Your extremely difficult Bertha Pappenheim," did not waver, insisting, "No one, who knows of injustice anywhere, may remain silent. Neither gender, nor age, nor religion, nor party can justify remaining silent. Knowing of injustice and remaining silent makes you an accessory."[24] Pappenheim reasoned that exposing Jewish vice in order to instigate reform within the Jewish community would ultimately curtail anti-Semitism. She even argued that the *wachsende Unsittlichkeit* [growing immorality] within the community was more dangerous to Jews than the *Haß der Völker rings um uns her* [hate of the peoples around us].[25]

At least one Eastern European Jewish intellectual took umbrage when Pappenheim's Jewish self-critique was aimed at Eastern European Jews. The Galician publicist Benjamin Segel issued a scathing critique of the work of the *Weibliche Fürsorge*, the Frankfurt social work agency founded by Pappenheim, in Galicia. Segel's two-part article, which was written in response to the annual report of the *Weibliche Fürsorge*, charged Pappenheim's colleagues with being ignorant of conditions in Galicia and with exhibiting the typical Western European chauvinism toward Galician

Jews. He is particularly critical of "Schwester Johanna's" report that her attempts to bring "order" to a hospital in Drohobycz (Ukraine) resulted in death threats from Galician Jews, who angrily threw stones at her when she attempted to institute visiting hours. Segel writes:

> I have heard similar reports from the colonies of German East Africa, Australia, and the regions where savages and cannibals live. You will get a cold shiver down your spine, when you consider the dangers that the heroic Sister Johanna so valiantly defied in order to uphold the Western European principle of order, and you comprehend "just what it entails, how much energy and good will is required to undertake such a campaign against the lack of culture", as the report so proudly stresses.[26]

Like Pappenheim, Franzos defends his Jewish self-critique as his duty as a Jew and a matter of conscious. In his preface to *Der Pojaz*, Franzos writes:

> I believe that I have done my duty towards my fellow Jews, that I have worked to help and not to harm them. Confident of this, the Chasidic who attack me and vituperate against me have not caused me to waver. Chasidic Jews have often told me to convert to Christianity, as Judaism had no room for someone with my views. But I tell myself, "This is the best proof that you have done your duty. If you had been so foolish, unjust, and cowardly as to turn your weapons only against Judaism's external enemies and not against the inner enemies of healthy development, then these men would have been satisfied with you but no one else, least of all your own conscience."[27]

The strategy of Jewish self-critique employed by both Franzos and Pappenheim was problematic for several reasons. Their critics were correct in the assumption that they provided fuel for anti-Semites. Pappenheim's writings on Jewish involvement in human trafficking, for example, were reprinted in the anti-Semitic propaganda organ *Der Stürmer*. The assumption that ridding Jews (especially Eastern European Jews) of their supposed faults would eliminate anti-Semitism falsely and dangerously implied that Jews themselves were responsible for anti-Semitism. Fighting anti-Semitism on this front also diverted their attentions from addressing actual causes of and perpetrators of anti-Semitic policies and violence and from adopting other potentially more effective strategies. It is also possible that Western reformers of Eastern European Jews were motivated in part by the desire to distinguish themselves from their Eastern brethren, a strategy that mistakenly assumed that German anti-Semites were wont to distinguish between assimilated Western and unassimilated Eastern Jews.

THE AUTHORS' GERMANOPHILIA

In Franzos's *Der Pojaz,* it is presumed that to become an actor, a true artist as opposed to a *schnorrer*, the Galician Jew must master the German language and German culture. The possibility that the Jewish artist's ascent to true art could transpire in the Polish or Ukrainian language, let alone Yiddish, is never broached. While *Der Pojaz* simply elides these possibilities, Franzos's preface to *Aus Halb-Asien* explicitly dismisses them. Yiddish is rejected as a "corrupt Jargon" undeserving of the epithet "cultured language." Polish is dismissed because it is more difficult for Yiddish-speaking Jews than German and would be an unnecessary "detour" on the way to Eastern European Jew's ultimate "destination," which is "the acquisition of Western culture."[28]

Franzos displays a general bias against Eastern European (especially Polish) culture: "If the Polish Jew has not risen to the stature of his German or French brethren, not he but the Polish Christian is to blame. For each land has the Jews that it deserves."[29] Franzos (who was once indicted for treason for a pan-Germanic speech he gave while amember of a German nationalist student fraternity) denies, however, that his call for *die Verbreitung deutscher Kultur* [spreading German culture][30] in Galicia is politically motivated. He insists that it is not for the good of the Germans, but for the good of the Galicians:

> Because Germany is one of the most educated nations of the world…and because the German spirit is naturally imbued with a certain selflessness and affection…because the most unique advantage of our German education, simple thoroughness, is preciselythe one that is the least inherent to the peoples of the East and therefore needed the most. For these reasons, I believe that a broader and deeper influence of our culture would be a salvation for the Half- and Unculture of the East.[31]

Franzos deliberately rejects the term *Germanisation* [Germanization], however: "Germanization is truly not what I have in mind here. Germanization is an un-German word for an un-German deed. Whoever loves his own national traditions would never want to take this most precious possession from another. What I am referring to here is the dissemination of German culture....The duty of German culture in the East is to awaken and promote the cultural strivings of the peoples there, to be like a pole in the garden, on which their own national culture can grow and climb."[32] Franzos held fast to the idyllic myth of a multi-ethnic and multi-national Austrian empire whose benevolent Germanophone emperors (with the help of German-speaking bureacrats, who, like Franzos's father, were stationed throughout the empire) protected the minority rights of the various peoples in his charge:

> As long as Galicia and the Bukowina were administered by German civil servants, there was peace, peace in national and religious matters. Prosperity was beginning to grow; and the justice and education systems were on the same level as in Western Austria. Because wind and sun were divided impartially between them, the Pole, Ruthenian, and Rumanian could work, in peaceful competition and encouraged and directed by the German example, toward the development of their intellectual life; and the Jew was able to join the German culture.[33]

Whereas Pappenheim, like Franzos, rejects Yiddish, which she also considered a jargon unworthy of the moniker "cultured language" and accordingly unsuitable as an artistic medium, she does not recommend that Galician and other Eastern European Jews overstep other languages in favor of German. While Arjeh's path is clearly defined as the German one and other options are not broached in "Der Wunderrabbi," Pappenheim advocates elsewhere for learning other languages. The protagonist of Pappenheim's story *Der Erlöser* [The Redeemer], for example, rents a room from native Parisians in order to improve his French and urges that his Yiddishist friend do likewise. In her travel letters, *Sisyphus-Arbeit* [Sisyphus Work], Pappenheim advised that Jewish girls in Turkey should learn Turkish for employment purposes, and she praises Jews in the Young Turk movement for their commitment to Turkish nationalism and Turkish language.[34] In *Zur Lage der jüdischen Bevölkerung in Galizien*, she recommends instruction in both Polish and German for Galician Jewish girls and English lessons for American-bound immigrants.[35] While Pappenheim certainly agreed with Franzos that German was the most easily accessible "language of culture" for Yiddish-speaking Jews, as a social worker she pragmatically insists that mastery of the dominant language of one's surroundings is the first priority.

THE PORTRAYAL OF MODERN CHASIDIM AND THE HEDER

Both Franzos's and Pappenheim's heroes risk their lives for their art. They contract life-threatening diseases that are caused or aggravated by having to study in secret because their studies are considered sinful within their Chasidic communities. Both Franzos and Pappenheim vilify modern Chasidim, charging Chasidic Jews with a variety of excesses and failings. In *Der Pojaz*, Franzos juxtaposes the Chasidic Jews of Barnow with the *misnagdim* of Buczacz:

> The Jews of Barnow are Chasidim…wild fanatics, who alternate between terrible asceticism and lavish feasting. They claim to be the "Blessed" among Jews because they drink from deeper sources of revelation, those of the Kaballah….In Buczacz on the other hand, live the *misnagdim*, stern, sober people, who honor the Bible above all, and the Talmud only insofar as it explains the Bible. The *misnagdim*, practical and cool people, live for better or worse according to the laws of their religion, but they consider the ten commandments to be more important than everything else, they explain miracles with natural means, and are not prone to excessive brooding.

> The Barnower are great fasters, but also avid drinkers. Life in Bucacz follows a moderate, monotonous course. In Barnow they carry on learned debates all day long and only work or usure during the breaks. The Buczaczer are dedicated to their crafts and business. The industriousness and sense of civil honor and duty are greater. The respect for intellectual work and charity for the poor or scholars is smaller.[36]

Franzos likens the *misnagdim* to Protestant Rationalists. Ritchie Robertson correctly assesses Franzos's strategy:

> Evidently their [the *misnagdim's*] religion is supposed to exalt rationality and ethics above ritual observance, and thus to qualify them for citizenship of an industrious Protestant state like Prussia….Franzos's readers are to understand that not all Eastern Jews are so obstinately alien and unassimilable as the Chasidism

of Barnow. To convey this message, however, Franzos has had to distort his picture of Eastern Jewish Life by combining the most unattractive features of Chasidism and Talmudic Judaism and charging Chasidism with both.[37]

Whereas Franzos, a wholly secular Jew, seems most concerned with the way Chasidism appears to outside (especially German) observers, hence the comparison to Protestants, Pappenheim, who was raised Orthodox and remained observant throughout her lifetime, is more interested in Chasidism's spiritual core. She criticizes what she perceives as the replacement of observance with *kavannah* to empty routine, the perversion of the "spirit of Jewish teachings" via the creation of a "priestly cast" of *tzaddikim* who abuse their position:

> Historically, Chasidism is a mystically pious, anti-Talmudic movement. Today, Chasidism holds the spirit of the pure doctrine of God and morality transfixed in forms and formulas, so that its adherents cannot see through the heap of trivialities to the heart of Jewish teaching….Although Jewish religion knows no Dogma and no priests as mediators between man and God, in Galicia, the so-called miracle rabbis have become a priestly caste, who use their influence in the most excessive and damaging ways. Their influence not only cripples the slightest stirring of forward-looking development, but kills the spirit of Jewish teachings.[38]

As a social worker/educator, she was most distraught by the *heder*. Pappenheim writes, Galician Orthodoxy requires boys to begin studying Hebrew, the Torah, and the Talmud at age three. All other knowledge is frowned upon, because 'if it isn't in the Talmud, you don't need it.' "She characterizes the pedagogy of the *heder*, as "monotonous drill" carried out by a teacher "who isn't good for anything else," with the aid of corporal punishment meted out with "sticks, leather belts, and whips."[39] Franzos's characterization of the Chasidic *heder*, which he refers to as a *Schandfleck des orthodoxen Judentums* [Mark of shame for Orthodox Judaism] and *Marterhöhlen für Körper und Geist* [Torture chambers for body and soul] is nearly identical:

> Nobody has ever been killed in a *heder*. That may be true, as long as you are talking about a clear and simple murder, the kind that can be punished by the gallows. But many a life has certainly been slowly strangled there: through the deplorable abuse of

uncultivated fanatics. It is certainly a beautiful and intelligent element of Jewish tradition that learning is a religious duty and erudition a service to God, and that the only sort of "nobility" recognized by Jews is the "nobility" of erudition. One could only wish that traditional Jews could show equal respect for other types of knowledge, not only from reading Hebrew, the Pentateuch, the Talmud and the Kabala.[40]

ALTERNATIVES TO TRAGEDY

The stakes are high for Franzos's and Pappenheim's budding Jewish artists. Pappenheim's Gabriel "Der Schwächling" and Franzos's Sender are confronted with the all-or-nothing attitude of Jewish authority figures. For Gabriel's father and Sender's rabbi, secular culture and Jewish religion are incompatible. Gabriel's father's rants leave him no choice but to betray his art, which he cannot, or his faith:

> Artist! That means living the life of a vagabond, not wearing tefillin, not keeping the sabbath, eating and drinking indiscriminately, and painting gods and saints....Did you forget that it is written, "You shall not make images of other gods," and are you so filled with the poison that you drank that you look me in the eye and tell me that you drew a god? Woe is me! I would have preferred that you were never born than that I should witness that my only child desert the faith of his fathers![41]

While Gabriel's father's wrath is directed specifically at his art and is grounded in the Jewish taboo against icons,[42] Sender's rabbi rejects any unnecessary exposure to non-Jewish culture. He forbids Sender's engagement to a Jewish girl who can read German, declaring, *Deutsch Lesen und Schreiben ist ein Makel fürs Leben, noch mehr—ein Gift ist es!* [Reading and writing German is a defect for life, what's more—it is a poison!]. When he learns that Sender has also learned German, he curses him and threatens to excommunicate him.

Both Franzos and Pappenheim caution that this all-or-nothing attitude could lead to the loss of members of the younger generation through conversion. Malke of *the Pojaz* describes the fate of one of her uncles, whose *lebenskluger aber überaus strenggläubiger* [wise in the ways of the world but exceedingly strict] father demanded that he become a medical doctor but remain *nicht minder fanatisch...wie er selbst* [no less fanatical than he is]:

> So Froim had to wear the caftan in high school, and while at university in Pest he had to board with Chasidim. It was Hell on Earth. The Christians mocked him and the Jews considered him sinful. Is it any wonder that he learned to hate the constraints of his religion and finally cast it off? The Chasidim made a Christian out of him!⁴³

With the example of Malke's other uncle, Franzos offers an alternative to apostasy:

> "My uncle Max, who is now a lawyer in Czernowitz, however, suffered through the same martyrdom but then only cast off the constraints and not the religion." Then she told enthusiastically what a wonderful man he was, a champion for the rights of his coreligionists but also for their moral ennoblement and liberation.⁴⁴

Franzos's conception of religion was a Judaism in name only. Franzos summarized his own relationship to Jewish religion in his autobiographical sketch "Mein Erstlingswerk": "There is one God above us all. All religions are equally benevolent because all of them obligate their followers to be humane. Ceremonial practices are unnecessary. Having been born a Jew, you are obligated to remain a Jew because this is God's will and because your coreligionists, who are still seen in an unfavorable light, are in need of good and educated men who ennoble and defend them."⁴⁵ This minimalist view of Jewish religion did not suffice for Pappenheim, who, although she insisted that she was politically and ideologically "neutral," was ideologically closest to German Neo-Orthodoxy, whose proponents maintained that secular pursuits (including art) and Orthodoxy were compatible and advocated the integration of Orthodox Jews into general Jewish culture.⁴⁶

Although she was not as understanding of converts as Franzos (her title *Ein Schwächling* implies her conviction that the convert himself, not maltreatment by anti-Semites or the failings of his community, is ultimately responsible for his own actions), Pappenheim was sympathetic to Gabriel's plea to his father, "God created beauty, and he gave me talent, so that I can nurture it so that it thrives, so I can become an artist. People will say I am blessed by God, not godless."⁴⁷ Philosopher Margarethe Susman reports that Pappenheim referred to art as *die höchste Emanation des menschlichen*

Geistes [the highest emanation of the human spirit]. According to Susman, Pappenheim stated, "Calling art a prophetic expression is one of the most naively beautiful moments in the Zennerenne".[48]

While Gabriel, like Franzos's Sender, must ultimately die as a result of the conflict between art and faith, Arjeh survives because of his parents' willingness to accept a modicum of secular education—not instead, but alongside of Orthodox practice.[49] Pappenheim sought to implement her ideal of the compatibility of Orthodox practice and secular pursuits, including the fine arts, in her social work with Jewish girls and women. In a report on the home she founded for unwed mothers and endangered girls, Pappenheim insisted, "Isenburg must be run strictly according to Jewish ritual and with a conscious Jewish spirituality".[50] She objected to the notion that there was a contradiction between Orthodox Judaism and the knowledge, appreciation, and enjoyment of secular culture, especially the fine arts. Indeed, her *Anregungen für die Weiterführung der Arbeit im Heim* [Suggestions for Continuing Work in the Home] include arranging lectures, children's plays, and music on Sunday evenings.[51]

Helene Krämer, who grew up in the Jewish girl's orphanage that Pappenheim directed prior to founding Isenburg, remembers: "She also tried to awaken in us an appreciation for art and aesthetics, and I remember visiting museums and sites in the immediate vicinity and beyond."[52] Johanna Stahl, another of Pappenheim's charges, remembers: "Only the best was good enough for our education. Lectures, concerts, theater, books, the especially lovely hours she spent reading especially well-written novellas to us while we did fine crafts."[53] In 1929, Pappenheim commissioned sculptor F. Kormis (who also sculpted her likeness) to craft a fountain, *Der vertriebene Storch* [the exiled stork] for the garden in Isenburg.[54]

The fine arts also played an important role in fundraising for Isenburg. In 1911, one of Pappenheim's plays was staged for fundraising purposes, directed by Fräulein Klinkhammer of the Frankfurt Schauspielhaus.[55] Other fund-raisers relying on the fine arts included a 1925 production of Goethe's *Jahrmarktfest zu Plundersweile* [Market Festival at Plundersweile] with actors from the *Neuen Theater*, the sale of plaques depicting the *Auffindung Moses* [discovery of the infant Moses] by Leo Horowitz,[56] and the sale of Pappenheim's own original hand-beaded necklaces.[57]

Not only did Pappenheim not eschew the fine arts as incompatible with Orthodoxy, but she also integrated the arts into religious observance at Isenburg, believing that they would not detract from but enrich religious celebration. For example, she composed a *Schabbeslied* [Sabbath song] for her charges and wrote a Purim-play, *Die Haselnusstorte* [The Hazelnut Cake], to be performed by the home's children. Sara Eisenstädt, a close associate, explains: "Bertha Pappenheim attributed great pedagogical value to aesthetic beauty."[58]

Both Franzos and Pappenheim propose models for reconciling the Eastern European Jewish artist with his (their artists are exclusively male) Jewish identity and community. Whereas Franzos shows little interest in preserving his artists' religion (an intact ethno-cultural identity and solidarity suffice for him), Pappenheim seeks to demonstrate the compatibility of artistic pursuits and Judaism. Neither author, however, seeks to resolve the tension between the artist and Chasidim because both Germano-centric authors viewed Chasidism as a major barrier to the desired modernization and Westernization of East European Jewry. Two post-Shoah American Jewish writers, Chaim Potok and Pearl Abraham, have revisited the question of the place of art and the artist within Chasidism.

Chaim Potok's *My Name is Asher Lev* seeks to resolve the tension between the arts and Chasidism, creating a tenuous place for one young artist within the Chasidic community. The Ladover Rebbe, realizing that he cannot stop Asher Lev from using his "gift," resolves to oversee Asher's education as a painter to ensure that he will not abandon his faith and that his gift will ultimately serve the community. It is notable that Potok's Rebbe also condones Asher's mother's university studies, with the understanding that her Ph.D. in Russian history will also benefit the sect. There are, however, limits to free artistic expression. Asher's Brooklyn Crucifixion series, which oversteps these bounds, results in a temporary break between Asher and the Chasidic community and Asher's return to France, where he had studied. In the sequel, *The Gift of Asher Lev*, Asher returns to the Brooklyn Chasidic community twenty years later. When Asher realizes that his son Avrumel has been chosen to succeed the Rebbe, he must choose between his family and community and his gift. Unable to work within the confines of the community, yet unwilling to defy the Rebbe's wishes, Asher returns to France, leaving his wife and son behind. It is notable that Asher had not abandoned Judaism in the two decades during which he distanced himself, physically and emotionally, from Chasidism. Whereas Asher managed to reconcile his identity as artist and observant Jew, he could not reconcile his need for free artistic expression with the confines and increasing demands of his Chasidic community. Asher Lev, although fictional, is widely considered to be based on both Potok, whose staunchly Orthodox father opposed his painting, and Marc Chagall, who also faced hostility from the Jewish community for his use of Christian imagery.

Pearl Abraham, who grew up within the Satmar sect of Chasidism, portrays in her debut novel *The Romance Reader*,[59] the story of Rachel, a Chasidic girl, whose voracious consumption of secular popular literature (especially romance novels) results in her rebellion and the failure of her arranged marriage. Abraham attributes her own break with Chasidism in part to her youthful consumption of secular literature (including Dickens, Hawthorne, and Shakespeare) at the ultra-Orthodox (but not Chasidic) girls' school that she attended in her childhood home of Monsey, New York. Whereas Rachel, the fictional consumer of secular literature, remains, for the time being, within the community, Abraham the artist breaks with Chasidism. Although she now lives outside the community, she reamins close to her family and insists that she has not rejected Chasidism: "I feel it is very much part of my life."[60] She continues, for example, to portray the contemporary Chasidic milieu and its folklore in her works. The protagonist of her recent novel *The Seventh Beggar*[61] is obsessed with the legendary *tzaddik* and story-teller Rebbe Nahman of Bratslav, and attempts to create a female golem. With the title *The Seventh Beggar*, which alludes to Rebbe Nahman of Bratslav's last (unfinished) story, she symbolically reintegrates herself into the Chasidic fold.

NOTES

[1] Karl Emil Franzos, *Aus Halb-Asien: Culturbilder aus Galizien, der Bukowina, Südrußland und Rumänien* (Leipzig: Duncker und Humblot, 1876); *Vom Don zur Donau: Neue Culturbldler aus Halb-Asien* (Leipzig: Duncker und Humblot, 1878); *Aus der großen Ebene: Neue Kulturbilder aus Halb-Asien* (Stuttgart: Bonz, 1888); *Die Juden von Barnow* (Stuttgart: Adolf Bonz, 1887).

[2] Karl Emil Franzos, ed., *Deutsches Dichterbuch aus Österreich* (Leipzig: Breitkop and Härtel, 1883). Georg Büchner, *Sämmtliche Werke und handschriftlicher Nachlass. Kritische Gesammt-Ausgabe* (ed. Karl Emil Franzos; Frankfurt a.M.: J.D. Sauerländer, 1879).

[3] Josef Breuer and Sigmund Freud, *Studien über Hysterie* (Leipzig and Vienna:

Franz Deuticke, 1895).

[4] Bertha Pappenheim, trans., *Allerlei Geschichten: Maasse-Buch. Buch der Sagen und Legenden aus Talmud und Midrasch nebst Volkserzählungen in jüdisch-deutscher Sprache. Nach der Ausgabe des Maasse-Buches, Amsterdam 1723* (Frankfurt a.M.: J. Kauffmann, 1929); *Die Memoiren der Glückel von Hameln* (Vienna: S. Meyer and W. Pappenheim, 1910); *Zeenah U-Reenah: Frauenbibel. Übersetzung und Auslegung des Pentateuch von Jacob Ben Isaac aus Janow* (Frankfurt a.M.: J. Kauffmann, 1930).

[5] Regina Neißer, "review of Bertha Pappenheim, *Kämpfe: Sechs Erzählungen*," *Dr. Bloch's Wochenschrift* 34:22 (1917): 372.

[6] All subsequent references to *Der Pojaz* refer to Karl Emil Franzos, *Der Pojaz: Eine Geschichte aus dem Osten* (Hamburg: Europäische Verlagsanstalt, 1994/2002).

[7] Bertha Pappenheim, "The Tzaddik," in *Kämpfe: Sechs Erzählungen* (Frankfurt a.M.: J. Kauffmann, 1916), 43-66. All further citations of "Ein Schwächling" refer to the 1916 version.

[8] Bertha Pappenheim, "Ein Schwächling," *Jahrbuch für jüdische Geschichte und Literatur* 5 (1902): 210-46. Pappenheim, "Ein Schwächling," in *Kämpfe: Sechs Erzählungen* 141-88.

[9] I am grateful to Helga Heubach for alerting me to this possible connection.

[10] Pappenheim visited Bezalel in 1911. Although she praised the institution's organization and pedagogical principles, she found it artistically *grauenhaft* [horrible]. Bertha Pappenheim, *Sisyphus-Arbeit: Reiseberichte aus den Jahren 1911 and 1912* (Leipzig: Paul E. Linder, 1924), 103.

[11] For recent studies of "Jewish Art," see the following studies and anthology: Margaret Olin, *The Nation Without Art: Examining Modern Discourses on Jewish Art* (Lincoln: University of Nebraska, 2001); Kalman Bland, *The Artless Jew: Medieval and Modern Affirmations and Denials of the Visual* (Princeton: Princeton University, 2000); and Vivian B. Mann, *Jewish Texts on the Visual Arts* (Cambridge: Cambridge University, 2000).

[12] A small incident in *Der Erlöser* [The Redeemer], another of the stories in Pappenheim's collection *Kämpfe*, attests to Pappenheim's rejection of Jewish nationalism in general and a Jewish national art in particular. A young Jewish artist, Wolf, has his girlfriend Reisle model for his sculpture "Israel erwache!" As a young orphan, Reisle was a victim of human trafficking and had converted to Christianity. Although Wolf believes that Reisle has reformed and returned to Judaism, she continues to wear a diamond-studded cross and to work as a prostitute, hardly a fitting model for the "awakening" Jewish nation and its national art.

[13] According to Henry Sapoznik, the number of rabbinic injunctions raised against wedding performers (both *badkhonim* and *klezmorim*), "shows how entertainment, even when linked to a specific requirement, remained suspect in the eyes of the clergy." Sapoznik notes, however, that the Chasidim "placed a higsh value on music and dance as an augmentation to prayer and study." Harry Sapoznik, *Klezmer! Jewish Music from the Old World to Our World* (New York: Schirmer, 1999), 17-18.

[14] Franzos attended a Domincan monastery school.

[15] Franzos, *Pojaz*, 6-7. These and subsequent translations from the German works of Franzos and Papenheim are by the author.

[16] Reprinted in Fred Sommer, ed., *Karl Emil Franzos: Kritik und Dichtung, eine Auswahl aus seiner Schriften* (New York: Peter Lang, 1992), 30.

[17] P. Berthold (Bertha Pappenheim), *Zur Judenfrage in Galizien* (Frankfurt a.M.: Gebrüder Knaur, 1900).

[18] Bertha Pappenheim, *Zur Lage der jüdischen Bevölkerung in Galizien: Reise-Eindrücke und Vorschläge zur Besserung der Verhältnisse* (Frankfurt a.M.: Neuer Frankfurter Verlag, 1903).

[19] Pappenheim, *Zur Lage*, 6

[20] Wolf S. Jacobson, "Beth Jacob und Bertha Pappenheim," *Blätter des Jüdischen Frauenbundes für Frauenarbeit und Frauenbewegung* 12.10 (Oct 1936), 1-2. Bertha Pappenheim, "Leitgedanken von Bertha Pappenheim," *Blätter des Jüdischen Frauenbundes für Frauenarbeit und Frauenbewegung* 12.10 (Oct. 1936), 3-4.

[21] Sholem Aleichem, *Blondzhende Shtern* (New York: Hebrew Publishing, 1920), *Stempenyu* (Odessa: A. Warchawer, 1888), *Yosele Solovey* (New York: Sholem Aleichem Folksfond, 1919); Chaim Potok, *My Name is Asher Lev* (New York: Fawcett, 1972), *The Gift of Asher Lev* (New York: Knopf, 1990).

[22] Pappenheim, *Sisyphus-Arbeit* 155, 164; "Zur Sittlichkeitsfrage" (speech presented at the 2. Delegiertentage des Jüdischen Frauenbundes, Frankfurt a. M., 2-3 October 1907), 19.

[23] Isak Unna, "Fräulein Pappenheim und die Stellung der Frau im Judentum," *Frankfurter Israelitisches Familienblatt* 5.40 (18 Oct. 1907), 2, "II. Delegiertentag des Jüdischen Frauenbundes," *Frankfurter Israelitisches Familienblatt* 5.39 (11 Oct. 1907), "Jüdischer Frauenbund," *Frankfurter Israelitisches Familienblatt* 5.39 (11 Oct. 1907), "Der 2. Delegiertentag des Jüdischen Frauenbundes," *Allgemeine Zeitung des Judentums* 71.38 (20 Sept. 1907), 448-49, "Zweite Delegiertenversammlung des jüdischen Frauenbundes," *Allgemeine Zeitung des Judentums* 71.42 (18 Oct. 1907), 500-02,

23 "2. Delegiertenversammlung des jüdischen Frauenbundes," *Die jüdische Presse* 38 (1907), 426-28.

24 Pappenheim, *Sisyphus-Arbeit*, preface.

25 Pappenheim, "Zur Sittlichkeitsfrage," 19.

26 Benjamin Segel, "Die Tätigkeit der Frankfurter 'Weiblichen Fürsorge' in Galizien," *Frankfurter Israelitisches Familienblatt* 9.22 (1 June 1911), 1-2; 9.23 (9 June 1911), 1-2.

27 Franzos, *Pojaz*, 10-11.

28 Reprinted in Sommer, *Karl Emil Franzos*, 43.

29 Ibid., 36.

30 Ibid., 32.

31 Ibid., 38.

32 Ibid., 32.

33 Ibid., 39.

34 Pappenheim, *Sisyphus-Arbeit*, 36.

35 Pappenheim, *Zur Lage*, 54, 56, and 65.

36 Franzos, *Pojaz*, 44-45.

37 Ritchie Robertson, "Western Observers and Eastern Jews: Kafka, Buber, Franzos," *Modern Language Review* 83:1 (January 1988): 94.

38 Pappenheim, *Zur Lage*, 41-42.

39 Pappenheim, *Zur Lage*, 12.

40 Franzos, *Pojaz*, 40.

41 Pappenheim, "Schwächling," 153-55.

42 That Pappenheim sat for numerous portraits (a painting by Leopold Pilichowsky in 1925, two drawings by Samson Schames ca. 1930, a drawing by Josef Oppenheim in 1934) attests to her liberal interpretation of the second commandment, which is frequently cited as the source of Jewish aniconism and the resultant marginalization of the visual arts.

43 Franzos, *Pojaz*, 249-50.

44 Franzos, *Pojaz*, 250.

45 Quoted in Carl Steiner, "Karl Emil Franzos," in *Major Figures of Nineteenth-Century Austrian Literature* (ed. Donald G. Daviau; Riverside: Ariadne, 1998), 223.

46 Mordechai Breuer, *Modernity Within Tradition: The Social History of Orthodox Jewry in Imperial Germany* (New York: Columbia University, 1992).

47 Pappenheim, "Schwächling," 154.

48 Margarete Susman, "Bertha Pappenheim's geistige Welt," *Bertha Pappenheim zum Gedächtnis*, special issue of *Blätter des Jüdischen Frauenbundes* 12 (1936), 36.

⁴⁹ I find in Chaim Potok's Asher Lev a modern version of Pappenheim's "Der Wunderrabi." In *My Name is Asher Lev*, the young artist's dilemma is also first detected by his mother, who is troubled by his abnormal behavior and his (in this case mental) illness. Like Arjeh's parents, the Rebbe decides that the artist and the community will best be served if the artist is allowed to develop his talents, albeit under the Rebbe's supervision.

⁵⁰ Bertha Pappenheim, *Aus der Arbeit des Heims des Jüdischen Frauenbundes in Isenburg: 1914-1924* (Frankfurt a.M.: R.Th. Hauser, 1926), 32.

⁵¹ Pappenheim, *Aus der Arbeit*, 32.

⁵² Helene Krämer, "Erste pädagogische Arbeit: Mädchenwaisenhaus," *Bertha Pappenheim zum Gedächtnis*, 5.

⁵³ Johanna Stahl, "Erste pädagogische Arbeit: Mädchenwaisenhaus." *Bertha Pappenheim zum Gedächtnis*, 6.

⁵⁴ Fred Kormis (1897–1986) was born in Frankfurt, a.M. He served in the Austrian army during World War I (he was a prisoner-of-war in Siberia from 1915 to 1920). He lived in Germany until 1933, when he emigrated to England via Paris.

⁵⁵ "Frankfurt a.M., 29. Januar," *Allgemeine Zeitung des Judentums* 3 Feb. 1911, 3 [Gemeindebote].

⁵⁶ Leopold Horovitz (1838-1917) was a Hungarian artist trained in Vienna. He was best known for portraiture (his sitters include Austrian Emperor Franz Joseph) and genre scenes.

⁵⁷ Helga Heubach, *Das Heim des Jüdischen Frauenbundes Neu-Isenburg Taunusstraße 9, 1907 bis 1942 gegründet von Bertha Pappenheim* (Neu Isenburg: Magistrat der Stadt Neu-Isenburg, 1986), 33, 99.

⁵⁸ Sara Eisenstädt, "Die Dienstag-Gäste," *Bertha Pappenheim zum Gedächtnis*, 24.

⁵⁹ Pearl Abraham, *The Romance Reader* (New York: Riverhead, 1995).

⁶⁰ Danitia Smith, "An Author's Chasidic Roots Become Her Inspiration," *New York Times*, 8 February, 2005, Late Edition, Section E, 1.

⁶¹ Pearl Abraham, *The Seventh Beggar* (New York: Riverhead, 2005).

The Politics and Priorities of Jewish Music Publishing in Eastern Europe

Susan M. Filler

Dissemination of Jewish music is usually researched according to its history, style, and performance. There is no known study of the history of Jewish music publishing as such; that is surprising, considering the general interest in such aspects of Jewish literature, drama, and film. In this essay, I want to offer an introduction to this neglected subject, primarily devoted to Jewish music publishing in central and eastern Europe, where it was a flourishing business until the Holocaust. It is important to note that, during and after the devastation of the Holocaust, publication of music in the Jewish community survived and continued in other countries, which makes it important to devote some attention to non-European locations, including North America and Israel.

Music publishing dates back to the late fifteenth century, but the business of mass production was not firmly established until the eighteenth century, especially in England, France, and the German-speaking countries, which were the leaders in the field. In Germany and Austria, Jews contributed significantly to the business, especially in the nineteenth century, in such houses as C. F. Peters of Leipzig, Bote & Bock of Berlin, and Universal Edition of Vienna. However, it is important to differentiate between publishers who included music by many composers, Jewish and non-Jewish, in varied styles and for varied uses, and those who specialized in music for the use of the Jewish community, even when that community was influenced by music of non-Jewish neighbors. In western European countries, the Jews were among the most assimilated in Europe; but in eastern Europe and in the immigrant enclaves in North America, especially in New York, the publication of folk music, synagogue music, and music for the Jewish stage flourished. The disposition of music publication in the Jewish communities depended largely on types of music, which may be divided into the following categories:

- religious music for the synagogue and home;
- folk music;
- symphonic music for the concert hall;
- stage music, including opera, theater and *klezmer*.

As evidenced in Alfred Sendrey's data, much of this music was not published at all or published privately by the composers.[1] While Sendrey's book was published over half a century ago, it is important to emphasize that what he noted as only available in manuscript is often still unpublished even today, and such sources—especially of ambitious orchestral works and Yiddish opera—probably survive only in libraries and archives.[2] It is interesting to note that Sendrey also included short musical works in Jewish periodicals, of which the most notable are *Österrichisch-Ungarische Kantorenzeitung* (based in Vienna), *Di Chazanim Welt* (Warsaw), *Ost und West* (Berlin), and *Ponimer un Ponimelekh* (Buenos Aires). The music published in periodicals was modest, usually limited to folk songs and synagogal chants. In this they are comparable to the publication of piano pieces and art songs in the musical periodicals of mainstream Europe that flourished at the same time.[3]

The following list of publishers by location is not exhaustive. It comprises those that appear to have been widely active in the period from the nineteenth century to the Holocaust and occasionally beyond it:

Publishers of Jewish Music

Austria

Vienna: Jibneh Edition (see also Berlin, Jerusalem & New York entries)
Vienna: Universal Edition

Germany

Berlin: Jibneh Edition (see also Vienna, Jerusalem & New York entries)
Berlin: Juwal (see also Tel Aviv entry)
Berlin: Bote & Bock
Berlin: Schlesinger[4]
Mainz: B. Schotts Söhne
Frankfurt am Main: J. Kauffmann
Leipzig: M. W. Kauffmann

France

Paris: Heugel & Fils
Paris: A. Durlacher

Russia/Soviet Union

St. Petersburg & Moscow: Edition Russe de Musica
Moscow: Verlag Engel
St. Petersburg: Gesellschaft für jüdische Volksmusik
Kiev: G. I. Indrzhishek (or G. I. Jindrzhshek)
Kharkov: Tsentralfarlag

Other Eastern European Countries

Zagreb: Omanut(h) (see also Tel Aviv & Zürich entries)
Vilna: A. G. Syrkin
Vilna: Farlag "Grinike Beymelekh"
Varshe [Warsaw] & Bialystok: Kultur-Liga
Varshe: M[enakhem] Kipnis
Lodz: A. S. Lehwental
Varna: M. Gadol

United States

New York: Yibneh Edition (see also Vienna, Berlin & Jerusalem entries)
New York: Bloch Publishing Company
New York: Hebrew Publishing Company
New York: Katzenelenbogen & Rabinowitz
New York: J. & J. Kammen
New York: Arbeter-Ring [later Workmen's Circle]

Israel

Jerusalem: Jibneh Edition (see also Vienna, Berlin & New York entries)
Tel Aviv: Olam Omanut (see also Zagreb & Zürich entries)
Tel Aviv: Dvir
Tel Aviv: Edition Hanigun

Other

Zürich: Omanut(h) (see also Zagreb & Tel Aviv entries)
Amsterdam: J. L. Joachimsthal
London: R. Mazin
Mexico City: Farlag "Yidishe Dertsiung"
Alexandria, Egypt: Edition Orientale de Musique

Leaving aside major publishers in Germany, Austria, France, and England, the leading publishers of music for the Jewish community were in the Russias, and this appears to be a direct result of the work of Jewish nationalist composers. This movement was strongly influenced by the example of Russian nationalist composers in the late nineteenth century, especially the so-called *Kuchka* [the Five, consisting of Cesar Cui, Mily Balakirev, Modest Musorgskii, Aleksander Borodin, and Nikolai Rimsky-Korsakov]; other influences may have included Hungary (especially the ethnomusicological research of Bela Bartok and Zoltan Kodaly) and the Czech Lands.[5] Jewish nationalism had actually made an early appearance in the opera Judith by Alexander Serov, who was partly Jewish and consciously chose the story of Judith and Holofernes for this opera, which is, however, written in grand opera style. It is possible that Serov, whose opera dated from 1863, was familiar with Jacques Fromental Halevy's opera *La Juive*.[6] It appears that such works influenced the Yiddish operettas of Abraham Goldfaden. The difference was that both Halevy and Serov had contracts with mainstream publishers, whereas Yiddish operetta was published piecemeal, first in eastern Europe, later in England and the United States.

The great wave of Jewish music research and publication in the Russias and the Soviet Union came after Serov's time and was not only influenced but actually encouraged by Russian nationalists, who do not appear to have been influenced by the pervasive anti-Semitism in their country.[7] The Society for Jewish Folk Music was established in 1908 in St. Petersburg In the following years, branches were established in Moscow, Kiev, and Kharkov, all of which supported research and publication of Jewish folk music. Such musicians as Joel Engel, Aron Marko Rothmüller, Lazare Saminsky, and Abraham Wolf Binder contributed to this activity. In the list above, the sections covering the Russias includes publishers with Yiddish and German as well as Russian names. It may have been under the influence of this movement that the chamber group *Zimro*, which consisted of Jewish musicians who had gone to school in St. Petersburg with Sergei Prokofiev, commissioned him to write a work that they performed on tour shortly after World War I; this *Overture on Hebrew Themes* would not have been written had not the members of the group given Prokofiev a book of Yiddish folk songs.[8] (It could very well have come from the work of the original Society in St. Petersburg, which had been active for about a decade when the overture was written.)

We note several publishing houses in Poland, especially Warsaw, which must have been a big market for Yiddish folk music and theater, and individual houses in Zagreb and Varna, which were probably outside the milieu of the Yiddish-speaking community in Poland. Not all of these enterprises survived. Omanut of Zagreb, which was actually a society for Jewish folk music that published its research privately, was one of the few that did survive; the founder, Aron Marko Rothmüller, established branches in Zürich and Tel Aviv when it was no longer possible to function in Yugoslavia. The German house Jibneh, based in Vienna and Berlin, survived by establishing branches in Jerusalem and New York, as did the Juwal Edition of Berlin, which moved its base of operations to Tel Aviv.

The first known Jewish composer who published liturgical music of any sort was Salamone Rossi, whose *Solomon's Songs, Psalms, Hymns,* and *Temple-Songs*, a collection of thirty works from the prayer book, was published in Venice in about 1620.[9] The Italians and Germans were primarily responsible for early music publications beginning in the late fifteenth century,[10] although mass production was still centuries in the future. Liturgical music took priority over folk or popular stage music in both Catholic and Protestant countries, and it surely influenced the Jewish communities later in the history of music publishing.

The work of the great cantors in the nineteenth century, including Salomon Sulzer, Samuel Naumbourg, and Louis Lewandowski, was published primarily in Berlin, Leipzig, and Vienna, later in the United States. There is no evidence of publication of their work in the eastern European countries, where their reforms were regarded with suspicion when they were known at all.[11] Even in the Jewish communities in Germany and Austria, there was controversy because these well-known cantors reformed the style along the lines of Christian liturgical music, especially the Protestant chorale;[12] these reforms were condemned by the Orthodox communities. The fact that some of the work of these innovators was actually published by mainstream publishers (for example, some of

Lewandowski's work was published by Breitkopf & Härtel of Leipzig) did not improve the situation. This schism continued even in the United States: separate communities with separate musical styles and published sources were established in New York and elsewhere.

In a previous presentation, I discussed the involvement of non-Jewish composers with Jewish music.[13] Among the examples I cited were Beethoven, Schubert, Ravel, and several Russian composers including Prokofiev and Musorgskii. All of these composers did business with specific publishers; for instance, Musorgskii with Belaief of Moscow and St. Petersburg, and Ravel with Durand of Paris.[14] They had contracts with these publishers, and in that way they were fortunate; composers writing for the Jewish community seldom had such contracts, and those who did were likely to be the cantors whose work was known. Most of the others had to place their works where they could; that was the reason many works remained in manuscript, were published privately by the composers themselves, or went to publishers who are virtually unknown today.

We do not know why the work of these musicians was published by their own rather than major publishers like Belaief, which was responsible for many works of the *Kuchka*. Anti-Semitism may have been a factor in the case of the publishers, although not the Russian composers themselves; or possibly such publishers were influenced by considerations of what would sell to the public beyond the Jewish community.

Up to this point I have discussed publication of religious and folk music. An interesting example of the latter is supplied by Menakhem Kipnis, a collector of Yiddish songs. His work appears to have been published primarily in Warsaw, privately by himself, and by E. Gitlin [plates 1 and 2]. The Kipnis family, which originally came from the Ukraine, boasted more than one musician, including the great bass Alexander Kipnis, who was apparently of the same generation as Menakhem (although we do not know the exact relationship between them), and Alexander's son Igor Kipnis, the harpsichordist.

Immigrants from Poland and the Russias who became involved with publication of music in the New World generally specialized in folk music and music of the Yiddish theater and operetta. Jacob Kamenetsky (later Jack Kammen) established J. & J. Kammen in New York, which specialized in that repertoire, as did the Hebrew Publishing Company (and R. Mazin in London, where some immigrants from eastern Europe had gone). The publication of music from Yiddish theater and operetta is comparable to

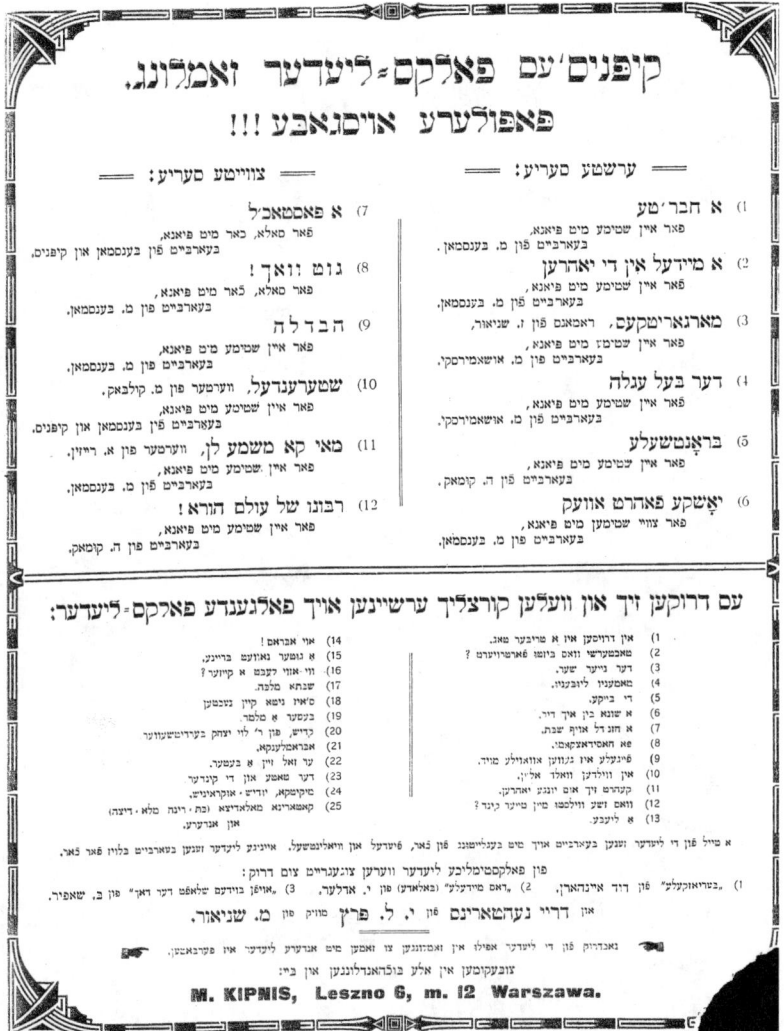

plate 1 Kipnis' music collection - selfpublisher

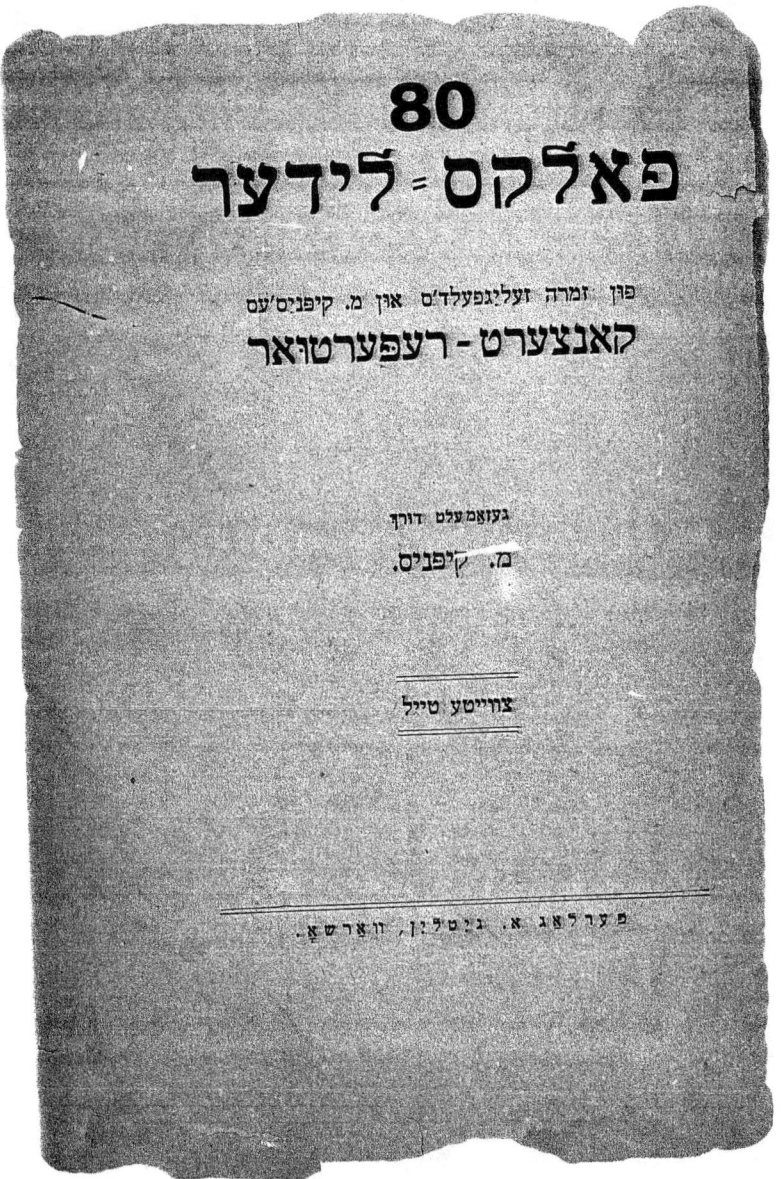

plate 2 Kipnis' music collection - published by E. Gitlin

that of Broadway show music in English in later generations: individual popular songs in sheet music, some song collections, and an occasional complete piano-vocal score of an operetta (especially the works of Goldfaden, who emigrated to New York in the late nineteenth century).

Orchestral scores are very rare, and this is a big disappointment to scholars today, who would really like to know what sort of instrumentation was used in these dramatic works. The reasoning behind such priorities is simple: big works like operettas and operas, or concert works for orchestra (which were written with increasing frequency by Jewish nationalist composers, who in many cases were influenced by Jewish folk songs), are technically demanding beyond the capabilities of many such publishers, expensive to produce—especially when the publisher must combine music written left to right with text in Hebrew or Yiddish from right to left, which must have been a major problem (in the New World it became increasingly common to present the text in transliteration)—and not likely to sell very well. Sendrey listed many works that he saw only in manuscript in libraries and archives, which must have been in this country since they were unlikely to have survived in manuscript through the Holocaust and the wars. Plate 3 shows the title page of a score of *Bar Kochba* by Goldfaden, published by the *Arbeter-Ring* [the Workmen's Circle] in New York as late as 1945; it appears to be reproduced from handwritten score [plate 4], although in Goldfaden's own time he had publishers in both New York and London, according to Sendrey's data.[15]

One important form of music in the Jewish community for centuries was *klezmer*, which is rarely seen in print. It appears that scholars in eastern Europe confined their work to folk music; even Sendrey very rarely listed publications of *klezmer* specifically defined as such, and Abraham Idelsohn described *klezmer* in purely verbal terms even in *Jewish Music in its Historical Development*, which is richly illustrated with musical examples in discussions of other forms of Jewish music.[16] Considering the popularity of this music among Ashkenazim, we should consider the reasons for this lack. Idelsohn quoted an account of a *klezmer* group dating from about 1800, which gives us some information:

> The five musicians engaged in other trades in addition to their playing. Two of them were violinists, one played the clarinet, one the violoncello and one the *Hackbrett* [Dulcimer]. "Only the first violinist played from written music, the others following by ear. The cellist, an old man, played with especial skill. He knew

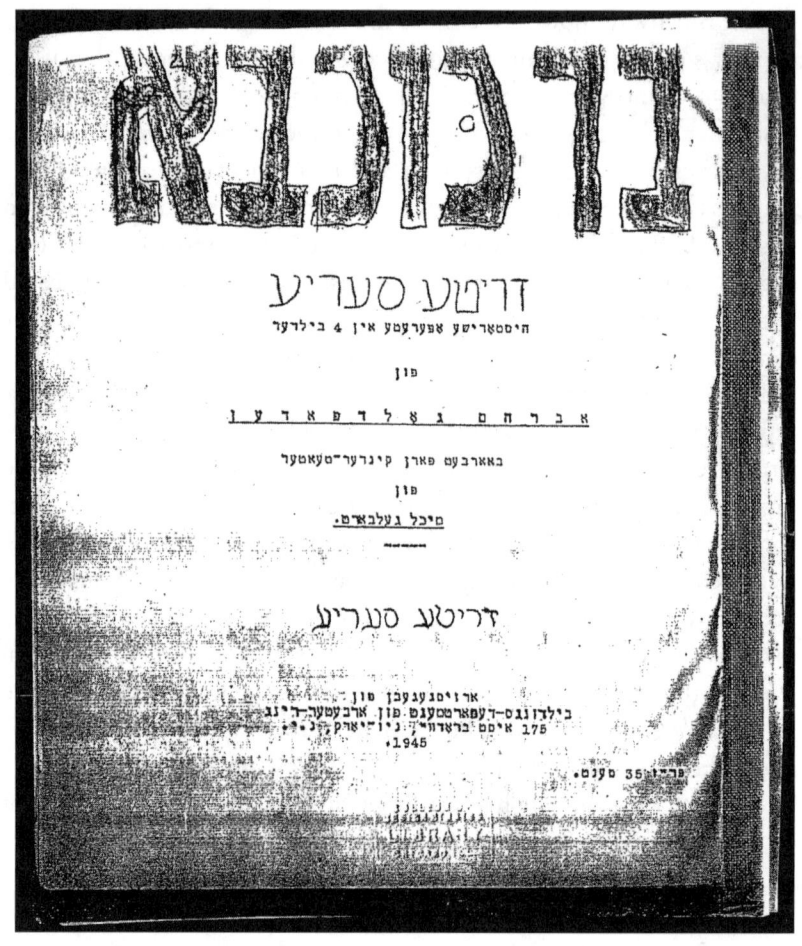

plate 3 Title page of *Bar Kochba*

plate 4 Handwritten score of *Bar Kochba*

nothing of notes, but had an excellent ear, observed each turn of the leading melody and was able to add accompaniment in perfect harmony."[17]

This account suggests that the average *klezmer*, until comparatively recent times, could not read music. The semi-improvisatory nature of *klezmer* music (it is not entirely improvisatory, since the style and often the melody are based on songs the klezmorim knew, whether folk songs or liturgical chants) was obviously influenced by this situation. Even today, when modern *klezmer* groups are educated musicians, it is often considered a matter of professional skill and pride for *klezmorim* to be able to create music without the printed page.

The example of the group *Zimro*, for which Prokofiev wrote the *Overture on Hebrew Themes*, is most unusual. The group consisted of string quartet, piano, and clarinet, which is fairly typical for *klezmer* music; but actually having a non-Jewish composer write down a work, and it was published too, is really exceptional. *Klezmorim* in the nineteenth century, such as Michael Joseph Gusikow, who was greatly admired by Felix Mendelssohn, and Mordechele Rosenthal, who became known as Rozsavölgyi Mark (gaining fame in Hungary by touring with a group of *klezmorim* disguised as gypsies), were grassroots musicians who learned by apprenticeship, often with members of their own families.

I want to conclude this introduction to Jewish music publishing by offering a few thoughts about methodology in organized research of the subject. First, there is evidence enough that, in spite of the Holocaust, Jewish music publication survived, and the best way to document that fact is to trace the movements of the publishers from country to country and from language to language.

Second, while there is little surviving documentation of the history of such publishing houses (at least compared to documentation of mainstream music publishers), comparison of Jewish music publishing with mainstream music publishing does not yield such a disparity as appears at first glance. The vast majority of the publishing houses capable of mounting anniversary *Festschriften* were bombed during the war, and it took many years for those houses to reconstruct their archives and resume publication. Also, such *Festschrift* volumes often do not tell the whole story. They should not be taken at face value.

As an example, I learned the story of the arrangements Universal Edition of Vienna made to transfer the works of the Jewish composers in its catalogue, including Gustav Mahler, to Boosey & Hawkes of London during the Nazi period, not from books but from representatives of Boosey & Hawkes in New York and London. Universal Edition itself has rarely commented publicly about the political foresight of the Jews who administered Universal Edition in effecting the transfer. Ultimately, Universal Edition sued to recover the rights to publication of the works after the war—something that is not spelled out in that house's publications either. It is an example of the need to track the history of such movements between music publishers carefully by dates as well as places.[18]

Third, we may be very thankful for the fact that Alfred Sendrey listed sources even in manuscript because it enables modern musicologists to recover such works in libraries and archives for critical editing and publication. Mark Slobin demonstrated how this could be done in his edition of Lateiner and Mogulesko's Yiddish operetta *Dovid's Fidele*, which was published in 1994.[19] The fact that Yiddish opera is not so popular today as it was a century ago does not alter its historical influence on the Broadway musical, and the resurgence of interest in Yiddish culture makes such work imperative.

Finally, we should look for documentation of Jewish music in places that we might not expect it. While the centers of Jewish music publication were in Europe and North America, it is worth looking for source materials in Latin America—for instance, the "Farlag Yidishe Dertsiung" in Mexico City—and in the Middle East, where scholars from Europe continued their work in Israel and even in one or two of the Arab countries.

In short, while documentation of the history of publication of Jewish music is fragmentary, it is a fruitful subject of investigation for those who have the minds of detectives and can piece evidence together.

NOTES

[1] Alfred Sendrey, *Bibliography of Jewish Music* (New York: Columbia University Press, 1951).

[2] The repositories Sendrey cited most often were the New York Public Library, the Library of Congress, the library of Hebrew Union College (Cincinnati), the Jewish Theological Seminary Library (New York) and the YIVO Institute for Jewish Research, all of which can be consulted today.

[3] Mainstream musicological periodicals that incorporated short works as musical

supplements included *Die Musik*, the *Archiv für Musikwissenschaft*, the *Neue Zeitschrift für Musik*, and the *Musikblätter des Anbruchs*, among others.

⁴ The well-known Beethoven specialist, Theodore Albrecht, recently presented a lecture to the Midwest Jewish Studies Association about Beethoven's business relationship with Schlesinger in the early nineteenth century. Albrecht produced excellent evidence that the relatively new publishing house of C.F. Peters attempted to persuade Beethoven to withdraw his compositions from Schlesinger and transfer them to Peters for publication. Albrecht has done extensive research into the relationship between Beethoven and the Jewish community of Vienna, and his conclusion in this lecture was that the offer to Beethoven from Peters was doomed to failure because he did not share the anti-Semitism Peters expressed in the course of their correspondence.

⁵ The *Kuchka* preceded the Jewish nationalist composers in Russia by a generation, having been active beginning in the 1860s. The research of Bartok and Kodaly (which included field recordings of folk music in many parts of eastern Europe) dates from the first decade of the twentieth century forward and is thus contemporary with the Jewish composers of Eastern Europe. Curiously enough, while the work of the Hungarians demonstrated stylistic distinctions between Hungarian, Romanian, Russian, Turkish and Gypsy music, it did not include information about Jewish music.

⁶ This opera was published by Schlesinger (a son of Beethoven's publisher in Berlin) in Paris in 1836. Serov, a very cosmopolitan musician, traveled outside Russia and made the acquaintance of Wagner; however, in his own operas, including *Judith*, he was apparently influenced less by Wagner than by French grand operas, including those of Halevy and Meyerbeer, and by Verdi. However, we should consider the possibility of multiple influences, since the early works of Wagner including *Tannhäuser* show the influence of Meyerbeer before Wagner turned against him.

⁷ Musorgskii and Shostakovich were the foremost examples of Russian composers who incorporated Jewish influences in some of their musical works. Others included Prokofiev (see below), Glinka, and Borodin.

⁸ Sergi Prokofiev, *Overture on Hebrew Themes* (Moscow: A. Gugheil, 1922).

⁹ Salamoe Rossi [Ebreo], *Ha-Shirim Asher li-Shelomo* (Venice: P. & L. Bragadini, 1620).

¹⁰ The *Harvard Dictionary of Music* identifies a German *Graduale* [a book of chants from the Catholic monastic liturgy] dating from about 1473 as the earliest example of music printing. However, a major breakthrough was achieved in the case of the *Harmonice Musices Odhecaton* published in Venice in 1501 by Ottaviano dei

Petrucci, which was printed from moveable type in three stages: first the staves, then the music, and finally the words. Interested readers should consult the edition of this work by Helen Hewitt and Isabel Pope, which was published by the Medieval Academy of America in 1942 and revised in 1946.

[11] A discussion of this problem is found in Aron Marko Rothmüller, *The Music of the Jews* (New York: A. S. Barnes, 1960), 100-12.

[12] The Protestant chorale dates from the time of the Reformation in Germany in the sixteenth century. Martin Luther himself apparently wrote some early chorales, which were later adapted by major composers including Heinrich Schütz, Dietrich Buxtehude, and Johann Sebastian Bach. The chorale is characterized by simple melodic lines, basic triadic harmony, stanzaic form, and four-square rhythm, which facilitated the participation of the people of a congregation.

[13] "The Other Side of the Coin: Non-Jewish Composers, Jewish Music," Midwest Jewish Studies Association, annual meeting, Spertus Institute of Jewish Studies, Chicago, October 2001 [unpublished].

[14] See, for instance, Ravel, *Deux Mélodies Hébraïques* (Paris: Durand & Fils). This includes two songs, "Kaddisch" (in Hebrew) and "L'énigme éternelle" (in Yiddish), both with French translations. It was published in 1920 in separate prints for voice and piano and voice and orchestra. The *Chants Populaires*, which included a "Chançon hébraïque," was also published by Durand & Fils in 1925.

[15] The two publishers responsible for most of Goldfaden's works after his emigration to New York were Hebrew Publishing Company (New York) and R. Mazin (London). Unfortunately, after Goldfaden's death in 1908, many of his works were dismembered, rearranged by other composers, and published by other publishers in both the United States and Europe, which raises questions about the extent of copyright protection for such works.

[16] Abraham Zvi Idelsohn, *Jewish Music in its Historical Development* (New York: Holt, Rinehart & Winston, 1929; New York: Schocken Books, 1967, 1973), 435-60. The chapter "*Badchonim* (Merry-Makers) and *Klezmorim* (Merry-Makers): Song and Singers in Folk Style" includes only two musical examples, neither of which is in the section on *klezmorim*.

[17] Ibid., 457.

[18] I am indebted to Sylvia Goldstein and Robert Cowan of the New York and London offices of Boosey and Hawkes, who verbally gave me this information. Both of them emphasized the significant role played by the widow of the founder of Universal Edition, Emil Hertzka, in transferring the publications to Boosey & Hawkes. It is also worth noting that Boosey & Hawkes published some works of Mahler that were entirely new prints rather than photographic reprints of the

Universal Edition scores. There is no evidence that those works were included when the rights were transferred back to Universal Edition after the war.

[19] Jacob Lateiner and Sigmund Mogulesko, *Dovids Fidele* (ed. Mark Slobin; New York: Garland Publishing, 1994). The source on which this edition was based had been published in 1899 by the Hebrew Publishing Company.

The Radical Assimilated: Hungarian "Urbanists" and Jewish Identity in the 1930s

Richard S. Esbenshade

"I can't become assimilated!" cried out Géza K. Havas in an article in the January-February, 1939, issue of *Szép Szó* [Beautiful Word], a Budapest "urbanist" journal.[1] This was not the lament of an obstinate Orthodox rabbi or even the son of one stuck halfway between two worlds, but of a thoroughly assimilated writer and critic steeped in classical Hungarian literary traditions, who refused to conform to the ever more unforgiving exclusive nationalist, anti-Semitic, and "Germanic" tendencies dominating intellectual discourse at the end of the 1930s.

Havas spoke, by and large, for a group of Hungarian intellectuals who became known as the "urbanists," in their stubborn belief in an inclusive Hungarian culture. Most of the urbanists were Jewish in the sense that they were born into Jewish (or recently converted) families, but by adulthood they had practically given up all connection with the organized Jewish community and any overt Jewish identity. Many in fact converted to Christianity, but typical was the stance of Havas's *Szép Szó* colleague Pál Ignotus, who wrote, in 1934—rejecting the mantra of the organized Jewish community, which stated: "My nationality is Hungarian, my religion Jewish"—"My religion is not Jewish. I converted, I did it from conviction—not religious conviction, since I'm not at all a believer in God, but from a socio-political one."[2]

Still, these journalists and critics, who would rather have been writing about French literature or borrowing from British legal practice to reform semi-feudal, authoritarian, interwar Hungary, were the first to oppose the growing anti-Semitism, in particular the coded, "non-extremist" anti-Semitism that percolated through Hungarian intellectual discourse in the years leading up to the World War II and the Holocaust. They in particular challenged the increasingly race-based and exclusive formulations of writers of their main antagonists, the increasingly national-minded "populists." And however much they may have been leaving behind or even denying their Jewishness, they could not escape being labeled as such by their opponents and interwar Hungarian society in general. Though Havas's death in the Günskirchen concentration camp in April 1945 was atypical for the urbanists—the others were by and large able to escape the country and the Nazi danger either before or during the war—his fate stands as a reminder of the identity none of them could escape.

I will use these writers and their complicated relationship to their own identity to take issue with a widespread one dimensional view of assimilation on the cusp of the Holocaust as pure tragedy. I would not want to deny that there is a tragic aspect to the urbanists' position, which cannot be separated from the immeasurably greater tragedy of the destruction of over half a million Hungarian Jews, most of whom were far more willing to identify with Judaism even while believing they had a place in Hungarian society. But it is too easy in hindsight to deny all value to the century-long process that brought Hungarian Jews to the point where they felt themselves as much if not more Hungarian than Jewish, to see assimilation as a "fool's game" that could only come from blindness to the inevitable and to the antagonism of their non-Jewish co-citizens.

The urbanists were, as intellectuals, triply marginalized: as assimilated Jews, from both Hungarian society and Jewish memory;[3] as liberal humanists in an age of extremism; and as East Europeans undergoing the traumas of late modernization. I postulate their conflicted but creative position, along the lines of recent work in Jewish cultural studies,[4] as a productive one for critiquing Hungarian national discourse, and positing an inclusive rather than exclusive form of the national idea.

In the past few years there have appeared two major treatments of the so-called "Jewish Question" in Hungary, by writers of divergent cultural-political positions. One, *Ahasverus and Shylock: The "Jewish Question" in Hungary*,[5] is by the literary scholar and critic Tamás Ungvári, who might well be described as a neo-urbanist. The other, titled simply *The Jewish Question in Hungary*[6] (tellingly, without the scare quotes), is by János Gyurgyák, a scholar and publisher associated with the center-Right "neo-populist" party that led the governing coalition between 1998 and 2002. Though the two books differ greatly in their perspective and their assessment, especially of the populist writers—who include most of those now recognized as the pantheonic Hungarian writers for the period—they both agree on the failure, the bankruptcy of the assimilation project. Both of these writers see themselves as countering an assimilationist orthodoxy that has allegedly dominated Hungarian-Jewish historiography.

Ungvári states in his book's very first sentence, "Every researcher of the cultural history of Hungarian Jewry has represented it as the triumphal march of assimilation"[7] he then proceeds to demolish this tableau with his description of the dead end "assimilationist trap" that undermined Jewish identity, distorted the Jews' position in society, and finally made impossible a unified and effective resistance to anti-Semitism and the Holocaust. Gyurgyák likewise sees the nineteenth century model of mass assimilation as having been:

> an illusion shared by many. I do not consider opinions pointing towards the failure of assimilation, and furthermore some concepts of dissimilation, as *ab ovo* anti-Semitic. This understanding will with all certainty be received with antipathy by the majority of the decisively pro-assimilation Hungarian and Hungarian-Jewish public opinion, which has chosen to and still chooses to identify dissimilationist views with anti-Semitism. I consider this a misconception with fatal consequences.[8]

This unlikely consensus between representatives of resolutely opposed cultural-political currents evokes support by interwar populists, who wanted to expel the urbanists and other Jewish writers from the national literature into a separate "Hungarian-Jewish literature" for certain "Jewish separatist" writers such as Károly Pap.[9]

Outside of Hungary, the work of Sander Gilman presents an unavoidable challenge to any who would defend the integrity of the assimilation process and its devotees. Starting with his pathbreaking work, *Jewish Self-Hatred*,[10] and further developed in subsequent works such as *Inscribing the Other*,[11] Gilman describes the history of Jewish writers in a German culture that—in the manner of Jean-Paul Sartre's dictum that "it is the anti-Semite who *makes* the Jew"[12]—refused to let them escape their Jewishness, and the net of stereotypes and associations that went with it. Their efforts towards a more perfect assimilation and unassailable cultural status and identity through the command of language, the currency of culture, were haunted by the charge of the "secret language of the Jews," which when it could no longer be targeted at Yiddish or "*mauscheln*"—a particularly Jewish mangling of "pure" German—shifted to their rhetoric, form of thinking and logic, and their artistic identity as mere journalists.

In the German cultural context, Gilman argues, Jews could not but internalize the stereotypes and could defend themselves only by projecting their alleged negative qualities onto others, usually but not always less assimilated Eastern Jews, who could constitute for them the bad Jews to their own good Jewish selves. Thus it was with writers from Moses Mendelssohn through Heinrich Heine and Sigmund Freud to Karl Kraus: the more they tried to prove themselves in the dominant culture and political context, the more they were inexorably sucked into the maelstrom of self-hatred.

Gilman's studies rest in large part on the specificities of German cultural history, but the outline of his exclusion of writers strongly parallels the questioning of the Hungarian urbanists' (and Jews' generally) place in Hungarian literature. While the correct use of language itself was less of an issue—though not absent, especially in the case of criticism of the poetic language of the "fringe urbanist" *Dezső Szomory*[13]—the German denial of an assimilation taken for granted intellectually, but never secure in reality is completely transferable to the Hungarian case, along with a constant subtext of the questioning of, if not language per se, certainly the rhetoric, style, and sensitivity of the Jewish critic. But the second part of Gilman's dynamic, the Jewish reaction, seems largely missing among the Hungarian urbanists. Gilman's German Jews were "glorifying difference rather than treating it with abnegation,"[14] while Hungarian urbanist writers to the end practiced that very abnegation of difference in relentlessly asserting their universalist response. Even the populists' perceived instances of anti-Semitism were castigated more as examples of their drift to the right and susceptibility to fascist/Nazi "infection" than as offenses against Jews specifically.

The application of Gilman's model to the Hungarian interwar situation also invokes the Eastern European context. While the East-West schema is itself often used to glorify difference unnecessarily, Hungary's membership in this geopolitical category does explain some crucial distinctions. Gilman roots his study in the dichotomy (especially in conception and discourse) between Western (assimilated, secularized) and Eastern (Yiddish-speaking, Orthodox) Jewry. Hungary distinguishes itself among Eastern European countries in its high proportion of Western Jews.[15] But the country's history is also marked by the pathologies of late or incomplete modernization, in part because of an anti-entrepreneurial aristocratic ("national") ethos. It would be an exaggeration, but not a great one, to say that Jews built capitalism in Hungary. The Magyar landed nobility controlled society and politics,

The Radical Assimilated

but, after the 1867 *Ausgleich* in which it took on de facto control over half the Habsburg empire, it needed the Jews' seven percent of the population to give Hungarian culture(measured by language) a majority to legitimate its rule over the Slovaks, Romanians, Croats, Serbs, Poles, Ruthenians, and others on greater Hungarian territory.[16] This led in the interwar period to a strong sense of backwardness among Hungarian intellectuals, a complex that spawned an abiding perception of cultural anxiety and, for Jewish intellectuals, a paradoxical consciousness of representing the vanguard of development but being caught in an "underdeveloped" culture, which they strove to assimilate into but could also at times disdain. The conflicts between the urbanists and populists cannot be understood without taking these complexes into account.

The urbanist intellectuals, at the end of a long procession of assimilation—from adopting the Magyar tongue to name-changing, intermarriage, pursuing noble titles, and the gentry lifestyle, through, for many, conversion (as portrayed in the recent film *Sunshine*)[17] had divested themselves of any outward or structural connection to Judaism, the organized Jewish community, or cultural Jewishness. Their religion was rationality and relentless critique of their society. Their community was the cafe milieu of Budapest intellectual life. Their coalescence in the face of the perceived anti-Semitism of their opponents, who in pressing discussion of "the Jewish Question" would not let them leave their origins behind, fits perfectly Sartre's previously cited formulation. This Jewishness has little to do with history or inherited identity—that which the urbanists seemed to be trying to escape—but is situational: "The Jew is in the situation of a Jew because he lives in the midst of a society that takes him for a Jew."[18]

But Sartre goes further: true identity becomes untenable in such a situation. It is the example par excellence of "bad faith": "[The Jew's] life is nothing but a long flight from others and himself. He has been alienated even from his body; his emotional life has been cut up in two; he has been reduced to pursuing the impossible dream of universal brotherhood in a world that rejects him."[19] Gilman as well identifies a betrayal of Jewish identity, seemingly inevitable, in assimilation. For all the psychological understanding, critical discourse awareness, and reflexivity he applies to his subjects, the power of the label "Jewish self-hatred" (which loses the scare quotes after its first use) puts a fatal stamp on the effort to fit in. The current multiculturalist orientation of American scholarship also tends to see assimilation as betrayal, if not as cultural genocide.

I would not deny the problematic nature of Jewish assimilation in Hungary from its beginnings, or its historical progression towards a dead end. Ungvári's thoroughly historical treatment argues that the assimilationist bargain was flawed from its inception: the peculiar, gentry nature of Hungarian capitalist development left the Jews, in a society still ordered semi-feudally and with a closed political life in particular off limits to Jews, with "nowhere to assimilate to." Emancipation was offered without clear expectations. Thus the Jews, constantly unsettled by the suspicion and social discrimination they faced and by charges (increasing in number and force as time went on) that they were not assimilating enough, tended to "over-assimilate," adopting Magyar aristocratic styles and manners to a degree verging on, and often spilling over into, caricature.

They were left thereby increasingly adrift from their Jewish identity, but never completely accepted as true Magyars, out-of-place hybrids in a national state striving (especially post-Trianon)[20] for homogeneity, but with no (especially after the defeat and total discrediting of Octobrism)[21] bourgeois nationalism to join in opposing the dominant official noble/landowner nationalism. This is the outline of the assimilation trap that caught the greater part of Hungarian Jewry, and especially the assimilated intellectuals, before being subject to the successive and ever more brutal waves of anti-Semitism of the interwar period.[22]

But I still strive to see the urbanists' commitment to the choice of assimilation, and their insistence on the right to equal participation in Hungarian culture, with no identity qualifications, as positive—certainly tragic in some sense, even naive, but also worthy of reclamation as an attempt to hold the emancipation promise of a non-discriminatory society and culture to its word and to develop the possibility of an independent critical position on society liberated from sectarian or communitarian restraints or biases.

In this article I use particular scenes from the so-called "populist-urbanist" debate to illuminate the position and identity of these, to use Isaac Deutscher's term, "non-Jewish Jews."[23] This ongoing polemic pitted the "populist" writers, whose sociographical studies and novels exposed the misery of the country's impoverished rural majority and who called for land reform and transformation of a still semi-feudal agriculture, against the "urbanists," who likewise rejected the aristocratic-conservative Horthy regime, but in the name of universal rights and the rule of law. The populists defined the Hungarian nation as peasant-based, thirsting for social

The Radical Assimilated

reform and geographically alone; the urbanists as open, cosmopolitan, and European. This conflict has, especially when it burst out into the open to divide political life after 1989, become recognized as a, or even the, critical divide in Hungarian culture. The urbanist identity, forged in conflict, cannot be understood outside of the discourse created in that conflict.

The first character in my story is (Baron) Lajos Hatvany. The son of a wealthy Jewish industrialist and landowner, Hatvany (1880-1961), used his family fortune to support urbanist and liberal journals and writers of various political stripes; he was a leader of the 1918 left-liberal revolution, spent 1919-27 and 1938-47 in exile, was imprisoned in 1928 for nation-slandering articles, and also converted to Catholicism in that year.[24] He was, in the words of Gyurgyák, a holder of "extremist assimilationist" views; his response to the proto-urbanist journal *Huszadik Század*'s [Twentieth Century] 1917 questionnaire on whether there is a "Jewish Question" included the forthright pronouncement "it is the duty of every enlightened Jewish father to raise his children Christian."[25] He advocated the eventual dissolution of Jewish identity, not through assimilation into the real existing "gentry Hungary," but rather into a new Hungary that itself was changed and formed by those who joined it.[26] Still, as a representative of an older generation, he maintained an abiding loyalty to the traditional ideal of assimilation. As he wrote in a 1929 letter to Martin Buber:

> My path as a Jew, in contrast to yours, led to an imagined assimilation. I felt myself Hungarian, I was at home here, I wrote and agitated as a Hungarian until they made me aware that I had no business here. Then after ten years in emigration and a revolting trial, prison and expulsion became my fate. Through all of that I am incorrigible, and I have to admit that I've become fused together with the country and the people.[27]

But he also, in an article revealingly titled "A Jewish-Hungarian Monologue," recognized the brick wall he ran up against:

> But woe be to that Hungarian, a hundred times woe...woe be to us, a hundred times woe, who just refer to that fact that we grew up on Hungarian soil, breathed Hungarian air, spoke Hungarian, gave Magyardom our body and soul, our marrow, our sweat, and still if we are disregarded and insulted in our Hungarianness, we can't even open our mouth to complain, because the wit of the political order charges "Jew! Jew!" (And the Jew also laughs in

our face: "They persecute your kind, and you throw yourselves at the persecutors! The ethnic Magyars are right to expel you for it.")[28]

In 1934, Hatvany was instrumental in the explosion of the first of the nasty polemics between the urbanists and populists—some fifty articles—over the populist movement's unofficial chief ideologue László Németh's autobiographical essay, "Person and Role," and especially the statement in it that "A put-in-its-place Jewish literature, unfolding in the direction of its capacities and problems: a blessing; a Jewish Hungarian literature that is overgrowing us and falsifying us too: a trap."[29] The distinction between "Jewish literature" and "Jewish Hungarian literature" hit at the heart of the stance that had maintained Hatvany's and the other urbanists' identities: their mastery of Hungarian language as the ticket to full membership in culture. Hatvany replied with an article titled, "The Storm Troops of the Spirit," accusing Németh of wanting to apply an Aryan-paragraph to Hungarian literature, and ultimately to re-ghettoize Jewish writers.[30] He defiantly stated:

> There is no Hitler, who could prohibit me from Goethe's poetry and heavy-blooded, German prose…in vain I know that I came from the East—the people of the Mediterranean Sea, Latins, and Greeks brought me up and towards the French and Italians, the writers of the South and West.[31]

This declaration encapsulates at the same time the internal contradictions of the urbanist stance and the deployment of identity on the terrain of ideological battle. Hatvany acknowledged his non-Western origins—fully aware of the debates raging among Hungarian intellectuals on the Eastern versus Western roots of Magyardom itself—while claiming a successful cultural path to full citizenship in Europe: Hungarian Jewry's assimilation road writ large. At the same time, the reference to Hitler evoked the always double-valenced presence of the Germans: at once Nazis and the bearers of Central Europe's highest cultural gifts. Hatvany claimed the right to identify—and to be in solidarity—with the "good" side of that culture, while more essentially aligning himself with the Latin heritage against the Germanic New Europe in the making, into whose camp he had just projected Németh.[32] This was a subtle way to claim that a fully assimilated Jewry, or at least its urbanist intellectual leadership, was more European than culturally underdeveloped "gentry Hungary"

The Radical Assimilated

(to which the populists, their plebian thrust notwithstanding, could be attached as opponents of modernity and progress) and that it was to them that the backward Magyars had to assimilate, rather than the other way around.

Németh responded with "Confession of a Storm Trooper."[33] He decried the "Jewish sensitivity, which covers the country like an endless net; if hit anywhere, the whole shakes,"[34] and called his opponents "Shylocks":

> In the golden age of Hitlerism, to the question of whether we have to swear on the racial idea, I answer: If race is an anthropological idea, no; if moral, yes. The physiological version that imperfectly covers the people cannot be an ideal; a stance appropriate to the fate of the people: yes. In Hungary the German ideal of pure race hasno place. Magyardom is by its situation and fate made dependent on other peoples. It will either learn to be their unifier or it will die. And as to whether it is capable, one of the main tests is the Jewish Question.[35]

Németh's rejection of the urbanist charges of Nazism while holding fast to the "Jewish Question" was a constant in the populist stance. His attempt to make of race a moral question and the expansion of his vision for literature to the whole national fate postulated assimilation not as an a priori impossibility, but as a failed project, since it led to false reckonings on both sides.[36] And this brought him to his claim that the "Jewish Question" in Hungary is not even primarily about the Jews, but "the matter of Magyar and Magyar,"[37] of renewal of the Hungarian national idea. Németh himself recognized that his "new humanism," as he called it, was skirting a fine line and sought to redeem himself by drawing distinctions among Hungarian literary Jews. He contrasted those of Hatvany's ilk, who remember when the country was in their hands, and now grind their teeth that they let it slip away, with the type who plunges into his people's past, feeling the country in which he lives as nothing more than a new roof after so many others in his long wanderings. This opened the possibility for the genuine "Jewish literature" he had called for previously, best represented by Károly Pap (1897-1944), who Németh had "defended many times even against Jews."[38]

Pap and Németh may seem at first strange bedfellows. Pap had taken part in the 1919 Hungarian Soviet revolution and paid for it with several years in prison. By the beginning of the '30s, many were already hailing him as "the writer of Jewry"—a term that had no meaning up to then, with Jewry never considered a separate group and its writers considering themselves in the mainstream of Hungarian literature. His most renowned and provocative work, *Jewish Wounds and Sins*,[39] traced the history of the "Jewish fate" and "suicidal psyche" with a mystical attitude that, according to intellectual historian Miklós Lackó, marks it as a characteristic product of the "radical humanities orientation" of the time.[40]

Pap saw the three Jewish responses to the "Jewish Question"—assimilation, Zionism, and the revolutionary alliance of radical Jewry with the oppressed of the accepting nation—as equally dead ends. Assimilation had led to an unholy alliance between exploiting Jews and the Magyar nobility, drawing the hatred of the oppressed onto Jewry. Zionism was likewise an escape from the Jewish fate that accompanies Jewry's scatteredness. The flaw of the revolutionary path, as in the 1918-19 experience, was that no one can carry out a revolution for someone else. The emphasis on destiny echoed the populists', and in particular Németh's, constant reference to and exploration of "Hungarian fate." On the basis of his historical discursus, the only possible solution for Hungary's Jews was to accept minority status among the Magyars, pull back into themselves, suffer, and purify for a more harmonious future.

Pap's book was greeted by the populists as a courageous break with the assimilationist orthodoxy and, even in the dominant organ of literary establishment liberalism, the *Nyugat* [West], as the voice of a new, dynamic, self-critical generation.[41] His was not the only Jewish voice against assimilation: Pál Kardos, offering in the populist *Válasz* [Answer] a "Jewish answer to the Jewish Question," in defense of Németh in the debate referred to above on his "Person and Role," assailed the urbanists for attacking the populists not for their lack of but exactly because of their democracy, humanism, and freedom, feeling themselves "Enlightenment Inc." who have a monopoly on what we might now call political correctness.[42] He went on to charge that this humanism "is so deeply tied to the desire to flee from Jewishness, the unconscious instinct of embarrassment at Jewish origins which is just the opposite of the most noble humanism." Kardos took care to deny that he is an anti-Jewish Jew: "I am a Jew, I remain a Jew, because I feel my being a Jew makes me unworthy neither of humanity nor of Hungarianness."[43]

Another urbanist who tangled with Németh was the aforementioned Pál Ignotus (1901-78). Ignotus's own family history traced a typical parabola for the urbanists: from rabbi (great-great-grandfather) to self-taught doctor, healer, and miracle rabbi (great-grandfather) to his grandfather, who after conventional medical training and practice became a journalist and finally editor-in-chief of the Budapest German-language daily *Pester Lloyd*.[44] His father, Hugó Veigelsberg, came into conflict with his own father at the beginning of his literary career and started writing under the single name Ignotus, which then stuck and became official and was handed down to his son Pál. The elder Ignotus, as co-founder of the most important literary-political journal of the pre-World War II period, the *Nyugat* [West], and comrade-in-arms of poet and journalism Endre Ady, the founder of Hungarian literary modernism and an icon to this day, was in the thick of the political and intellectual battles of the previous generation and himself became the target of Németh's attacks.

The younger Ignotus showed early interest in populist themes, then went through a socialist phase, and during the time of the anti-Semitic post-revolutionary "white terror" turned towards his inner Jewishness. In his 1947 memoir *Csipkerózsa* [Hedge Rose], he described this attempt: "In a matter of weeks I fell out of love with the Jewish primal soul, just as I had done over a period of years with the Magyar primal soul. . . . Because there and then, in 1919, it became clear to me that there is no such thing as a populist or national or racial primal soul."[45] He converted in 1926 (but "socio-politically") and embarked on a career as, in his own words, the most "irascible urbanist,"[46] writing in *Nyugat*, *A Toll* [The Pen], the *Szép Szó* (which he co-founded with the abiding literary icon of his generation, Attila József), and other liberal publications, in the spirit of the most uncompromising radical liberalism and Europeanism, until his emigration to London in 1939. Against friends' advice, he returned to Hungary in 1949, was arrested and imprisoned as an English spy, and was released a few months before the 1956 revolution, in which he participated before his second and final emigration in 1957.

Ignotus responded to Németh's indelicate reference to his attackers as "Shylocks" with an article titled "As one of the Shylocks."[47] In that article he stuck to exposing Németh and the other populists' dangerous references and formulations, which in his view drifted evermore in the direction of an ascendant National Socialism. But in the article cited previously, "Who in Fact is the Philosemite?" he responded to charges of "philosemitism" in a more personal and revealing way. He defended himself by criticizing those Jews who had "over-assimilated," and what is more, to the worst of

Hungarian culture and values; he stated that he found the "gentry Jew" no less disgusting than the "gentry gentry." He also mentioned the "house-Jews" of anti-Semitism, who go so far as to condone or even tacitly support out-and-out anti-Semites in order to "prove" their Hungarianness.[48]

He declared that intellectual anti-Semitism "appears as a crusading attack on the cosmopolitan spirit, against rationalism striving for clarity and unambiguousness and in general against all of those qualities which we've come to consider part of the urban intellectual."[49] He challenged the charge against him of representing Jewish interests, since the Jewish community accused him of unnecessarily rocking the boat by sharpening things.[50] He militantly identified himself with the stamp of the "destructive spirit" attributed to the Jews, which most ran away from like the plague.[51] Despite his defense of his conversion, quoted at the beginning, he stated that he never tried to hide his origins, environment, or his Talmudic ancestors—"being a Jew is a fact. But not a fact that should be an excuse, and also not a moral postulate"—and that he had never tolerated any attempt to limit speaking out on Hungarian issues because of those origins.[52]

Ignotus explored his relationship to Jewish identity and assimilation further, in perhaps more depth than any of the other urbanists, in *Csipkerózsa*. He treated with understanding but rejection the "mimicry" of the previous generation, which:

> knew that Magyardom is a nation, Jewry on the other hand—the Jewry with Hungarian mother tongue and Hungarian citizenship—is a denomination; so one in one's Jewish merchant self can still be "just as good a Hungarian" as the country squireling from Szabolcs, and if on top of it he changes religion and career, then there is simply "no difference between them."[53]

He instead strove towards the example of the "bad Hungarians," the troublemakers, from István Széchenyi[54] to Endre Ady and Attila József, without whom Hungary would be "a cemetery or a trash heap." It is this "strangeness" that the whole Magyar world must assimilate to, for "it's only possible to become assimilated to those who are assimilated, and especially it's only worth it to them. Assimilation between those who have outgrown their tribe must be mutual."[55] When describing his 1919 identity crisis, he evokes Gilman's pathology: "Even at the most adolescent moments of crisis of Magyar posing and *Jüdischer Selbsthass* [Jewish Self-Hatred] my sensibilities held me back from following in my soul the servile

The Radical Assimilated

superciliousness of 'patriotic Jewry' with which it differentiates itself from the 'Galicians.'"[56] And finally he described his questioning of the whole idea of group identity that led him to his matured sense of self:

> What is this farce? What am I trying to do by now making myself into a "Jew" in such a pure-blooded and primal form, as before that a "Magyar"? What kind of cowardice can be nesting in me, that I cling to such spurious, fabricated root-hairs, in order to see my outline in the world? Why don't I see myself as I am? Why don't I recognize the city, the street, the environment from which I came? Why do I invent believed bonds between myself and others...and really what need is there for such bonds, even if they were real?[57]

Béla Zsolt (1895-1949) had protested against the death penalty for imprisoned communists—and been hauled into court because of it—together with several of the leading populists a few short years before. He was editor of the urbanist journal *A Toll* ["The Pen"], which he transformed from a neutral literary weekly into a biting literary-political gathering place for a wide spectrum of leftist views, until he was forced out of the editorship by the intervention of the Interior Ministry. His own merciless pen continued to play a provocative role in literary and cultural life through the 1930s. He was the author of popular plays and novels skewering foibles of the Jewish middle class, and highly critical of the Jewish elite and big capitalism, but, as other assimilated urbanists, highly attuned to fascist danger and any whiff of anti-Semitism.

Zsolt was provoked by a single line from populist Gyula Illyés that he "becomes unsettled in the face of that writer, who was born in the city."[58] Illyés was the author of the most widely translated populist work of the period, *The People of the Puszta*, about the peasants he grew up with; by the time of his death in 1983 he would become the unofficial grand old man of Hungarian letters. This attack, implying that Budapest was not completely Magyar, struck a chord with Zsolt, one stretching back to the triumphant march into the "criminal city" of interwar ruler Regent Miklós Horthy after the defeat of the Hungarian Soviet Republic of 1919, which he subsequently "cleansed" in the anti-Semitic White Terror of 1919-20. Zsolt charged Illyés with "sneering exclusivity, behind which lies a hushed anti-Semitism hidden by tactics and intellectual prudishness," which "would put back into the ghetto" those who "made the eternal values necessary for awakening the peasants."[59]

Illyés's response, in an article titled "Intellectual Blood Libel," accused Zsolt of creating racial conflict and being blind to a movement that "only sees people" (not races).[60] His statement that the populists would not harm the "Pest spirit and literature, which today rules the whole country with its good and bad products, mainly bad,"[61] was a thinly veiled reference to the Jewish media, with the implicit charge that Zsolt was engaging in defending Jewish interests. Illyes's defense employed a typical strategy—blaming Jews for causing anti-Semitism by throwing around charges anytime their interests were criticized. The populist movement was a "child" and tagging it as anti-Semitic could be a self-fulfilling prophecy: "If you call it Kurt, it will likely grow up to be Kurt, rather than János."[62] The reference to "Kurt" echoed Hatvany's storm trooper charge: the populists, and Illyés especially, whose bombshell article "Destruction" presented the prospect of lands vacated by the disappearing Magyars being taken over by strong, fertile ethnic Germans, saw themselves as defending Magyardom at least as much against Germans as against Jews.[63] The urbanists' readiness to resort to "Nazifying" the populists risked tipping the political balance towards already ascendant Germandom.

This contrasting of the left-behind ghetto and the eternal values that could save Hungary was characteristic for the urbanists. Later, in 1938, in an article appropriately titled "Alone," Zsolt made it clear that he would prefer not to dwell on Jewishness:

> Perhaps we would never have written down the word "Jew," if the right-wing politics had not put Jewry into the center of every Hungarian question, practically of the Hungarian fate. We would have written of capitalism, socialism, feudalism, the gentry, bourgeoisie, dictatorship and democracy, but when the nationalist press over and over wrote the slogan Jew next to Hungarian, it would have been real cowardice, if we were to prevaricate, use euphemisms and not stand up in open defense of a category, on which they openly laid the responsibility for war and peace, communism and capitalism, the emigration of landless peasants in peacetime, the landless peasants' landlessness after the war.[64]

And he continued to declare that his fight was not just for the targets of anti-Semitism: "We stood up in defense of not only Jewry…but also to defend the clearsightedness of the Hungarian people against anti-Semitism."[65]

Zsolt's political journalism addressed the "Jewish Question" only when he felt he had no choice, but his plays and novels were relentless in exposing the contradictions and foibles of the Jewish *kispolgár* [petty bourgeois]. In the words of his biographer Péter Nagy Sz., "With practically monomaniacal consequentialness throughout his whole career one thing interested him: the Hungarian Jew."[66] Nagy Sz. acknowledges the fine line Zsolt was treading in his critical attitude to his Jewish subjects—"It is said that Béla Zsolt, often in extreme fits of temper, defended that very stratum, which in his novels he rather attacked with depressive self-hatred and despising passion"—but then goes on to state that "Béla Zsolt was the journalist and sociographer of Jewish self-knowledge, and not of Jewish wounds and sins."[67]

He was also "the chronicler of Jewish assimilation. [He] examined in his texts this halfway, deformed assimilation's forms of private life, dead ends, and failures,"[68] and he exhibited:

> violence and desperation upon seeing that that stratum, which he knew best, was incapable of being the bearer and trustee of democracy, since its capacities, interests, and characteristics at most make it fit for just a negative assimilation, a fitting into a half-feudal, gentry, neobaroque Christian-aristocratic middle class.[69]

But Zsolt's commitments and world view left him unable to see an alternative to some kind of assimilationist path, producing a tortured inner stance easily visible through his transparent characters. In the words of Dr. Hell, the "hero" of what is considered his most potent novel, *Kinos ügy* [Unpleasant Affair], "What an unbearably tiring work is this permanent Jewish state of nerves, to tinker with everything until your insides turn over, to get to the bottom of everything just to ascertain how joyless and useless it is for you."[70]

The last representative, Ferenc Fejtő (1909-), was born to a Jewish Hungarian-Croatian family in Zagreb and converted to Catholicism at the age of 18. He later spent almost a year in prison for underground communist activities, was a founder of the urbanist periodical *Szép Szó*, was despite his conversion harassed by fascists, and fled an indictment for "inciting class hatred" into exile in 1938. He briefly returned after the war but then fled again, has lived since then in Paris (he is the only one of these figures still alive), and published voluminously on East European affairs (as François).

Fejtő was provoked in 1937 by fellow Social Democrat Peter Veres, who was attempting to elaborate a concept of racial socialism in a debate that took place in the Social Democratic organ, *Szocializmus*. Fejtő called him on this:

> The racial question in today's Hungary means the "Jewish Question"....That however, there is a "Jewish Question," I believe, doesn't mean that there are Jews, in that sense in which Péter Veres usually uses the word. There was also a "Witches' Question" in the Middle Ages, they burned the witches...but the witches only existed in people's imagination....Today also there are people, who according to their birth certificates are Jewish believers, or who converted, or who are the descendants of Jews; there are those, on whose exterior these origins are visible...but Jews in Hungary in that sense, who don't want to be members of the Hungarian nation, and melt into one of the classes making up that nation, to by means of the common language come into spiritual unity with it and strengthen that unity with their children: these hardly exist.[71]

He warned that the racial theory wants to "lead the Jew back into an intellectual and social ghetto."[72] Fejtő asked the obvious question—why Veres (and, by implication, Németh, Illyés, and the other populists) used the word "race" instead of "nation."

Veres, in his response, decried the "impossible situation that on the Left one can't say the word 'race' or 'Jew,' because a certain intellectual terrorism, for which the Jewish intellectuals have wider media opportunities, immediately denounces such a writer out of the progressive camp."[73] He finally burst out in anger:

> Why must the Jews be ashamed of or hide their race? Have they truly shameful racial characteristics?...Assimilation is a hundred times more difficult for the Jews than for any other race. The more they desire it, the more difficult it becomes, for their nervous conformity is one of their main characteristics....Jewry never married the Magyar blood-stock, the peasantry, not even by chance. Reciprocally they had no need for each other: not the Jew for the peasant, nor the peasant for the Jew, while the peasant with other peoples could marry without any particular

obstacle.[74]

Fejtő responded by pulling the "German card"—he warned that German agitators were using the same concept of race Veres was defending to pull Hungarian citizens of German origin (the *Schwabians*) out of the national community, in effect accusing Veres of being soft on the Nazis.[75]

The highly assimilated urbanist writers, effacing their Jewish origins at every step, militantly proclaimed their right to equal status as Hungarians and yet mobilized at the first sign of anti-Semitism on the part of their opponents, but always in terms of the most universal humanism. They never opposed anti-Semitic manifestations as Jews, rather always as partisans of (an itself very embattled) democratic liberalism. They were unfortunate enough to live in a place and time when their beliefs and political stance were completely isolated: their bourgeois-radical position was discredited by Hungarians' association of the revolutions of 1918-19 with the traumatic loss of half of the country's territory and a third of the Magyar population in the post-World War I Trianon peace settlement, and their commitment to rationality and pure intellectualism seemed obsolete in an age dominated by appeals to instinct and blood. While never giving up their basic criticism, the consistent charges by their opponents of representing Jewish interests forced them to confront their problematic self-identity. This is evident in the ending of Zsolt's novel *Villámcsapás* [Stroke of Lightning], in which the main, autobiographical character lamented:

> I have failed as a Hungarian, because I could not be patriotic in the appropriate spirit for the feudal and capitalist interests. I have failed as a Jew, because I couldn't recognize in the Jew the bias, the conservatism, the clericalism, the prejudice, the intellectual laziness, and the lack of scruples which I hated in the non-Jews. I couldn't be Zionist or Jewish in a political sense, because Europe is my home. At the same time I have failed as a European as well, because the larger part of Europe denied and disgraced European traditions. I have failed as a world citizen, since there is hardly place in the world for the citizen who wants to live peacefully and in a civilized manner. I have failed as a humanist, because I had to realize that no one is more defenseless, than s/he who wants to remain humanist at any cost, and the ideas and institutions of humanism cannot be defended otherwise than with—in case of

necessity—inhuman means.⁷⁶

Far beyond "mere" self-criticism, this statement (published in 1937) was a thorough indictment not only of assimilation and Hungarian development, but of the whole political and moral dead end that Europe found itself in as it hurtled towards the tragedies of war and Holocaust. And just as this political critique points, however obliquely, to more positive political possibilities and to better roads not taken, Ignotus, in his embrace of the everpresent charge of rootless cosmopolitan, did the same for identity:

> It's not the question, whether the Jew, the Jew in particular, can be just as "roots-rich" a person somewhere as (let's say it like this) the Aryan. Rather it is whether it is required for someone to put down "roots." Isn't the fact of belonging to Magyardom, the compulsion to solidarity as a citizen of the country, and the even more unfalsifiable compulsion which language means enough "roots"?⁷⁷

A key question for evaluating assimilation is that of the relationship between the individual and group identity. We are often told that assimilation is bad for the Jews—but is it bad for the particular Jews who choose it? Is it bad faith, or of the inevitably difficult and painful search for self-realization? The Hungarian urbanists, with their liberal or radical individualist convictions reaching deep into their bones, were not unaware of collective problems, but were congenitally averse to collective solutions, or identities. They wanted something more than what could be offered by existing society and politics. They saw their assimilationist choices not as negative or as leaving something, but as creating something new on a higher plane. Thus they were able to break through the anti-Semitic context, not without pathologies and complexes, but finally in a positive way, approaching the meaning of *polgár* [bourgeois/citizen] in the best sense.

The populists too, paradoxically, even perversely and misguidedly, were on a comparable search on behalf of the Hungarian people (though without any qualms about collective identity) for renewal, for a way forwards out of history and not back into it. Thus they recognized in Jews such as Károly Pap the kind of critical thinking and vision they missed in much of their own literary and political traditions. In fact, an anti-assimilation perspective was often justified by exactly the idea of Jewish

The Radical Assimilated

racial strength, giving them an unfair advantage in the struggle to succeed in the embattled, peripheral Hungarian economic and cultural position.[78] The imagined Jews, in spite of and against all the real Jews' efforts to assimilate, here fill the rhetorical role of "model race" for the Magyar to admire and emulate.

The urbanists can be faulted for many things, not least for treating assimilation as a completely individual matter and not concerning themselves with the dilemmas of the assimilated Jewish community as a collective, much less of the non- or less assimilated Orthodox and other traditional Jewish communities, who they saw as hopelessly backward. But I believe they should also be given credit for articulating a different kind of Hungarian national identity, inclusive and forward-looking, at exactly the moment when, ironically, their antagonists the populists (and, in a more extreme form, many others) were retreating to an embattled, fearful, limited identity expressed in book and journal titles like "In the Minority" and "We are Alone."[79]

This largely (but perhaps not completely) failed project admittedly seemed already then obsolete; and now, post-Holocaust, doubly so. But it still takes on for me a valence and a poignancy beyond the empty and sterile neoliberal platitudes that might be its translation today. As Isaac Deutscher said of his non-Jewish Jews, "whenever religious intolerance or national emotion was on the ascendant…they were the first victims," but "living on the borderlines of nations and religions…they comprehend more clearly the great movement and the great contradictoriness of nature and society."[80] Gilman himself both calls into question the concept of Jewish self-hatred, lifting it as a category applied by anti-Semites to Jews into the realm of the anti-Semitic dynamic he is describing, and, through Philip Roth and his character/alter ego Nathan Zuckerman, revealing "the hidden truth about Jewish self-hatred"—that it is part of the human condition…the struggle of every human being with his or her sense of growth and eventual decay."[81] Stripped of its pathologizing description, it is the potential of the marginal actor, uniquely equipped for self-reflexivity, for vision and analysis.

Béla Zsolt, who though barely escaping the Holocaust experienced his own tragedies—his stepdaughter was deported and killed, and his own health was ruined, leading to an early death, after which his wife committed suicide—never ceased to believe in his role among the "importunate unwanted advocates" for the stigmatized and all those without rights. It may seem perverse that, after the first punitive Jewish Law of 1938, he still maintained that "even as Jews stripped of our status as Hungarians, we feel a hundred times more community with the peasant proletarian from Balmazújváros than with the Jews of other countries."[82] But, in line with the uncompromising combativeness that he and the other urbanists showed throughout, he managed a kind of triumph that holds the potential to rescue the positive side, not just of Hungarian culture (and, I do maintain, some kind of Hungarian-Jewish synthesis), but of the so thoroughly flawed ideals represented by the idea of Europe: "They can take our Hungarianness, our tools, our pens, our bread from us—but Europe is ours. And now, when we close the debate, we declare just the same, that exactly because we remain Europeans, we are Hungarians."[83]

Thus, while in a sense defending assimilation, the urbanists really strove to move beyond it, at least in the obsolete nineteenth century sense they saw in the "Magyar-posers" around them. The populists saw, in a perverse sense perhaps presciently, identity politics as the wave of the future, which they advocated for Jews and Gentile Magyars alike. From this vantage point, the urbanists can be seen as occupying a post-national position, represented in recent discourse by Jürgen Habermas and others. The more abiding framework is that of particularist versus universalist politics and conceptions of identity. Of course, there were unintended tangible consequences for both positions, as is inevitable for intellectuals engaging in ideological endeavors. The urbanists were operating in a social and ideological context that was far from ready for post-national appeals; thus they drove themselves into isolation and irrelevance. The populists found an all-too-ready audience, but one that assimilated them to the dominant racialist and ultimately exterminationist currents swirling at the time.

The idea of Europe has revealed itself, in the course of the twentieth century and into the twenty-first, as just as flawed as the other ideals pursued by the 1930s intellectuals. But there is still value in fighting for the best of it in an inclusive sense, of which Jews are fully a part. Pál Ignotus, too, saw the urbanists' contribution as crucial for claiming this progressive possibility, though expressing it in his characteristically negative way: "The Jews force not only themselves into an absurd situation, but also impoverish the country, if they remove from the nation's spiritual storeroom that more critical, more sarcastic, more analytical perspective, the acquisition of which eases their social situation."[84]

This sensibility is eminently, though not exclusively, "Jewish" and a part of a conscious Jewish identity—but one reaching in the direction of the universal, not the particular. If this too is Gilman's legacy of "Jewish self-hatred," and it may well be, then however much I may cringe at his terminology, I and my urbanists are with him.

ACKNOWLEDGMENTS

Research for this article was supported in part by Fulbright/Institute for International Eduction and the International Research and Exchanges Board (IREX).

NOTES

[1] Géza K. Havas, *Nem tudok asszimilálodni!* [I can't become assimilated!], *Szép Szó*, January-February 1939; repr. in *Talpra, halottak! Publicisztikai írások 1937-1944* [Rise Up, Corpses! Journalistic Writings 1937-1944] (sel. and ed. János Kenedi; Budapest: Gondolat-Nyilvánosság Klub-Századvég, 1990), 141-45.

[2] Pál Ignotus, *Ki hát a 'filoszemita?* [Who Really is the 'Philosemite'?], *A Toll* [The Pen] 5 (1934); repr. in *Vissza az értelemhez* [Return to Reason] (sel. and ed. András Bozóki; Budapest: Hatodik Síp Alapítvány-Új Mandátum, 1997), 140. Tellingly, Ignotus in his 1947 autobiography, although referring to the fact of its having happened and treating in detail his failed attempt to embrace his Jewish essence (discussed below), completely passes over the occasion and details of his conversion. Pál Ignotus, *Csipkerózsa. Budapesti és londoni emlékek* [Hedge Rose: Budapest and London Memories] (Budapest: Múzsák, 1989). The memoir was originally published in series between 23 January 1947 and 16 September 1948 in the weekly *Haladás* [Progress], edited by fellow urbanist Béla Zsolt.

[3] Though most of the urbanists had selected journalism republished after 1989 in a "neo-urbanist" spirit—especially in the series *Ars Scribendi*; for example, Géza K. Havas, *Talpra, halottak!*; Béla Zsolt, *A végzetes toll. Publicisztikai írások* [The Fatal Pen: Journalistic Writings] (sel. and ed. András Bozóki; Budapest: Nyilvánosság Klub-Századvég, 1992)—the explicitly Jewish publishing house *Mult és Jövő* [Present and Future] put its energies into republishing writers such as the "Jewish separatist" Károly Pap: *Pap Károly művei 1-8* [The Works of Károly Pap] (8 vols.; Budapest: Múlt és Jövő, 1998-2001). In a wider sense, post-Holocaust Hungarian Jewish memory has tended to emphasize Zionist efforts and separate Jewish institutions in the interwar period and "write out" amalgamation and mixed identities; see, for example, "memory books" of various vanished Jewish communities, mostly

published in Israel. Richard S. Esbenshade, "Beyond Passivity: Relations between Jews and Non-Jews in the Hungarian Provinces during World War II" (Masters' thesis, University of California, Santa Cruz, 1996), 53-56.

[4] See Jonathan Boyarin and Daniel Boyarin, eds., *Jews and Other Differences: The New Jewish Cultural Studies* (Minneapolis: University of Minnesota Press, 1997), and especially Jonathan Boyarin and Daniel Boyarin, "Introduction / So What's New?" in ibid., vii-xxii.

[5] Tamás Ungvári, *Ahasvérus és Shylock: A 'zsidókérdés' Magyarországon* [Ahasverus and Shylock: The "Jewish Question" in Hungary] (Budapest: Akadémiai, 1999), published in English as *Ahasverus and Shylock: The "Jewish Question" in Hungary* (Budapest: Akadémiai, 1999). The Hungarian language edition will be referred to here.

[6] János Gyurgyák, *A zsidókérdés Magyarországon: Politikai eszmetörténet* [The Jewish Question in Hungary: A Political History of Ideas] (Budapest: Osiris, 2001).

[7] Ungvári, *Ahasvérus és Shylock*, 13.

[8] Gyurgyák, *A zsidókérdés*, 18.

[9] See below.

[10] Sander Gilman, *Jewish Self-Hatred: Anti-Semitism and the Hidden Language of the Jews* (Baltimore: Johns Hopkins University Press, 1986).

[11] Sander Gilman, *Inscribing the Other* (Lincoln: University of Nebraska Press, 1991).

[12] Jean-Paul Sartre, *Anti-Semite and Jew: An Exploration of the Etiology of Hate* (trans. George J. Becker; 1948; repr. New York: Shocken, 1995), 13. Emphasis in original.

[13] See Ungvári, *Ahasvérus és Shylock*, 252-63.

[14] Gilman, *Jewish Self-Hatred*, 285.

[15] Using the perhaps one-dimensional but not misleading index of language, Ferenc Fejtő cites statistics of 56.3% of Hungarian Jews (59.1% in Budapest) declaring Hungarian as their mother tongue in 1880, 63.8% (74.2%) in 1890, 71.5% (85.6%) in 1900, and 76.5% (90.1%) in 1910—and this under the Habsburg Monarchy, when German was still widely spoken, especially among Jews. Ferenc Fejtő, *Magyarság, zsidóság* [Magyardom, Jewry] (História Könyvtár Monográfiák) [História Library Monographs] 14; trans. Gyula Zeke; Budapest: História-MTA Történettudományi Intézete, 2000), 98.

[16] Rolf Fischer, "Anti-Semitism in Hungary, 1882-1932," in *Hostages of Modernization: Studies on Modern Anti-Semitism 1870-1933/39* (ed. Herbert A. Strauss; Berlin: Walter de Gruyter, 1993), 872.

[17] István Szabó, dir., *Sunshine* (Hungary/Germany/Canada/Austria: 1999).

[18] Sartre, *Anti-Semite and Jew*, 13.

[19] Ibid., 135.

[20] The 1920 Trianon Treaty divested Hungary of two-thirds of the national territory and over half of her population, leaving some four million Magyars in the neighboring lands of Czechoslovakia, Romania, and Yugoslavia. This perceived betrayal by the victorious Allied powers, summed up in the name of the Paris suburb where the treaty was signed, became the touchstone of Hungarian politics through the interwar period and a perceived thorn in the body of the nation that remains to this day.

[21] Octobrism is the liberal-democratic (also often referred to as "bourgeois-radical") ideology that brought Count Mihály Károlyi to the head of the first post-Habsburg independent national government in October 1918. In March 1919, he resigned in favor of the Hungarian Soviet regime, which was toppled after four months by the counterrevolution led by Miklós Horthy, who ruled as regent through the whole interwar period.

[22] Ungvári, *Ahasvérus és Shylock*, 14, 17-22, 77-92.

[23] Isaac Deutscher, *The Non-Jewish Jew and other Essays* (ed. Tamara Deutscher; London: Oxford University Press, 1968).

[24] Biographical data for this and following writers can be found in László Péter, ed., *Új Magyar irodalmi lexikon* [New Encyclopedia of Hungarian Literature] (László Péter, ed.; 2nd rev. ed.; 3 vols.; Budapest: Akadémiai kiadó, 2000).

[25] *Huszadik Század* [Twentieth Century] 36 (1917): 92-93; cited in Gyurgyák, *A zsidókérdés*, 531-32.

[26] Ibid., 532.

[27] Cited in Gyurgyák, *A zsidókérdés*, 533.

[28] Lajos Hatvany, "Egy zsidó-magyar monológja" [A Jewish-Hungarian Monologue], *Korunk* [Our Age] (1927); cited in Gyurgyák, *A zsidókérdés*, 534. The distinction between Magyar ethnicity and the Hungarian language and state/geographical formation is conventional in English, though the Hungarian language does not distinguish between the two.

[29] László Németh, "Ember és szerep," *Kalangya* [Shock of Corn] (1 January 1934); repr. in *A Népi-Urbánus Vita Dokumentumai 1932-1947* [Documents of the Populist-Urbanist Debate, 1932-1947] (ed. Péter Nagy Sz; Budapest: Rakéta, 1990), 28.

[30] Lajos Hatvany, "A szellem különítményesei," *Újság* [News] (27 May 1934); repr. in *A Népi-Urbánus Vita Dokumentumai*, 94.

[31] Ibid., 101.

[32] Pál Ignotus explored his own conflicted relationship with German culture and

power in *Csipkerózsa*, 110ff.

[33] László Németh, "Egy különítményes vallomása" [Confession of a Storm Trooper], *Budapesti Hirlap* [Budapest News], 17 June 1934; repr. in *A Népi-Urbánus Vita Dokumentumai*, 121-29.

[34] Ibid.

[35] Ibid., 128.

[36] At a later juncture, he expressed this stance more baldly: "Jewish assimilation, I believe, has not succeeded anywhere in the world....It stuck on two things: they threw themselves too avidly on the host peoples' zones of fate, culture and politics, from which decency and blood equally might have held them back, and at the same time, when they tried to monopolize the nations' futures, they couldn't resist the calling of international currents steaming with their ancient belief and racial thinking." László Németh, "Kisebbségben" [In the Minority], in *Kisebbségben* (4 vols.; Budapest: Magyar Élet, 1942), 1:66.

[37] Németh, "Ember és szerep," 28.

[38] Németh, "Egy különítményes vallomása," 128-29.

[39] Károly Pap, *Zsidó sebek és bünök. Vitairat. Különös tekintettel Magyarországra.* [Jewish Wounds and Sins: Polemical Essay, with particular Attention to Hungary] (Budapest: Kosmos, 1935).

[40] M. Lackó, *Sziget és külvilág: Válogatott tanulmányok* [Island and Outer World: Selected Essays (Budapest: MTA Történettudományi Intézete, 1996), 126. The Hungarian expression *radikális szellemtudományos iranyzát*, for which my translation is inadequate, indicates a mixture of history, literature, and mythology drawing especially on German anti- or post-Positivist currents and their substantial quotient of irrationalism, though without the fascist or proto-fascist implications.

[41] See Gyula Illyés and Aladár Komlós, "Zsidó sebek és bünök: Pap Károly könyve" [Jewish Wounds and Sins: Károly Pap's Book], *Nyugat* 28:37 (1935); repr. in *A Népi-Urbánus Vita Dokumentumai*, 180-89.

[42] Pál Kardos, "Zsidó válasz" [Jewish Answer], *Válasz* 1:2 (1934); repr. in *A Népi-Urbánus Vita Dokumentumai*, 135-40. Pap and Kardos were the only participants in the debate to respond explicitly as Jews—the urbanists, however much they might have identified themselves as Jews individually, to a person responded as universalist humanists.

[43] Ibid., 140.

[44] This biographical information from András Bozóki, "Ignotus Pál és kora" [Pál Ignotus and his Era], in Bozóki, *Vissza az értelemhez*, 287.

[45] Ignotus, *Csipkerózsa*, 110, 114.

[46] Pál Ignotus, "Elvek, frontok, nemzedékek" [Ideas, Fronts, Generations], *Irodalomtörténet* [Literary History] 3 (1973): 633-43; quoted in Bozóki, "Ignotus Pál és kora," 288.

[47] Pál Ignotus, "Mint egyike a Shylockoknak . . ." [As one of the Shylocks], *A Toll* [The Pen] 76 (1934); repr. in *A Népi-Urbánus Vita Dokumentumai*, 51-54.

[48] Ignotus, "Ki hát a 'filoszemita'?," 138-39.

[49] Ibid., 139.

[50] Ibid., 142.

[51] Ibid., 143.

[52] Ibid., 140.

[53] Ignotus, *Csipkerózsa*, 32.

[54] Nineteenth century visionary of national consciousness and development, who founded the Academy of Sciences and National Casino and also designed and pushed through construction of the first bridge across the Danube.

[55] Ignotus, *Csipkerózsa*, 33-34.

[56] Ibid., 102.

[57] Ibid., 115.

[58] Béla Zsolt, "A nagyerdö és a nagyvilág" [The Big Woods and the Big World], *Újság* [News] (27 May 1934); repr. in *A Népi-Urbánus Vita Dokumentumai*, 110. Németh expressed a similar sentiment: "I live here in Budapest, but in my heart I'm an emigrant in the country." "A Tanu megszünik" [The *Witness* is Ceasing Publication], *Tanu* [Witness] 5-6 (1936): 75.

[59] Zsolt, "A nagyerdö és a nagyvilág," 110-11.

[60] Gyula Illyés, "Szellemi vérvád" [Intellectual Blood Libel], *Magyar Hirlap* [Hungarian Newspaper] (3 June 1934); repr. in *A Népi-Urbánus Vita Dokumentumai*, 113.

[61] Ibid., 114. See also Gilman's discussion of the stigma of "Jewish journalism," for example in the case of Karl Kraus. Gilman, *Inscribing the Other*, 173-90.

[62] Ibid., 115.

[63] Gyula Illyés, "Pusztulás: Utijegyetek" [Destruction: Travel Notes], *Nyugat* (15 September 1933), 189-205.

[64] Béla Zsolt, "Egyedül" [Alone], *Újság* (14 August 1938); repr. in *A végzetes toll. Publicisztikai írások*, 222-23.

[65] Ibid., 224.

[66] Péter Nagy Sz., *Zsolt Béla* [Béla Zsolt], (Budapest: Akadémiai, 1990), 97.

[67] Ibid., 8. Nagy Sz. later acknowledges "Jewish self-hatred."

[68] Ibid., 9.

[69] Ibid., 98.

[70] Béla Zsolt, "Kinos ügy" (1935?); quoted in Nagy Sz., *Zsolt Béla*, 133.

[71] Ferenc Fejtő, "A 'faji' szocializmusról" [On "Racial" Socialism], *Szocializmus* [Socialism] (June 1937); repr. in *A Népi-Urbánus Vita Dokumentumai*, 344-45.

[72] Ibid., 345.

[73] Ibid., 298.

[74] Ibid., 299-300.

[75] Ferenc Fejtő, "Fajkérdés és szocializmus. Viszonválasz Veres Péternek" [The Race Question and Socialism: Second Reply to Péter Veres], *Szocializmus* (July 1937): 307.

[76] Béla Zsolt, *Villámcsapás: Schwarz András önéletrajza* [Stroke of Lightning: The Autobiography of András Schwarz (Budapest: Pantheon, n.d. [1937]), 212. The literary critic Aladár Komlós noted, in this same vein, "The propagandists of the 'criminal Budapest' slogan couldn't find more arguments for their position by anyone than exactly him, who in his public writings is the slogan's most talented opponent." Aladár Komlós, *Zsolt Béla*, [Béla Zsolt], in *Írók és elvek: Irodalmi tanulmányok* [Writers and Ideas: Literary Essays] (Budapest: Nyugat, 1937), 115.

[77] Ignotus, "Ki hát a 'filoszemita'?," 141.

[78] See comments by Németh on Ignotus the elder and Jewish "racial discipline" in Németh, "Ember és szerep," 27-28.

[79] Németh, *Kisebbségben* [In the Minority]; *Egyedül Vagyunk* [We are Alone] was an extreme right-wing journal appearing between 1941-44.

[80] Deutscher, *Non-Jewish Jews*, 34-35.

[81] Gilman, *Jewish Self-Hatred*, 383.

[82] Zsolt, "Zárszó" [Last Word], in *Kőért kenyér. Vezércikkek, 1921-1939* [Bread for Stone: Lead Articles, 1921-1939] (Budapest: Tábori és Társa, 1939), 264.

[83] Ibid.

[84] Ignotus, *Csipkerózsa*, 35.

The Transformation of Jewish Vilna, 1881-1939

Theodore R. Weeks

The city that is presently Lithuania's capital, variously known as Vilne, Vilna, Wilno, and now Vilnius, holds a special place in Jewish history. It is the "Jerusalem of Lithuania," a center of Jewish learning, home of the Vilna Gaon of the late eighteenth century, and in a sense the "capital" of the *mitnagdim*, the learned opponents of the more free-wheeling Chasids of the south. In the twentieth century, Vilna became a hotbed of Jewish socialism and a center of Zionism. The city was the home of the Jewish Historical Instititute, YIVO, founded in the mid-1920s and later transferred to New York. In the Russian Empire, Vilna was one of the most important Jewish centers, along with Warsaw and the brash upstart Odessa.

By the late nineteenth century, however, Vilna's best days as a Jewish center were over. The restrictive policies of the Russian (and later Polish) authorities, a stagnant economy, and the ravages of World War I all contributed to the shrinking and increasingly impoverished state of Vilna's Jews in this period. At the same time, Jewish life continued and even flourished in Vilna during this period. This paper will sketch some of the most important changes that Jewish Vilna underwent between the pogroms of summer 1881 and the beginning of World War II in autumn 1939. The purpose here is not to attempt a comprehensive view of Jewish Vilna, but merely to point out how the Jewish community of the multi-ethnic city changed over this period of nearly three generations.

VILNA IN 1881

In 1881, Vilna was a sleepy provincial town of around 80,000 souls. It served as the administrative capital for the Russian Empire's "Northwestern provinces," comprising most of present-day Lithuania and Belarus. The city was indeed larger than Minsk, Vitebsk, Mogilev, Grodno, and other such metropolises, but probably not terribly different in most aspects of everyday life. As in those cities, Jews made up a large percentage of the population: almost forty-six percent according to official sources. A contemporary statistician noted that if temporary military residents were left out of the city's population figures, Jews actually made up a bare majority of Vilna's inhabitants.[1] It would not be unfair to describe Vilna in 1881 as a Jewish city with Polish accents and Russian rulers. The very center of the city was dominated by Jewish residents and businesses. While Polish and Russian businesses, signs, and conversation might dominate on St. George's Boulevard (now Gedimino) or on Castle Street (Zamkovaia, now Pilies), in the small streets in between Jews and Yiddish set the tone. Aside from their numbers, Jews were also more likely to be natives of Vilna: in 1875 almost two-thirds of the city's Jewish population had been born in the city, while only two-fifths of Catholics and not even one-fifth of Orthodox believers could make that claim.[2]

Economically, Jews in Vilna made up the bulk of the city's middle class between Polish landowners and Russian officials on the one side and mainly Catholics (and probably Polish) servants and laborers on the other. Jews were largely excluded from government jobs, though a small number worked as teachers in the city's Jewish teachers' institute (which up to 1873 had been the government-sponsored Rabbinical School).[3] Most Jews earned their living as artisans, merchants, shopkeepers, and agents of various types. In 1875, several thousand Jews worked as laborers, but this kind of physical work was much more typical for Catholic Vilners.[4] It was as artisans and shopkeepers that Jews dominated in the city's occupational structure. Half of all construction workers, two-thirds of leather workers, and nearly all tobacco workers were Jews.[5] The figure of the Jewish tailor [*portnoi* in Russian] and shopkeeper are almost legendary—but in this case, the legend is based on solid statistical evidence. Less commonly spoken of are Jewish prostitutes. A one-day census in 1875 found 120 women active in this trade, likely a gross underestimate, of whom half were Jewish.[6]

In 1881, Jewish education continued to be carried out mainly in exclusively Jewish schools, most commonly the *heder* and for more advanced students the *yeshiva*. However, St. Petersburg was interested in educating a Russian-speaking Jewish elite and had established a Rabbinical School for this purpose in 1847. While the Rabbinical School had been shut down in 1873, it reopened shortly thereafter as a Teachers' Institute and in that form existed until 1915.[7] Hirsz Abramowicz later recalled his own experiences in this and other government schools for Jews, where all subjects—even religion and prayers—were taught in Russian. As Abramowicz remembered, speaking Yiddish in public was forbidden these students, even outside of the school itself.[8] Among these *maskilim*, the preferred spoken language was Russian, never Yiddish, but this group was still quite tiny in 1881. In 1875, a Russian statistician found that over a quarter of Vilna's Jews were literate or semi-literate in Russian, which gives some idea of the spread of the language within the Jewish community.[9]

Far more typical was the *heder*, where boys learned rudimentary Hebrew skills and usually little else. Despite constant attempts by both Russian authorities and *maskilim* to reform these small, usually cramped and unhygienic schools, most Jewish lads received their only formal education here.[10] It has been estimated that in the late nineteenth century there existed one *heder* for approximately every twenty-eight boys of school age.[11] The *heder* teachers, as is often recounted in memoirs, were usually far more interested in their own studies than in teaching a crowd of small boys. The 1875 census found 202 *melamdim* [*heder* teachers] in Vilna, only thirty-six percent of whom were literate in Russian.[12] Most likely the number of actual *melamdim* was higher. The learning of Hebrew letters was often accompanied by harsh words and physical blows for the lazy or dull. At the same time, it is almost certain—though hard to prove—that Jews were the most literate people in Vilna. Even among Orthodox people in Vilna, around one-third were illiterate or half-literate in 1875. Very few adult Jewish men could not at least make out Hebrew letters, and, as we have seen, over one-fifth of them were also literate in Russian.

The Russian authorities' distaste for Jews is well known. However, in Vilna it may be argued that the Russians mistrusted and despised the Poles even more than the Jews—at least, this was the case for the most infamous Russian governor-general of Vilna, Count M. N. Murav'ev, "the hangman."[13] On the whole the Russian governors and governors-general felt little sympathy for the Jews, but tended to see the Poles, in particular the Catholic clergy, as far more menacing. Younger Jews, however, were often singled out as seditious troublemakers, as in 1881, when the governor of Vilna province wrote in an annual report that the younger generation of Jews was being influenced by "enemies of public order." He concluded, however, that this phenomenon was of "insignificant dimensions."[14]

A far more interesting question is the behavior of Russian officials in 1881, the year of widespread pogroms in southern Russia. While few historians now believe that officials actually fomented the pogroms, it is a matter of historical record that no significant pogroms occurred in the empire's "Northwest provinces"; that is, the region around Vilna.[15] Just as no entirely satisfactory answer has been given to why pogroms took place when and where they did, it is probably not possible to state confidently why pogroms failed to occur in the Northwest.[16] However, one reason that pogroms did not spread into this region could be the decisive action of the governor-general of Vilna, Count Eduard Ivanovich Totleben.

Immediately upon receiving word of the Elizavetgrad pogrom in mid-April, Totleben sent out orders to military and civilian authorities warning them to take all possible measures to prevent any clashes between Christians and Jews. A circular of May 6, 1881, to the governors of Vilna, Kovno, and Grodno provinces clearly stated measures to be taken. First, all false rumors and agitation among the people was to be "vigilantly pursued"; authorities were to pay "painstaking attention" to "unknown individuals." If a disturbance broke out, local authorities were ordered to suppress it immediately and inform local military units. If need be, these military units were to aid civilian authorities in reestablishing order.[17] The correspondence between Totleben, local authorities, and the Ministry of the Interior in Petersburg shows that all were concerned with maintaining public order. In the end, despite alarming rumors and fears, Vilna's Jewish community was spared.[18]

A unique witness to the situation of Jewish Vilna was Dr. J. Rülf, a rabbi from Memel who visited the city in late summer 1881. As Rülf explained in the foreword to his short book, the anti-Jewish attitudes expressed by the Russian Minister of the Interior, M.Ignat'ev, combined with the tragic events of 1881, pushed him to pay a personal visit to Russia to experience firsthand the realities of Jewish life there. His short sojourn in Russia, a bit over a week in total, was spent in Vilna and Minsk. As an acculturated but religiously Orthodox German Jew, Rülf felt both alienated from and attracted to Vilna's Jewish population. His commentary alternates between condescension, affection, and a sense of superior protectiveness.

Arriving in Vilna late at night, Rülf rises early and sets off for the main synagogue. Walking from "German Street," where his Jewish-owned hotel is located, he notes that the court of the synagogue [*Schulhof*] takes up a large area "cut through with different irregular streets running hither and thither, badly paved and not entirely clean." Houses crowd the street, some containing apartments and others housing different charities and associations [*khevros*]. Each association had its own prayer house [*beyt midrash or kloyz*]. The decorations in the Great Synagogue he describes as "massive, very old [*uralt*] and gnawed on by the tooth of time."[19]

After breakfast at his hotel, Rülf gets a guided visit to the city's charitable institutions from the state rabbi, Dr. A. Gordon. Visiting a Talmud Torah where poor children are both housed and taught, he remarks that the children are better behaved than in such institutions in Germany. He spends the morning visiting a hospital, clinic, and old folk's home. Despite the large number of charities, the streets abound in beggars, crying "*zedoko tazil mimowes*" [in Rülf's transcription: charity saves from death]. Indeed, Rülf notes a kind of beggar found nowhere else: a beggar for beggars who keeps only a small portion of alms given him, passing most along to a yeshiva. Even on shabbes, beggars are busy—but on this day accepting alms in the form of bread.[20]

Rülf noted that the Jewish community in Vilna was not unified. Dozens of prayer houses and small synagogues existed, practically one for each Jewish association [*khevrah*], with only the Great Synagogue and the cemetery uniting all. To quote Rülf again, though the town was full of churches—"and what pretty churches"—their architecture "reminds one just as much of synagogues as of churches."[21] Vilna lacked a chief rabbi, though it did have a crown rabbi, Dr. A. Gordon. Most Jews did not consider crown rabbis, trained at state institutions, their true spiritual leaders, but they depended on them to carry out many functions such as performing marriage ceremonies. Several different rabbinical courts existed in the city, each with its own clientele. As the abundance of beggars suggest, most Jews in Vilna were far from prosperous. Entire streets were lined with tiny Jewish shops, all competing with each other for their daily bread. Jewish artisans and workers were also prevalent in the city, and many artisans also personally sold the goods they made.[22]

Rülf praised the "deep piety" of the Vilna Jews. Rabbis and their families enjoyed great respect in the community. Unlike many traditional Orthodox Jews, however, the Vilners were "tolerant to the highest degree." Moderate and frugal, Vilna's Jews were also hardworking, especially the women. Girls did not receive any education, but by the age of six were already helping out at home and often becoming skilled seamstresses. Unfortunately their artisanry was very poorly paid, as most Russians, Rülf contended, purchased such items from abroad. While admitting that among younger Jews there were some "nihilists," Rülf suggests that Vilna's Jews would soon be patriotic Russian citizens, if only the government would change its ways. Along these lines Rülf strolls by the governor-general's palace and remarks that Todleben was known as a "order-loving, decisive, and just" administrator: "a real German man" [*ein wahrhaft deutscher Mann*].[23] Unstated but understood is the sentiment: if only more Russian officials were like him!

VILNA IN 1905

In the generation between the pogrom year 1881 and the revolutionary year 1905, the Russian Empire changed considerably. Tsar Alexander III had died in 1894, and his son Nicholas II now ruled. Nicholas shared his father's distaste for Poles and Jews, but lacked the firm hand and charisma of Alexander III. As for Vilna itself, it had grown considerably since 1881. According to the first empire-wide census of 1897, Vilna boasted a population of 154,532, a figure that went up another third by 1914.[24] The town retained its mainly Jewish character with roughly half of the population Jewish, over fifteen percent Russians, and just under twenty percent Polish.[25] The Russian authorities had adorned the city with two large monuments, one of Count M. N. Murav'ev who had suppressed the 1863 uprising (built in 1897) and the other of Catherine the Great (1904).[26] The Catherine statue had been sculpted by native son Mark Antokolsky, who died before the monument was unveiled.[27] On a more practical level, both electricity and telephone service were inaugurated in Vilna on the eve of 1905.[28] While the growth and economic development of the city could not compare with that of industrial cities like Warsaw or Łódź, Vilna was in any case moving forward.

Jewish life in Vilna had also not stood still. In 1903 a grand new synagogue in the Moorish style was built on the edge of the Jewish quarter.[29] Here more "respectable" Jews could worship in sumptuous surroundings, avoiding the grime and ruckus of the Old Synagogue. However, even here Orthodoxy was maintained; religious reform had few adherents among Vilna's Jews. While reform had made little progress, out-and-out rejection of Jewish religious norms was not rare among Vilna's youth. In 1897, the Jewish Bund, the first Jewish socialist party, had been founded in the city, and by 1905 it is estimated that one quarter of the city's Jewish workers were members of that party.[30] Long before this, the Russian authorities had uncovered "illegal circles" of "socialist-revolutionary" Jewish youth, for example in 1875 at the Jewish teachers' institute.[31]

But those were schoolboy affairs compared to the Bund, which quickly spread "revolutionary propaganda" among the town's workers—almost a dozen brochures were confiscated by local authorities by 1898.[32] Four years later, a Bund sympathizer, Hirsh Lekert, fired two shots at the detested Vilna governor, Victor von Wahl. Despite the governor's minor wounds, Lekert was tried and executed a mere three weeks later.[33] Not without reason did the governor of Vilna province in his 1903 report call the Bund "the most serious and most zealous Jewish movement."[34]

Political Zionism was also gaining strength in Vilna. Theodor Herzl visited Vilna in 1903 and was greeted as "king of the Jews."[35] At the same time, St. Petersburg sent out a circular warning local authorities to keep a close watch on Zionist activities, which it considered "in contradiction with the principle of the Russian state idea."[36] From 1905 to 1911 Vilna served as the location for the socialist *Poalei tsiyon's* central organization and publishing activities.

1905 was a revolutionary year throughout the Russian Empire and in Vilna, too. The Bund and social-democratic parties were the most prominent leaders of the strikes, demonstrations, and the like during the year.[37] The year began with a strike on 11 January in response to bloodshed in St. Petersburg ("bloody Sunday"), and calm was not restored until the following year. As always in agitated situations, Vilna's Jews feared attacks from their Christian neighbors. Self-defense squads were formed, though these were forbidden by the Russian authorities.[38] Writing in 1907, Vilna provincial governor D. Liubimov complained that "false rumors" were spread that the authorities were tolerating or fomenting pogroms and that "Jewish self-defense," led by revolutionaries, had been set up in response to these rumors.[39]

In October 1905, Tsar Nicholas II issued a manifesto promising, among other things, some kind of parliament [Duma] for Russia. Elections for the first Duma took place in Vilna in April 1906, with the Bund and other revolutionary parties boycotting. The Zionist Shmariahu Levin succeeded in being elected to the first Duma with the help of the liberal Kadet party.[40] With the quick demise of the first Duma, Jewish representation for Vilna also ended. No Jew was sent from the city or province of Vilna to the remaining three Dumas (1907-17). For Jews, as for most subjects of the Russian Tsars—and especially for non-Russians—the 1905 revolution brought mainly unfulfilled promises. Legal restrictions and official discrimination continued in education and government employment. Worse yet, these years saw an economic downturn. Only on the eve of

World War I did the economy begin to look up again.

WORLD WAR I

When the German Empire declared war on Russia in early August 1914, Vilna was a major garrison town with some 30,000 soldiers. It also held an important position on the vital railway from St. Petersburg to Warsaw. From the start it was clear that the city's inhabitants would be directly, and most likely adversely, affected by the war. As is well known, the first few weeks of the war went surprisingly well for the Russian army, which penetrated deep into the German province of East Prussia. Rapidly, however, the Russian gains against the Germans were turned around at the stunning defeat of Tannenberg. From that point in August 1914 onward, the Russian armies were in perpetual retreat from the Germans. Warsaw was lost in August 1915, and many refugees descended upon Vilna.[41] From the perspective of Jewish Vilna, the Russian military authorities appeared to be trying to cover up their own gross ineptitude by blaming defeat on spies and saboteurs, in particular singling out Jews for such accusations. Despite all harsh measures adopted against the civilian population, the Russian army continued its retreat, abandoning Vilna on the eve of Yom Kippur, 17 September 1915.

Hirsz Abramowicz recounts that most Vilna Jews welcomed the Germans, reasoning that things could in any case not get worse. German troops did engage in some looting, according to Abramowicz, but there were no attacks on civilians and soon order was restored. Unfortunately, the German authorities were hardly more favorable to the Jews than the Russians had been. Trade in grain was forbidden, severely curtailing many Jews' livelihood. Similarly, the Germans' restrictions on movement within the occupied region [soon called *Oberost*] infringed on Jewish merchants and pedlars. Worse yet, the Germans soon introduced a system of requisitions, in particular of grain and other produce, but also of cows, horses, and other livestock. Two heavily Jewish occupations, dealing in fish and smuggling, also attracted the Germans' attention.[42] In general, living conditions were harsh and even grim. Unemployment was high and the Polish-dominated city council tended to help their own unemployed before those of other nationalities. Conditions were so bad that some Jews volunteered to leave for work in Germany, while others left Vilna for America. Some aid from foreign Jews made it to Vilna, but this too came to an end with the United States' entry into the war in April 1917.[43]

Germans not only established their administrative center in Vilna, they also set up schools (in German for Jews, claiming that Yiddish was merely corrupt German) and publishing, including a daily newspaper. In 1916, the *Wilnaer Zeitung* published an informal guidebook to Vilna, which was so popular that it was published as a booklet and went through three printings before war's end. The author, apparently a German soldier, describes Vilna in condescending but not altogether negative terms. At first, the author writes, Vilna appears to be only a confused mish-mash of small streets lacking any kind of order or coherence. The only street with "big city character" is George's Street (today's Gedimino); otherwise the town resembles Nürnberg or Rothenberg with its narrow streets. The town's "German Street" was full of signs "in the most impossible German offering the broadest possible array of items for sale." Though not mentioned specifically, the signs were almost certainly the work of Vilna's Jewish merchants.[44] Similarly the scene in front of the railway station, where travelers are accosted by individuals with Yiddish accents [*"schennes Zimmer?"*] offering meals and lodging.[45]

The Jewish part of town or Ghetto is also described in some detail. "As on an island in the sea the people of Israel live on their own streets, just like long ago, in the middle of the large city Vilna." Tradition and piety predominate in this "city within a city." A description of the crowded, narrow, and not particularly hygienic conditions in this quarter merits quotation:

> A dark cloud appears to hover over these roofs, no matter what the weather. Walking in these gloomy streets arouses claustrophobia in a western person [i.e., a German]. All senses rebel against the stroller's impressions. The eye sees misery, the ear hears dissonant sounds, and the nose—oh the nose!—the nose has very good reason to feel personally insulted.[46]

Endless numbers of tiny stores line the streets, offering everything possible for sale. Everywhere one looks there are hawkers and children under foot. Only on shabbes do the stores close, and only then does the hubbub on the street die down. But finding the Great Synagogue is no easy matter, as "it hides itself" amid a warren of little streets and tiny courtyards, each harboring another small prayer house. Here, within a few steps, all the necessities of Jewish life are available: places to buy and sell, places to pray, a bathhouse, and a large library (the famous Straszun library).⁴⁷ Even in the middle of World War I, apparently, Jewish life continued little changed in Vilna.

By 1917, most of Vilna's inhabitants were going hungry.⁴⁸ Mortality rates shot up, especially among the youngest and oldest parts of the population.⁴⁹ Banditry increased, and it appeared that all semblance of law and order was breaking down. The German authorities seemed entirely incapable of dealing with the situation and were certainly not helped by the terrible harvest of 1916-17. At the very least, Vilna had hoped that the Germans would succeed in maintaining order, but by late 1917 and 1918 chaos and lawlessness gave the lie to any pretense of German *Ordnung*.⁵⁰ Of course, nobody could know how desperate the Germans' own situation really was. Despite the Russian revolution and the harsh treaty of Brest-Litovsk in spring 1918, life did not improve in Vilna. The German capitulation of November 1918 translated into chaos in Vilna. There is no need to go into detail here; suffice it to say that in the next two years control over the city passed from Lithuanians to Soviets to Poles to Soviets and finally back to the Poles. By 1920, when a fragile peace was finally implemented, exhaustion was perhaps the most prevalent emotion among Vilna's population.

The end of the war brought no respite for the suffering population of Vilna. Khaykl Lunski described 1919 as a year of epidemics and famine, even worse than the war years. In 1914, Lunski noted, one often heard cries and weeping, but by 1919 the misery and exhaustion was so great that no one could even cry any more.⁵¹ Hirsz Abramowicz describes almost total desolation under Soviet rule in April 1919: "Hunger was pervasive. It was against the law to buy or sell anything....Bread was difficult to find and a bowl of plain soup was also a rarity....Anyone who was able to do so fled Vilna."⁵² April 1919 also witnessed a pogrom by Polish troops.⁵³ Only the Treaty of Riga of March 1921 would end the back and forth attacks between Poland and Soviet Russia.

VILNA UNDER POLISH RULE

The Treaty of Riga did not decide Vilna's fate. Indeed, the USSR had earlier (July 1920) granted control over the city to the Lithuanians, handing over the city on August 26, 1920, as the Red Army retreated from Vilna.⁵⁴ Unhappily for the Lithuanians, Polish units under general Lucjan Żeligowski marched into the city in October 1920, to the exulting of the Polish citizenry and the anger of Lithuanians. Żeligowski set up a

The Transformation of Jewish Vilna, 1881-1939

kind of mini-state dubbed "Central Lithuania" [*Litwa środkowa*] around Vilna. No government recognized this entity, though Warsaw covertly encouraged it. Even the supporters of "Central Lithuania" saw its existence as fleeting, only long enough to elect delegates who would, no doubt, press for incorporation into Poland. Vilna's Jews were, to say the least, sceptical of Żeligowski and his Warsaw supporters. After all, 1919 and 1920 had been marked by a number of attacks on Jews and looting of their stores in Vilna. Nearly all of these had been the work of Polish units.[55] To be fair, the Warsaw government and Żeligowski himself had condemned these incidents, but Jewish opinion in Vilna was certainly not favorable to the Poles. On the other hand, Jews feared that in a contest between Lithuanians and Poles there would certainly be one loser—the Jews, who would be blamed for any stance they might take.

Both the authorities of "Central Lithuania" and the newly-created Lithuanian government, now "temporarily" in Kaunas, went out of their way to woo the Jews. Jews noted with interest and sympathy the creation of a ministry for Jewish affairs in Kaunas and the Lithuanians' granting of broad autonomy to Jewish communities.[56] In Vilna itself the Polish authorities did what they could to convince Jews that the upcoming elections would be democratic and fair. Jewish parties were initially divided on the election, the Bund favoring participation. In the end, however, most Jews decided to abstain from voting. The three mainly Jewish (over seventy-five percent) electoral districts registered a voter turnout of between ten and fifty percent, compared with over ninety percent in the fifty mainly Polish districts.[57] In the city of Vilna itself, of nearly 80,000 voters just over half went to the polls. Those abstaining were probably mostly Jews.[58]

It came as no surprise that the delegates elected voted overwhelmingly to ask for Central Lithuania's incorporation into Poland, which occurred very rapidly in 1922. While most Vilna Jews clearly viewed their position as Polish citizens with misgivings, at least no one took the opportunity to criticize this opinion. Immediately after the elections the journalist J. Kronenberg published a diatribe against the Zionists, calling them harmful for the Jews of Poland. In the pamphlet Kronenberg argues that when "Polish society as a whole" rejoiced upon Żeligowski's taking of Vilna, the city's Jews should have joined in this joy. Instead, Kronenberg continued, Zionist leaders like Yitshak Grunbaum and Jacob Wygodzki encouraged hostility towards Żeligowski and things Polish. Not incidentally, the Zionist press apparently attacked Kronenberg personally, calling him an agent of Żeligowski. Kronenberg concludes in an exalted vein that the Poles extended their hand in friendliness to the Jews, "and that hand was brushed aside."[59] Kronenberg's pamphlet would deserve no mention at all if it did not reflect a larger—though more Polish than Jewish—attitude: that the Jews had cast their lots with "the other side" and would henceforth be treated accordingly.

The Polish government's attitude on the Jewish question was neither uniform nor consistent. But speaking generally, two issues must be conceded. From the start, the newly reborn Polish state viewed itself not as a multi-national or multi-ethnic state, but primarily as the homeland of ethnic Poles and Catholics. While foreign pressure, in particular the western allies after World War I, forced the Poles to guarantee rights as national minorities to Ukrainians, Jews, Germans, and Belarusians, such guarantees were not generally translated into reality.[60] Secondly, relations between Poles and Jews were never particularly cordial (speaking generally) in the inter-war period, but became far worse as the 1930s advanced. Both of these phenomena, Poland as the nation-state of Poles and chilly relations degenerating into frigid and even violent ones, can be observed in Vilna in the 1920s and 1930s.

Economically, Jews saw their position decline in this period. From the start, the Polish government saw its primary responsibility as encouraging ethnic Polish business and trade. When a state tobacco monopoly was set up early in the 1920s, Jews were almost entirely shut out of this business, in which they had previously played a prominent part. The following year prime minister Władysław Grabski's anti-inflation measures hit Jewish businesses hard. These years also witnessed wrangling between Jews and the Polish authorities on issues such as government schools for Jews and Jewish autonomy. In the end, the government would permit only religious autonomy but not, as many Jewish leaders wanted, national-cultural autonomy. Jews in Vilna, as elsewhere in Poland, welcomed Piłsudski's May 1926 coup, but conditions did not greatly improve afterwards.

The German writer Alfred Döblin visited Vilna and other Polish cities in the mid-1920s and commented on the agitated, uneasy atmosphere. The newspapers, Döblin noted, were full of stories of Bolshevik plots and attacks by bandits. Passing a cinema, he noted that its advertisements were in both Polish and Yiddish. Throughout the city signs were often in Yiddish. But Vilna's Jews were clad not in traditional kaftans, but in European clothing. "All of them [dressed] European and yet speaking no Polish. This is another kind of Jew from Warsaw."[61] Döblin visits the Jewish quarter, admires the heritage of the Gaon, and meets with both sides of the "Hebrew-Yiddish language battle." Even as some children are being taught in Hebrew and some in Yiddish, others go learn their lessons in Polish.[62]

Döblin's account is purposely fragmentary and anecdotal, offering a series of images without detailed commentary, reaching no conclusion. One thing, however, is clear: Vilna's Jewish community under Polish rule was diverse: politically divided (Bund, Zionists, Socialists, etc.), using various languages, following Jewish religious law to varying degrees, attempting to eke out a living in a variety of ways, and trying to survive in an unfavorable political and economic situation.

An article by a Jewish economist of 1931 spoke of the "downfall of a Jewish city," referring to Vilna. Tracing this economic decline from the devastations of World War I, Jakob Lestschinski pointed out that Jewish businesses in the city had shrunk by at least one-third. For certain professions, such as tailors and seamstresses, the job loses were almost double compared to 1914. The situation was hardly better among shoe and stocking manufacturers. The reasons for this extreme economic shrinkage were many. For one thing, the Polish government favored ethnic Polish artisans and businessmen, giving them cheap bank credits and encouraging Polish civil servants to patronize them.[63] Even more important, Vilna was now an isolated outpost, cut off from trade with Lithuania and from the USSR alike.

Given the generally backward condition of the Polish economy, Vilna's peripheral position in the state only increased its economic woes. For Jews, the general economic malaise was exacerbated by the fact that the Polish state almost entirely excluded non-Poles from government jobs. Thus in Vilna in 1931, a single Jew worked in the state post and telegraph office (among almost 1,000 employees) and only eight for the railroad (out of 2,883). In state administrative offices, schools, courts, and the like, the situation was only marginally better. The worsening economic situation may be gauged by the fact that in 1938, nearly half of the Jews in Vilna applied for relief at Passover.[64]

Perhaps adversity does encourage cultural development. In any case, for all the problems that the Jewish community in Vilna faced in the interwar period, these scant two decades were also ones of cultural ferment. Jews ran not one but several school systems alongside the official Polish one.⁶⁵ Zionists, Bundists, and a variety of smaller parties were active in the city. Well over a dozen dailies and many more weekly and monthly periodicals were published in Yiddish, Hebrew, and Polish.⁶⁶ Yiddish theater and literature also prospered, perhaps most famously in the literary movement *Yung Vilne*.⁶⁷ The stature of Vilna as a center of Jewish, and especially Yiddish, culture is reflected in the decision to found the Jewish/Yiddish Scientific Organization (YIVO) there in 1925.⁶⁸ YIVO's dual scholarly purpose is reflected in the ambiguity of the first word in its title—both "Yiddish" and "Jewish." The institute aimed both to further Jewish learning (though in a mainly secular, modern spirit) and to do this in Yiddish. Linguistic, historical, sociological, and ethnographic research were encouraged and fostered by YIVO. The institute also published various monographs and scholarly journals. After World War II, YIVO continued its existence in New York City.⁶⁹

JEWISH VILNA ON THE EVE

For all the cultural and scholarly work taking place in Vilna, the political situation underwent considerable deterioration from the mid-1930s. In 1934, Poland signed a non-aggression pact with Nazi Germany, and the following year Piłsudski died. From that point onward, anti-Semitism of both the "genteel" and "violent" varieties grew significantly.⁷⁰ This is not to say that anti-Semitism was a new phenomenon in Poland or in Vilna. As Czesław Miłosz has recently pointed out, while anti-Semitism at the university became much worse in the 1930s, already in 1922 there were calls for a *numerus clausus* limiting the number of Jewish students.⁷¹ In fact, the percentage of Jews enrolled at Uniwersytet Stefana Batorego (USB) in Vilna grew quite steadily until the 1930-31 academic year (1,192 students, over thirty-five percent of total enrollment) and thereafter fell off rapidly, down to only 400 Jewish students in 1938-39.⁷²

In particular, the university witnessed several clashes between National Democrat (ND – anti-Semitic) students and Jews. At the beginning of the 1931-32 academic year the ND student organization organized attacks on Jewish students throughout Poland, including Vilna. Starting on November 8, 1931, these anti-Semitic activists prevented Jewish students from entering the university. Two days later, a scuffle between the anti-Semites and Jewish students led to the death of the Pole Stanisław Wacławski. One Jewish student, Szmuel Wulfin, was sentenced to two years' imprisonment for participating in the stone-throwing that led to

Wacławski's death.⁷³ After these incidents the ND students demanded that Jews be segregated from Polish students and obliged to sit on separate benches on the lefthand side of lecture halls.

From the mid-1930s, amidst increasingly economic misery and mounting political instability, anti-Semitism became ever more prevalent. The economic boycott campaign that had simmered from the 1880s gained strength as Jewish businesses found it harder and harder to stay afloat.⁷⁴ At the same time, government measures against the Jews increased, including laws restricting and ultimately forbidding entirely kosher butcheries. Jews strolling in the city parks were attacked by anti-Semitic thugs, and Jewish vacationers on the outskirts of the city were subjected to similar indignities.⁷⁵

The Polish government did not condone physical attacks on Jews, though it must be admitted that anti-Jewish policies created an atmosphere propitious to anti-Jewish violence. The official line after 1935 may be summed up in the words of a prominent politician, General Stanisław Skwarczyński, in 1938: "[Jews] pose an obstacle to the normal evolution of the masses of the Polish nation"; hence the Polish government should seek "a radical decrease in the number of Jews in Poland."⁷⁶ This reduction in Poland's Jewish population was sought primarily through emigration, but in the later 1930s very few possibilities for legal emigration existed.

In fairness it must be said that many Poles protested the shortsighted chauvinism of their government at the time, but one cannot deny that by the late 1930s many Polish Jews, including those in Vilna, found it difficult to be optimistic about their future in the Polish state. On the other hand, emigration did continue—including to Soviet Birobidzhan and illegally to Palestine.⁷⁷ Still, life went on despite all difficulties. In the 1930s, still around one quarter of the city's population was Jewish, running their own schools, publishing a number of newspapers and journals, and producing plays in Yiddish (and in Hebrew). For all the difficulties and economic dislocation of the 1920s and 1930s, Jewish Vilna was still full of life.

A unique witness to the last "normal" year of Jewish Vilna comes from the American Yiddishist and historian, Lucy Dawidowicz. Coming from New York, Dawidowicz spent the academic year 1938-39 at YIVO in Vilna, leaving the city only as war loomed on August 24, 1939. She describes a Vilna in which observant, traditional Jews no longer dominated. In her words, "the upholders of the Gaon's tradition were embattled, even if they did not yet consider themselves beleaguered."⁷⁸ Middle-class Jews in Vilna were generally bilingual, though perhaps speaking Polish with a Yiddish accent. The Jewish upper crust tended to speak Russian at home, considering that language and culture superior to either Polish or Yiddish.[79] Most Vilna Jews in 1938 were trying to adapt to the modern world, "in search of ways to reconcile their dual identity as Jews and as Poles," in Dawidowicz's words.[80] Once can certainly challenge Dawidowicz's account, but paging through contemporary photographs of Jewish groups included in Leyzer Ran's monumental *Jerusalem of Lithuania* seems to corroborate her words: men are usually clean-shaven, dressed in jacket and tie; women wear frocks or skirts and blouses that exactly resemble those of their Polish contemporaries.[81]

More evidence of the vitality of Jewish Vilna "on the eve" may be found in the *Vilna Almanac* published in 1939. The almanac contains such articles as "Why Vilna is called the Jerusalem of Lithuania," a memoir by the longtime Jewish activist and doctor Dr. Jakob Vigodski, material about YIVO ("at its Bar Mitzvah"), journalists, sculpture, Jewish business, educational groups, museums, rubber manufacturing, Zionist groups, dentists, Talmud Torahs, and much more. Several dozen cultural organizations are listed from the "*Vilner yidishe kunst-gezelshaft*" [art society] to "*Arbeter-sport-klub*" [workers' sports club] and a variety of charitable societies. Several pages list the names, addresses, and office hours of Jewish professionals from Dr. K. Baranowska, internal medicine, to Zalman Shapiro, children's dentist. The almanac ends with many advertisements in Yiddish and Polish from diverse businesses, radios to dry goods, beer to Jewish banks, insurance to lotteries, furs "Alaska" to the "Palais de Danse" at Mickiewicza 11.[82] Despite the hard economic times, political tensions, and complications of Jewish life within Poland, Jewish Vilna in 1939 was full of life, only darkly suspecting the catastrophe about to break over it.

ACKNOWLEDGMENTS

The research and writing of this paper were made possible by grants from the Memorial Foundation for Jewish Culture and the Kennan Institute for Advanced Russian Studies at the Woodrow Wilson Center for International Scholars in Washington, DC.

NOTES

[1] N. Zinov'ev, *Vil'na, po perepisi Aprelia 1875 goda* (Vil'na: Tipografiia A. G. Syrkina, 1881), 18-19.

[2] Ibid., 30.

[3] On the Rabbinical Institute, see Verena Dohrn, "Das Rabbinerseminar in Wilna (1847-1873). Zur Geschichte der ersten staatlichen höheren Schule für Juden im Russischen Reich," *Jahrbücher für Geschichte Osteuropas* 45:3 (1987): 379-400.

[4] According to the census of 1875, 3,134 Jews worked as laborers (*"fizicheskii trud"*) while there were 5,491 Catholics in that category, Zinov'ev, *Vil'na*, 44.

[5] Ibid., 45.

[6] Ibid., 55. According to Zinov'ev, sixty of the prostitutes were Jewish, ten Orthodox, and forty-three Catholic.

[7] Mojżesz Heller, "Wilno jako ośrodek żydowskiego życia kulturalnego," in *Wilno i ziemia wileńska. Zarys monograficzny* (Wilno: Wydawnictwo wojewódzkiego komitetu regjonalengo, 1930), 263; and Israel Klausner [Kloizner], *Vilnah, Jerushalayim de'Lita, doroth rishonim, 1495-1881* (Tel Aviv: Bet Lohmei ha'getaoth, 1988), 330-46.

[8] Hirsz Abramowicz, *Profiles of a Lost World: Memoirs of East European Jewish Life before World War II* (trans. Eva Zeitlin Dobkin; Detroit: Wayne State University Press, 1999), 117-25. Here Abramowicz describes Joshua Steinberg, *maskil*, government censor, graduate of the Rabbinical School, and later teacher there; and Samuel Gozhanski, later a founder of the Bund, who ironically called Abramowicz to task for speaking Yiddish.

[9] Zinov'ev, *Vil'na*, 33. The exact statistics were: 21.4% literate, 5.0% half-literate [*polugramotnyi*] for Jews; 37.7% and 7.3% for Catholics; and 66.4% and 5.3% among Orthodox.

[10] On the *heder* in the East European context, see Shaul Stampfer, "*Heder* Study, Knowledge of Torah, and the Maintenance of Social Stratification in Traditional East European Jewish Society," *Studies in Jewish Education* 3 (1988): 271-89.

[11] Leyzer Ran, *Jerusalem of Lithuania* (New York: Laureate Press, 1976), 2:283.

[12] Zinov'ev, *Vil'na*, 50.

[13] O. N. Shteinberg, "Graf M. N. Murav'ev i ego otnosheniia k evreiam g. Vil'ny v 1863-1864 gg. (Iz zapisok ravvina)," *Russkaia starina* 3:2 (February 1901): 305-19.

[14] *Russian State Historical Archive* (St. Petersburg; RGIA), f. 1284, op. 70, 1882, d. 176, l. 11.

[15] On the 1881 pogroms, see Omeljan Pritsak, "The Pogroms of 1881," *Harvard*

Ukrainian Studies 11:1-2 (June 1987): 8-43; and Irvin Michael Aronson, *Troubled Waters: The Origins of the 1881 Anti-Jewish Pogroms in Russia* (Pittsburgh: University of Pittsburgh Press, 1990).

[16] The Russian government's own investigation of the pogroms often concluded that Ukrainians simply took it for granted that Jews were there to be beaten, and they tended to lay blame on the victims themselves for "economic exploitation." RGIA, f. 821, op. 9, 1881, d. 126.

[17] Lietuvos Valstibinis Istorijos Archyvas, Vilnius (hereafter: LVIA), f. 378, PS 1881, b. 52, ll. 10-13.

[18] It does need to be noted that Totleben's colleague in Kiev, A. R. Drentel'n, while personally anti-Semitic, also attempted to prevent attacks on Jews. Why exactly Drentel'n was unsuccessful in preventing pogroms, while Totleben had better luck, has not yet been satisfactorily explained. On Drentel'n and the situation in Kiev, see Michael F. Hamm, *Kiev: A Portrait, 1800-1917* (Princeton: Princeton University Press, 1993), 123-26.

[19] Dr. J. Rülf, *Drei Tage in Jüdisch-Russland. Ein Cultur- und Sittenbild* (Frankfurt a/M: Verlag von J. Kauffmann, 1882), 4-6.

[20] Ibid., 10-24.

[21] Ibid., 36-37.

[22] Ibid., 26-43.

[23] Ibid., 45-58.

[24] J. Jurginis, V. Merkys, and A. Tautavičius, *Vilniaus miesto istorija nuo seniausi? laik?iki Spalio revoliucijos* (Vilnius: Mintis, 1968), 303.

[25] *Goroda Rossii v 1910 g.* (St. Petersburg: MVD, 1914), 90. The exact figure given for Jews was 46.5% of the population.

[26] On these monuments, see Theodore R. Weeks, "Monuments and Memory: Immortalizing Count M. N. Murav'ev in Vilna, 1898," *Nationalities Papers* 27:4 (December 1999): 551-64; and A. Vinogradov, *Pamiatnik imperatritse Ekateriny II v g. Vil'ne* (Vil'na: Vilenskii Vestnik, 1902).

[27] On Antokolsky, see Abramowicz, *Profiles*, 251-59.

[28] *Vilniaus miesto istorija*, 338-39; RGIA, f. 1284, o194, 1905, d. 79, l. 17v (Vil'na province report for 1904).

[29] This is the only synagogue presently functioning in Vilnius, the so-called "Choral Synagogue," known in Hebrew as "Taharat ha-Kodesh." G. Agranovskii and I. Guzenberg, *Litovskii Ierusalim. Kratkii putevoditel' po pamiatnym mestam evreiskoi istorii I kul'tury v Vil'niuse* (Vilnius: Lituanus, 1992), 35.

[30] Henri Minczeles, *Vilna, Wilno, Vilnius: La Jérusalem de Lituanie* (Paris: Editions la découverte, 1993), 92-93; Gottfried Schramm, "Wilna und die Entstehung

eines ostjüdischen Sozialismus 1870-1900," in *Deutsche Juden und die Moderne* (ed. Shulamit Volkov; Munich: R. Oldenbourg, 1994), 129-40.

[31] LVIA, f. 378, PS 1875, b. 193.

[32] LVIA, f. 446, a1, b. 249.

[33] Minczeles, *Vilna*, 99-100. For a more personal account, see Abramowicz, *Profiles*, 132-42. Lekert's assassination attempt occurred on May 6, 1902 (old style); he was hanged on May 28.

[34] RGIA, f. 1284, o194, 1904, d. 52, l. 5.

[35] Minczeles, *Vilna*, 97-98; Pinchas Kon, *Geheimberichte über Herzls Besuch in Wilno im Jahre 1903* (Vienna, 1928).

[36] RGIA, f. 1284, o190, 1903, d. 101, l. 1.

[37] On the Bund's role in 1905, somewhat glorified, see G. Aronson, et al., *Geshikhte fun bund* (New York: Farlag unzer tsayt, 1962), 2:167ff.

[38] Klausner, *Vilnah*, 32-47.

[39] RGIA, f. 1284, o194, 1907, d. 31, l. 3.

[40] Vladimir Levin, "Russian Jewry and the Duma Elections, 1906-1907," in *Jews and Slavs* 7 (ed. Wolf Moskovich; Jerusalem: The Hebrew University of Jerusalem Center for Slavic Languages and Literatures, 2000), 238.

[41] In general on the issue of refugees, see Peter Gatrell, *A Whole Empire Walking: Refugees in Russia during World War I* (Bloomington: Indiana University Press, 1999).

[42] For a contemporary's reminiscences, see Abramowicz, "World War I and Its Aftermath in and around Vilna," in *Profiles*, 177-208.

[43] Klausner, *Vilnah* 107-25. In general on conditions in Vilna during World War I, see Jurginis et al., *Vilniaus miesto istorija*, 374-81.

[44] Paul Monty, *Wanderstunden in Wilna*, (3rd ed.; Vilna: Verlag der Wilnaer Zeitung, 1918), 9, 17, 19.

[45] Ibid., 30.

[46] Ibid., 59.

[47] Ibid., 61-67.

[48] On the situation in 1916 and 1917, see Lidas Gira, "Vilniaus gyvenimas po vokiečiais," *senovè* 1:2 (1921), 21-38, and 1:3 (1922), 410-24.

[49] According to Minczeles, mortality rates went up from 292 in 1916 to 548 in 1917 among those under five years of age, and from 227 to 621 among those 61 to 70 years old. Minczles, *Vilna*, 135.

[50] Vejas G. Liulevicius, *War Land on the Eastern Front: Culture, National Identity, and German Occupation in World War I* (Cambridge: Cambridge University Press, 2000), 181-84.

[51] Khaykl Lunski, *Mehaghetto havilnai: tipusim vetslalim* (Vilna: Agudath hasofrim vehazhurnalistim haivrim, 1921), 7. On the author, best known as a librarian at the Strashun library, see Abramowicz, *Profiles*, 260-64.

[52] Ibid., 209.

[53] Minczeles, *Vilna*, 150-52.

[54] Piotr Łossowski, "Das Wilna-Problem in der polnischen Außenpolitik 1918-1939," in *Zwischen Staatsnation und Minderheit. Litauen, das Memelland und das Wilnagebiet in der Zwischenkriegzeit* (special edition of *Nordost-Archiv* [Lüneberg]), new series 2/1993, no. 2, 281.

[55] Klausner, *Vilnah*, 140-50, 162.

[56] Solomonas Atamukas, *Lietuvos...pabaigos* (Vilnius: Alma Littera, 2001), 116-27. Ezra Mendelsohn makes the point that at least in the first years of the Lithuanian state, good relations between Jews and Lithuanians were to both nations' advantage. In the 1930s, however, this relationship became more fragile. Ezra Mendelsohn, *The Jews of East Central Europe between the World Wars* (Bloomington: Indiana University Press, 1983), 217-25.

[57] *Wybory do sejmu w Wilnie 8 stycznia 1922. Oświetlenie akcji wyborczej i jej wyników na podstawie źródeł urzędowych* (Wilno: Wydawnictwo Generalnego Komisarjatu Wyborczego, 1922), 57. For more on the Jewish attitude toward the elections, see 37-40 and 68-69.

[58] Minczeles, *Vilna*, 161. The exact figures were 79,348 voters in a population of 129,954. 54.8% of voters actually took part in the elections, a percentage very close to that of Poles in the city (p. 104): 56.1%.

[59] J. Kronenberg, *Sprawa wileńska a sjoniści* (Warsaw: Nakładem autora, 1922), 13.

[60] Klausner, *Vilnah*, 177-83; Israel Cohen, *Vilna* (Philadelphia: Jewish Publication Society of America, 5704/1943), 388-94. In general on politics in interwar Poland, see Antony Polonsky, *Politics in Independent Poland, 1921-1939: the Crisis of Constitutional Government* (Oxford: Clarendon Press, 1972). On the Jews and Polish policy toward them, see Celia Heller, *On the Edge of Destruction: the Jews of Poland between the Two World Wars* (New York: Columbia University Press, 1977).

[61] Alfred Döblin, *Reise in Polen* (Olten und Freiburg im Breisgau: Walter-Verlag, 1968), 116-18.

[62] Ibid., 132-49.

[63] Jakob Lestschinski, "Wilna, der Niedergang einer jüdischen Stadt," *Jüdische Wohlfahrtspflege und Sozialpolitik* (Berlin), 2 (1931): 21-33.

[64] Cohen, *Vilna*, 405. Cohen gives the figure of 25,000 out of 60,000 Jews in

The Transformation of Jewish Vilna, 1881-1939

Vilna applying for Passover assistance in 1938.

[65] Mojżesz Heller, "Wilno jako ośrodek żydowskiego życia kulturalnego," in *Wilno i ziemia wileńska. Zarys monograficzny* (Wilno: Wydawnictwo wojewódzkiego komitetu regjonalnego, 1930), vol. 1, 263-68; Abramowicz, *Profiles*, 219-48 (on vocational education).

[66] On the Vilna Jewish press, see Ran, *Jerusalem of Lithuania*, 2:364-70; Minczeles, *Vilna*, 304-10.

[67] Minczeles, *Vilna*, 312-13, 331-50; Elias Schulman, *Yung Vilne 1929-1939* (New York: Farlag Getseltn, 1946); Sima Kaganowicz, "Teatr żydowski w Wilnie," in *Wilno i kresy północno-wschodnie. Materiały II. Międzynarodowej Konferencji w Białymstoku* (ed. Elżbieta Feliksiak and Antoni Mironowicz; Białystok: Towarzystwo Literackie im. Adama Mickiewicza, 1996), 255-68.

[68] *Das jiddische wissenschaftliche Institut (1925-1928)* (Berlin: Auslandszentrale des Jiddischen Wissenschaftlichen Instituts, 1929); Klausner, *Vilnah*, 546-59.

[69] Minczeles, *Vilna*, 280-96.

[70] Klausner, *Vilnah*, 189.

[71] Czesław Miłosz, *Wyprawa w dwudziestolecie* (Cracow: Wydawnictwo Literackie, 2000), 278-79. To prove his point, Miłosz quotes an article from *Przegląd Wileński* (17 December 1922) arguing against ND-inspired demands to limit Jewish enrollment at the university.

[72] Klausner, *Vilnah*, 288-89. See also Irena Sławińska, "Z życia naukowego akademików USB w Wilnie," in *Wilno i kresty północno-wschodnie*, 283-96.

[73] Klausner, *Vilnah*, 291-95; Ran, *Jerusalem of Lithuania*, 40.

[74] Ibid., 41-43 gives several examples of Polish calls to boycott Jews, anti-Semitic election sloganeering, and the like.

[75] Klausner, *Vilhah*, 191-203.

[76] Quoted in Edward D. Wynot, Jr., "'A Necessary Cruelty': The Emergence of Official Anti-Semitism in Poland, 1935-1939," *American Historical Review* 76:4 (1971): 1046-47.

[77] Klausner, V*ilnah*, 279-87; Ran, *Jerusalem of Lithuania*, 244.

[78] Lucy Dawidowicz, *From that Place and Time: A Memoir 1938-1947* (New York: Bantam Books, 1989), 117.

[79] Ibid., 106. A Polish contemporary corroborates Dawidowicz's remark that the Jewish intelligentsia often spoke Russian at home: Stanisław Mianowski, *Świat, który odszedł. Wspomnienia Wilnianina 1895-1945* (Warsaw: Oficyna wydawnicza Rytm, 1995), 172.

[80] Dawidowicz, *From that Place*, 107.

[81] A similar impression of "modern Jewish Vilna" may be derived from Morits

Grosman, *Yidishe vilne in vort un bild* (Vilna: Farlag-drukeray Hirsh Mats, 1925). For a child's memoirs of the 1930s in Vilna, see Samuel Bak, *Painted in Words: A Memoir* (Bloomington: Indiana University Press, 2001).

[82] A. I. Grodzenski, ed., *Vilner almanakh* (Vilna: "Ovnt Kurier," 1939; rep. ed. Isaac Kowalski; Brooklyn: Moriah Offset, 1992).

Russian Literature and Jewish Death

Gary Rosenshield

It is not really known who uttered the oft-quoted saying about nineteenth century Russian literature: "We all came out of Gogol's 'Overcoat'"; that is, we are all the literary descendants of Nikolai Gogol. If the statement addresses the attempt to portray the little man in a serious, existential manner, it is off the mark. But if the issue is the representation of Jews, one can say with more justice that the Jew in Russian literature came out of Gogol's *Taras Bulba*. Just as almost every Jewish character in the English literary tradition up to the nineteenth century bears the mark of Shylock from Shakespeare's *Merchant of Venice*, so almost every Jewish character in Russian literature owes something physically and/or morally to Gogol's Yankel and other Jews from *Taras Bulba*.

It has been said that Gogol does not show hatred for Jews, rather he treats them with contempt. The scrawny Jew, usually male, with his strange gaberdines, alien language, and wild gesticulations, cuts a rather ludicrous figure throughout *Taras Bulba*. Gogol exploits Yankel and his cohort for comic purposes, for Yankel as a character or caricature is as irresistible to Gogol as any comic figures in *Dead Souls*.[1] There are many aspects of the Jews that one can and should address in a full assessment of their portrayal in Gogol,[2] but the aspect of Jewish representation that I would like to address here, especially because of its reverberations in later Russian literature, is the image of the Jew in death, violent death. Gogol presents the Jew in death no less ludicrously than in life. The crucial passage in this regard occurs in Chapter 4 of *Taras Bulba*, when the Cossacks call for hanging all the Jews for the crimes they have committed against the Russian population.[3] But before they can carry out their intentions, a Jewish orator makes an attempt at staying the Cossack rage:

> "Illustrious masters!" cried one tall Jew as long as a stick, thrusting his pitiful face, distorted by terror, from among a group of his companions: "Illustrious masters! A word, only let us say one word! We'll tell you something you have never heard before – so

important that there is no saying how important!" "Well, let them speak," said Bulba, who always liked to hear the accused. "Noble lords!" the Jew articulated. "Such lords have never before been known, upon my soul, never! Such kind, good, valiant gentlemen have never been in the world before!" His voice failed and shook with terror. "How could we think any harm to the Dnieper Cossacks! Those who are leaseholders in the Ukraine are not our people at all! By God, they are not! They are not Jews at all! The devil knows what they are; such that one can but spit upon them and turn them out! Here they will say the same. Isn't it true, Schloma, or you, Samuel?" "By God, it's true!" answered Schloma and Samuel from among the crowd, in tattered caps, both white as clay. "We have never had any dealing with the enemy," the tall Jew went on, "and we don't want to know anything of the Catholics: may they dream of the devil! We have been brothers with you. . . ." "What? The Dnieper Cossacks are your brothers?" one of the crowd shouted. "You'll never see that, you damned Jews! Into the Dnieper with them, comrades, drown all the heathens!" These words were the signal. They seized the Jews by their arms and began flinging them into the water. Pitiful cries rang out on all sides, but the hardhearted Cossacks only laughed at the sight of the Jews' legs in slippers and stockings kicking in the air.[4]

It was unwise for the Jews to suggest that they were brothers to the Cossacks. Gogol's Cossacks treasure brotherhood above all else. The Jews' suggestion that they are part of the Cossack brotherhood further infuriates the Cossacks. The normally stern Cossacks cannot help laughing at the Jews drowning in the Dnieper. There are no other deaths in the novel at which the Cossacks laugh. Death is serious business for the Cossacks, whether it is their own deaths or the deaths of their enemies. It is never taken lightly, unless it is Jewish death, which is presented as being inherently ridiculous.

The above scene is the impetus behind Turgenev's short story, titled "The Jew" [*Zhid*, 1847], which tests the notion that the violent death of anyone can be ridiculous, even the death of a Jew.[5] To perform his experiment, Turgenev takes the Jewish physical and moral stereotype much further than Gogol. Like Gogol, he draws a sharp contrast between the moral and physical health of the Russian and Jewish protagonists. The

Russian narrator is described as the essence of good-heartedness and manly beauty: "He was a large, tall, broad-shouldered man; his dark face, 'one of those wonderful Russian faces,' his honest, intelligent gaze, his gentle smile, his manly and resonant voice—everything about him was pleasing and attractive."[6] Girshel, the Jew, is described in far more physical detail than Gogol's Yankel and far more negatively. Girshel was "small, thinnish, pock-marked, and red-headed. He was continually blinking his tiny, reddish eyes. He had a long crooked nose, and he coughed incessantly."[7] His constant coughing is associated throughout with sickness and disease, and thus is presented as the antithesis of the Russian, who simply exudes health and vitality. Girshel is always fidgeting, bowing obsequiously, wagging his head, waving his hands, spreading out his fingers, shaking his side-locks, closing his eyes, leering, and skipping back and forth. While spying against the Russians, "he suddenly ran off a little to one side, quickly and timidly looked around…uttered a cry, crouched down, cautiously craned his neck and began again to look around and listen closely."[8] He starts like a hare and sniffs at the air. When he is apprehended, "Girshel shriveled up. He shook like a leaf and let out a sickly rabbit-like cry."[9] Girshel is caught and sentenced to death by hanging. Rather than accept his fate and die with dignity, he sobs like a baby, trembles like a leaf, begs for his life, shrieks and writhes like an animal. Before he is hanged, Girshel, probably in desperation, yells that he is now willing, for real, to sell his daughter to the narrator if the narrator saves his life.

Despite the title, Turgenev's story is less about Jews than about Russians, in particular the Russians' reaction to the death of the Jew. In this respect, Turgenev radically diverges from Gogol. For the Cossacks and probably also for the narrator of *Taras Bulba*, Jewish death is inherently ridiculous: there is no aspect of Jewish life that is not alien and ludicrous. For everybody in Turgenev's story, however, the German general, the common soldiers, and especially the narrator, Girshel's death is presented as existentially serious. To one extent or another, they all feel compassion for the Jew in his terrible plight. On the other hand, no one can help laughing at the Jew, for indeed, just as Gogol described him, the Jew is as ridiculous in death as he is in life.

The narrator tells us that the "soldiers were standing in a circle, and just imagine, my friends, they were laughing, laughing at poor Girshel. I became infuriated and screamed at them."[10] The narrator presents himself as not only indignant at those who are laughing at a man about to die, but also baffled at how anyone can laugh at someone facing summary execution. But he has been so busy trying to intercede for Girshel that he has not looked at him. When he finally sees Girshel, he understands why the soldiers are laughing:

> I understood then why they had been laughing at the Jew when Sara and I came running from the camp. He was really ridiculous [*smeshon*] in spite of all the horror of his situation. The tormenting anguish of parting with life, his daughter, and his family expressed itself in the unfortunate Jew in such strange and grotesque gesticulations, cries, and skips, that we all smiled involuntarily, though it was horrible—oh so horrible—to us too. The poor wretch was half dead with fear.[11]

To see how this Gogolian image of Jewish death survives, though transformed, well into twentieth century Russian literature, we need only go to the work of an odd literary pair: the Jewish writers Anatoly Rybakov and Isaac Babel. Rybakov's novel *Heavy Sand* [*Tiazhelyi pesok, 1978*] uses the momentous events of the Bolshevik Revolution and the Holocaust to challenge many aspects of the negative Jewish stereotype, both physical and moral, in Russian literature and culture. The narrator counters the unprepossessing Jewish stereotype with family members who are exemplars of physical beauty. He counters the charge of dishonesty by showing his grandfather abhoring shady business dealings; the charge of cowardice by presenting his relatives warding off a pogrom in their native town; the charge of disloyalty by portraying his relatives fighting for Communism during the Revolution, Civil War, and the Great Patriotic War. But he saves his most powerful scenes for valorizing Jewish death, which is in most cases portrayed as heroic as *Taras Bulba*'s. Just as Taras's death is likened to a crucifixion, so is the death of Dina, the narrator's sister:

> The inhabitants of the ghetto were all lined up on the square, where a cross had been erected. They brought Dina out, naked, beaten, covered in blood, her face a bluish color. They tied her to the cross....At a sign from Stalbe, the executioner hammered the first nail into Dina's hand. Dina fainted and Stalbe ordered water to be thrown over her. They poured water over her and she came to....He struck her with his lash. "Maybe you'll sing, all the same?" And Dina started to sing. No, it wasn't singing. A wheeze came from her chest and blood came from her throat.

They had damaged her lungs. She choked, wheezed something, then wheezed something again, all the time getting quieter and quieter. I couldn't say what it was she was trying to sing, maybe a Jewish song, or a Ukrainian or a Russian song, or perhaps the "Internationale," the hymn of our youth and our hopes.[12] Dina hung dead on the cross for three days.[13]

In the end, the majority of Jews refuse passively to accept a humiliating death. They go to their death like martyr-heroes, including the narrator's brothers, sisters, father, mother, and grandfather. Jewish death is neither ridiculous nor inconsequential; it is the highest affirmation of the human spirit. It is meant to eclipse the apotheosis of death in the Russian national epic, that of Taras Bulba himself.[14]

In the last section of this study, I will examine the representation of Jewish death in Isaac Babel, perhaps Russia's greatest prose writer of the Soviet period. Here I will use the first story of *Red Cavalry*, "Crossing the Zbrucz," which is emblematic of Babel's treatment of Jewish death throughout the collection. In "Crossing the Zbrucz," Babel presents his Jewish narrator experiencing, reacting to, and representing the atrocities committed against his own people. Babel may have witnessed a pogrom in his youth, but in his Odessa stories he focuses mostly on the city's colorful Jewish gangsters. Although he joined the army in October 1917, not until his participation in the Soviet-Polish War did he personally witness large-scale atrocities against the Jewish population of the former Pale of Settlement. When Babel entered the former Pale, he experienced a double shock: not only was he horrified at the atrocities committed against the Jewish population, but he also came upon a Chasidic Jewish civilization that seemed to bear little relation to the Jewish environment in which he grew up—a civilization that he realized was marked for extinction.

As soon as the narrator of *Red Cavalry* crosses the river Zbrucz, his assumptions about Communism and his own Jewishness are questioned. So is his artistic world. At the beginning of the story, the narrator uses the war as material for his art. He also uses art to distance himself from the horror and the gore; that is, Jewish death:

> Fields of purple poppies flower around us, the noonday wind plays in the yellowing rye, the virginal buckwheat rises on thehorizon like the wall of a distant monastery. The quiet Volyn recedes from us into a pearly mist of birch groves, it is creeping

away into flowery knolls and entangling itself with enfeebled arms in thickets of hops. An orange sun rolls across the sky like a chopped-off head, a gentle radiance glows in the ravines of the thunderclouds and the standards of the sunset waft above our heads. The odor of yesterday's blood and of slain horses drips into the evening coolness. The Zbrucz, now turned black, roars and pulls the foamy knots of the rapids. The bridges have been destroyed, and we ford the river on horseback. A magnificent moon lies on the waves. The horses sink into the water up to their backs, the sonorous currents ooze between hundreds of horses' legs. Someone sinks and resonantly defames the Mother of God. The river is strewn with the black rectangles of carts, it is filled with rumbling, whistling and singing, clamoring above the moon-serpents and the shining chasms.[15]

While there is death, Jewish death, all around, the narrator aestheticizes the scene of the previous day's battle, painting a picture of abundant life and almost pristine beauty—of purple poppies, yellowing rye, virginal buckwheat, pearly mists, and a majestic moon. The discordant elements—the orange sun rolling across the sky like a chopped-off head, the odor of yesterday's blood, and the black river—are all harmonized: the orange sun creates a gentle radiance and a panoply of solar standards, the odor of yesterday's blood drips into the evening coolness, the black river receives the light of the majestic moon. The narrator turns from the gore of battle to the majestic beauty of nature, just as nature herself seems to transform slaughter into beauty. Though the bridges have been destroyed and the troops are cursing, the focus is on the sonorous currents, the whistling, the rumbling, and the singing. Babel implicitly presents his narrator-reporter as a self-conscious artist, actively working at his metaphors, which—however daring and original bear the stamp of the workshop.

As in the other stories in *Red Cavalry*, the narrator tries to hide his Jewish identity: among the Cossacks in order to gain acceptance, among the Jews in order maintain his distance. In "Crossing the Zbrucz," he distances himself from his pregnant Jewish landlady, at whose house he has been billeted, by playing "the role of Cossack."[16] Although he finds evidence of Polish looting, desecration, and mayhem in the "ransacked wardrobes...scraps of women's fur coats, human excrement and shards of the special dishes that Jews use once a year at Passover,"[17] he responds not like a fellow Jew but like an alien Cossack: he orders the old woman to clean up everything, rebuking her for the mess for which she is obviously not at all responsible.

He further distances himself from the two red-haired Jews in the house by describing them in terms of the nineteenth century Gogolian stereotype: "The two Jews rise from their chairs. They hop about on felt soles, clearing the debris from the floor, they hop about in silence, monkey-like, like Japanese in a circus; their necks swell and revolve."[18] The narrator associates the Jews with the excrement that surrounds them. He next presents them as alien, Japanese; then as animal, monkey-like, and inhuman, marionettes with swelling and swerving heads.

But after the magnificent opening paragraphs, the severed head, the smell of blood dripping, and the black holes grow more ominous. We learn that there has been a pogrom in the village, and we see the narrator try even harder to distance himself from the Jews and their death. He lies down next to a third Jewish male, who, covered up and pressed into the corner, seems to be sleeping. Falling asleep, the narrator begins to dream. As he dreams of the division commander, Savitsky, shooting out the eyes of a brigade commander for a military error, he is awakened by the pregnant Jewish landlady, who tells him that he is thrashing and crying out in his sleep and pushing her father. Since the woman addresses the narrator as *pan* [Polish for Sir], she obviously does not identify the narrator as a Jew. As she uncovers the sleeping man, the narrator sees for the first time the true horror of the situation. The old man lying next to him, the landlady's father, is not asleep, but dead. His throat has been torn out and his face cleft in two. Dark blue blood clings to his beard like pieces of lead. The narrator has not only witnessed the ravages of the pogrom, he has also lain down side by side with Jewish death itself. Carole Avins writes: "All the stories of pogroms that Babel had heard are summed up in the story's final lines":[19]

> "Sir [*Panie*]" the Jewish woman says, as she shakes out the feather mattress, "The Poles were murdering him, and he begged them: 'Kill me out in the backyard so that my daughter doesn't see me die.' But they did what they wanted. He passed away in this room thinking about me. And now I want to know," the woman said suddenly with terrible force, "I want to know where else in the entire world can you find a father like my father."[20]

The father as the personification of Jewish death is the story's ethical time bomb. At first, noted only in passing, he works himself into the story, destroying the aesthetic, and therefore moral, distance that the narrator has attempted to put between himself and Jewish suffering and death.

The narrator dreams about death because of the recent pogrom. The dream about the brigade commander being shot through the eyes corresponds to the landlady's fumbling with her fingers on the narrator's face. As Savitsky does with the brigade commander, she catches up to the narrator and rebukes him. She opens his eyes and also his ears. As soon as the narrator hears what happened to the landlady's father and how she speaks about her dead father (whom she is probably too afraid even to bury), description stops. For the first time he really sees: the father could have been his own father. The story ends with her words not his. The aesthetic and moral distance that he tried to place between himself and the Jews of the town disappears.[21] Willy-nilly, he has become the spokesman of existential Jewish death. Babel begins by distancing himself and the reader aesthetically, but, in the end, in this first story, the narrator is forced to lie down, and forces us to lie down, with our own father, who has had his throat cut out right in front of our eyes. Not one word of description follows the landlady's remarks, only an ellipsis. We are left not with an image, but with a howl—and then silence: "All has been murdered by silence" [*vse ubito tishinoi*].

Alfred Kazin somewhat naively writes that the *Diary* and *Red Cavalry* contain the "sad hope that art can somehow reconcile such opposites as Jew and Cossack, intellectual and brute, and transmute the 'small and horrible' world into something larger, softer, more human."[22] On the contrary, the art of synthesis and resolution gives way to disruption, unresolved tension, and moral outrage. In little more than a page an aesthetics is superseded by an ethics, the flamboyant image by a voice that grows louder after silence. We are left with the tragedy of Jewish death, an adumbration of the greater tragedy that was yet to come. Russian literature has come a long way from Gogol. But in the end it is Gogol who again and again must be overcome.

NOTES

[1] For a representative critical view of Gogol's comic portrayal of the Jew, see Joshua Kunitz, *Russian Literature and the Jews* (New York: Columbia University Press, 1929), 35-43. Vasilii Gippius, an eminent Gogol scholar, writes: "All the scenes with Yankel are calculated to create a comic effect (N. V. Stankevich could not recall them without laughing); even the cruel scene where the Jews are thrown into the water is depicted in the style of farce" (*Gogol'* [Leningrad: Mysl' 1924], 75). Gogol's comic or ridiculous Jew is a staple of the European literary and cultural tradition. The comic Jew often appears in the Ukranian nativity puppet theater, which differs little, and ultimately derives, from the medieval European mystery play. But the historical narratives of Gogol's own time offer many examples of the comic Jew in the various roles that Gogol casts him.

[2] For example, the Jews as anti-Cossacks or un-Cossacks, the Jews as *homini economici*, Jews and religion, Jews and loyalty, Jews and black magic, Jews and the city, Warsaw in particular, Jews and hygiene, Jews and cowardice, Jews and common sense, that is, the lack of it, Jews and space, Jews and children, Jews and women, Jews and the liquor trade, Jews and the devil, Jews and Christ, Jews and Judas, Jews and the Orthodox Church, Jews and Poles, Jews and Tartars.

[3] Gogol generally uses the word Russian in its widest sense; that is, to include all Eastern Slavs (present-day Ukrainians and White Russians). He tends to see things in common, rather than differences, between Great Russians and Ukrainians. Much is still being written on the Russian and Ukranian antipathies and sympathies in *Taras Bulba*. The debate, an old one, arose while Gogol was still writing. It is still raging. For a recent article that focuses on the competing (and irreconcilable) evidence regarding Gogol's national sympathies and that analyzes Gogol's attitude toward Russia and Ukraine, see P. Mikhed,"'Privatizatsiia' Gogolia?: Vozvrashchaias' k 'russko-ukrainskomu voprosu,'" *Voprosy Literatury* 3 (May-June 2003): 94-112.

[4] *The Complete Tales of Nikolai Gogol* (ed. Leonard J. Kent; Chicago: University of Chicago Press), 2:54.

[5] Very little has been written on Turgenev's early story. Turgenev's portrayal of the Jew is invariably treated as a caricature, which it certainly is, but critics have not, understandably, examined the reasons for Turgenev's exploitation of the caricature. Again, for a representative critical view of the story, see Kunitz, *Russian Literature*, 48-52. But see also E. A. Gutlitz, "Struktura i smysl rasskaza Turgeneva '*Zhid*,'" in *I. S. Turgenev: Voprosy biografii I tvorchestva*, (ed. Mostovskaia; Leningrad: Nauka, 1990), 57-67; S. E. Shatalov, *Problemy poetiki I. S. Turgeneva* (Moscow:

Prosveshchenie, 1969), 80-85.

[6] I. S. Turgenev, *Sobranie socinenii* (Moscow: GIKhL, 1961), 5:90. All translations done by the author.

[7] Iid., 5:91

[8] Ibid. 5:97.

[9] Ibid., 5:97.

[10] Ibid., 5:101.

[11] Ibid., 5:102-3.

[12] At the end of Evtushenko's, "Babii Iar"—one of the first Soviet texts to broach the subject of anti-Semitism—the persona says, "Let the 'Internationale' thunder out."

[13] Anatoli Rybakov, *Heavy Sand* (trans. Harold Shukman; New York: Penguin, 1981), 348-49.

[14] For a more detailed discussion of Jewish death in *Heavy Sand*, see my "Socialist Realism and the Holocaust: Jewish Life and Death in Anatolii Rybakov's *Heavy Sand*," *Proceedings of the Modern Language Association* 111 (1996): 240-55.

[15] Isaac Babel, *Collected Stories*, (trans. David McDuf; London: Penguin, 1994), 91.

[16] See Carole Avins, "Kinship and Concealment in *Red Cavalry* and Babel's 1920 *Diary*," Slavic Review 94:3 (1994): 702; Patricia Carden, *The Art of Isaac Babel* (Ithaca: Cornell University Press, 1972), 130.

[17] Babel, *Collected Stories*, 101-02.

[18] Ibid., 92.

[19] Carole Avins, "Introduction: Isaac Babel's '*Red Cavalry*' Diary," in *Isaac Babel. 1920 Diary* (trans. H. T. Willets; New Haven: Yale University Press, 1995), li.

[20] Babel, *Collected Stories*, 102-03.

[21] Alice Stone Nakhimovsky (*Russian-Jewish Literature and Identity* [Baltimore: Johns Hopkins University Press, 1992]) curiously asserts that the "narrator's coldness undergoes no obvious change at the story's end" (p. 93) and that only in the last story of the collection do we see any explicit "statement of identification" (p. 97). Avins more accurately sums up the story's last lines when she asserts that "the words of the bereaved daughter force the narrator to revise his interpretation of his surroundings, to see the people and the setting through a different lens" ("Kinship," p. 702).

[22] Alfred Kazin, "A Jew on Horseback," *New York Review of Books* (22 June 1995), 6.

"...even beyond Pinsk": *Yizker Bikher* [Memorial Books] and Jewish Cultural Life in the Shtetl

Jeffrey Veidlinger

Throughout the Russian Empire the late Tsarist period saw the emergence of new cultural institutions that challenged the traditional hierarchies of society. These institutions included mutual aid societies, credit cooperatives, joint stock ventures, and cultural societies. Jewish shtetls were in no way immune to this process. Among the Jewish population, cultural associations helped modernize the way that Jewish youth saw both the outside world and their inner selves. As a result of the proliferation of voluntary associations that characterized the early twentieth century in Russia, this period has often been identified as a missed opportunity for the fullscale development of a civil society in Russia.[1] This article will look at the social impact of this phenomenon as seen through the prism of *yizker bikher* [Memorial Books] with a focus on literary societies, libraries, and drama circles, some of the most widespread voluntary cultural associations.

Memoirs that were published in *Yizker bikher* attest to the profound impact that these societies had on the Jewish community. By providing insider views of social, economic, and political life in the shtetls, these sources present valuable perspectives on the development of social organizations through the eyes of some of their participants. *Yizker bikher* were published in the aftermath of the Holocaust as a means of preserving the memory of individual shtetls. Typically, memorial book committees were established between 1950 and 1980 in places like New York and Tel Aviv, where the newly-formed committees sought out émigrés from the town in question willing to put down some of their reminiscences in writing. The contributions to *yizker bikher* are amateur writings, often composed without recourse to original sources. As a result, they often contain factual errors, anachronisms, and inconsistencies. The testimonies in *yizker bikher* are simply as fallible as memory itself.

The authors of the memoirs were predominantly in their youths at the time of the events they describe. Therefore, there is great emphasis on concerns of the young, which include drama clubs, libraries, and literary circles. With all their limitations, the *yizker bikher* provide unrivaled sources of impressions and recollections of ordinary residents. They are glimpses into a world that was largely beneath the radar and had little impact on archival records and official registries.[2] The *yizker bikher* affirm that in the eyes of those who remember life in the interwar shtetl, the proliferation of voluntary cultural associations, and particularly of drama circles, literary societies, and libraries, had a profound impact on the youth of the shtetl.

One of the many values of the *yizker bikher* is that they candidly tell of clandestine activity in a period during which much Jewish cultural activity was under legal constraints. Yiddish theater in the Russian Empire had been under a formal ban since 1883. Although its enforcement was relaxed after 1905, it continued to be enforced in some provinces as late as 1909. The overall effectiveness of the ban was mixed. Although it hindered the development of professional Yiddish theater in the Russian empire, local police authorities were known to grant permission for select performances throughout the period of the ban and other performances took place clandestinely. Most famously, troupes received permission to perform in German and then proceeded to present Yiddish plays without the knowledge of the authorities.[3]

Legal restrictions also hindered the development of reading rooms and libraries. Laws of 1867 and 1890 forbade the establishment of any libraries without permission from the local gubernatorial authorities. In order to obtain permission, applicants were required to submit a statute to the authorities describing the management and resources of the library. Letters and chronicles in educational journals of the period provide ample evidence of the difficulties inherent in this process. Many local authorities feared the repercussions of allowing the masses access to reading material and modern ideas or simply had little interest in educating the general public—and so they routinely ignored or denied such petitions.

Therefore, many libraries were established clandestinely. Even those rare libraries that did receive the requisite permission were still usually restricted. The law of 1890 limited the acquisition of books by free public libraries to a list prepared by the Ministry of Enlightenment. This list, which was in effect until 1906, included no Yiddish books. Therefore, any library that did not charge admission was forbidden from carrying Yiddish language books. As a result, Jewish libraries were often established and run clandestinely. These operations required the cooperation of the entire library's membership.[4]

The impetus for the establishment of cultural associations in the shtetls was usually one of the major political movements effecting the youth of the period, Zionism or Bundism. Both movements saw the youth as their primary targets of propaganda and hoped to reach this demographic through cultural societies and social organizations. Many of the contributors to *yizker bikher* recall their first relationship with the major political movements occurring through their participation in drama circles, reading groups, or libraries. Indeed, in the memoirs of many of the rank and file participants within these movements, social activities often seem to take precedence over political activism. The reading of Zionist literature, though, and observance of Zionist plays had propagandistic effects on the audiences. Yaakov Levin recalls a Zionist play he saw in Kobrin in 1909:

> It seemed like a fairy tale, the first play, *Hebrew Farmers in the Holy Land*, that was performed in the Zionist hall in our town. Less than three *minyans*[5] participated, all of whom were invited by their friendsand acquaintances, the few Zionists in the town, in order to see a Zionist play about the Land of Israel…this was the goal of the play: to show Hebrew farmers in their land working their soil: plowing, planting and harvesting.[6]

Zionists also helped establish public spaces for reading secular Hebrew books and carrying on discussions in Hebrew. Many Russian library activists had pointed out that teahouses and taverns had greater liberty in disseminating reading material than libraries; the Zionist teahouses successfully took advantage of this legal loophole. In 1900, for instance, the Hebrew-language newspaper *Hamelits* reported that a teahouse had been established in Grodno, intended "to be a house for the Zionists in our city to gather here occasionally in the evening to discuss subjects of interest relating to national affairs or literature, etc., over a hot drink."[7] Those gathered were encouraged to speak Hebrew, and the teahouse subscribed to several Jewish newspapers in Hebrew and Russian. In Slutsk, the Zionist organization Kadimah also reported that it was in the process of establishing a teahouse that would subscribe to ten newspapers.[8] These Zionist teahouses served as surrogate libraries and community centers for the youth of the city.

A native of the Belorussian town of Deretsin who had been studying in Vilna recalls the formation of a Bund cell in his hometown: "Almost every Saturday afternoon, the members of the Bund would be called out of their homes through various signals and passwords. They used to go one by one out into the forest, around three kilometers from the shtetl. There they used to hold large meetings and discussions until nightfall. Then they would silently and separately return home."[9] Another memoirist of the same town recalls his inauguration into the Bund: "One Saturday afternoon, when I was going for a walk in the gooseberry orchard, as was the custom then, Soreh-Leyke, the blind klezmer's daughter, came up to me, and asked me if I would like a little book to read."[10] One of the Deretsin Bund's chief accomplishments was the establishment of a library housing over 1,000 books. Nevertheless, the conspiracy of sneaking out of the house on the Sabbath to enjoy romantic summer afternoons with friends seemed more important to some than the greater goal of liberating the workers.

For clandestine libraries, books often had to be smuggled in from abroad and then stored with members of the society, who would move the books between them. The workers' library in the Volhynian town of Hosht, for instance, was a clandestine library: "Therefore the library was not kept in a single place, but wandered around from one person to another, under the strictest supervision."[11] After the library of Nisviz' was closed by the police in 1905, the collection of about 1,000 books was hidden in private homes for the next twelve years until a new library and reading room could be founded after the February Revolution.[12]

Gradually these informal circles and libraries became institutionalized even prior to the 1906 legalization of many amateur associations. Avrom Slutsky tells how an informal gathering of youth was transformed into a more formal society in Lenin in the early 1900s:

> In the shtetl, one could find intelligentsia and men of means who owned private libraries. In some of them, one could from time to time read a book, but it was not convenient for us young people from poor parents to call upon the well-to-do aristocrats very often. One read what came into one's hands. From time to time a traveling book-seller would come to the shtetl. People would

buy from him Shomer's[13] or Eliakum Zunser's[14] books, or stories and jokes about Hershele Ostropoler.[15] This type of literary work would from time to time be read by one of us at a gathering [*farzamlung*] of boys and girls.[16]

In Slutsky's case the turn towards deliberate voluntary association came when he and a group of friends secretly subscribed to a Bundist journal: "A circle [*krayz*] of listeners quickly formed around us, who with great thirst would listen to what one of us read."[17] This was a more formal association than the gatherings that occurred around the readings of novels and romances. For one, sharing the cost of a subscription was a more longterm financial investment than splitting the cost of a romance novel and required a lasting commitment. Further, the conspiracy of subscribing in secret required trust and commitment. Slutsky also clarifies the distinction between the informal gatherings and the formal circle of subscribers by referring to the former by the term *farzamlung* [or gathering] and the latter as a *krayz*, echoing the Russian *kruzhok* [or circle], with its connotations of earnest literary discussion.

The move toward institutionalization was repeated throughout the Pale, as informal groupings of friends emerged into formal, institutionalized, and modern societies. Following the February 1906 rescinding of the most onerous restrictions on public libraries, including many of the limitations on acquisitions, it became possible to establish legal free public libraries with Yiddish books. The new liberties regarding libraries led to the establishment of a library movement among segments of the Russian Jewish intelligentsia, who were inspired by a parallel movement among the Russian population. The Society for the Spread of Enlightenment Among the Jews of Russia (OPE) responded by subsidizing the establishment of legal libraries and providing information and guidance in librarianship. The newsletter of the OPE, which began publication in 1910, included news about libraries and several articles written by the Jewish library activist Abraham Kirzhnits about modern bibliography and library studies.[18] In 1914 the OPE also published a guidebook for Jewish libraries.[19]

Dovid Roykhl recalls the summer of 1909, when he returned to the Volhynian town of Kremenits from his studies in Odessa. In Odessa he had belonged to a *krayzl* [little circle], and upon his return he united with several fellow students from neighboring towns in Podolia and Volhynia with the goal of acquainting the youth of the region with the activities of enlightened circles active in the cities. He established a group of activists who would disseminate journals through subscriptions that could be paid for by the locals in installments. They got thirty-four subscriptions in Kremenits. The group then negotiated agreements with booksellers in Vilna and later Warsaw by which they could receive a forty percent reduction by paying in cash for books, a reduction that they would then pass onto the consumer. In this manner, an informal circle was transformed into a more formal literary society.[20]

The library of Lipkany, Bessarabia, was typical of the new type of formal library. According to the Lipkany *yizker bukh*, the library, which was established in 1907, "was managed by a democratically elected executive that devoted a lot of time to its development."[21] The library of Kamin-Koshirskii in Northern Volhynia established a monthly membership fee so that it could hire a few librarians who would remain in the library every Sunday, Tuesday, and Thursday from 6:00 p.m.-10:00 p.m. to assist the readers. According to one recollection, there were 150 members.[22] Typically, legal libraries were run by a general assembly, comprised of all adult members of the library, which usually met biannually, in December and over Passover. The general assembly was also responsible for electing an executive committee that would serve two years. Often all subscribers had the right to request the purchase of books by writing the title into a notebook that was kept in a visible location. Once a month, the committee in charge of the library was responsible for perusing the notebook and either ordering requested books or providing a reason for a book's rejection.

The *yizker bikher* present portraits of libraries as bustling centers of intellectual and social exchange, where the mostly young men and women who frequented the establishments could meet in a realm beyond the strictures of traditional society. An evening at the library was a communal activity. Not only was reading itself often communal, but the library also functioned as a surrogate community center, taking the place of the *bays midrash* [prayer house] for secularizing societies. In Baranovits, for example, the Jewish Literary-Artistic Society, which was founded in 1907-08, established a reading room and a library, as well as a small theater hall and a stage, taking over the second floor of the private residence that housed it. "It was located in the very center of the city," according to one former resident, "and everybody could feel at ease and at home there....In the years before the First World War, [it] was a lively nerve center of social life in Baranovits and the only place in which cultural activity was concentrated. Here theater performances, concerts, anniversary celebrations, Hanukah celebrations, and traditional Purim balls would take place, as well as literary evenings and other activities"²³ When celebrities visited the city, they would also perform at the library. Similarly in Kamin Koshirskii, the library, which was also kept in a private home, was in the words of one former resident, "the cultural center of our shtetl. There the youth would get together, regardless of political affiliation" and would meet for literary chats and meetings.²⁴

Like libraries, theater was also a communal activity, as well as being a source of enlightenment, entertainment, and distraction. As a resident of Polish Luboml recalls:

> The putting on of plays involved great effort not only for the actors, who had to overcome the opposition of their parents, memorize their parts, prepare the appropriate costumes, etc., but also for the devoted helpers, the "technical corps," who had difficult tasks: to get censorship permits from officials, which required traveling to the big city (Lublin or Warsaw); finding somebody to use his "pull" to get that permit; to prepare the hall and stage; to bring in benches from the synagogue (mostly by stealing), and chairs from private homes; finding large lamps to light the hall (also taken from the synagogue); borrowing stage props, such as furniture; bringing a make-up specialist from the big city; engaging musicians [*klezmer*] to play before and during the intermission, as well as for the dances that followed the performances and lasted well after midnight.²⁵

In this sense, both literary societies and drama circles brought together new social groupings who were united by taste and interest.

Voluntary associations provided the primary means by which new ideas were spread from a freethinking elite to larger audiences. The primary instigators, according to the *yizker bikher*, were often young Talmud students. "In those days," recalls Khayim Rabinovitsh of Deretsin, the first years of the twentieth century, "suddenly among the newly-arrived book-worms in our *bays midrash* there appeared a certain type of youth who would hide various profane books under the *gemarah* on his stand". I remember one of these bookworms, a relative of the Rabbi Leyb Luner, a young man, a child prodigy, who brought to Deretsin all kinds of Hebrew books and Russian journals…from time to time he chatted with us about worldly and scientific things, and would give us one of his books to read.²⁶

Aspiring intellectuals who lacked access to secular institutions of learning also recall using literary societies as a surrogate for formal education. Mikhal Rubensteyn writes of Ivenits in Belorussia:

> The shtetl was far from a train and from a large city. Besides the *heders* [schools] there were no educational institutions in the shtetl. Therefore the youth took it upon themselves to educate themselves. In the evenings, they used to meet in the attic of Ber-Yesheyhu Rabinovich's house and read newspaper and books in Yiddish, Russian, or Hebrew, and have discussions on various themes.[27]

In memoir after memoir, books are portrayed as the channel through which enlightenment was passed from one individual to another and from one social grouping to another.

Many literary societies and drama circles were established by students returning home for the summer or by summer visitors of all stripes. "After 1905, the time of confusion in Russia," wrote a native of Lipkany in Bessarabia, "when a little freer air began to blow, one could find in Lipkany a group of young nationalist and worldly educated students who, having studied in larger cities, became infected with progressive ideas and the spirit of those times."[28] One such example comes from Dubosari on the Dniester. As Issaac Hurwitz recalls, over the summer of 1901 a young man named Calman Beilis arrived in town from Gorodok to visit his brother. Beilis told the local youth about a theater group in his shtetl and inspired the locals to establish their own:

> It was late summertime and the swimming area at the Dniester soon became a meeting place for us, a young group of friends, with Beilis. We saw in him a force that would give a push forward to the backwards, provincial, Dubosari, these lively young men and women. After a few meetings with Beilis, it was clear to us, the more progressive Dubosari youth, that we must also do something. With his initiative and help we put together a group of around ten friends [to put on plays].[29]

Buoyed by initial success, the theater group became more and more serious as the year progressed, continuing through the fall. "The week after *sukkes*, we began to practice two or three times a week in the *heder* of the teacher Israel Meir."[30] Eventually, in a highly symbolic move, the group succeeded in renting the town theater hall by promising that they would be performing only in Judeo-German and not in Yiddish, thereby moving out of the *heder* and its parochial connotations and into the public sphere.

As their level of institutionalization increased, the members of drama circles also started to think in financial terms. As one member of the drama circle of Navaredok recalls:

> for the first plays we the actors...would walk from house to house in order to sell tickets. We succeeded mostly by appealing to people's charity and support. After a little time, though, our treasury was supported completely by ticket sales and I recall many plays for which it was hard to obtain tickets. We became a true theater, but we remained amateurs and kept our day jobs.[31]

Although few drama circles developed into for-profit organizations, many realized their potential for fundraising. When the Tarbut educational and cultural organization in Kamin-Koshirskii was in need of money, for instance, a Dramatic Section was established to perform a popular Yiddish play. Not having a concert hall, the section used a local granary, in which they installed a stage. The production succeeded in raising large funds; once established, the Dramatic Section continued performing plays for many years.[32]

In Korelits, a theater group raised money for the fire brigade.[33] After the February Revolution, even the Habima of Lipkany revived itself for the purpose of raising money to found a Jewish school for poor folk.[34] Even those theater circles that achieved some financial success were usually unable to transform themselves into professional endeavors. In the words of one former actor from Polish Volomin:

> The members of the drama circle were young people, who spent the entire day busy at work, in the glassworks, at the workbench. In the evenings, they came to the rehearsals, often tired, weary, but full of energy and zest and in contrast to professional actors, they didn't think at all about pay for their performances, but often added from their saved pennies to cover the deficits that were in the box office before and after the performance.[35]

Although youth are frequently mentioned as instigators in the establishment of literary societies, drama circles, and libraries, there were also some cases in which older men of enlightenment inclinations are credited with holding reading circles where newspapers or the stories of Mendele

Moykher Sforim or Sholem Aleichem would be read. In other cases, it was the wealthy members of the society who supported the establishment of a library. In these cases, enlightenment was usually packaged and presented to willing followers rather than discovered mutually. For instance, in Ukrainian Brzeziny, theater was used as a means of enlightening the masses. In this case, the theater, established in 1910, was led by an intellectual who used the stage as a training ground:

> The work began with several lectures on theater and performance. The director also explained to the players the essence of each of the characters in the play. The director's first commandment was that the performer must not allow himself to be dragged down by the audience; on the contrary, he must lift up the people with him to a higher artistic level.[36]

The Habima theater of Lipkany was formed "not simply by young men and women who did not know exactly what theater was, but rather by the very Jewish intelligentsia who knew their goal and what they wanted to accomplish with Yiddish theater."[37] One of its directors was Jacob Sternberg, who would go on to become director of the Vilna Trupe in Bucharest. The theater even possessed its own orchestra and toured the region. It was disbanded with the outbreak of war in 1914.

There was a similar tension within the public library movement between those who saw public libraries as a means of guiding the masses into discovering appropriate reading material through recommendations from trained librarians and those who believed that librarians and libraries should only facilitate easy access to the reading material desired by the masses. Dvoyre Kutnik tells of her father's establishment of the first library in Luninyets:

> He decided to open a library for the common people....My father ordered and received from Warsaw and Vilna various shipments of books in Yiddish and Hebrew. The Hebrew books were for the most part enlightened [Haskalah] books....The Yiddish books did not have great success at the beginning. Then my father, who understood the psychology of the small-town readers who want "interesting" books, ordered Shomer and Bloshteyn's[38] novels.... With time my father got the people to read the new Yiddish classics.[39]

Voluntary associations also served to expand geographic borders and reinforce ties between communities. Smaller communities looked to urban centers for advice and material, much as satellite *kehillot* [Jewish communities] had turned to larger *kehillot* in former times with religious and legal queries and requests for intercession. The Jewish community of Kamin-Koshirskii could not afford its own library in 1918, so a library committee was formed that struck a deal with the library committee of the Jewish community of nearby Kovel, through which a certain number of books would be sent from Kovel to Kamin-Koshirskii each week and then sent back the following week. This agreement continued for two years, but when the shtetl was forced to rebuild after the pogroms of 1920, they decided to raise some extra money to build their own library of Yiddish and Hebrew books.[40] The newly formed literary society of Kremenits looked for guidance to the Jewish Literary Society of St. Petersburg, writing a letter asking for recommendations of Yiddish-language thick journals.[41] Other libraries and drama circles turned to the OPE for guidance.

Increased travel helped standardize reading lists and theatrical repertoires and quickly spread ideas throughout the region. Many drama circles, for instance, were inspired by traveling troupes that visited the shtetl, usually during summer tours. For instance, soon after a famous traveling troupe came to Luninyets in 1909, a drama circle was formed emulating its repertoire. The regionally famous theater group of Meziritch-Podlaski was also founded on the inspiration of a traveling troupe that often visited the *shtetl*.[42]

Ultimately, by removing religious strictures, particularly regarding the separation of young men and women, voluntary associations often functioned as social equalizers. Women were included in many of these societies, which often became the first social organizations in which young Jewish men and women could freely interact. One woman from a town near Vilna recalls how she managed to join classes being offered by a Russian tutor by providing him with meals in return for lessons. "Our circle of self-education was soon significantly enlarged. Our religious parents, understandably, were against our activity (for what does a Jewish daughter need *bildung* [education], only to stray from the proper path?). We were forced to learn with the Karaites in a little *shtibele* on the courtyard where nobody would notice us."[43] This group soon came under the influence of the socialist movement and helped organize strikes as well as establish a library. The stage was also an equalizing force, in which even someone from the bottom of the social ladder, like Feyge Pomerantz, the daughter of the Luboml water-carrier, could become a local celebrity, admired by her peers and coveted by the local boys.[44] Other young girls came into their own on the stage, performing against the wishes of their parents, who often thought that theater was a waste of time and particularly unseemly for women.

It was not only gender differences, but also class differences that societies helped overcome. Kutnik, whose home housed the public library in Luninyets recalls: "Every Friday afternoon in our house visitors came from among the dressmakers, servant girls, clerks, and workers—cobblers and tailors, who would remember, coming from the baths, to stop by Avraham Hershl the melamed's to take a book for Shabes…the library had a great influence on the readers."[45] Within voluntary associations new communal leaders could emerge, a talented actor could supplant a knowledgeable rabbinical student as the pride of the town, for instance, or individuals of low social standing could propel themselves through their talents to become a leading luminary.

Men and women alike recall how these societies helped open their eyes to a larger world. "It did not take long for several of us small-town more developed youth (you understand, with talmudic education and religious upbringing) to begin to see for ourselves a new world with entirely different horizons," wrote one.[46] "The small-town folk became familiar with the larger world," wrote another, "it opened their eyes and they realized that there is a large world with problems outside of Luninyets and even beyond Pinsk."[47]

NOTES

[1] See, for instance, Joseph Bradley, "Subjects into Citizens: Societies, Civil Society, and Autocracy in Tsarist Russia," *American Historical Review* 107:4 (October: 2002): 1094-1123; David Wartenweiler, *Civil Society and Academic Debate in Russia, 1905-1914* (Oxford: Clarendon Press, 1999); and Edith W. Clowes, et al., *Between Tsar and People: Educated Society and the Quest for Public Identity in Late Imperial Russia* (Princeton: Princeton University Press. 1991). For Jewish voluntary associations, see Christoph Gassenschmidt, *Jewish Liberal Politics in Tsarist Russia, 1900-1914: The Modernization of Russian Jewry* (New York: New York University Press, 1995).

[2] For more on *Yizker bikher,* see Jack Kugelmass and Jonathan Boyarin, eds.

and trans., *From a Ruined Garden: The Memorial Books of Polish Jewry* (2nd ed.; Bloomington: Indiana University Press, 1998).

[3] For more on the ban on Yiddish theater, see John Klier, "'Exit pursued by a Bear': The Ban on Yiddish Theatre in Imperial Russia," in *Yiddish Theatre: New Approaches* (ed. Joel Berkowitz; Oxford and Portland: The Littman Library of Jewish Civilization, 2003), 159-74; and D. A. El'iashevich, *Pravitel'stvennaia politika i evreiskaia pechat' v Rossii, 1797-1917* (St. Petersburg and Jerusalem: Mosty Kul'tura and Gesharim, 1999), 473-80.

[4] For the legal status of libraries, see A. N. Vaneev, *Razvitie bibliotekovedcheskoi mysli v Rossii v nachale XX veke* (St. Petersburg, 1999). For the legal status of Jewish libraries, see A. Izrailitin, "O merakh k razvitiiu obshchedostupnykh bibliotek sredi evreiskogo naseleniia v Rossii," *Knizhki voskhoda* (February 1905): 99-135.

[5] A *minyan* is a prayer quorum of ten men.

[6] Jacob Levin, "Kobrin beshnot 1909-1913," in *Sefer Kobrin: megilat hayim ve-hurban* (ed. B. Shvarts and Y. H. Biletski; Tel Aviv: n.p., 1951), 88-89.

[7] *Hamelits* 254 (November 19, 1900).

[8] *Hamelits* 69 (March 21, 1903).

[9] Khayim Rabinovitsh, "Haskalah, bund, zelbshuts," in *Sefer Deretsin* (ed. Y. Raban; Tel Aviv: Irgun yotse'e Deretsin, 1971 or 1972), 81.

[10] Joe Silkovitsh, "Shturmishe yorn," in Ibid., 94.

[11] Avraham Yaron, "A lebn iz untergegangn," in *Seyfer Hosht: yizker-bukh* (ed. Reuven Fink;Tel Aviv: Irgun yotse'e Hosht, 1957), 150. For more on workers' libraries and the development of clandestine libraries in the 1890s, see David Shavit, "The Emergence of Jewish Public Libraries in Tsarist Russia," *Journal of Library History Philosophy & Comparative Librarianship* 20:3 (Summer 1985): 239-52.

[12] Binyomin Yoali (Yevelevski), "Tseirei-Tsion Poalei-Tsion," in *Sefer Nisviz'*, (ed. David Sztokfisz; Tel Aviv: Irgun yotse'e Nisviz', 1976), 101-03.

[13] Nahum Meyer Shaykevich (1849-1905) was a Yiddish novelist and playwright whose lowbrow romances and suspense novels achieved unprecedented popularity among the Yiddish reading public.

[14] Eliakum Zunser (1836-1913) was a popular *badkhn*, whose songs and poems were widely read.

[15] Hershele Ostropoler was an eighteenth century jester, whose antics were incorporated and embellished into popular legends, plays, and jokes.

[16] Avraham Yitskhak Slutski, "Der kulturelekh matsev in undzer shtetl," in *Kehilat Lenin: sefer zikaron* (ed. Moshe Tamari; Tel Aviv: Vaad yotse'e Lenin, 1956 or

1957), 253.

[17] Ibid.

[18] See, for instance, A. D. Kirzhnits, "Bibliotechnoe delo u evreev i zadachi Obshchestva Prosvesheniia (Vnutrenniaia organizatsiia evreiskikh bibliotek," *Vestnik obshchestva rasprostraneniia prosveshchesniia mezhdu evreiami v Rossii* 13 (March 1912): 3-28; and A. D. Kirzhnits, "Itogi obsledovaniia evreiskikh bibliotek," *Vestnik obshchestva rasprostraneniia prosveshchesniia mezhdu evreiami v Rossii* 19 (January 1913): 31-49.

[19] *Spravochnik po evreiskomy bibliotechnomu delu* (St. Petersburg, 1914).

[20] Dovid Roykhl, "vi m'hot amol farshpreyt yidishe literature," in *Pinkas Kremenits* (ed. Abraham Samuel Stein; Tel Aviv: Irgun hotsaat ole Kremenits, 1954), 376-78.

[21] Aaron Shuster, *Lipkan fun amol* (Montreal: A. Shuster, 1957), 62.

[22] Jacob Plot, "Di arlozorov bibliotek," in *Sefer ha-zikaron li-kehilat Kamin Koshirski veha sevivah*, (ed. Avraham Shemuel Shtain; Tel Aviv: Irgun yotse'e Kamin Koshirski, 1965), 487-90.

[23] N. Kroshinksi, "unter der rusish-tsarisher hershaft," in *Baranovits: sefer zikaron*, (ed. Avraham Shemuel Shtain; Tel Aviv: Irgun yotse'e baranovits be-yisrael, 1953), 71.

[24] Plot, "Di arlozorov bibliotek."

[25] Yisroel Garmi, "World War I and Its Aftermath," in *Luboml. The Memorial Book of a Vanished Shtetl* (Hoboken: Ktav Publishing House, 1977), 81-82.

[26] Khayim Rabinovitsh, "Haskalah, bund, zelbshuts," in *Sefer Deretsin* (ed. Y. Raban Tel Aviv: Irgun yotse'e Deretsin, 1971 or 1972), 81.

[27] Mikhal Rubenshteyn, "Ivenits un ire tsionistn," in *Sefer Ivenits, Kamin, veha-sevivah*, (Tel Aviv: Defus Arazi, 1973), 79.

[28] Aaron Shuster, "Melamdim un lerers," in *Kehilat Lipkany* (ed. M. Silon-Silberman; Tel Aviv: Irgun yotse'e Lipkani, 1963), 60.

[29] Eyzik Hurvits, "Der 'breshis' fun yidish teater in Dubosar," in *Dubosari: sefer zikaron* (ed. Joseph Rubin; Tel Aviv: Irgun yotse'e Dubosari, 1965), 221.

[30] Ibid., 223.

[31] Zahava Rabinovich-Engel, "Ha-teatron be navahrdok," in *Pinkas Navaredok* (ed. Eliezer Yuershalmi; Tel Aviv: Relif·komi·tet 'a.sh. Aleksander-Harkabi be-Artsot haberit·ve-Irgun yots'e Novahredo·k be-Yisra'el, 1963), 118.

[32] Jacob Plot, "Beit-hasefer, hatekhiah," in Shtain, *Sefer ha-zikaron,* 482.

[33] Yaacov Abramowich, "Basheftikung fun di Korelitsher yidn," in *Korelits* (ed. Michael Walzer-Fass; Tel Aviv: Irgune yots'e Korelits, 1973), 155.

[34] Shuster, *Lipkan fun amol,* 66-68.

[35] Malka Yelen-Grinberg, "Di komunistishe bavegung," in *Sefer zikaron kehilat Volomin* (ed. Shimon Kanc; Tel Aviv: Irgun yotse'e Volomin, 1971), 199.

[36] Malka Rose (Rozenblum), "Yiddish Theater in Our Shtetl" (trans. Renee Miller; ed. Fay Bussgang; http://www.jewishgen.org/Yizkor/brzeziny/brz112.html), 124.

[37] Shuster, *Lipkan fun amol*, 65. See also Moshe Zilberman-Silon, "Geven a khoylem," in Silon-Silberman, *Kehilat Lipkany*, 51-52. Numerous writers in the Lipkany memorial book remember the Lipkany theater as being particularly good, but their recollections differ enough to suggest there may have been several theater groups in Lipkany.

[38] Oyzer Bloshteyn (1840-1898) was one of the most popular Yiddish novelists of his time.

[39] Dvoyre Kutnik, "Di ershte yidishe bibliotek," in *Yizkor kehilot Luninyets/Koz'anhorodok* (ed. Yosef Zeevi; Tel Aviv: Irgun yots'e Luninyets ve-Koz'anhorodok, 1952), 146-47.

[40] Plot, "Di arlozorov bibliotek."

[41] Dovid Roykhl, "vi m'hot amol farshpreyt yidishe literature," in Shtain, *Pinkas Kremenits*, 377.

[42] Meyer Edelbaum, *Di yidn-shtot Meziritsh* (Buenos Aries: Mezritsher Landslayt-farayn in Argentine, 1957), 264

[43] Sonia Ayerof, "Ivie in di yorn 1904-1907," in *Sefer zikaron li-kehilat Ivyeh* (ed. Moshe Kaganovich; Tel Aviv, Irgune yots'e Ivyeh, 1968).

[44] Garmi, "World War I and Its Aftermath," 81.

[45] Kutnik, "Di ershte yidishe bibliotek," 146-47.

[46] Rabinovitsh, "Haskalah, bund, zelbshuts," 81.

[47] Kutnik, "Di ershte yidishe bibliotek," 146-47.

New Jews: David Bergelson and Birobidzhan

Harriet Murav

Soviet Yiddish literature has been widely neglected. Very few works from this vast literature are available in English, except, as Mikhail Krutikov points out, those that are critical of Communism. In the introduction to their anthology *Ashes Out of Hope* (1977), which includes Bergelson, Kulbak, and Der Nister, Irving Howe and Eliezer Greenberg write: "It has seemed pointless to waste space by printing what Yiddish writers had to compose during the worst years of the Stalin period."[1]

But to characterize Soviet Yiddish literature of the Stalin period and beyond as merely the result of force or nothing more than the use of approved socialist realist plot outlines (boy meets tractor, but on the Jewish street) is to miss the mark. I offer another perspective on the predominantly negative image of Soviet Yiddish literature by focusing on a story that might at first glance seem to be a prime example of literary-political correctness, David Bergelson's "Barg-aruf"[Uphill], dedicated to the Jewish Autonomous Region of Birobidzhan and published in the Birobidzhan literary journal *Forpost* [Outpost] in 1936. The story consists of a series of vignettes about Birobidzhan, including, for example, the construction of a new building and the arrival of new settlers from depression-ravaged America, Bergelson's text reproduces such conventional socialist realist motifs as the triumph over nature, but I hope to show that his subtle interweaving of traditional Jewish texts and his own extraordinary language fracture and dissolve the socialist realist aesthetic.

By the time he published "Barg-aruf," Bergelson was recognized as a master of Yiddish prose for such early works as "The Deaf One" and *Arum voksal* [At the Depot, 1909]. Bergelson's Soviet-era novel *Baym Dnepr* [At the Dnieper, 1932, 1940], translated into Russian in 1983, remains unavailable in English. Bergelson left Russia for Berlin in 1921 and returned in 1933, motivated at least in part by the Soviet government's enthusiastic support of Yiddish. In 1934, Bergelson attended the First Congress of the Soviet Writers' Union, at which he received high acclaim from the Yiddish writer Itzik Fefer and the critic Iakov Bronshtein, who was arrested and shot in 1937. Fefer, like Bergelson and other Yiddish writers, was shot in 1952 as part of the campaign against "nationalism." Bronshtein, using the overblown language of the time, said that *At the Dnieper* "guillotined" the formerly idealized bourgeois nationalist Jewish environment.[2]

Bergelson's own remarks at the congress were far more enigmatic. On the one hand, he praised Stalin as the "great leader of the world proletariat," but he also said that "as a Jewish writer" one of the strongest speeches he had heard at the congress, given by the national poet of Dagestan, Suleiman Stal'skii, was one that he did not understand a single word of.[3] To praise a text that is completely opaque falls outside of the socialist realist demand for utter transparency, clarity, and cohesiveness.[4] Bergelson's delight with a text that he could not understand hints at his own literary technique, which foregrounds the opaque and the unsaid. Bergelson used this technique with particular skill in "Barg-aruf," as I will show.

"Barg-aruf" and other Bergelson works of the 1930s are tied to one of the most important Soviet Jewish experiments of the era, the Jewish Autonomous Region of Birobidzhan, established in 1928. While political and military concerns in part motivated the Soviet decision to create a Jewish settlement in the Far East, Birobidzhan offered Jews "economic rehabilitation and social respectability through agricultural work; the preservation and promotion of language, culture—and implicitly—of the Jewish people itself—through compact settlement."[5] The promotion of the Jewish people was, however, an enterprise fraught with ambivalence, since it was part of a larger policy aimed at the withering away of all forms of nationalism.[6]

"Barg-aruf," written in Yiddish, which the Soviet Union defined as the national language of the Jews, celebrates the foundation of the Jewish Autonomous Region and yet also reveals the profound contradiction of Soviet nationality policy even before the destructions of the late 1930s. In the opening vignette, the secretary of the district committee receives a negative report from the regional committee. He regrets his poor record of accomplishment, but nonetheless counts as a positive step the beginning of a "struggle against Jewish nationalism and against great-Russian chauvinism" [*a kampf...kegn yidishn natsionalizm un kegn groysrusishn shovinizm*].[7] The contradiction lies in the simultaneous development of "Jewish nationalism" in the Birobidzhan project as a whole, and in this story in particular, and the struggle against it.

However, to speak of Soviet nationality policy as if Jews were not active participants in its formulation is misleading. As Zvi Gitelman points out, even before Birobidzhan, the Jewish sections of the communist party promoted campaigns that "cleared the way for a new type of Jewishness and Jewry."[8] Instead of describing the Jews as merely passive victims of Soviet nationality and culture policies, it is preferable to borrow a grammatical term and use the middle voice, in which subjects perform actions on themselves, or, at the very least, the distinction between subject and object is unclear. The middle voice is a dominant trope of Bergelson's "Barg-aruf."

One dimension of the new type of Jewry was the new Jewish male. The stoop-shouldered, anemic, sickly Jewish male, the *shtetl luftmensh*, was to be transformed into an able-bodied, muscled, heroic worker. As Bergelson writes in a brochure on Birobidzhan: "In the struggle to master and develop the natural resources of this region a new type of Jew has emerged."[9] Birobidzhan propaganda features, for example, images of clean-shaven smiling Jewish agricultural workers with bulging muscles and sun-browned skin, their gaze directed toward their bright future. In Emmanuel Kazakevich's *Sholem un Khava: Roman in ferzn* [Sholem and Khave: A Novel in Verse], a Birobidzhan love story published in 1941, the narrator says, "And one lives life with the future/ Because 'now' has no worth" [*un lebn lebt men mit der tsukunft/ Vayl s'hot keyn vert nit der 'itst'*].[10]

Mikhail Kalinin, the president of the Soviet Union, said that Birobidzhan was "giving birth" to a new kind of Jewish nationality, "to people with big fists and strong teeth."[11] In Kazakevich's novel, the Jews settling the taiga "sate their bellies with coarse food/ And glow with a quiet fire" [*Mit shverer shpayz dem boikh gezetikt/ Un vi geglit mit shtiln bren*].[12] An emphasis on the strong, healthy Jewish body can also be found in Bergelson's story, "Barg-aruf"; Kalinin's focus on strong teeth appears in Bergelson's description of the worker Molover eating his food: "His healthy white teeth chew quickly, his cheek muscles bulge" [*Zayne gezunte vayse tseyn kayen gikh-gikh, zayne bak-muskuln zaynen ongetsoygn*].[13]

The physically powerful positive hero of 1930s literature, film, and visual culture is a hallmark of the socialist realist aesthetic. I have already indicated that socialist realism demanded a comprehensible, cohesive message. The single most important message was the transformation of the individual through the transformation of the surrounding world, the overcoming of nature, and the defeat of the class enemy. The process was to be a joyous struggle. In his speech at the First Congress of the Soviet Writers' Union, Maxim Gorkii said: "Socialist realism affirms existence as action, as creativity, the purpose of which is the unceasing development of the most valued individual capacities of the person, for the sake of his triumph over the forces of nature, for the sake of his health and longevity, for the sake of the great joy of living on the earth."[14]

In his brochure, Bergelson describes Birobidzhan as "the scene of a joyous struggle," and in "Barg-aruf" the character Velvl has the nickname "happy-go-lucky" [*freylekh khapenish*].[15] As Velvl works to build the new building in which the community will celebrate November 6, Revolution Day, he experiences intense happiness: "The higher he lifted himself together with the scaffolding under the hot sun, the more he felt that what he was doing was more joyous play than work" [*vos hekher er ineynem mit di reshtovanies hot zikh unter der heyser sun ufgehoybn, alts mer hot er gefilt, az yener zakh, vos er tut do iz mer a shpilevdike freyd eyder an arbet*].[16]

However, the joy of socialist construction and self-reconstruction has a dark underlining. Current scholarship is taking another look at the image of the whole, integral body of the socialist realist hero. In an article published in 1989, Eduard Nadtochii argues that the model of the socialist realist hero is marked by ambivalence. On the one side, the hero must abandon his individual body in order to join the collective body, like everyone else. But, on the other side, he remains an individual, and as such must suffer. Nadtochii draws attention to the torments to which the socialist realist hero is subjected: he is drowned, burned, maimed, frozen, and dies. As Nadtochii points out, the socialist realist text masks these punishments under the guise of the hero's self-sacrifice.[17]

In her dissertation, titled *Bodily Remains: The Positive Hero in Stalinist Fiction*, Lilya Kaganovsky similarly argues for a revision of the dominant image of the positive hero.[18] Kaganovsky shows that notwithstanding the stereotype of the clear-headed, party-minded, healthy, and strong hero of the 30s and 40s, a closer inspection of literature and film of the time reveals an abundance of mangled, wounded bodies. As Kaganovsky and other critics point out, Stalin's new heroes turn out to be cripples (Kaganovsky discusses, for example, Pavel Korchagin, the paralyzed blind hero of Nikolai, Ostrovsky's *How the Steel Was Tempered*; Ivan Pyr'ev's film, *The party Card*; Gladkov's *Cement and other works*). According to Kaganovsky, a line from Andrei Platonov's 1934 "Garbage wind" [*Musornyi veter*] serves as an emblem of this tendency in socialist realist art. The hero remarks: "The time of the whole, warm, dear human body had passed: each person was obliged to be a crippled invalid" [*proshlo vremia teplogo, liubimogo, tsel'nogo tela cheloveka: kazhdomu neobkhodimo byt' uvechnym invalidom*].[19] The new Stalinist order of things requires that the hero be injured in some way. As Kaganovsky writes, "The hero's physical or psychic scarring is precisely that which allows him to function" in the society imagined by socialist realism.

The socialist realist aesthetic of the injured hero has important ties to the Gulag aesthetic of punishment, about which I have written in *Russia's Legal Fictions*. I repeat the argument here. I. L. Averbakh's *From Crime to Labor* [*Ot prestupleniia k trudu*], published in 1936, argued that the goal of Soviet corrective labor was the "transformation of the most foul human material into fully valued active builders of socialism. The transformation was to take place by means of concentrated labor on gigantic objects, which shook the imagination by their grandeur."[20] The completed project was not primarily the "gigantic object," but the injured and transformed prisoner, the new builder of socialism. The prisoners were to be remade by the labor they performed on such gigantic projects as the White Sea Canal. This remaking included the aesthetic element that Averbakh calls the "pathos of the construction," the shock of the gigantic scale of the construction, and the violence of forced labor. The Gulag aesthetic, the remaking of the prisoner, directly parallels the socialist realist aesthetic, what Evgeny Dobrenko calls the "making of the state writer" in the context of power.[21]

Bergelson's text plays the "obligation to be wounded" against the Jewish covenantal model of the wound that obligates. In Genesis, circumcision is the sign of the everlasting covenant between God and the Jewish people: "You shall be circumcised in the flesh of your foreskins, and it shall be a sign of the covenant between me and you" (Gen 17:11).[22] God promises Abraham that from him will come "nations" and kings and that the land of Canaan will be their possession. Circumcision is the sign of the mutual obligation between God and the Jews, and it is a sign among Jews of their belonging to the nation of Israel, synchronically and diachronically. The Genesis circumcision commandment obliges fathers to circumcise their sons, the next generation. Circumcision is the wound that signals a promise of plenitude. In Deuteronomy, circumcision is a metaphor. Moses tells the recalcitrant Israel of God's love and urges a recommitment from them: "Circumcise therefore the foreskin of your heart, and be no longer stubborn" (Deut. 10:16). Other traditional Jewish texts reemphasize the corporeal and corporate nature of the covenant. After eating bread, Jews thank God for "the covenant which You sealed in our flesh."

In the Jewish tradition with which Bergelson was familiar, circumcision is a wound that is a sign of a promise; it is the wound that binds and obligates members of the community to God and to each other. In the socialist realist model, the transformation of the individual through socialist construction also has the effect of binding the individual to the collective To use Bergelson's language from the First Congress of the Soviet Writer's Union, the socialist realist writer must "illuminate all the bonds that tie the laboring unit to the collective" [*osvetit' vse perepleteniia. kotorymi sviazyvaetsia trudovaia edinitsa s kollektivom*].[23] In the Soviet context of the 1930s, the wound that obligates becomes the obligation to be wounded, and this is precisely what "Barg-aruf" reveals.

The biblical trope of the covenantal sign and the socialist realist aesthetic intertwine in powerful and disturbing ways in Bergelson's text. Birobidzhan was supposed to solve the Jewish problem by providing Jews with a national territory. Bergelson's narrative glosses the problem as the prior exclusion of the Jews from secular history. The construction worker Velvl and the editor of the Birobidzhan newspaper engage in a dialogue about the current new moment in Jewish history. The choice of these two interlocutors, the worker and the editor, is stock-in-trade socialist realism because the two represent the proletariat and party consciousness. The language they use, however, is far from stereotypical socialist realism. Velvl recites the prior history of the Jews in highly marked language: "Their fate tossed them from land to land, and not anywhere in any land was their history written on the ramparts, the walls, the towers, not with the roads that went through them, or the bridges that were thrown across them, or with the building of cities" [*un in ergets in yene lender iz ir geshikhte nit farshribn gevorn nit of keyn moyern, nit of keyn vent un nit of keym turems, nit mit durkhleygn vegn, tsi mit ibervarfn brikn, tsi mit oysboyen shtet*].[24] The Jews could not leave a record of their presence on the great public works of civilization and progress.

The editor continues the metaphor of history as inscription, adding that the Jews "carry their history around like a type of little prayer book under their arm" [*un zeyer geshikhte trogn yidn arum vi epes a min siderl unter der pokhve*].[25] Up to now, up to the dawn of socialism, the history of the Jews

New Jews: David Bergelson and Birobidzhan

had no material, positive existence; it was a deterritorialized, depoliticized tale of exclusion and homelessness, and it was a history, moreover, known only to them, like the prayer book they would carry to the synagogue. But with the rise of socialism, everything changed. The tale of woe is no more; instead, the text of Jewish history is to be realized materially, concretely, territorially. The editor continues, "And now the party tells you: 'Jews, take part in our great socialist construction, write your history on the walls, write it on the ramparts, write it on the factories, on the cities, and on the land" [*Un itzt zogt tsu aykh di partey: "Yidn bateylikte in undzer groyser sotsialistisher boyung, shraybt ayer geshikhte of vent, shraybt zi of moyern, shraybt zi of fabrikhn, of shtet un of land!"*].[26]

This language, which suggests a relation between participation in history as progress and work on physical construction, eerily reflects the language of Gulag rehabilitation, with its emphasis on the remaking of the prisoner by means of work on gigantic constructions. The language also echoes the text of the traditional Jewish prayer, known as the *Shema*, that begins with the line, "Hear, O Israel." Israel is enjoined to "write" God's words: "And thou shalt write them upon the doorposts of thy house and upon thy gates."[27] Bergelson's text repeats and transforms this commandment in the party's commandment to the Jews to "write your history on the walls, write it on the ramparts."

The inscription of the Jewish people in history by means of socialist construction comes with a price. The new covenant of the socialist collective requires a new, terrible circumcision, a wound that is not a sign, but an injury. Kaganovsky argues that in canonical socialist realist texts the positive hero's body is "legible only through its display of lack."[28] The hero is recognizably heroic only in his injury and mutilation. But in Bergelson's text, the punishment is only hinted at. Receiving his negative report from the regional committee, the district "secretary had the face of a man who allows himself to get a whipping, only he himself must think whether the whipping comes for him alone, and if not, for whom else?" [*hot er gehot a ponem fun a mentshn, vos lozt zikh gebn shmits, nor aleyn darf er nokh a trakht ton, tsi di shmits kumen nor im eynem, un oyb nit—iz vemen nokh?*].[29]

Bergelson repeats the motif of metaphorical and self-inflicted pain in the worker Velvl, whom I have already mentioned. Velvl has the misfortune to miss the girl he left behind and foolishly asks for leave just as the work reaches its most frantic pace. Sensing that he has committed an error, he "grimaces harshly as if he had hit his own finger himself while hammering a nail" [*zikh shtark farkrimt, vi er volt bam farshlogn a tshvok getrofn mitn hamer in an eygenem finger*].[30] Here, as in the example above about the secretary who "lets himself" receive a whipping, is the middle voice, in which the subject performing the action and its recipient are the same. In another emblematic scene, the semaphore at the train station is torn up from the ground by the ferocious Birobidzhan wind. As the worker Sholem Bubes labors to replace it, his face takes on the appearance of a "fiery wound."[31] Leaving a trace in history—the semaphore in the taiga—requires bodily injury.

Bergelson's vignettes describing socialist construction in the taiga of Birobidzhan shift the emphasis from the transparent message of victory to an emphasis on the unsaid and the unfulfilled. The new covenant is not between God and Israel, but between Stalin and Israel. The sign of the father works through absence and distance. Stalin enters Bergelson's text through terror and fear, his great power signaled by an enormous portrait, an icon, that Velvl carries as he rushes off to complete his tasks in the new building. Stalin the new father of the people is only a punishing and wrathful God. I quote the elusive opening of the story:

> Nonetheless, this time, as always after the late rains, the work began anew in the young city and in all the young human nests, in the mountainous and in the flat places of the entire area. Like flaming fiery horses the days before the October holidays rushed in, and with them, the summer warmth returned....Like flaming, fiery horses, the days before the October holidays chased over villages and settlements along hidden trails, along mountain peaks, and around fields, everywhere throwing off sunny embers, everywhere kindling the desire to mount them, hold them by the manes and ride and ride....They brought joy to some. Others they frightened.[32]

The opening line suggests, without articulating it clearly, a prior condition that would obviate the yearly cycle of renewed work and the return of warmth. In spite of this circumstance that would interrupt the cycle, what usually happened, happened this time as always. The unspoken negative is the founding moment of the story and constitutes one of its dominant motifs. Indeed, at the end of the story, we find a string of unspoken negatives. An American family arrives in Birobidzhan, and as

New Jews: David Bergelson and Birobidzhan

they make their way in a snowstorm from the station to their quarters, their escort shouts, "'It's like Winnipeg,' as if someone had frightened them with 'it's worse than Alaska.'" He points out the post office, "as if someone had frightened them with, 'it's the end of the world, a wasteland'"[*ek velt, a midber*].[33]

The "October holidays," twice repeated in the opening passage, refer to a time of special significance in the Jewish calendar: the New Year and Yom Kippur, and especially the days between the New Year and Yom Kippur, the period known as "the Days of Awe," when Jews wait to see whether they have been inscribed in the Book of Life. The link to the Jewish tradition of the fall holidays, with their communal confession of sins of both commission and omission, emerges in the opening vignette. The secretary of the Birobidzhan regional committee learns that he has not fulfilled a single plan: the necessary plots of land have not been cleared, the required number of apartments and barracks have not been constructed, not enough hay and silage was prepared, and so forth. The enumeration of the secretary's list of sins, together with the mention of the October holidays unmistakably echoes the Yom Kippur confession.

Ironically, for Bergelson's fictitious district secretary, the only indication of positive accomplishment is the lack of greater consequences. The secretary considers that, given all his failures, the regional committee ought to remove him and the entire leadership in the area and that, if it have not done so, it is a sign that something was accomplished [*iz a simen, az epes iz in rayon dokh opgeton gevorn*].[34] Evidence of accomplishment, which would consist of the abundance of food, provisions, land, and the positive presence of socialist construction, can be seen only in the absence of punishment for the failure to achieve success. In this episode, Bergelson provides a gloss on how to read his text. Absence, negativity, lack, and distance provide meaning.

In his introduction to a collection of Birobidzhan stories published in 1980 in Russian and English, Chaim Beider quotes the last lines of "Bargaruf." Notably, the story as a whole is absent from the collection. I cite from the English translation:

> The sifting snow has stopped, the wind had died down and everywhere you look the snow lies smooth as a counterpane. And the sun.... The sun above you, below you, in the hillocks and in the sky, so bright—could it possibly be any brighter?[35]

According to Beider, this passage shows that "the story ends on a joyous note." Nothing could be farther from the truth. The extraordinary brightness of the sun on the white snow calls to mind Bergelson's words from the tribune of the First Congress of the Writers' Union about the blinding whiteness of the sheet of paper on which the Daghestani poet wrote his completely incomprehensible poem about Lenin and Stalin. Bergelson said, "I did not understand a single word of this speech, but nonetheless this extraordinary poem about Lenin's and Stalin's national policy was written on a piece of paper of blinding whiteness."[36] The sun shining on the snow of Birobidzhan is also blinding, and the blinding sun on the snow "everywhere you look" makes it impossible to read the traces of human habitation there. The all-important material inscription of the Jews on the land is illegible, and the meaning of Birobidzhan as a solution to the Jewish problem remains completely opaque.

NOTES

[1] Irving Howe and Eliezer Greenberg, *Ashes out of Hope: Fiction by Soviet-Yiddish Writers* (New York: Schocken Books, 1977), 25. For a recent approach to Soviet Jewish culture that offers a revision of Howe's negative view, see Jeffrey Veidlinger, *The Moscow State Yiddish Theater: Jewish Culture on the Soviet Stage* (Bloomington: Indiana University Press, 2000).

[2] *Pervyi vsesoiuznyi sezd sovetskikh pisatelei stenograficheskii otchet* (Moscow: Sovetskii pisatel', 1934), 220.

[3] Ibid., 271.

[4] For the aesthetic of socialist realism, see Régine Robin, *Socialist Realism: An Impossible Aesthetic* (trans. Catherine Porter; Stanford: Stanford University Press, 1992), 260.

[5] Zvi Gitelman, "Introduction," *Stalin's Forgotten Zion: Birobidzhan and the Making of a Soviet Jewish Homeland* (Berkeley: University of California Press, 1998), 8.

[6] For a discussion of the contradictions of Soviet nationality policy, see, for example, Yuri Slezkine, "The USSR as a Communal Apartment, or How a Socialist State Promoted Ethnic Particularism," *Slavic Review* 53:2 (1994): 414-52. All English translations in this article are by the present author.

[7] David Bergelson, "Barg-Aruf," *Forpost* (1936): 38.

[8] Gitelman, "Introduction," *Stalin's Forgotten Zion*, 6.

[9] David Bergelson, *The Jewish Autonomous Region* (Moscow: Foreign Language

Publishing House, 1936), 48.

[10] Emmanuel Kazakevich, *Sholem un Khave: Roman in ferzn* (ed. Kushnirov; Moscow: Der emes, 1941), 28.

[11] Mikhail Kalinin, cited by Robert Weinberg, *Stalin's Forgotten Zion: Birobidzhan and the Making of a Soviet Jewish Homeland* (Berkeley: University of California Press, 1998), 46.

[12] Kazakevich, *Sholem un Khave*, 74.

[13] Bergelson, "Barg-Aruf," 39.

[14] *Pervyi vsesoiuznyi s"ezd sovetskikh pisatelei stenograficheskii otchet*, 16.

[15] Bergelson, "Barg-Aruf," 42.

[16] Ibid.

[17] Eduard Nadtochii, "Druk, tovarishch, i Bart (neskol'ko predvaritel'nykh zamechanii k voprosheniiu o meste sotsialisticheskogo realizma v iskusstve xx veka)," *Daugava* 8 (1989): 115-220.

[18] Lilya Kaganovsky, *Bodily Remains: The "Positive Hero" in Stalinist Fiction* (University of California at Berkeley, 2000).

[19] Andrei Platonov, cited in Kaganovsky, *Bodily Remains*, 1.

[20] I. L. Averbakh, *Ot prestupleniia k trudu*, (ed. A. Ia. Vyshinskii; Sovetskoe zakonodatel'stvo, 1936), 23. The author of *From Crime to Labor* was Ida Leonidovna Averbakh, who was the sister of the prominent literary critic Leopold Averbakh and the wife of Genrikh Iagoda, the head of the NKVD.

[21] Evgeny Dobrenko, *The Making of the State Writer: Social and Aesthetic Origins of Soviet Literary Culture* (Stanford: Stanford University Press, 2001).

[22] All Biblical citations are taken from the Revised Standard Version of the Bible.

[23] *Pervyi vsesoiuznyi s"ezd sovetskikh pisatelei stenograficheskii otchet*, 271.

[24] Bergelson, "Barg-Aruf," 42.

[25] Ibid.

[26] Ibid., 43.

[27] Morris Silverman, *High Holiday Prayer Book* (New York: The Prayer Book Press, 1984), 7.

[28] Kaganovsky, *Bodily Remains*, 21.

[29] Bergelson, "Barg-Aruf," 38.

[30] Ibid., 48.

[31] Ibid., 52.

[32] Ibid., 37.

[33] Ibid., 66.

[34] Ibid., 38.

[35] Chaim Beider, ed., *Native Land: A Selection of Soviet Jewish Writers* (Moscow:

Progress, 1980), 16.

[36] *Pervyi vsesoiuznyi s"ezd sovetskikh pisatelei stenograficheskii otchet*, 271.

Nokhem-Meyer Shaykevitsch: Another Classic of Yiddish Theater?

Andrey Bredstein

In the 1870s, the Yiddish theater already had all the necessary components, created by the cultural renaissance that East European Jews experienced in the middle of the nineteenth century.[1] There were playwrights (Etinger, Aksenfeld, Gotlober, and others), there were performers (folk singers and *badkhonim* [wedding bards] like Elyokum Zunzer and the famous Broder singers) and, there was an audience, "which, by reason of *Haskole* [Enlightenment] and a rather benevolent political regime that had just emerged from the forbidding restraints of fanaticism, fell upon the new medium of culture and amusement with a ravenous appetite."[2]

In 1876, Jassy, Romania, had a particularly large number of merchants and traders because the Russian army supply headquarters was located in the region. There was a certain demand for amusement, satisfied mostly by Romanian wine and folk performers. So, when the folk poet Avrom Goldfaden came to Jassy that year, he found favorable conditions for organizing a Yiddish theater. He wrote his first play, *Di bobe mitn eynikl* (1876), hired two actors, and started with performances that attracted many enterprising people,[3] one of whom was a young writer Nokhem-Meyer Shaykevitsh (1846-1905). The Yiddish theater in Romania made a great impression on him and considerably influenced his life.

For any institution, including such a complicated one as theater, the period of creation and early development is especially important, not only because of its historical value, but also because it helps to understand better other phenomena and processes that led to the further development of this institution. In this paper I try to analyze facts related to the early days of modern Yiddish theater (1878-83), particularly focusing on Shaykevitsh, whose contribution toward establishing and developing the Yiddish theater as Goldfaden's brother-in-arms (rather than his competitor) was of significant importance.

Since early childhood Shaykevitsh distinguished himself as a brilliant storyteller. Later, he became famous as the author of over 200 novels, partly historical and partly reflecting Jewish life in the small towns and villages of Russia in the middle of the nineteenth century. Shaykevitsh also wrote about seventy plays, most of which were produced first in Russia and later in America. While beloved by his numerous readers, critics and other writers attacked his work as harmful and stamped it as *shund* [trash]. The culmination was Sholem Aleichem's pamphlet *Shomers mishpet* (1888), in which the author reproached Shaykevitsh for his bad literary taste and called for banishing him from Yiddish literature. Ten years later, Shaykevitsh tried to defend himself in a pamphlet *Yehi Oyr* (1898), showing that his literary goal was to satisfy every plane of intelligence, from the householder to the servant girl who could not understand the exquisite works of the later Yiddish writers. Starting in the 1930s, a number of scholars and critics (Avrom Reyzen, Shoel Ginzburg, Zalmen Reyzen, Yankev Glatshteyn, Avrom Vevyorke, and Sophie Grace-Pollak, among others) have tried to establish a new understanding of Shaykevitsh and his work.

The literary career of Shaykevitsh started in Vilna. There, in 1876, he came to Shmuel-Yosef Fin, the renowned editor of *Ha-karmel*, and offered him a Hebrew novel, *Victims of Inquisition*, for publication in the journal. Fin was very impressed with the first effort of the young author, yet suggested that he should write something in Yiddish. The next morning Shaykevitsh brought him a story, *Sonim fun di mekhutonim*. The story was immediately accepted, and the author received his first modest three ruble honorarium. Fin urged Shaykevitsh to continue and expected an even better follow-up. He was not a disappointed: Shaykevitsh followed this advice and kept bringing new stories on a daily basis. Within less than a week, Fin started negotiations with the well-known publishing house Shriftzetser and Rozenkrants and obtained a contract for Shaykevitsh's first book.

However, when the Russo-Turkish War in the Balkans (1877-78) broke out, Shaykevitsh obtained a position as a contractor in a military purveyor company in charge of supplying Russian troops; in this capacity he made a number of business trips to Bucharest and Odessa. It was in Bucharest that Shaykevitsh got acquainted with the newborn Yiddish theater and its founder, Avrom Goldfaden. Seeing the commercial success of the new enterprise, Shaykevitsh decided to try the theater for himself.

By that time he was married and had to support his wife and children. Earlier he had had a number of jobs, but none of them improved his financial situation. At the same time it appears that theater attracted Shaykevitsh much more than trade: when the war was over, he decided not to return to Vilna to his rich father-in-law Yekhiel Vigodski, who had offered him the position of a contractor, but instead sought employment in one of two Hebrew periodicals in Odessa (*Hamelits* and *Haboyker Oyr*). Shaykevitsh was fortunate: Avrom-Ber Gotlober, the editor of *Haboyker Oyr*, offered him a position at his magazine, which he had long been dreaming about, and in early 1878 he settled in Odessa with his family.

Shortly before that, in late 1877, Goldfaden's troupe and several other companies (led by Mogulesco, Grodner, Spivakovski, and Roze Fridman, among others) left Romania together with the traders and moved to Russia, especially its southern regions. This geographical shift marks a new phase, the Odessa period in the history of Yiddish theater.

Among the most important historiographic sources for reconstructing events of this period are theater reviews. For the Yiddish theater, in many cases, they are practically the only available source of information about productions, actors, directors, etc.[4] However, one has to bear in mind that most of these reviews and articles were written at a very low level: professional theatre critics (including Jews) usually did not know the Yiddish language, nor did they have any interest in it. Thus, most reviews were written primarily by amateurs, who lacked both talent and professional vocabulary, but were eager to satisfy readers' interest. Being a new and unknown amusement (in early 1878), Yiddish theater provoked curiosity and caused all sorts of rumors in the Russian regional press. In April 1878, one of the few Odessa newspapers wrote about forthcoming performances of a Yiddish company: "We heard that a Jewish drama and operetta company from Galatz will soon perform in the Marinskii Theater; among other plays *Recruitment of the volunteers in Poland in 1871* (an operetta in three acts) will be performed for the first time."[5]

The troupe was directed by Yisroel Rozenberg, "a comic actor, well-known among local Jews, who successfully depicts funny features of the hardened Jewish fanatics."[6] Rozenberg came from Bucharest in August 1878: "We do not know whether Mr. Rozenberg will perform in Odessa, but there is no doubt that it will be successful because it will be the first performance in Yiddish in Odessa."[7]

Because Rozenberg did not have plays approved by the censor, he had to call his amateur performances "literary evenings." There were no other Yiddish companies in Odessa in 1878, and so one can assume that it was his performances that Shaykevitsh had seen during his business trips there.

In early 1879, Goldfaden learned about performances in Odessa and in March of that year came with his troupe: "On Sunday Mr. Goldfaden, the manager of a Jewish company and a dramatist, arrived from Bucharest. He is going to perform a number of plays in Odessa."[8] Like Rozenberg, Goldfaden did not have plays approved by the censor and thus could not perform in a leased theater; rather, he started in April with "literary-musical evenings" in the Handicraft Club.[9] The reporter of *Odesskii Vestnik*, A. Zilberbroyt, wrote:

> On Saturday, April 7, the Jewish company from Bucharest managed by "the famous folk poet"…started its performances with operetta *Koldunye*….We wonder not so much about the bold title that Mr. Goldfaden has usurped or the fact that the regular theater performances (the characters appear in costumes and make-up) are presented as "literary-musical evenings," as why Mr. Goldfaden decided to move his activity in Odessa.[10]

From this theater announcement one can see that Goldfaden was not welcome in Odessa. His arrival created competition for Rozenberg, who may have even sponsored this article. However, Rozenberg's theater was soon closed by the police. Goldfaden quickly rented the Marinskii Theater,[11] had all his plays approved by the censor, and started performing. Shaykevitsh visited Yiddish plays performed by Goldfaden's company throughout 1879, except for September and October when the company was in Kishinev and Nikolayev. By that time, several stories that he had written three years earlier under his pen name Shomer were already well known, and his popularity began to grow. He decided to explore other literary forms and within a few weeks wrote his first novel in Yiddish, *Der blutiker adye*, which later became a tremendous success. The Mats publishing house bought the novel and ordered a second one. By the end of 1879, Shaykevitsh wrote two more novels, *Der gliklekher pastekh* and *Rashkele kozak*. All three novels were published in the same year and quickly sold out.

As Shaykevitsh's popularity grew, Avrom Ber Gotlober persuaded him to write a play for Goldfaden's troupe. Shaykevitsh recalls:

> I started thinking about which play I should write and finally decided to write a play about life in a small Lithuanian town, in

which I would depict the fanaticism of those provincial rabbis, the absurdity of the public representatives, and present some persons of that dark time.[12]

The play he wrote, *Der trefnyak oder Der yidisher porets*,[13] was an adaptation of his novel, *Der yidisher porets*. Before this play was sent to the censor, the director of the Marinskii Theater Homer (Homero)[14] bought it for 100 rubles and fifteen rubles per performance, but then quarreled with the actors and left the company. By that time, the former director of a French theater in Bucharest, Yosef Lerner, came to Odessa and managed to become a director of this company. In summer 1880, Lerner had several of his own plays approved by the censor and was ready to perform them together with Goldafaden's and Y. Lateiner's repertoire.[15]

From the very beginning, Lerner had a very serious attitude toward censorship in particular and a tenuous relationship with the local authorities in general. One can see how important these issues were from the following theater announcement. When the former manager Homer left his position, he still tried to get some profit out of the Yiddish troupe during that summer of 1880 by claiming that he has bought some plays from Zigmund Mogulesko and Lateiner, which both of them denied:

> Theater announcement. In refutation of Mr. Homero's claim we find it necessary to state, that never and by no contract did we sell him our plays, which are still our irremovable property.[16]

Presumably Lerner tried to create a substantial repertoire and looked for playwrights. His previous experience as a journalist provided him with a good knowledge of the expectations that the audience in Odessa would have. By that time, Shaykevitsh had written six more novels[17] and was becoming a best-selling Yiddish author: the sales of only one of his novels, *Der katorzhnik*, reached 40,000 copies within several years.[18] His first novel *Der yidisher porets*, was well known among the readers and his new play, based on this novel, looked quite attractive to Lerner—which is why he offered Shaykevitsh 150 rubles per month to become a fulltime playwright.

Lerner started performing in August 1880, with Shloyme Etinger's *Serkele* in his own adaptation and Isroel Aksenfeld's *Der oytser*. Although the *Leksikon fun dem yidish teater* states that both plays failed,[19] the reviews tell quite the opposite:

> On August 26...the new comedy *Der oytser* was performed for

the first time. The theater was packed; the play was a real success. After the performance Mr. Lerner and Mr. Mogulesco were called before the curtain.[20]

In the middle of September, *Der yidisher porets* was ready to be performed after a rehearsal period of two months. The actors met twice a day, which was quite unusual, and as a result all the actors learned their roles by heart.[21] The play included some musical numbers, with the text written by Shaykevitsh. The first performance was scheduled for the September 17 and expectations were high. Four days before an announcement read:

> They say, the play is very interesting and what is the most important—well staged. It has totally new Jewish characters. On the whole, one can comment upon Mr. Lerner's way of producing plays quite indulgently.[22]

Lerner decided not to renew the lease at Marinskii and moved his company into the completely renovated Handicraft Club (the stage had been enlarged, boxes were added, and armchairs were installed in the first three rows). This move could have been made in order to save some money: the Marinskii was much bigger and thus more expensive to rent. Between the last performance at the Marinskii (*Der dibuk* by Lateiner) on September 21 and the opening of the season on a new stage on October 1, the company went to Kishinev, Moldavia,[23] where five performances were scheduled but not performed because the company did not get permission from the local authorities.[24]

As one can judge from articles in the Odessa papers, the Jewish audience in 1880 was not homogeneous, and the sympathies of the gallery were definitely not the same as of those in the front rows; if the former preferred verses with dancing and music, the latter were not excited about it and looked for a more intellectually loaded content. The better educated spectators could not be satisfied with the carnivalesque art of traditional *purimshpiler* and expressed their attitude in the numerous reviews and articles:

> We cannot but reproach Mr. Lerner for trying to be popular with the occupants of the gallery; he avoids plays devoted to current Jewish problems, as for example, *Der oytser*, and entertains the audience with Goldfaden's repertoire. This week the whole repertoire is compiled of Goldfaden's plays, except for Wednesday, when the new play by Shaykevitsh, *Der yidisher porets*, will be

performed…Leave Goldfaden alone, Mr. Lerner, at least for some time.[25]

Goldfaden perhaps did not want or simply could not adapt himself to these new demands and trends. He continued writing the same sort of plays, although they started to seem old fashioned and boring to at least a part of the audience. At the same time, Shaykevitsh wrote plays that matched the expectations of these better educated spectators and could recognize the general demand of the time, which was toward serious material ("serious" being a keyword in many reviews):

> Mr. Entrepreneur is going to leave Goldfaden's overplayed plays for a while and will give the audience something more serious. For the winter season Mr. Lerner has twelve serious plays, among which are *Der kholem*, a comedy in five acts by Mr. Shaykevitsh, and *Uriel Acosta*, a tragedy by Mr. Gutzkow translated by Mr. Lerner, who also wrote the music for this play. Among other new plays with a serious content they name *Der yidisher porets* and *Di takse*.[26]

Performed for the first time in the fall season of 1880, *Der yidisher porets* was praised by the critics for both its content and language:

> The comedy by Shaykevitsh stands out against the background of other plays by Jewish home-bred playwrights because of its doubtless merits. Well staged, well shaped roles, warm and true feelings in tragic episodes together with the absence of vulgarity and caricature which is so beloved by previous Jewish authors, just to mention a few of them. One has to add correct and clear language, which is not an easy thing to achieve, and an interesting although not too tangled intrigue, artfully presented in every act.[27]

Together with the changes in repertoire, one can notice a certain shift toward more complex reviews: their authors started discussing such technical details as staging, roles, and quality of language, whereas all they could say earlier was, "the play was a real success."

The success of Shaykevitsh's plays brought a certain increase in revenue, and Lerner could therefore afford to rent the Marinskii again. He soon started working on another play by Shaykevitsh:[28]

The new play *Der kholem* by Mr. Shaykevitsh, the talented author of the popular *Der yidisher porets*, is being rehearsed right now. Mr. Shaykevitsh introduces new characters from the Jewish middle class. Among the merits of the new play, one can name a vivid, clear language and theatrical effectiveness. One does not have to sing the praises of this play though: the name of its author speaks for itself. Mr. Shaykevitsh is long known among the Jewish readers as a talented writer.[29]

"Theatrical effectiveness" and quality of Yiddish are again the focus of the reviewer. Seeing that *Der yidisher porets* featured actual problems that involved his audience, Shaykevitsh decided to portray the same characters in his new play; i.e., the Jewish middle class. It would be hard to find a better place in Russia at that time because nowhere else was the position of the middle class as strong as in Odessa.

However, when *Der kholem*[30] was performed on December 1, 1880, reviewers killed it, sharply criticizing its lack of ideas and its complete artificiality:

> The play has lots of characters who talk nonsense mixed with the most scabrous verses accompanied by a Jewish [music] *à la* Offenbach. There are also many irrelevant and badly made caricature scenes. Although the author is relatively well known by his *Der yidisher porets*, the audience was quite indifferent to this play—it never called the author (to his great disappointment), and there was even some whistling after the performance. This sad event, i.e., the complete fiasco of the new play (if it is possible to call the new talentless work by Shaykevitsh a play), leads us toward really…joyful thoughts….The taste of Jewish audience has improved lately…and all of a sudden it was presented with such an insipid dish as the new comedy *Der kholem* which does not have a single character scene of manners, not a single idea, not a single intelligent phrase—literally nothing![31]

It is hard to establish the level of objectiveness of this review. One may only suggest that if the play was really that bad, Lerner's theater would not have been able to attract people and earn a profit. Another explanation can be found among traditions of Russian journalism that make it possible to "order" reviews with certain content. Anyway, the production was quite successful, and Lerner could extend the lease of the Marinskii Theater for another three years. For the winter season of 1880-81, he invited a Russian opera company; in order to create it, he went to Petersburg and Moscow in early January.

In December 1880, the new comedy in four acts, *Der toes*,[32] by Shaykevitsh was performed for the first time:[33]

> The difference of approaches between audience and reviewer was clearly seen at the performances of Shaykevitsh's two last plays—*Der kholem* and *Der toes*. The former had been a fiasco because, as many have said, it turned out to be tedious; the latter however was, to a certain extent, a success—although taking in consideration the inner content, richness of plot and creativity of the basic idea, [it is obvious that] *Der kholem* is much better than *Der toes*, which is modeled after Golfaden's plays....[34]

> The little success which *Der toes* had at first does not have anything to do with its merits, but rather with the art of Mr. Lerner and the director, who managed to stage it so well together with a good performance of the actors.[35]

The success of his plays led Shaykevitsh to try to become an entrepreneur, and in early 1881 he created his own company, consisting of Yisroel and Aneta Gradner, Khaymovitsh, Klener, Koyfman, Gelis, Zaks, and other actors.[36] According to Shaykevitsh's daughter Rose, he advertised in the paper, and for a couple of weeks his home was filled with the aspiring actors.[37]

He was planning to tour in the southern region of Russia, and for this purpose wrote a new play, *Der baltshuve*,[38] based on his novel of the same title. In the spring 1881, Shaykevitsh went with this play to Nikolaev, where he rented a theater and, under the name of "German theater," successfully performed *Der baltshuve*. The reason for calling the theater "German" rather than "Yiddish" was purely commercial: it was more prestigious to go to the German theater, and the troupe could thus earn more money. The outcome however was meager. Shortly before the performance (April 15-17), a pogrom burst out in Elisavetgrad, and only a few Jews attended. Shaykevitsh dismissed his troupe, leaving behind his play as a gift to the actors. The later reappeared with this play in Kherson, Ekaterinoslav, Kharkov, and Kiev.

Shaykevitsh did not give up his idea of tours; in July, he appeared with a new company in Kharkov and performed his own plays in the garden theater Bavara:[39] *Di yesoyme, Der yidisher porets*, and several others.

As the Yiddish playwright Yankev Vaksman wrote in his memoir,[40] the plays were performed successfully, but too frequently, and the audience gradually decreased in numbers. In order to improve the financial situation, Shaykevitsh tried to perform a famous Russian play, *Inspector General* by Gogol, in his own adaptation.[41] The majority of the audience were Russian civil and military government personnel, who understood this as a mockery of a great Russian classic, and the governor prohibited the performances of this play.[42]

The next city of the tour was Kishinev. Shaykevitsh managed to receive a permit from the governor and performed with great success his *Der baltshuve*, *Der yidisher porets*, and for the first time his new historical drama, *Di shpanishe inkvizitsie*, and an operetta, *Der neder*.[43] His company consisted of Khaymovitsh, Karp, Tsukerman, Boyke, Nakhamkus, Koyfman, Zaks, and Levitski.

While Shaykevitsh was touring around the province, Lerner performed his new play *Di yesoymim* on September 1, 1881, in Odessa.[44] This play has been scheduled to open on May 23, 1881;[45] because of some conflicts between Shaykevitsh and Lerner, it was not performed until the fall, when their relationship improved again.

In early 1882, Shaykevitsh returned from his tour to Odessa and, together with Lerner and Goldfaden, opened a new "German theater" in Marinskii. Among the actors were Mogulesko, Spivakovsky, Yisroel and Aneta Grodner, and Edelshteyn; there was also a large choir and an orchestra. The distribution of the partners' roles can be gleaned from the letter written by Goldfaden to Shaykevitsh in which Goldfaden suggested that he create farce and operettas, while his addressee write drama.[46]

Shaykevitsh's success as a writer and playwright had such an impact on his readership that as early as in the mid-1880s there appeared publications like those of Shomer, claiming that they represented "a faithful, highly entertaining novel in the style of Shomer." There were authors who appropriated Shomer's pen name, turning it into Shomer from Sadlik, Shomer from Slutsk, Shamir, and similar variations. His name became a guarantee not only for an interesting read, but also for an interesting spectacle; it is no wonder that many companies included his plays in their repertoire [see table].

In August 1882, the company went on a tour in Kishinev. Returning to Odessa in October, during the winter season it performed Goldfaden's plays, *Shulamis* and *Bar-Kokhbe*, together with Shaykevitsh's *Ayzerne froy*,[47]

Der protsentnik[48] (Rose Shomer-Batshelis added a play *Di kokete damen*),[49] and a third play, not mentioned anywhere but in the newspaper: "December 30,...the drama *Der volf in shofn fel* created from the famous Jewish novel *Der katorzhnik* by Shaykevitsh was performed with tremendous success. The staggering finale made many of the spectators cry."[50]

In the spring of 1883, Shaykevitsh tried to perform his old adaptation of *Revizor* [Inspector General], which caused him much trouble in Kharkov. There is evidence that among the Jewish audience this play was a success;[51] however, it is obvious that Russian spectators did not like this adaptation. It was sharply criticized in the local press and was not staged as often as other plays by Shaykevitsh:

> On March 16, the Jewish company performed a Jewish version of *Revizor* [Inspector General] by Gogol for the first time. The performance was a complete fiasco. The adapter of this wonderful comedy tried to make all the characters look Jewish by dressing them in old-fashioned kapotes and yarmulkes and adding a whole row of ugly musical fragments.[52]

The Yiddish theater was slowly achieving stability. The audience was growing accustomed to it and no longer treated it as something new. The tone of the reviews written in 1883 was free from both rapture and hatred; it had become more calm and objective. By that time, there was an established repertoire consisting not only of the old-fashioned plays with dancing and singing, but also including plays with modern content, able to satisfy the growing demand of the Jewish middle class. The repertoire of the Yiddish theatre in Odessa in 1878-1883 included at least 48 plays, as far as it can be seen from the papers. One-fifth of these plays (9) belong to Shaykevitsh. In fact, he was one of most prolific playwrights, yielding only to Goldfaden, who wrote more than one-third (17 plays) of that repertoire [see table].

The desperate need for new plays had finally stopped being the urgent problem of Yiddish theater. Among those who had filled this need was Shaykevitsh. In a relatively short period of time, he made a significant contribution—acting both as a playwright and as a theater manager—by creating repertoire and attracting audience.

Table of Repertoire of Yiddish theatre in Odessa (1778-1883)

Author	Plays	%
Goldfaden	17	35
Shaykevitsh	9	19
Lerner	6	14
Lateiner	5	10
Katsenelenbogen	2	4
Kurtis	2	4
Adler [?]	1	2
Bazelinski	1	2
Lilienblyum	1	2
Mogulesco	1	2
Skib	1	2
Ter	1	2
Other	1	2
Total	48	100

NOTES

[1] In this article, the transcription of Yiddish titles is based on the YIVO system for transcribing words in Yiddish. Personal names follow the same system unless they have a long tradition of some other spelling (like the Library of Congress system). Russian titles and names are all transcribed according to the Library of Congress system.

[2] Miriam Shomer-Zunzer, *Yesterday: a Memoir of a Russian Jewish Family* (New York, 1978), 179.

[3] Nahma Sandrow, *Vagabond stars: a World History of Yiddish Theater* (New York, 1977), 41.

[4] E. Binevich, "Istorija jevrejskogo teatra v Rossii (1876-1883)," *OEN:Serija preprintov I reprintov* 38 (1997):1.

[5] *Odesskii vestnik* 22 Apr. 1878:2.

[6] *Odesskii vestnik* 20 Aug. 1878:3.

[7] Ibid.

[8] *Vedomosti Odesskogo Gradonachalstva* 20 Mar. 1879:2.

[9] Although called a club, it had a stage and a hall with a balcony, and could accommodate about one hundred people. See B. Vaynshteyn, "Di ershte yorn fun yidishn teater in Odes un in Nyu-York," in *Arkhiv far der geshikhte fun yidishn teater un drame* (Vilne–Nyu-York, 1930), 244.

[10] *Odesskii vestnik* 14 Apr. 1879:2.

[11] Originally built and used as a circus, this building was once reconstructed into a popular theater. After the main city theater was distroyed in fire in 1873, Marinskii became the center of the theater life of Odessa until the famous Opera theater was built in 1887. Marinskii was gradually forgotten and finally rebuilt once more into a regular apartment complex.

[12] *Mentshnfraynd* 1891:129.

[13] Published in 1888 in Vilna.

[14] Having had a quarrel with Goldfaden, Homero hired his own company and for a short time (after Goldfaden had to leave the theater) was the manager of the Yiddish theater.

[15] *Odesskii vestnik* 25 Jun. 1880:2.

[16] *Vedomosti Odesskogo Gradonachalstva* 16 Jul. 1880:1.

[17] *Der yidisher porets, Der baltshuve, Der katorzhnik, Di blinde yesoyme, Di agune,* and *Der kosherer yid.*

[18] Rose Shomer-Batshelis, *Undzer foter Shomer* (New York, 1952), 92.

[19] "Shaykevitsh," Leksikon fun yidishn teater, 1959 ed.

[20] *Odesskii vestnik* 28 Aug. 1880:1.

[21] Shomer-Batshelis, *Shomer*, 99.

[22] *Odesskii vestnik* 13 Sep. 1880:3.

[23] *Odesskii vestnik* 17 Sep. 1880:2.

[24] *Odesskii listok objavlenii* 30 Sep. 1880:2.

[25] *Odesskii vestnik* 16 Sep. 1880:2.

[26] *Odesskii vestnik* 24 Sep. 1880:2.

[27] *Odesskii vestnik* 5 Nov. 1880:1.

[28] *Vedomosti Odesskogo Gradonachalstva* 28 Oct. 1880:2.

[29] *Odesskii vestnik* 16 Oct. 1880:2.

[30] The text approved by the censor, dated 1880 (*Der kholem, a komedie in 4 aktn un 8 kartines*), is preserved in the Shomer-Archive at YIVO.

[31] *Odesskii listok* 5 Dec. 1880:2.

[32] The text approved by the censor, dated 1880 (*Der toes, a komedie in 4 aktn*), is preserved in the Shomer-Archive at YIVO.

[33] *Odesskii vestnik* 25 Dec. 1880:2.

[34] Ibid.

[35] Ibid.

[36] "Shaykevitsh," Leksikon fun yidishn teater, 1959 ed.

[37] Shomer-Batshelis, *Shomer*, 89.

[38] This play was also performed as *Di yesoymim* or *Di tsvey yesoymim*. The novel

Der baltshuve was first published in 1880 in Vilna. The play was never published; a censorship copy dated 1881 is preserved in the Shomer-Archive at YIVO.

[39] Presumably it is a typo – the correct name for this theater is Bavaria.

[40] Yankev Vaksman (1866-1942), Yiddish playright. In 1882, he joined a Jewish acting company and toured with it around provincial towns. See Y. Vaksman, in *Arkhiv far der geshikhte fun yidishn teater un drame*, 85.

[41] "Shaykevitsh," Leksikon fun yidishn teater, 1959 ed.

[42] *Der revizor* was published in 1883 in Odessa, but the work was obviously begun much earlier: in the Shomer-Archive at YIVO there is a censorship copy of *Zikh aleyn ongefayft, a komedie in 4 aktn, umgearbet fun dem rusishn oys oys der barimter pyese "Revizor,"* dated 1880.

[43] *Der neder* was never published. The manuscript and the censored texts, dated 1880 (*Der neder*) and 1882 (*Bas tsien, oder Der neder*), are preserved in the Shomer-Archive at YIVO.

[44] *Vedomosti Odesskogo Gradonachalstva* 3 Sep. 1881:2.

[45] *Odesskii vestnik* 23 May 1881:1.

[46] This letter is mentioned by Shaykevitsh's daughter Miriam. See Shomer-Zunzer, *Yesterday*, 179; compare with Shomer-Batshelis, *Shomer*, 93.

[47] This play is based on Shaykevitsh's novel, *Di Ayzerne froy oder dos farkoyfte kind*, published in 1882 in Vilna.

[48] *Der protsentnik* was never published. Two censorship copies, both dated 1880 (*Protsentnik* and *Der shkontist, a komedie in 5 aktn un 10 bilder*), are preserved in the Shomer-Archive at YIVO.

[49] Shomer-Batshelis, *Shomer*, 93. The play *Di kokete damen* was first published in Odessa in 1882.

[50] *Odesskii vestnik* 1 Jan. 1883:3.

[51] "Shaykevitsh," Leksikon fun yidishn teater, 1959 ed.

[52] *Suflyor* 24 Mar. 1883:3.

From "Little Man" to "Milkman": Does Jewish Art Reflect Jewish Life?

John D. Klier

The use of fiction as a conduit for the understanding of Jewish history has a solid pedigree.[1] In a famous article, the turn-of-the-century critic of Yiddish literature, David Frishman, praised the work of Mendele Mocher Sforim (S. I. Abramovich) for encompassing the entire spectrum of Jewish life in the squares and alleys of the small markets towns, or shtetls, of the Russian Empire in the first half of the nineteenth century. In words that were both prophetic and poignant, he claimed that "if a flood were to destroy all that mankind had created, leaving this one book, we should be quite capable of using it to reconstruct the overall picture of Jewish life and Jewishness in the small towns of Russia during the first half of the nineteenth century.... Not a detail is omitted."[2] Gerald Stillman shared this view, asserting that Mendele's work "presents a social history of the period which cannot be obtained from any history book."[3] Professor Maurice Friedberg speaks in almost identical terms of the work of Sholom Aleichem (S. Rabinovich) as "wondrously realistic social history" that tells us more about the economic life of East European Jewry than we learn "from the books of all the experts of that time—the historians, the economists, and the statisticians—taken together...Sholom Aleichem's writings enrich the scholarly histories of Jews in tsarist Russia—such as those of Simon Dubnow and Salo Baron— with sound and smell and color. They make their dry bones live."[4]

Impressive claims indeed! However, a warning signal has been sounded in a recent article by Professor Dan Miron of the Hebrew University of Jerusalem. He points us to another portrait of the shtetl, painted in the memoirs of Vulf Abramovich, the brother of Sholom Rabinovich. The shtetl is Voronkov, Sholom Aleichem's home town, which his artistry transformed into the archetypal Jewish shtetl of Kasrilovka. The picture which Vulf presents of youthful scrapes takes place in quite a different landscape from his brother's stories, for this is a town physically dominated by the local Christian church, which served as a focus and target for boyish mischief. As Miron observes, everything is present in Kasrilovka, except non-Jews. The shtetl of Jewish literature, called a *mestechko* or *posad* by its other inhabitants, has been "radically judaised." Once the shtetl has been turned into a purely Jewish landscape, it can be "sanitized, exposed as benighted or reactionary, soporific, resistant to initiative and innovation or, alternatively, portrayed nostalgically and romantically as the quintessence of spirituality and communal intimacy, the nucleus of a besieged civilisation that nevertheless enjoyed internal harmony and perfect internal communication."[5]

How can we best choose between these two divergent views: Is the shtetl located in a landscape or a dreamscape? Our answer is facilitated if we recall the argument in Miron's classic work on Yiddish literature, *A Traveller Disguised*. Miron points out that the first Yiddish-language chroniclers of the shtetl, with Abramovich in the lead, had turned to that language in order to publicize the ideals of the Jewish enlightenment movement, the Haskalah. The partisans of the movement, the *maskilim*, sought a radical transformation of the traditional community that surrounded them. Burdened as they were with a heavy ideological agenda, the literary works that they produced were not intended to follow the canons of literary realism any more than were those of Gogol or Dickens. Thus, *Fishke the Lame*, Benjamin the Third, or Mendele himself are as "real" as Gogol's Chichikov or Dickens' Mr. McCawber. Indeed, they are best seen as caricatures and grotesques, designed to entertain and, especially in Abramovich's case, to teach.[6] As Miron summarises, "Kabtsansk and Kasrilovke are poetic constructs informed by the ideologies of their time and shaped to fit the idiosyncratic visions of individual writers."[7]

Keeping in mind the need to recognize the author's perspective, we find that the classics of Eastern European Jewish literature are extremely eloquent, but not in the form of photographic or literal representations of a vanished world. Rather, they have much to tell us about the concerns of the contemporary Jewish artists and serve to illuminate the situation of Jews within the context of the surrounding Russian society. This thesis can be demonstrated by reference to two of the greatest Russian-Jewish writers, Sholem Iakov Abramovich (1836-1917) and Sholem Rabinovich (1859-1916). As the title of this essay suggests, it will focus on a number of representative works, ranging from Abramovich's *The Little Man* and *Fishke the Lame* to Rabinovich's later *Tevye the Dairyman*, *The Railway*

Stories, and *The Bloody Hoax.*[8] The emphasis is not on the literary qualities, but the ideology that underlies the work.[9]

S. I. Abramovich recounts how he began writing for the Jewish masses in pursuit of three goals: to teach them "science" (i.e., secular western learning) and good taste, to chose literary topics drawn from the life of the people themselves, and to offer guidance to a better, more useful life. These were, of course, the goals of the early Russian Haskalah, identified with writers such as I. B. Levinson. Under the influence of the Berlin Haskalah, the preferred language of the movement was Hebrew, written in the biblical style. Thus, Abramovich's first efforts were in Hebrew. He soon came to realize that any approach to the masses that hoped for success would have to take place in their vernacular language, the despised *zhargon* [Yiddish]. Moreover, this literature would have to center on the problems of day-to-day life rather than remote plots taken from biblical times. The decision to write in a "common," much-scorned tongue was not an easy one, especially for an author driven by elevated ideals.

Abramovich recalled his dilemma, torn between a desire to achieve literary recognition, and a determination to serve the Jewish masses:

> What profit accrues to a writer for all his work and thinking, if he does not serve his people....How great then was my dilemma when I considered that if I were to embark on writing in the "shameful" tongue, my honorable name would be besmirched....My love for utility, however, overcame my hollow pride, and I decided, come what may, I will write in Yiddish, that cast-off daughter, and work for the people....I fell in love with Yiddish and bound myself to that language forever. I found for her the perfumes and fragrances that she needed, and she became a charming lady who bore me many sons.[10]

The Jewish world that Abramovich confronted was not the solid and rooted Jewish world of popular imagining, but a world that was in the throes of socioeconomic upheavals. The emancipation of the peasantry from serfdom in the Russian Empire in 1861 initiated the destruction of the old, feudal, patriarchal economic system of the Russian countryside. In the Pale of Settlement, Jews were an integral part of the economy, serving as agents of the feudal economy inherited from the old Polish-Lithuanian Commonwealth. In particular, Jews served as the principal mercantile link between the town and the village. One economic undertaking in the Pale of Settlement, those areas of the Russian Empire where most Jews were required by law to live, was quintessentially Jewish: the trade in spirits. To be sure, the distillation and sale of vodka was a state monopoly, but the messy details themselves were leased to Jewish tavern keepers. The non-Jewish townsmen, and the flood of peasants who arrived in the shtetl on market days, would have encountered the Jews as the buyers of their harvest and livestock, and the purveyors of goods and services. A day of trade was customarily followed by a visit to the tavern, and its Jewish proprietor.

The abolition of serfdom did not cause this world, and its set of relationships, to vanish over-night. Nonetheless, the winds of change sweeping over Russian were felt by all, and prescient contemporaries were well aware of the challenges that lay ahead. The Jewish journalist and historian Il'ia Orshanskii, writing in 1869, appreciated the negative implications of the modernizing economy for the Jews. He warned that "the impoverished situation of our co-religionists in Russia is a transitory phenomenon, a temporary one, and will be eliminated to the degree that Jewry adapts itself to new structures of life, forgetting old trades and occupations which are now obsolete, and learning new ones."[11]

Orshanskii was a commentator, not a prophet, and he was unable to foresee the role of outside forces, such as regional variations in the speed of change, the pace of industrialization, the changing face of Russian agriculture, or officially imposed economic restraints that were to befall the Jewish population. Nor was he fully aware of the demographic explosion that would elevate the Jewish population of the Empire from approximately 800,000 in 1800 to over five million by century's end.[12]

The consequence of these diverse forces was the growing pauperisation of the Jewish population throughout the Empire. A decade after Orshanskii's article, an article in the Russian-Jewish newspaper *Nedel'naia khronika Voskhoda* lamented the poverty of the Jews of Pinsk, who had heretofore made a living through the grain trade and navigation on the rivers Pin and Dneper. The newly constructed Kiev-Brest railroad had deprived many of them of their livelihood.[13] It was a lament that was to find frequent echo. A new Jewish type now took center stage, the *Luftmensch*, who made his living out of thin air.

Orshanskii wrote at almost the same moment as Abramovich published his novel *Fishke the Lame*, with its searing portrait of poverty and beggary in the Jewish world. It was left to the remnants of the traditional, semiautonomous Jewish community [the *kahal*] to confront this phenomenon, represented by the legions of itinerant beggars who arrived seeking charity. In the eyes of Abramovich and other *maskilim*, the *kahal*, and all the traditional institutions of Jewish life were abject failures in dealing with this situation. The task was to offer Jewish society a critique of this failure.[14]

Thus, Abramovich's focus is the corrupt world of the communal leadership of "Foolstown" or "Idlersville." He depicts the leaders of the *kahal* as corrupt and self-servingmen, who no longer even pretend to serve the interests of anyone save the communal elite. Still worse are the leaders of the various brotherhoods, especially the Burial Society [the *khevrah kaddisha*], who use their power to terrorize the community with the threat of a "donkey's burial" and who charge exorbitant burial fees even for the poor. The communal leaders are especially condemned for the mal-administration of the government-mandated kosher meat tax [the *korobochka* tax], which numerous critics denounced as unfairly applied and corruptly administered. The small amounts of money that trickle down for the use of the community, moreover, are expended on institutions that harm rather than help the community. At the top of Abramovich's list is the *heder* [the traditional Jewish school for boys]. Rather than educating young boys for any useful and productive life, the *maskilim* complained, it inculcated useless knowledge and harmful superstitions, all in a physical environment that undermined the young scholars' health.[15]

In the economic realm, the communal leadership were guilty of complete apathy towards the chronic poverty of Jewish society. If anything, by sponsoring a system of charity, they were seen to encourage the itinerant beggary described in *Fishke the Lame*. Abramovich's clear message is that ignorance is the mother of poverty and destitution, and that the latter are not an inescapable burden sent by God, but social ills susceptible to human remedies, if only the will is present. Mendele Moykher-Sforim, Abramovich's narrator, lacked Orshanskii's awareness that change was in the air. Indeed, his very profession, that of itinerant book peddler, was one soon to be rendered obsolete by the appearance of a modern communications infrastructure, with the railways leading the way. The peddler, along with the fairs that were so much a part of his life, was unknowingly facing extinction.

It is noteworthy that the city, even that quintessential "nest of Jewry" like Odessa—an engine of economic growth and commercial success for Jews in the future—appears as a remote and alienating place for Abramovich's characters. To the rustic Fishke, for example, Odessa offers no sense of place. The streets are broad and regular, unlike the mud-clogged byways of the shtetl. They are populated by shaven men and unshaven women. Most scandalous of all, to his practiced eye as a former bath-house keeper, the ritual baths of Odessa are clean and sanitary: how can they possibly be kosher? Nor would Fishke, had he been aware of its existence, approved of the progressive Jewish school in Odessa that was Abramovich's chief means of support. The author could not hope to earn his daily bread from his pen.

To Abramovich, even when writing in the 1860s in progressive Odessa, the goals of the Haskalah appeared far distant. *The Little Man*, in fact, ends with a call for his readers to seek out the symbolic *maskil*, "Mr. Gutman." Those *maskilim* who do appear in Abramovich's chronicles are invariably marginalised figures. There is more than a touch of irony in Abramovich's description of Fishke's wonderment at the progress of a *maskil* around the streets of Odessa seeking to sell his books from door to door—an urban Mendele Moykher-Sforim. Unlike Mendele, who invariably receives a joyous welcome from his customers, the *maskil* finds doors slammed in his face. Abramovich was writing when the Russian Haskalah had already matured into a movement rather than the earlier efforts of a few lone wolves, but it still had far to go to touch the hearts and minds of most Russian Jews.[16]

What a contrast appears when we transverse the three decades that separate Abramovich's "Little Man" of 1864 from the first appearance of Rabinovich's "Tevye the Milkman" in 1894. The changes only hinted at in the former have come to maturity in the latter, a maturity that may be witnessed in the position of Yiddish literature itself. Rabinovich felt no need to apologize for writing in Yiddish. Far from being the outcast daughter of Abramovich's analogy, he depicts Yiddish as a national treasure, an integral part of Jewish culture. The self-esteem of Jewish culture itself was more deeply rooted, as will be noted below, and Rabinovich's concerns were far removed from the didactic preoccupations of Abramovich.

The physical world of Rabinovich's literary imaginings reveals that the changes only hinted at in his predecessor's work have come fully to fruition. It is a recognizably modern world. Indeed, the narrative action of one cycle of stories, appropriately known as the *Railway Stories*, occurs entirely in a third-class railway carriage.[17] The opening scene of *The Bloody Hoax* is set in a restaurant, under "the newly-invented electric light." At one point the novel's heroine is saved from rape by the opportune interruption of a telephone call.[18] Another feature of this world is often overlooked in exploring Rabinovich's creativity: the role of the modern periodical press. Both authors wrote their works in serialized forms for the Yiddish press. But Rabinovich also had access to a host of modern newspapers in Yiddish, Hebrew, and Russian, in which the events of the day were readily at hand. (An extreme example is *The Bloody Hoax*, which Rabinovich was writing in installments even as the Beilis trial was reported in the press.) As a consequence, his works are much more topical than Abramovich's.

The cultural changes revealed in his oeuvre are just as noteworthy. Rabinovich's characters switch easily from Yiddish to Russian and even make Russian verbs out of Yiddish words: *akhamesovali* from *khometz* "to make ritually unclean." (This is not just a Rabinovich fancy: I have found a similar process at work in official Russian, where the report of a police investigation casually uses the word *shabashovat'*; i.e., to be someone's guest for the Sabbath, or *shabbos*.)[19] Real people are woven into Rabinovich's narrative, such as the anti-Semitic politician N. V. Purishkevich, the prominent Zionist leader Dr. Max Mandelshtam, and the near-legendary family of Jewish millionaires, the Brodskys, the Kiev sugar barons. Tevye "makes a fortune" by selling dairy products to the nouveau riche Jews who spend their holidays at country dachas. He just as quickly loses it through the stock market speculations of his cousin Menachim Mendel. (This was a fate that befell Rabinovich himself.) Tevye's daughter Hodl is exiled to Siberia with her Jewish revolutionary husband. Beilke becomes the unhappy wife of a wealthy and irreligious contractor, a type thrown up by emergent Russian capitalism and comparable to the merchant class characters of the Russian playwright A. N. Ostrovskii.

Contemporary events continually intrude, such as the Dreyfus Affair and pogroms, including one that is forestalled when the undependable local train, "the straggler special," is late. *The Bloody Hoax* is a literary retelling of the contemporary Beilis ritual murder trial in Kiev. The *heder* is no longer the focus of educational aspirations for Jews. Rather, it is the Russian commercial school, the "Gym-na-zi-um" of the tale of the same name. Tevye quotes Russian proverbs along with his mangled pearls of Talmudic wisdom. It is a world of change and, above all, of mobility. As Tevye says, "Today, Pani Sholom Aleichem, we met on the train, but tomorrow may find us in Yehupetz, and next year in Odessa, or in Warsaw, and maybe even in America."[20]

The setting of Rabinovich's fiction, especially his later stories, is now recognizably Russian, even when the action is concentrated in the shtetl, into which the external world keeps intruding, like the railway train with its passenger-load of *pogromshchiki*. As Dan Miron observes:

> The internal Jewish arena—which in most of the more typical shtetl stories (where the shtetl is sometimes portrayed as a type of autonomous Jewish state) contained all meaningful relations and interactions—is now replaced by another one, the "extrinsic" world of the train….The protagonists of the *Railway Stories* constantly need to deal with Russian bureaucrats, policemen, members of military draft boards, anti-Semitic principals and teachers of Russian secondary schools, doctors, attorneys, even priests.[21]

The Bloody Hoax in fact is very much an urban novel, not uncommon in Russian (as in the Petersburg of Dostoevsky's imagining), but heretofore rarely encountered in Yiddish or seen as a place of mystery and danger. The city of Kiev is itself virtually a character in the novel, with its stock exchange, theatre, university, cafes where stock-jobbers meet, and even the municipal prison. The concerns that dominate the life of its Jewish population, such as the obsessive quest for a *pravozhitelstvo* [residence permit], are very contemporary.

Most importantly, Rabinovich confronts problems of self-identity which are totally absent in the work of Abramovich, who viewed the world very much in terms of Us (the Jews) and Them (the non-Jewish population). If for the *maskil* Abramovich the Jews were too Jewish, for Rabinovich, writing within and for a modernizing society, the Jews were becoming too Russian. The damage done by the wiles of cultural assimilation are everywhere on display. Thus, the story "Ritual Fringes" has as its premise a Jew who lights a samovar on the Sabbath, eats meat on the solemn fast day of Tisha b'Av, fails to kosher his Passover dishes, and is denounced as a "pork lover," "the beardless one," and a "heretic."[22] Abramovich, in *Mottel the Cantor's Son*, chronicles one of the most striking features of Jewish life at the *fin de siècle*, mass trans-Atlantic migration.

Yet, while Jews have begun the painful processes of acculturation and integration, reciprocity has not been forthcoming from the Russian community. One of the most telling scenes in *The Bloody Hoax* depicts the Jewish population of Kiev camped out at the railroad station in flight from a threatened pogrom in the wake of a ritual murder accusation. Suddenly the night is filled with the ringing of bells. The Jews are terrified that this signals a pogrom, until they suddenly realize that it is Easter and the bells are signaling the beginning of the most joyous celebration of the Christian church calendar.[23]

The dilemma, then, is two-sided: How can the Jews retain their self-identity when faced with the twinned pressures of assimilation and anti-Semitism? A scene at the start of the academic year at St. Vladimir University in Kiev provides a graphic illustration. Like all the higher educational institutions of the Empire, the university has a Jewish quota. The percentage is fixed, but the exact number to be admitted in any given year is dependent upon the total number of non-Jewish students enrolled. Faced with exclusion, one of the Jewish students, Lapidus, converts to Christianity to gain admission. His new status is symbolized by the toy-like ceremonial sword that is part of his student uniform.[24] This scene is certainly drawn from life; after the introduction of the *numerus clausus* in 1887, the Russian press regularly carried reports of qualified Jewish students who had been denied admission and later reappeared at university registries with a baptismal certificate, claiming admission. In 1888, two conservative and judeophobe newspapers, *Grazhdanin* and *Novoe vremia*, conducted a polemic on the quality and sincerity of the Christians thus produced.[25]

The renegade Lapidus, while not portrayed as irredeemably evil and more ridiculous than malevolent, is nonetheless the most negative character in *The Bloody Hoax*. The secret policeman-rapist is at least capable of shame. Lapidus is so eager to ingratiate himself with Christian society that, even after having been beaten up by anti-Semites in search of a token Jew upon whom to vent their wrath, he writes to the pogrom-mongering local newspaper offering to provide information on the Jews' use of blood. "How did our people ever produce such a creature? That's what makes it so sad," observes one character in response.[26] Rabinovich clearly sympathizes with the words of the student Tumarkin, who has also been rejected by the admissions office but recoils in horror at the very idea of betrayal via the baptismal font:

> Comrades! When I speak of those people who have abandoned everything that is holy, those who are prepared to sell their own souls, a fire ignites within me and I haven't enough words with which to damn them....Some wish to defend these people...as it

is written in our Talmud, Judge not they friend until thou hast stood in his place. If those who desert us at such a bitter time in their own self-interest or to further their careers do sometimes deserve our sympathy, the apologists who defend them are not worth the earth they walk on! And if our downtrodden, rebuffed people is obliged to maintain its Jewishness even more strongly in such bitter times, then we, the youth, are certainly obliged to do so!²⁷

The plot of *The Bloody Hoax* revolves around two students, a Christian and a Jew, who trade identities, so as to test the former's claim that the Jews do not live badly in Russia. The imposter trades his unmistakably Russian, clerical name, Popov, for the quintessentially Jewish name Rabinovich (which, as we recall, is Sholom Aleichem's real name). The humor derives from the fact that, while he comes to respect the Jewish world, Popov-Rabinovich cannot fully comprehend its logic and mores. He is unable to avoid acting like a Russian when placed in "Jewish" situations, perfectly illustrating the Yiddish proverb, "like a *goy* in a *sukkah*." Thus, he is unwilling to tolerate rudeness from a policeman who calls him a "Yid": "He sprang from the carriage and headed straight for the policeman to discuss philology with him." Likewise, he belligerently objects when the police conduct a midnight search of his quarters, instead of behaving in the meek and mild way expected of any Jew.²⁸ In many ways Popov-Rabinovich is a wish-figure: a rooted, physically brave, self-confident individual who is willing to stand up for himself, in contrast to Jewish self-abnegation and passivity. When his landlord's son, Syomke, is beaten up, Popov-Rabinovich explodes "like a provoked animal." Syomke's father explains:

> What advice can you give me? I already know what you'll say—..."self-respect," "honor." I know it, believe me as well as you. You are absolutely right. It's humiliating, especially when they attack a child who is totally without blame....But we mustn't forget that we are Jews and that we live in a bitter time. It will pass, believe me, it will pass. There will come a time when they'll regret it. You'll see. And Syomke? Well, with God's help he will grow up and forget. As I am a Jew, he'll forget. We have a saying, "it will heal by the time of the wedding."²⁹

Popov-Rabinovich can only wonder in response that they are "a strange people these Jews, with a strange psychology!"[30] Such concerns are a world away from those of Abramovich, with his sense of national self-deprecation. His Jews are no more than victims, a mere "nag" to be beaten and abused as part of the natural order of things. The mindset of Jews in Abramovich's works, in contrast, is to be silent out of a sense of moral superiority over the boisterous "sons of Ham."

The objective of this essay has been to explore the value of the classics of pre-revolutionary Jewish fiction as "wondrously realistic social history." My conclusion confirms that it can serve this function, but with the proviso that literature best reveals the internal Jewish world and its evolving preoccupations and values, rather than serving as a precise documentary chronicle of Jewish life as lived in the Russian Empire. In short, fiction reveals how Jews thought they lived, as opposed to how they really lived. Let us recall what is missing. The "radical judaization" of the shtetl strips away its broader social context. The literary geography on display offers no sense of Jewish-Gentile interaction, although this must have been the daily experience of every Jew. Well-developed gentile characters, with a few striking exceptions, are missing from Rabinovich's archetypal shtetl, Kasrilevke. When, in the story "The Great Panic of the Little People," the Jewish residents of Kasrilevke temporarily abandon the shtetl, the author tells us that "the village had become deserted, forlorn as a graveyard. Not a soul remained."[31] Yet it takes only an observant eye to populate the shtetl with non-Jews. There are gentiles who form part of Jewish households, such as Fyodor, the *shabbos goy*, and Pockmarked Hapke, who "talked Yiddish as though it was her mother tongue,"[32] and the "swarthy Lithuanian maid" of Mordecai-Nossen, the rich merchant. Russian authorities—the postmaster, the police chief, and Makar Khalodne, the municipal clerk who is the shtetl's resident anti-Semite—hover in the background. And where are Mordecai-Nossen's customers, most of whom, we are told, were Christians?[33] They, like all non-Jews, appear only in passing.

Where, in particular, is that centerpiece of Jewish economic life in the village, the tavern? Jewish characters pop in and out of them, but it is invariably their resident bedbugs, not their role as "Jewish space," that attracts the narrator's attention. As Magdalena Opalski has demonstrated, it was left to Polish fiction to explore the diverse and mythic world of the Jewish tavern.[34]

With its critical and didactic intentions, Jewish fiction often paints a misleading portrait of Jewish life, such as the generalized portrait of women running the family business, while their feckless men folk pray, study and gossip.³⁵ Indeed, one of the achievements of Rabinovich is to create in Tevye the milkman what the jargon of the time would call "an authentic Jewish working class hero," who, let it be noted, is engaged in productive labor. And if the men folk of Jewish fiction are overly stereotypical, what can we say about the caricatures which pass as women? They are either foul-mouthed shrews or idealized young maidens.³⁶ Only at the turn of the century, under the influence of more naturalistic trends in Russian literature, do we begin to encounter the missing figures of Jewish life, the horse thieves, smugglers, and bandits—and even female Jewish revolutionaries. This trend, in fact, can be said to represent another kind of cultural integration.

Jewish fiction can best serve to provide snapshots of a moment or milestones on the path of modern Jewish history. Thus, Abramovich and Rabinovich portray two sharply contrasted Jewish worlds whose shapes are formed from their entirely different set of concerns. One (Abramovich) sees the Jews as too far removed from the cultural values of the wider society, while the other (Rabinovich) laments Jewish malleability when faced with the lures and demands of Russian society.

In a recent talk the Israeli Hebrew-language author David Grossman recalled his childhood enchantment with the world of Sholom Aleichem and the feeling of kinship that his works created in him. These works provided a tunnel from modern Israel to a parallel universe inhabited by Tevye and his friends and family in Eastern Europe. If we use this intellectual passage carefully, employing context and empathy as our guides, Jewish literature can indeed bring us greetings from the past. To quote Tevye, as he bids good-bye to his creator: "Be well and have a good trip. Say hello for me to all our Jews and tell them wherever they are, not to worry: the old God of Israel still lives!"³⁷

NOTES

[1] Iris Parush, "The Politics of Literacy: Women and Foreign Languages in Jewish Society of Nineteenth-Century Eastern Europe," *Modern Judaism,* 15 (1995):183-206.
[2] Gerald Stillman, "Introduction," in *Selected Works of Mendele Moykher-Sforim* (Malibu, 1991), 16.

[3] Ibid.

[4] Maurice Friedberg, "Introduction," in Sholem Aleichem, *The Bloody Hoax*, (trans. Aliza Shevrin; Bloomington and Indianapolis, 1991), ix.

[5] Dan Miron, *The Image of the Shtetl* (Syracuse, 2000), 4.

[6] Dan Miron, *A Traveller Disguised: A Study in the Rise of Modern Yiddish Fiction in the Nineteenth Century* (New York, 1973). For an example drawn from Hebrew-language Jewish literature, see David Patterson, *The Hebrew Novel in Czarist Russia: A Portrait of Jewish Life in the Nineteenth Century* 2nd ed. (Lanhan; 1999); and David Aberbach, *Realism, caricature, and bias: the fiction of Mendele Mocher Sefarim* (London, 1993).

[7] Miron, *Image*, 9.

[8] It is hardly possible to establish a canonical version of these works, especially for Abramovich, since they were often written and rewritten, as well as recast from Yiddish into Hebrew. Thus, versions of *The Little Man* date from 1864, 1865, 1866, 1879, and 1907. Rabinovich's *Tevye* and *Railroad Stories* were both written over a decade, while his novelist treatment of the Beilis Affair, *The Bloody Hoax*, is better known in its dramatic form of "Hard to Be a Jew" [*Shver tzu zayd a yid*]. I use the following English versions: Marvin Zuckerman, et al., eds., *Selected Works of Mendele Moykher-Sforim* (Malibu, 1991); Sholem Aleichem, *The Bloody Hoax* (trans. Aliza Shevrin; Bloomington, 1991); Marvin Zuckerman and Marion Herbst, *Selected Works of Sholem-Aleykhem* (Malibu, 1994); Sholom Aleichem, *Old Country Tales* (trans. Curt Levant; New York, 1999).

[9] I am consciously using the given names of the two authors rather than their pseudonyms as is usually the practice, since the pseudonyms themselves have become part of the myth of Jewish literature. As Miron has shown, it is sometimes difficult to separate Abramovich the writer from his fictional creation Mendele.

[10] Zuckerman, *Selected Works of Mendele Moykher-Sforim*, 41-42.

[11] *Den'*, 15:22/VIII/1869.

[12] See *Evreiskoe naselenie Rossii po dannym perepisi 1897 g. I po noveishim istochnikam* (Petrograd, 1917).

[13] *Den'*, 42:16/X/1882.

[14] Technically, the autonomous Jewish community, the *kahal*, had been abolished by the Russian government in 1844. In fact, most of its institutions remained in place and were still functioning. For one example, see John D. Klier, *Russkaia voina protiv 'Khevra kadisha'* [The Russian War against the Khevrah kaddisha], in D. A. El'iashevich, *Istoriia Evreev v Rossii: Problemy Istochnikovedeniia I Istoriografii* (St. Petersburg, 1993), 109-15. A more comprehensive study is found in Isaac Levitats, *The Jewish Community in Russia, 1844-1917* (Jerusalem, 1983).

[15] Technically, the *heder* was a private school, organized in their own homes by teachers, or *melamdim*. Community taxes supported a charity *heder*, the *Talmud Tora*. In practice, Mendele makes no distinction between the two types of traditional schools, which had identical curricula. See the discussion in Steven J. Zipperstein, *Imagining Russian Jewry: Memory, History, Identity* (Seattle and London), 41-62.

[16] See Michael Stanislawski, *Tsar Nicholas I and the Jews: The Transformation of Jewish Society in Russia, 1825-1855* (Philadelphia, 1983); and the essays in *New Perspectives on the Haskalah* (ed. Shmuel Feiner and David Sorkin; London, 2001).

[17] Abramovich does use the railroad as the setting for one of his stories, "Shem and Japheth on the Train," but it serves only as background and is presented as a novelty. Zuckerman, *Selected Works of Mendele Moykher-Sforim*, 375-96.

[18] Sholem Aleichem, *The Bloody Hoax*, 3, 184.

[19] *Istoricheskii Arkhiv Ukranini-Kiev*, fond 442, opis 158, delo 1064 (1847), ll. 1-12.

[20] Zuckerman, *Selected Works of Sholem-Aleykhem*, 377.

[21] Miron, *Image*, 278.

[22] Sholem Aleichem, *Old Country Tales*, 226-33.

[23] Sholem Aleichem, *Bloody Hoax*, 160-63.

[24] Ibid., 62.

[25] For a summary of the debate, see *Novoe vremia*, 4498:6/IX/1888 and 4501:9/IX/1888.

[26] Sholem Aleichem, *Bloody Hoax*, 339-40.

[27] Ibid., 27-28.

[28] Ibid., 158, 38.

[29] Ibid., 115.

[30] Ibid.

[31] Sholem Aleichem, *Old Country Tales*, 119.

[32] A proper study remains to be done on language use in mixed Jewish-Ukrainian communities. There are numerous indications that many non-Jews spoke some Yiddish.

[33] Sholem Aleichem, *Old Country Tales*, 102-13.

[34] Magdalena Opalski, *The Jewish Tavern-Keeper and His Tavern in Nineteenth-Century Polish Literature* (Jerusalem, 1986).

[35] Tova Cohen, "Reality and Its Refraction in Descriptions of Women in Haskalah Fiction," in *New Perspectives on the Haskalah* (ed. Shmuel Feiner and David Sorkin; Littman Library; London and Portland, 2001), 144-65. As Cohen points out,

this lifestyle was restricted to a small elite, the *lomedim* [scholar] circles.

[36] Ibid., 145.

[37] Zuckerman, *Selected Works of Sholem-Aleykhem*, 377.

The Politics of Philanthropy: Migration, Emigration, and the Transformation of Jewish Communal Governance in Bialystok, 1885-1939

Rebecca Kobrin

In 1907, after visiting Bialystok, a small city on the western edge of the Pale of Settlement. Zvi Hirsch Masliansky, itinerant preacher and noted speaker of New York's Lower East Side Educational Alliance remarked:

> If Vilna was "City and Mother among Israel," then Bialystok was "City and Daughter in Israel." Bialystok was not as large or as old as Vilna nor was it known for its *geonim* [wise men] or *maskilim* [enlightened thinkers], universities, or old historic cemeteries....Bialystok was a new city, known throughout the world for its textile manufacturing, celebrated as the center of [the revolutionary] "Hibbat Zion" movement [and] renowned for its charitable organizations whose kindness was a model for other cities....In sum, if Vilna was Jerusalem of Lithuania then Bialystok was Jaffa of Lithuania—[like the first] new settlement in our land.[1]

Indeed, Bialystok shared several notable traits with Jaffa, Palestine's burgeoning new port, as both places owed their growth to the influx of Jewish migrants who brought with them a pioneering spirit that not only built new industries, political parties, and social-welfare organizations, but also redefined the contours of Jewish communal life in each of these growing cities. Although many are familiar with the role Jewish migrant pioneers played in Jaffa's development, far fewer are cognizant of the equally critical role Jewish migrants played in the development of nineteenth century Polish urban life, where they revolutionized local economic and political life [fig. 1].

While only 2,000 Jews lived in Bialystok in 1807, by the late nineteenth century Jews comprised over seventy-five percent of the city's 62,993 residents.[2] As Jews streamed into this city, they not only enjoyed economic opportunity and stimulated economic expansion; they also faced long periods of unemployment. These economic hardships encouraged the development of new Jewish welfare and philanthropic organizations that, as Masliansky suggested by mentioning them in the same breath as the revolutionary Zionist movement, were innovative institutions that fundamentally redefined Jewish communal life.[3]

Periods of severe economic recession also pushed thousands of Jews to decide to leave this city between 1870 and 1914.[4] Despite the vast oceans often separating these Jewish émigrés from their former home, they remained in close contact with Bialystok through philanthropic organizations that regularly sent remittances to their former home. The intensity of émigrés' financial commitment to their former home after World War I prompted Pesach Kaplan, editor of Bialystok's largest Yiddish newspaper *Dos naye lebn* [The New Life], to proclaim in 1925: "Bialystok is unique," not only as a result of "its populace" but more importantly because "wherever there are a few Bialystoker Jews, regardless of their number, they immediately organize themselves into a colony, [in order to] remain connected to their beloved motherland" and support it in its time of need.[5] With loyal subjects scattered throughout the world dedicated to its financial maintenance, Bialystok, in Kaplan's eyes, was akin to an "imperial center." Émigré philanthropy had prodded Jews still living in Bialystok to rethink the contours of Jewish communal life, imagining themselves at the center of a new transnational political entity.

Despite Kaplan's claims of uniqueness, Bialystok was by no means exceptional or unusual: Jewish migration, both within the Russian Empire and beyond its geographic borders, transformed Jewish communal life and politics throughout Eastern Europe in the late nineteenth and early twentieth centuries.[6] These mass population shifts had a profoundly unsettling effect on Russian-Jewish society as Jewish migrants founded new revolutionary organizations to address their needs. While many have considered the role tsarist policies played in the diminution of *kehilla* authority—the traditional authority in nineteenth century Russian-Jewish society—few have adequately queried the ways in which the strains caused by internal Jewish migration informed this political transformation.[7] How, and in what ways, did the profound population shifts of the late nineteenth century influence existing systems of control and authority?[8]

The Politics of Philanthropy

What types of challenges did Jewish migrants and Jewish émigrés present to local Jewish communal authorities as well as the larger state?

While few have looked at migration, in recent years much attention has been paid to the challenges facing traditional authorities in late imperial Russian-Jewish society, with studies on Zionism or the Bund[9] garnering the lion's share of scholars attention.[10] Whereas the Bund and Zionism mobilized a new Jewish politic in one arena, the following case study, of two philanthropic organizations in Bialystok founded by migrants, illustrates how new charitable organizations were equally crucial in challenging traditional systems of authority, creating additional grounds for political instability, democratizing systems of Jewish communal governance, and provoking the restructuring of Jewish communal life.[11] Time and space do not allow for a full discussion of the central role philanthropic organizations played in East European Jewish communal life. Suffice it to say that, by the turn of the century, philanthropists increasingly became seen as powerful political actors, and, as Derek Penslar notes, "the application of Jewish power was primarily economic in nature."[12] *Linas Hatsedek*, a medical aid organization founded in Bialystok by acculturated Jewish migrants in 1885, and the Bialystoker Center, a charity established by Bialystoker Jewish émigrés in New York in 1919, vividly highlight not only the ways in which philanthropy became a key arena for Jews to exercise power and debate their relationship with the larger society, but also how philanthropic organizations were used by a new cadre of Jewish elites, created through such venues as entrepreneurship or the Imperial university, to gain influence in the Jewish community.[13] Operating alongside the traditional leaders of the community, who were rabbinic authorities or wealthy, the leaders of these new communal welfare agencies transformed philanthropy from a bastion of conservative politics into a revolutionary force, fundamentally altering how Jews in Bialystok envisioned the contours of their communal identities and engaged political authorities.[14]

WELFARE REFORM AND JEWISH COMMUNAL POLITICS IN LATE IMPERIAL RUSSIA

Bialystok's rapid economic expansion in the nineteenth century was fueled by reports of economic opportunity; yet, this city, like other developing industrial centers in Eastern Europe, also experienced periods of acute economic recession.[15] Bialystok became a central transit point in the Russian railway's Warsaw-St. Petersburg route in 1859, enabling Jews to stream into the city.[16] Aside from promoting the city's demographic expansion, the Jewish population grew thirty fold, the hundreds of Jews who flooded the city fueled industrial expansion: while only eighty-nine textile mills existed in Bialystok in 1867, by 1898, 372 operated in the city, of which eighty percent were owned by Jews.[17] Jews constituted nearly eighty-four percent of the factory work force and comprised eighty-eight percent of the city's shopkeepers.[18]

Business was seasonal. As personal memoirs and reports of the *gubernia* [district] governor narrate, it was also quite commonplace, despite economic opportunity, for Jewish migrant newcomers to lose their jobs in slack times. Max Pogorelsky, a young man who arrived in Bialystok in the 1880s, recalled that after being unemployed for several months, he finally was offered a job where "I would work from seven in the morning until eight in the evening. Before holidays, I worked the entire night and for all this, I earned only two rubles a week after six months."[19] Under such circumstances, it was not surprising that Jewish migrant workers often found themselves mired in poverty and were almost totally dependant on charity for survival.[20]

Since the tsarist empire did not maintain an official welfare policy or system of public relief, Bialystok's poor, as in almost every city in the empire, were cared for by a dense array of public and private institutions that received support primarily from wealthy individuals and some funding from the state and municipal authorities.[21] In theory, the *kehilla*, the local Jewish communal authority, was ultimately responsible for dispensing charity and addressing Jewish migrants' needs. Even after the Tsar's official abolition of the *kehilla* in 1844, this institution still exerted great power in the community as a legal authority and as a regulator of religious and charitable affairs.[22] A critical source for its authority was its exclusive right to serve as the intermediary between the Jewish community and the secular powers.[23]

As events in Bialystok suggest, by the late nineteenth century, the *kehilla*'s inability to address the needs of the growing number of Jewish migrants, both indigent Jews and rapidly acculturating Jews who had come to Bialystok in search of opportunity and status, compromised the *kehilla*'s position in the community, prompting the wealthier and more acculturated Jewish migrants to establish their own competing organizations. These new charitable organizations often operated outside of the *kehilla*'s purview.[24] Once the *kehilla*'s monopoly on power was broken by these new organizations, tsarist authorities began consulting other internally unsanctioned groups within Jewish society, unleashing a contest for power within Russian-Jewish society that, as Benjamin Nathans argues, defined Russian-Jewish history for much of the next century.[25]

The proliferation of these new charitable organizations must also be seen in the context of late nineteenth century Russian welfare reform.[26] Beginning in the 1880s, as part of a larger reform effort, the tsarist state grew increasingly concerned over the governance of Jewish communal welfare and expressed a great interest in regulating Jewish voluntary welfare associations. Tsarist authorities began to see the unsupervised activities of traditional Jewish charitable organizations as suspect and demanded their reorganization as part of their effort to combat "Jewish isolation" and the Jewish community's oligarchic governance.[27] With these goals in mind, tsarist authorities encouraged Jewish communities to reorganize and centralize their communal and welfare services by abolishing traditional Jewish associations [*hevrot*] and replacing them with modern voluntary associations [*obshchestvo*].[28]

As a result, there was a rapid proliferation of Jewish charitable organizations: the editor of *Khronika Voshkoda* observed in 1899 that there were numerous "Societies to Aid to Poor" springing up "all over the place, in every community," directly challenging the authority of old Jewish societies and the "notables" who ran them.[29] As Khronika Voshkoka reported, these notables, who were notorious for their corruption resisted giving up their power, and conflicts ensued between older *hevrot* and these newer organizations. In several larger cities, like Bialystok, these modern voluntary associations became the bastion of a younger, secular-educated cadre of Jewish leaders who studied in other cities or migrated from afar and were attracted to participating in Jewish organizations that openly identified with the larger Russian society, as exemplified by their use of Russian-language names. These young men sought to challenge the traditional authority figures, who often had exclusive access to *korobka* funds [the kosher meat tax], a major source of funding and power in most Jewish communities.[30]

As they strove to insert themselves in Russian society, acculturating Jews saw philanthropy as serving not only the needs of the Jewish poor but, also their own needs as new Jewish elites who deserved greater recognition in the community. These Jews, who were lawyers, doctors and industrialists, hoped these new voluntary associations would both serve as a vehicle for empowerment and provide them with a means to put forth their agenda: integration into the surrounding society. This goal, they believed, would be best achieved through philanthropic organizations, since such institutions could effectively convey that the true face of Judaism and Jews was caring for all, regardless of faith, and clearly demonstrate Jews' commitment to the advancement of the multi-national Russian Empire.[31]

"THEIR KINDNESS WAS A MODEL FOR ALL": PHILANTHROPY, MIGRANT WELFARE AND THE CREATION OF A NEW CADRE OF JEWISH LEADER

Typical of these new types of social welfare organizations founded in this era of migration and reform was the self-help and medical aid organization *Linas Hatsedek* [literally, To Lodge the Righteous], established in Bialystok in 1885. This organization distinguished itself from the outset by organizing itself in a "democratic" manner, allowing both men and women to participate in its elections, demanding that all its members, regardless of income, serve equally, and tending to the needs of both Jews and Gentiles. Moreover, in their governance of this new self-help organization, the migrant founders of *Linas Hatsedek* articulated a new vision for the place of Jewish organizations in Russia's multinational society, openly challenging *kehilla* leaders who maintained a telescopic and exclusivist approach to Jewish philanthropy.

The founding myths concerning the impetus to establish *Linas Hatsedek* demonstrate how a new cadre of leaders reacted to the inadequate response of the *kehilla* to the pressing needs of the new Jewish urban poor in order to gain power in the community. According to one story, a neglected migrant Jew living alone in 1885 was bitten by rats and died. His tragic death prodded members of the community to found a new organization to care for the ill members of the working class because *Bikur Holim*, the *kehilla*-sponsored organization charged with this task, was run by a "despotic dictator" who did not tend to those poor ill workers in need.[32] A less gruesome tradition links the founding of *Linas Hatsedek* to the death of Meyer Szochet, a hospital attendant, who fell ill and died because of neglect. At Szochet's funeral, a group of Jews, whose families remained behind in smaller towns, established *Linas Hatsedek* to make sure that no other ill Jew in Bialystok would ever find himself in a similar situation.[33] Both versions are apocryphal, yet they sum up, as such tales often do, the main concerns and central facts of the case: in Bialystok, a city filled with poor Jewish migrants living apart from their families, the fear of falling ill and dying because of lack of care was paralyzing.

While indigent migrant Jewish workers feared dying alone, acculturated Jewish newcomers to the city, such as Joseph Chazanowicz, who gave critical support to this organization in its formative years, were concerned by the growing health problems of Jewish migrant workers. Russian Jews were often singled out in popular literature and the press for their poor health, and growing poverty among Jews often made that reputation well deserved. The crowded and unsanitary conditions of the city only made things worse. For acculturated Jews seeking to put a positive face on the Jewish community for the larger Russian society, sickly Jewish masses, who were liable to put other populations in danger (through cholera epidemics, for example), were a phenomenon to be avoided at all costs.[34]

Thus, the interests of these two groups came together to found *Linas Hatsedek*, which, in contrast to the *kehilla*-sponsored *Bikur Holim* [lit., To Visit the Sick] organization, whose members had to be approved by Bialystok's chief rabbi, was cast from the outset as a populist organization established "by the people."[35] Aside from providing care to the ill, over time and in response to the demands of its members, *Linas Hatsedek* established an ambulance service, a food bank to distribute food and clothing to the poor, and its own infirmary.[36] With an imposing building on Bialystok's main thoroughfare, *Linas Hatsedek* was recognized as the most reputable Jewish philanthropic organization in Bialystok [fig. 2]. By 1913, *Linas Hatsedek* was one of the most widely used charitable organizations in Bialystok, serving over 29,000 patients.[37]

Linas Hatsedek's success was due to its revolutionary organization as much as to communal need. First and foremost, *Linas Hatsedek* was the first Jewish welfare organization in the region not linked, directly or indirectly, with the *kehilla*. This independence allowed *Linas Hatsedek* to abandon the rigid hierarchical organization characteristic of other *kehilla* institutions and to organize itself in unprecedented ways.[38] *Linas Hatsedek* prided itself on being a "democratic" society, requiring all of its male members to serve on overnight shifts tending to the sick, regardless of their wealth or status in the community. Wealthy industrialists worked alongside uneducated factory workers to care for the ill and to operate *Linas Hatsedek*'s medical equipment. While wealthy members at times paid poorer ones to serve in their place, at *Linas Hatsedek*'s annual banquet rich and poor alike competed for prizes rewarding the member who had

fig. 1 Bialystok

fig. 2 *Linas Hatsedek* building

The Politics of Philanthropy 241

participated in the most night duties during the course of the year.³⁹

Perhaps even more radical than its cross-class membership was *Linas Hatsedek*'s inclusion of both men and women in its membership. Echoing trends in the larger Russian society, where the wives of Russian nobles, high officials, and wealthy merchants participated in local philanthropic causes, Jewish women in Bialystok established and ran many private relief institutions in Bialystok; yet official state-affiliated institutions remained the domain of men.⁴⁰ *Linas Hatsedek*, recognizing the immense resources women offered, allowed women not only to participate in the institution's nightly watches, but even to vote in its annual elections and sit on its governing board.⁴¹

This ideal of inclusiveness not only applied to its membership, but also extended to the constituencies this organization sought to serve. The founders of *Linas Hatsedek*, as part of their effort to distance themselves from the *kehilla* and advance a new vision of the role Jewish philanthropy could play in the Russian Empire, claimed that they would "serve any ill resident of Bialystok, regardless of their faith, nationality or class."⁴² In practice, *Linas Hatsedek* primarily helped Jews, since they made up the vast majority of the city's population. Nevertheless, the organization's leadership made great efforts to realize its multi-national ideology, as exemplified by the tireless efforts of Dr. Joseph Chazanowicz, *Linas Hatsedek*'s leader during its first two decades, who used this organization to articulate a new vision of Jewish philanthropy, transforming how Jews and even non-Jews viewed their place in Bialystok and the larger Russian Empire.⁴³

A NEW LEADERSHIP FOR A NEW TYPE OF JEWISH ORGANIZATION

Considered by some "the most remarkable Jewish personality of Jewish Bialystok," Joseph Chazanowicz, a doctor and future Zionist activist, epitomized this new cadre of educated and acculturated Jewish migrants who flocked to Bialystok in the nineteenth century, seeking to make names for themselves in this new, growing city.⁴⁴ Born in 1844 in Grodno, Chazanowicz was raised by his paternal grandparents after his mother's death.⁴⁵ His grandparents, committed to the ideals of the *haskalah* [Jewish Enlightenment], supplemented Josef's *kheyder* [traditional religious school] education with extensive training in Hebrew and Russian and sent him to the local Russian gymnasium.⁴⁶ In 1866, he enrolled in university in Konisberg, Prussia, to study medicine.⁴⁷ After completing his degree, he worked in St. Petersburg, serving as a Russian military doctor, but returned to the Grodno in 1878 to wed and then moved to Bialystok to open a medical practice. After his wife tragically died, Chazanowicz decided that instead of remarrying, he would devote himself to the affairs of the community.

Chazanowicz was typical of the hundreds of Jewish men who embraced medicine in the late nineteenth century, transforming the practice of medicine in the Russian Empire and creating new elites in Russian-Jewish society.[48] By 1889, for example, Jewish men represented thirteen and one half percent of Russia's practicing physicians, even though Jews accounted for less than four percent of the Russia's total population in the Russian Empire.[49] This disproportionally large number of Jewish doctors— constituting ten percent of medical students at the end of the century— gave the medical profession in Russia a stigma of social inferiority.[50]

While Russia's Jewish male doctors—like all ordinary *vrachi* [doctors] who completed the five-year program at university—garnered little pay, they did not have a lowly status like their Russian counterparts. A medical degree, on the contrary, earned them the coveted right to live outside the Pale of Settlement. According to a law promulgated in 1879, any Jew of either sex studying to become or practicing as a doctor [*vrach*], doctors' assistant [*fel'dsher*], or even midwife [*povival'naia babka*] enjoyed the right to live anywhere in the Empire.[51] While many used their medical training as their ticket out of the Pale, others, like Chazanowicz, chose to return to the Pale, where their degree translated into respect and higher social status.

Chazanowicz used the higher status accorded him because of his medical degree not only to assume the mantle of leadership in *Linas Hatsedek,* but also to put forth a new vision of the role Jewish philanthropic organizations should play in the Russian Empire as Jews sought integration [*sliianie*] into Russian society. While in other cities in the Russian Empire Jews represented a minority in need of incorporation, in Bialystok, as in a few other cities in the Pale, the case was in fact the opposite: Jews comprised the vast majority of the population, offering Jewish communal leaders a rare opportunity to present a model for integration. Appreciating his circumstances, Chazanowicz pushed *Linas Hatsedek* to provide its services free of charge to every resident of Bialystok, including local Poles and Russians.[52] He had the organization's charter proclaim that it would "serve any ill resident of Bialystok, regardless of their faith, nationality or class," immediately differentiating it from the *kehilla*.⁵³

As Chazanowicz's tireless efforts during Bialystok's 1896 cholera epidemic demonstrated, he was firmly committed, not just in rhetoric, to providing aid to all, whether they were Jews, Poles, Russians, or Ukrainians. Working for days without sleep, Chazanowicz put himself in grave danger, earning himself the nickname "the crazy doctor."⁵⁴ More important, his steadfast commitment to serving all members of the community led the district governor to appoint Chazanowicz Bialystok's official city doctor, lending the tsarist's state stamp of approval to both *Linas Hatsedek* and the new cadre of Jewish leaders running this organization.

Beyond transforming how tsarist authorities viewed Jewish charity, Chazanowicz's efforts also succeeded in altering the ways in which other ethnic groups inhabiting Bialystok saw Jewish philanthropy: despite its Hebrew name, *Linas Hatsedek* was not seen as an exclusivist Jewish organization. A turn-of-the-century Bialystok Polish proverb describing the assets of a young suitor bespeaks *Linas Hatsedek*'s success in establishing itself in the popular imagination as a welfare institution of Bialystok, not merely of Bialystok's Jewish community:⁵⁵

Zgrabny – jak ułan z Dziesiątki
Zgrał sie – jak rzeka Biała
....Punktualnie – jak w Pogotowie *Linas Hatsedek*
He is as handsome as an uhlan from the tenth regiment
He is as melodious as the Biała river
....As punctual as the members of *Linas Hatsedek*'s Emergency service.⁵⁶

As much a part of the Bialystok landscape as the Biała river, *Linas Hatsedek*'s volunteers were admired throughout the region, helping this organization eclipse the *kehilla* in stature and entrench itself in popular consciousness as the model charitable institution [fig. 3]. *Linas Hatsedek*'s pluralistic approach to charity became the pride of Bialystok's Jewish community: as journalist Nahum Prylucki summed up in 1935: "In describing the work and achievements of the *Linas Hatsedek* society, I have never used the word Jews or Jewish....This was deliberate, since, although it was founded and directed by Jews, supported by Jewish funds, and bears a Jewish name, no one is ever asked about his faith or nationality."⁵⁷

As it grew in prominence under Chazanowicz's guidance, *Linas Hatsedek* had to concoct several inventive fundraising techniques to support all of its programs. During the recession of 1900, for example, when few Jews in Bialystok had spare money, Chazanowicz sent appeals to several Yiddish newspapers in the United States, where he "called on our brothers who are residents of Bialystok but are dwelling across the sea to help us here in Bialystok with our bitter situation."[58] Chazanowicz emphasized that the Bialystok Jewish community was truly a trans-national community, and that Bialystoker Jews were "still members of Bialystok" regardless of where they lived.[59]

Chazanowicz's letter suggests both that fundraising needs prompted Jews in Bialystok to articulate a new vision of the parameters of their community and that trans-Atlantic migration was reshaping life in Bialystok by creating new constituencies from which struggling social welfare agencies could try to garner support. Chazanowicz's call to Bialystoker Jewish émigrés abroad for aid was far from the last time that Bialystoker émigré philanthropy would be called upon to rescue Jewish organizations in Bialystok, as we shall see below in our discussion of the interwar period when, after the devastation of the First World War, Jews in Bialystok solicited help from their compatriots abroad. Responding enthusiastically to their calls, Bialystoker Jewish émigrés raised over $5,000,000 (nearly $62,000,000 at present values) that not only rebuilt Jewish communal institutions, but also fundamentally transformed the complexion of Jewish communal politics.

BETWEEN ALTRUISTIC AID AND POLITICAL SUBVERSION: THE BIALYSTOKER RELIEF COMMITTEE AND BIALYSTOK JEWRY

Perched on the Russian-German border, Bialystok, like many cities in the former Pale of Settlement, was at the center of heavy fighting during World War I. Despite prevailing expectations of a short and decisive war, the Great War crept along, with civilians in Bialystok enduring as much hardship as the common solider on the front.[60] Tsarist forces' scorched-earth tactics created an acute famine in the region and destroyed most of the city's factories, leaving the vast majority of Bialystok's Jewish community poverty-stricken and starving: the city's Jewish population plummeted from 70,000 in 1913 to only 37,186 in 1921.[61]

The war's end, far from restoring peace and prosperity to the region, unleashed a period of terrifying anti-Semitism.[62] After Bialystok was incorporated into the Second Polish Republic in 1920, hyperinflation, anti-Semitic boycotts of Jewish businesses, and the closure of the border with Russia, the largest pre-war importer of goods from Bialystok, further devastated the city's struggling economy.[63] In 1921, for example, forty percent of Bialystok's Jewish workers were unemployed, and many who remained employed worked only three days a week.[64]

As news of the destruction of their former home made its way to America, David Sohn, a young journalist from Bialystok who had immigrated to New York in 1912, convened a conference to discuss how the émigré community could help those still living in Bialystok [fig. 4].[65] "We were not accustomed to hearing such passion at society meetings" recalled Joseph Lipnick, chairman of Bialystoker *Bikur Holim*, the largest Bialystoker Jewish émigré organization in America. These in attendance immediately felt compelled to send their savings to Bialystok.[66] "All were so enthused by Sohn's words," he continued, that thirty-five different Bialystoker émigré groups decided to join forces to coordinate their philanthropic efforts on Bialystok's behalf.[67] This new organization, called the Bialystoker Center, "truly hummed like a bee-hive," and "dozens of volunteers were needed to sit day and night in the office to accept money, issue receipts, and write letters to friends in Bialystok for those who could not write" [fig. 5].[68]

Such an enthusiastic response to Sohn's description of the dire circumstances in Eastern Europe not only testifies to Sohn's eloquence and influence, but also bespeaks Bialystoker Jewish émigrés' high hopes for the future of Jewish life in their former home. The events of the Second World War often overshadow the fact that the years following the First World War marked an exciting turning point in the history of East European Jewry. The most obvious change was political: formerly subjects of empires, the Jews were now citizens of republics. National borders were transformed as Poland became an independent republic for the first time in over a century. In Poland, the minority rights clauses insisted that Polish authorities grant Jews the right and the resources to develop Jewish cultural and political organizations. The treaty assured that all minority groups would be allowed to govern themselves and use their own language for official purposes. Bialystoker Jewish émigrés had particularly high hopes for Jewish life in Bialystok, where Jews had comprised over seventy percent of the population before the war, and it was assumed they still constituted a majority of the population.

Despite these seemingly auspicious conditions, the years following the war proved to be extremely trying for Jews in Bialystok. Economically

fig. 3 *Linas Hatsedek* volunteers

דוד סאָהן אין בערלין, אין יאָר 1920, אויף
זיין רעליף שליחות קיין ביאַליסטאָק. מיט זיין
איניציאטיוו איז דאן געגרינדעט געוואָרען דער
‏„ביאַליסטאָקער פאַרבאַנד" אין בערלין.

DAVID SOHN in Berlin, in 1920, while on his relief mission to Bialystok. On his initiative the "Bialystoker Farband" was then organized in Berlin.

fig. 4 David Sohn

The magnificent, 10-story building of the Bialystoker Center and Home for the Aged, at 228-230 East Broadway, New York, which serves as headquarters for Bialystoker the world over. Three hundred aged and ailing men and women are cared for at the Home.

fig. 5 Bialystoker Center, New York City

devasted from the war, the loss of the Russian market in the early 1920s and the lack of Polish government support for the redevelopment of the textile industry made it difficult for many Jewish workers and their families to survive. In Bialystok, migration from the surrounding hinterlands intensified the competition for jobs.[69] Hyperinflation in Poland escalated food prices beyond the reach of most of the working class, and currency reforms, intended to curb Polish inflation, actually forced the collapse of the few remaining textile factories in Bialystok.[70]

In 1918, Bialystok Jewry had great faith that the newly-reconstituted *kehilla* would be able to address their problems.[71] Created as a result of the Minorities Rights Treaty, the *kehilla* in interwar Poland was a democratic institution that was supposedly funded and supported by the Polish government [fig. 6].[72] In reality, Polish authorities offered little support to any local *kehilla*. With limited resources, the *kehilla* in Bialystok, like many others throughout the country, saw its funds rapidly disappear as desperate Jewish migrants streamed into Bialystok in search of employment; with few job prospects, they turned to the *kehilla* for aid, draining it of any remaining funds.[73] Then in 1920, the *kehilla* lost all of its influence and credibility in the community when several elected officials absconded with the limited funds available, using the money to pay for an extended summer vacation in the countryside.

The *kehilla*'s struggles prodded the Bialystoker Center in New York to send a representative to Bialystok to ensure that their philanthropic largess did not fall into corrupt hands. When Sohn, the first Bialystoker Center emissary, arrived in Bialystok, he was embraced with enthusiasm and respect. As Bialystok journalist Max Babitsh remarked upon meeting Sohn in Bialystok in 1920, "Sohn appeared to us in Bialystok as if he had come from a different world," for while "we were so tortured and dispirited," he stood "confident and proud."[74] *Dos naye lebn* [The New Life] compared Sohn to the messiah, declaring that "salvation has arrived.... Our American brothers and sisters have not forgotten us."[75] Salvation came first and foremost in the form of money, and Sohn brought with him over $150,000. Because of the loss of faith in the *kehilla* leadership, Sohn's arrival also boosted morale, since Jews in Bialystok saw Sohn as an "untainted" leader who could offer sound advice and leadership.[76]

As in other communities dispersed throughout the region, émigré money played a critical role in the reconstruction of Jewish life and reinforced regional identifications between Jews in Poland and abroad.[77]

248 · The Jews of Eastern Europe

קאנדידאטן ליסטע

פֿון די פּארטייען און גרופּעס צו די וואלן אין דער אידישער קהלה אין ביאליסטאק, וועלכע קומען פֿאר דעם 17—15,1918 (י"ב—י"ד סכּת תרע"ט)

#	משפחתו, שמו ושם אביו פֿאַמיליע, נאָמען און פֿאָטערס נאָמען	שנותיו יאָר	רחוב נומר נאָם נומר	הערה בּעמערקונג

רשימת הקנדידטים קאנדידאטן ליסטע № 11
אידישע דעמאָקראטישע פּארטײ.

1	פֿינקעל אברהם ב"ר מרדכי	55	8 צענסטאחאווער
2	קורליצקי תורה־ליב " זלמן	40	פּאָם 11
3	ארליאנסקי יצחק " מנחם	49	פּעלד 1
4	פֿינגער יצחק " זלמן	48	פּאָם 12
5	לעװינץ מענדל " יהושע	43	ביעלאסטאצאנער 15
6	באָקשט אברהם " ישעיהו	42	[ראָזאנער] ניזוועלם 6
7	גוטמאן שמיחו " הירש	42	ראזאנער 4
8	רזשוצק יעקב " עקיבא	50	ניזועלם 28
9	באצער אפרים " נחליהו	39	לינדען 39
10	ליטװאנסקי אליהו " זלמן	43	אלעקסאנדער 24
11	זאבלאדאווסקי אליהו ב"ר דוד	71	גוקאלי 33
12	באמסקאוסקי משה " לײב	55	5 "
13	פרילוצקי יעקב " לײב	38	2 "
14	מאריין יעקב " משה	38	אידזש 19
15	בארדנאא יעקב " יצחק	45	לונדער 4
16	װעליזשאנסקי משה " יונה	45	ראזאנער 1
17	נױרזשאן שמעון " לײב	47	קופֿמאן 8
18	קרעסלער ישראל " משה	48	אלעקסאנדער 5
19	מאנגעס נתן " פֿינקעל	42	לינדען 4
20	ראבינאוויץ חיים " שמואל	44	פּעלר 4

רשימת הקנדידטים קאנדידאטן ליסטע № 12
דעמאָקראטישע יוגנט

1	גאלדמאן שואל ב"ר משה	24	אלעקסאנדער 57
2	לין נחמן ב"ר דוד	24	פּאָם נאָם 20
3	מעלון מנחם ב"ר ואבן־מאלף	24	קופֿמאן 21
4	עקסמאן אדל ב"ר מאיר אברהם	24	לאָראָער 2
5	בערנשטיין רבקה ב"ר זלמן	24	שלאם 14
6	לעװין בונסין ב"ר יהודא	25	קופֿמאן 21
7	נעמוצעאווסקי סוטע ב"ר בנימן	22	אלס באַאיארץ 34
8	רובנצ׳ין ברכה ב"ר שאול	22	לינדען נאָם 48
9	ראבינאוויטשטאמנוחה דבורה ב"ר לואעי־ליב	23	אלינע 6
10	גלאנגאווסקי נחום ב"ר קלמן	24	פּעלר 5

רשימת חגנדידטים קאנדידאטן ליסטע № 13
א גרופע ביאליסטאקער בעלי־בתים

1	קופליאנסקי אברהם יצחק ב"ר שמואל	63	פּאָם נאָם 20
2	גדיץ חיים ב"ר יעקב	53	גוקאלי 17
3	גדאנסקי משה ב"ר יוסף	58	ראזאנער 8

fig. 6 Party and Candidate List, 1918 Bialystock *Kehilla* Elections. On this page are the names, ages, and addresses of the designated representatives of the Jewish Democratic Party and the Democratic Youth Party. Courtesy of the Rare Books and Manuscript Division, Chen Merhavia Collection, National Library, Jerusalem

The Politics of Philanthropy 249

Between 1919 and 1921 alone, Bialystoker Jewish émigrés sent back over $1,000,000 (nearly $13,000,000 at present values) to individuals in Bialystok and $108,000 to rebuild Bialystok's Jewish communal institutions.[78] Since many Bialystoker émigrés were unable to wire money to their relatives in Bialystok, the vast majority of the funds that representatives brought with them went directly to needy relatives. With few employment prospects, those employed earning only fifty-two percent of the pre-1914 figure, and the dollar worth over 4,550 Polish marks in 1921, these funds kept many families from starving.[79]

Émigré also provided all the funding to Jewish communal institutions committed to caring for the Jewish poor, such as those providing unleavened bread [*matzah*] to the needy on Passover, the local kosher soup kitchen, the Jewish hospital, *Linas Hatsedek*, and the Jewish Old Age Home.[80] With the several thousand dollars it received from émigrés, *Linas Hatsedek* extended its services beyond caring for the ill and began distributing food, new shoes, and clothing to Jews in Bialystok. Malka A, a woman who received clothes and shoes from *Linas Hatsedek* in 1921, remembered vividly that when she showed up for her first day of school at the local Polish grade school, she was immediately identified as being Jewish and teased for her "new Jew shoes." As she explained, "Only a Jewish child in Bialystok could have new shoes in 1921."[81]

The economic chasm noted by school children was evident throughout Bialystok as Jewish leaders turned to émigrés to finance special reconstructive projects in the Jewish community. For example, Dr. Synaglowski, the head of Bialystok's ORT [*Obshchestvo Remeslenovo Truda*: Society for the Encouragement of Handicrafts] was deeply concerned about Jewish workers' high unemployment rates and inadequate training. Organizing a dinner at the Bialystoker Center in New York City, he raised over $7,000 in one night to build a new vocational and agricultural training school for Jews in Bialystok.[82] In 1925, Eugene Lifshitz, an elected representative of Bialystok's *kehilla*, came to New York to raise money for a cooperative bank that could grant loans to businessman to stimulate the economy. Responding to his appeal, the members of Bialystoker Center raised $40,000 and soon established an interest-free loan society for Jews [*Payen Bank in Bialistok*] to support private entrepreneurship in the Jewish community.[83]

Aside from providing critical financial support for welfare programs and new enterprises, émigrés also offered advice concerning how to rebuild the community, encouraging Jewish leaders to incorporate "American" standards of organization into their institutions. In 1923, in response to the looming orphan crisis in the city, Rochelle Rachmanowitz, director of the largest Jewish orphanage in Bialystok, *Ezres Yesoymim* [Society to Aid Orphans], obtained a large grant from several donors in New York. After receiving these funds, Rachmanowitz, who had been informally caring for the city's Jewish orphans for decades, suddenly established a formal school, dividing all her charges by age, purchasing uniforms for them, and setting up a prescribed curriculum for each age group to follow.[84] Moreover, she also modernized her institution's annual report, which she then sent around the world with a formal, posed photograph of her staff to illustrate that *Ezres Yesoymim* was an efficient charity worthy of more charitable support [fig. 7].[85]

Ezres Yesoymim's transformation was replicated throughout Poland, as Shaul Stampfer notes in his study of interwar Chasidic yeshivot, where Chasidic leaders, despite their earlier vehement critiques of the limitations of formal yeshiva study, decided to establish formal institutions in the 1920s because they offered "an important advantage in fundraising."[86] Since the informal Chasidic bes midrash "certainly did not fit the Western patterns of formal education, organized study, and certification of completion," as the yeshiva did, Chasidic leaders chose to reorganize and recast their educational system to encourage American Jews "to send funds."[87]

In Bialystok, even the local non-Chasidic rabbinical school, Bes Medresh Bes Yoysef began keeping strict records, issuing textbooks to guide its students, and publishing balance sheets and annual reports as part of their effort to tap into the rich resources offered by émigrés.[88] Beyond the educational realm, the Jewish hospital in Bialystok also reorganized its financial accounting and rendering of services in order to attract more overseas donations.[89] Thus, the lure of additional funds, along with the actual and perceived demands of émigré philanthropists, transformed not only how Jewish institutions in Bialystok presented themselves, but also their very organization and operation.

Émigré Philanthropy and Bialystok's Yiddish Press
The blossoming of Bialystok's Jewish press during the interwar period also vividly demonstrates the ways in which émigré philanthropy played a pivotal role in reshaping Jewish communal politics, particularly Polish-Jewish relations, during this complex and contentious time of shifting borders and nation-building. The subject of Polish-Jewish relations in the

twentieth century is a long and complex one that cannot be fully treated here.[90] Nonetheless it must be noted that relations deteriorated steadily during the First World War, and the creation of the Second Polish Republic exacerbated the already strained Polish-Jewish relations in Bialystok, which did not improve as a result of the influx of American Jewish funds.

Fueling Polish antagonism was the adamant opposition of Jewish residents to their incorporation into the Second Polish Republic, a sentiment openly expressed on the pages of the Jewish press. In 1919, the editors of the Russian-language *Golos Belostoka* [The Voice of Bialystok], the first newspaper published by Jews in post-war Bialystok, demanded a plebiscite to decide whether the city should become part of Poland, Russia, Lithuania, or its own special zone.[91] *Dos naye lebn*, the city's most widely-circulated Yiddish newspaper, claimed that, according to the basic fundamental principle of ethnic self-determination, Bialystok belonged in either Lithuania or Russia, since less than one-third of the city's residents were Polish.[92] The Jewish press's lukewarm reception of the Polish state troubled the new government, who, in an effort to ensure that Bialystok would be an indisputably "Polish" city, created one municipal unit out of the city of Bialystok and the surrounding Polish suburbs in May 1919. In the end, though, this gerrymandering of Bialystok proved unnecessary, since the Jewish population of Bialystok boycotted the 1919 municipal elections after new regulations required that every member of the municipal government speak and write only in Polish.[93] The issue of language ultimately prompted the Polish government to expel the Jews from the Bialystok municipal government in September 1919.[94]

After the expulsion of Jews from municipal government, Jewish newspapers became the main vehicle through which Jews in Bialystok voiced their opinions about the region's shifting political boundaries. The experiences of *Dos naye lebn* clearly demonstrate the central role émigré funds played in maintaining this Jewish forum for political debate. In 1919, the editorial staff of *Dos naye lebn* advanced the idea that since Poland had never clearly defined its Eastern borders at the Versailles conference, the inclusion of Bialystok in the Second Polish Republic must be viewed as an illegal annexation.[95] Needless to say, such claims angered local Polish officials, who brought a libel suit against *Dos naye lebn* as part of their effort to paralyze this newspaper financially and hopefully close it down.[96] Mounting legal costs did in fact strain the newspaper's finances. But instead of shutting down the presses, *Dos naye lebn*'s editor, Pesach

Kaplan, wrote to Sohn, executive director of the Bialystok Center in New York, for help.[97] Sohn came to the rescue and immediately sent Kaplan money to defray legal expenses; in addition, Sohn contributed articles to *Dos naye lebn* about current events in America so that the newspaper would not have to support correspondents abroad.

As Sohn became more cognizant of the pressures and issues facing Jewish newspaper editors, he began sending dozens of grants, ranging from fifty to three hundred to almost every Jewish-sponsored newspaper published in Bialystok.[98] As the sole arbiter of which Bialystoker newspapers to fund, Sohn was seen as holding in his hands the fate of many publications and organizations. A 1925 letter from the editorial staff of Bialystok's *Naye bialistoker stime* [Bialystok's New Voice] underscores Sohn's power: the letter pleaded with Sohn to "influence the Bialystoker *landslayt* [countrymen] in America...so that we could get the funds necessary to start such an important newspaper," which "all cultural leaders and journalists in Bialystok agree is essential," but insufficient funding has prevented from being published.[99] As Sohn offered funds to the various newspaper editors, he also offered advice based on his experience working as a journalist in Bialystok and New York. Jewish newspaper editors, interested in receiving support in the future, listened carefully to his advice, fundamentally altering how almost every Jewish newspaper in Bialystok approached such issues as marketing, budget management, and staff retention.[100]

As Jewish newspapers in Bialystok were flooded with funds and advice from Sohn, Jewish editorialists began to advance the idea that their city was not a Polish city but an international one, with devoted "citizens" scattered throughout the world. With its frontpage reporting on current events in the United States, focus upon the Bialystoker émigré enclave as the locus of world news, frequent publication of feature articles by Sohn, and regular reprinting of articles from the Bialystoker Jewish émigré Yiddish quarterly, *Der Bialystoker Stimme*, published in New York, *Dos naye lebn* located its readers from the outset in an ideological universe whose very center was the United States.[101]

Thus, the Polish government's attempt to censure and control Bialystok's Jewish press failed miserably. Less concerned over government approval because of émigrés' unquestioning financial support, editors of Jewish newspapers continued to express their controversial opinions about the Polish state freely, molding their papers to suit American proposals and diffusing among their readers a vision of Bialystok as an international city,

The Politics of Philanthropy

whose destiny was not tied to debates in the Sejm but rather to current events taking place in locales far beyond Poland's geographic borders.

CONCLUSION

During the late nineteenth and early twentieth centuries, East European Jewish society was "the site of tremendous ferment," as Benjamin Nathans has described it, not only as a result of the development of new ideological currents and the tsarist state's uneven embrace of reform, but more fundamentally because millions of Jews uprooted themselves from their familiar social networks and migrated both within the Russian Empire and beyond its geographic borders. As they moved to new communities scattered throughout the Empire, Jewish migrants established new organizations, both philanthropic and political in nature—that transformed the shape of Jewish communal politics, the Jewish community's vision of their relationship with the state, and even the complexion of inter-ethnic relations.

While many have discussed the hand radical Jewish political movements, such as the Bund or Zionism, played in bringing East European Jewry into era of modern Jewish politics, few have adequately addressed the gradual yet revolutionary changes wrought by new charitable organizations, such as *Linas Hatsedek* or the Bialystoker Center, that increasingly involved women in Jewish communal affairs, solicited the support of the non-wealthy, and in general shifted Jewish communal governance away from the oligarchic model of the *kehilla*.[102]

The central role played by the Bialystoker Center and Sohn in rebuilding Bialystok and supporting a Jewish press that subtly challenged Polish authority members illustrates the importance of applying a trans-national lens to the study of Jewish Eastern Europe. Émigré philanthropists should not be viewed as mere altruistic welfare workers who wrote checks from afar hoping to ease the suffering of their compatriots abroad. Interwar émigré philanthropists acted as revolutionary forces, using their funds to restructure Jewish communal life in the manner they saw fitting and supporting institutions that challenged the authority of the Polish state.

The bifurcation of scholarship on East European Jewry in the United States and Poland often obscures the ways in which Jewish emigration not only transformed the lives of those who made the journey, but also fundamentally shaped the lives of those who remained behind in Eastern Europe. By helping Jews in Bialystok maintain a rich and diverse cultural life and subtly question the authority of the Second Polish Republic, émigré activism prompted Jews in Bialystok to re-envision their community as geopolitically located in the independent Polish state, but actually part of larger entity, a trans-national community made up of Bialystoker Jews scattered throughout the world. In short, beyond reshaping the demographics of East European Jewry, nineteenth century Russian-Jewish migration, not only within Russia but even beyond its borders, dramatically altered the organization, governance, and functioning of local Jewish communities first in Russia and later in the Second Polish Republic.

Finally, as the case of Bialystok highlights, scholars must re-examine the impact that all the different patterns and flows of Jewish migration had on both East European Jewish society and the Russian Empire as a whole. Jewish migration was both a local and trans-national phenomena that created new social groups who challenged traditional national categories. Appreciating the complex dynamics engendered by the processes of Jewish migration and settlement is essential if scholars hope to grasp the multifaceted forces that fueled the "road to modern Jewish politics" and prodded the restructuring of East European Jewish communal life during the epochal late nineteenth and early twentieth centuries.

fig. 7 *Ezres Yesoymim* staff

NOTES

[1] Zvi Hirsh Masliansky, *Zikhroynes: Fiehrtsig yohr lebn un kemfen* (New York, 1908, reprint 1924), 66.
[2] *Pervaia vseobshchaia perepis' naseleniia Rossiiskoi imperii, 1897 goda* (St. Petersburg, 1904) vol. 11, 22.
[3] Masliansky, *Zikhroynes*, 66.
[4] Approximately 70,000 Jews emigrated from Bialystok between 1850 and 1939. See Joseph Chaikan, "Bialystok Transplanted and Transformed," *Bialystoker Stimme* 233 (1944): 41, 45. David Sohn, head of the Bialystoker Center in New York, claimed that 50,000 Bialystoker Jews lived in America. See David Sohn, "Bialystok," in *Bialistoker Bilder Album: bilder album fun a barimter shtot on ire iden iber der velt* (New York, 1951), 16. Michael Flicker, president of Irgun Yotzei Bialystok in Israel, claims that a survey conducted during the war (1944) found 15,000 Bialystoker Jews residing in Palestine. Although no surveys were conducted in Argentina, memoir materials and *landsmanshaftn* membership figures suggest that between 8,000 and 10,000 Jews from the Bialystok region settled in Argentina. See L. Zhitnitski, "Landsmanshaftn, in argentina," *Argentiner yivo shriftn* 3 (1945): 156-59. It is estimated there were approximately 3,000 Bialystokers living in Melbourne by 1939. See Yakov Pat, "Bialistoker yidn in oystralia," quoted in Howard Rubinstein, *The Jews in Victoria*, 1835-1985 (Sydney, 1986), 190-91; Anna Gepner, oral interview, August 17, 1998.
[5] Pesach Kaplan, "Unzer likhtige fargangenheyt," *Dos naye lebn*, 1925, quoted in I. Shmulewitz, et al., eds., *Bialistoker yizker bukh* (New York: Bialystok Historical Society, 1982), 37.

In transliterating Russian, Polish, and Hebrew words, I have generally followed the systems used by the Library of Congress. In general, Yiddish words, phrases, titles, and names of organizations, places, and persons have been rendered according to the transliteration scheme of the YIVO Institute for Jewish Research, except that no attempt has been made to standardize non-standard orthography, most notably *Der Bialystoker Stimme*, which possesses a Yiddish title that was transliterated at the time of publication by its editors, who did not follow the YIVO guidelines. Hebrew words that appear as integral parts of Yiddish titles or phrases are spelled as they are pronounced in Yiddish. When referring to Jewish natives of a particular place, I use the Yiddish form (Bialystoker for a person from Bialystok). All translations are mine unless otherwise indicated.

[6] Shaul Stampfer notes that "the pervasiveness of migration left few local-born Jews in most East European cities." See Shaul Stampfer, "Patterns of Internal Jewish Migration in the Russian Empire," in *Jews and Jewish Life in Russia and the Soviet Union* (ed. Shaul Yaakov Roi; Portland: University of Oregon Press, 1995), 37; Steve Corrsin, *Warsaw before the First World War* (Boulder: East European Monographs, 1989), 145; Tomasz Wisniewski, *Jewish Bialystok: A Guide for Yesterday and Today* (Ipswich: Ipswich Press, 1998), Appendix III.

[7] Michael Stanislawski, *Tsar Nicholas I and the Jews* (Philadelphia: Jewish Publication Society, 1983); Jacob Katz, *Tradition and Crisis: Jewish Society at the End of the Middle Ages* (New York: New York University Press, 1992); Eli Lederhendler, *The Road to Modern Jewish Politics: Political Tradition and Political Reconstruction in the Jewish Community of Tsarist Russia* (New York: Oxford University Press, 1989); Benjamin Nathans, *Beyond the Pale: The Jewish Encounter with Late-Imperial Russia* (Berkeley: University of California Press, 2002).

[8] For the most part, scholarship on Jewish migration has focused on demographics, "crisis" moments, such as 1881, or the experiences of Jewish émigrés in their new host countries. Jacob Lestchinsky, a pioneer in Jewish demography, wrote extensively on East European Jewish migration. See Jacob Lestchinsky, "Die Zahl der Juden auf der Erde," in *Zeitschrift für Demographie und Statistik der Juden* (Berlin: Farlag Publishers, 1925), 1-8; Jacob Lestchinsky, *Prezesledlenie i przewarstowienie Żydów ostatniem stuleciu* (Warsaw, 1933), which he expanded upon in his *Jewish Migration for the Past Hundred Years* (New York: YIVO, 1944). Liebmann Hersch, "Jewish Migrations during the Last Hundred Years," in Central Yiddish Culture Organization's *The Jewish People—Past and Present* (New York: Jewish Encyclopedic Handbooks, 1946), was also a pioneering works on Jewish migration. Two examples of the "crisis" model approach to Jewish migration are David Berger, ed., *The Legacy of Jewish Migration: 1881 and Its Impact* (New York: Brooklyn College Press, 1983); and Jonathan Frankel, *Prophecy and Politics: Socialism, Nationalism and the Russian Jews* (Cambridge: Cambridge University Press, 1981). Moses Rischin's *The Promised City: New York's Jews, 1870-1914* (Cambridge: Harvard University Press, 1962) is a comprehensive work that set the stage for much of the subsequent scholarly interest in East European Jewish immigrant life in the United States as well as numerous other locales, arguing that we should approach this topic from the vantage point of settlement and arrival. See, for example, Gerald Sorin, *American Jewish Immigrant Radicals, 1880-1920* (Bloomington: Indiana University Press, 1985); Haim Avni, *Argentina and the*

Jews: A History of Jewish Immigration (Tuscaloosa: University of Alabama Press, 1991); Judith Elkin, *The Jews of Latin America* (New York: Holmes and Meier, 1998); and Nancy Green, *The Pletzl of Paris: Jewish Immigrant Workers in the Belle Epoque* (New York: Holmes and Meier, 1986).

While many notable studies examine urbanization in the Russian Empire, few look specifically at the impact of Jewish internal migration. See Barbara Anderson, *Internal Migration during Modernization in Late-Nineteenth Century Russia* (Princeton: Princeton University Press, 1980); Daniel Brower, *Estate, Class and Community: Urbanization and Revolution in Late Tsarist Russia* (Pittsburgh: University of Pittsburgh Press, 1983); and Michael Hamm, *The City in Late Imperial Russia* (Bloomington: Indiana University Press, 1986). In fact, the noted Russian historian Peter Gattrell does not even recognize internal Jewish migration as a mass population shift; he claims that "in peacetime [before the First World War], relatively few non-Russian minorities engaged in widespread migration within the boundaries of the Russian Empire." See Peter Gattrell, *A Whole Empire Walking: Refugees in Russia during the First World War* (Bloomington: Indiana University Press, 1999), 5.

[9] Abbreviated name for the *Algemeyner Idisher Arbeter Bund in Liteh, Pylin un Rusland* [Jewish Workers Alliance in Lithuania, Poland, and Russia].

[10] Zvi Gitelman, ed., *The Emergence of Modern Jewish Politics: Bundism and Zionism in Eastern Europe* (Pittsburgh: University of Pittsburgh Press, 2003); Lederhendler, *The Road to Modern Jewish Politics*.

[11] Gitelman, *The Emergence of Modern Jewish Politics*, 13.

[12] Derek Penslar, *Shylock's Children: Economics and Jewish Identity in Modern Europe* (Berkeley: University of California Press, 2001), 3. Concerning the political role Jewish welfare activists played in Eastern Europe, see Steven Zipperstein, "The Politics of Relief: The Transformation of Russian Jewish Communal Life During the First World War," in *Studies in Contemporary Jewry*, ed. Jonathan Frankel (New York: Oxford University Press, 1988), 22-40; Ezra Mendelsohn, *Zionism in Poland: The Formative Years, 1915-1926* (New Haven: Yale University Press, 1981), 46-49.

[13] Nathans, *Beyond the Pale*, 201-307.

[14] Gitelman, *The Emergence of Modern Jewish Politics*, 13. For discussions of similar developments in other cities in Imperial Russia, see Nathans, *Beyond the Pale*, 123-164; Natan Meir "The Jewish Community of Kiev: Community and Charity in an Imperial Russian City" (Ph.D. Dissertation, Columbia University, 2004), 164-99.

[15] Hamm, *The City in Late Imperial Russia*.

[16] The birth, death, and marriage records of the Jewish community from 1862, for example, reveal that the vast majority (sixty-nine percent) of Jewish residents in Bialystok hailed from surrounding cities such as Grodno and smaller hamlets in the region, such as Tykochin, Janow, and Knysan. See *Akta Stanu Cywilnego Okręgu Bożniczego w Białymstoku*, 1835-1899 nr. Zespol 264, 1-113. Archiwun Państwowe w Białymstoku.

[17] Avraham Herschberg, *Pinkes bialistok: grunt-materyaln tsu der geshikhte fun di idn in Bialistok biz nokh der ershter velt-milhomeh* (New York: Bialystok Historical Society, 1949), 41-42.

[18] Ibid., 49-53.

[19] Max Pogorelsky, "Why I Left the Old Country and What I Achieved in the U.S.," *YIVO Autobiography Collection, 1939*. Collection RG102: Box 16, Autobiography #194. YIVO Archives for Jewish Research.

[20] Stanisław Kalabiński, "Stan zatrudnienia w przemyśle Białostocczyzny w latach 1870-1914," *Studia Histoyczne 2*, (1972): 82-85.

[21] Adele Lindenmeyr, *Poverty Is Not a Vice: Charity, Society and the State in Imperial Russia* (Princeton: Princeton University Press, 1996), 99.

[22] Stanislawski, *Tsar Nicholas I and the Jews*, 123-25, 185-86.

[23] Ibid., 123-25, 185-86. Eli Lederhendler has provocatively argued, building on Max Weber's definition of the state as the legitimate arbiter of violence, that the *kahal's* monopoly on access and recourse to the state was the central defining characteristic of power in "pre-modern" Jewish politics. See Lederhendler, *The Road to Modern Jewish Politics*, 3-13.

[24] For more on the dense network of new charitable institutions established in Białystok in this period, see Herschberg, *Pinkes bialistok*, vol. 1, 315-41.

[25] Benjamin Nathans provides a detailed analysis of this contest for power in his discussion of the mercantile elite in St. Petersburg and their access to government officials. See Nathans, *Beyond the Pale*, 38-69. For a general overview of the *kehilla*, see Stanislawski, *Tsar Nicholas I and the Jews*, 123-25, 185-86; Katz, *Tradition and Crisis*.

[26] Lindenmeyr, *Poverty Is Not a Vice*, provides an excellent overview of this entire movement.

[27] RGIA f. 821, d. 108, ll. 143-47.

[28] S. Ia. Ianovskii, *Evreiskaia blagotvoritel'nost'* (St. Petersburg: Gos. tip, 1903), 16-19.

[29] *Khronika Voskhoda* No. 39, Sept. 19, 1899, 1194-97.

[30] Ianovskii, *Evreiskaia blagotvoritel'nost'*, 19. On the *korobka*, which Michael

Stanislawski has termed "the basic internal tax of the Jewish community," see Stanislawski, *Tsar Nicholas I and the Jews*, 40.

[31] Discussions of Jewish philanthropic agencies in St. Petersburg and Kiev illustrate how members of this new Jewish elite used philanthropy for similar goals throughout the Empire. See Nathans, *Beyond the Pale*, 123-64; Meir, "The Jewish Community of Kiev," 164-99. Such was the case in Western Europe as well. See Rainer Liedtkes, *Jewish Welfare in Hamburg and Manchester*, c. 1850-1914 (Oxford: Clarendon, 1998), 10-12.

[32] *Zikhroynes un maysim fun linat holim bialistok* (Bialystok, 1923), 4.

[33] See Tomacz Wisniewski, "The Linas Hatsedek Charitable Fraternity in Bialystok, 1885-1939," *Polin* 7 (1992): 122, and footnotes 4, 5.

[34] For a full discussion of Jewish healthcare in this period see, Lisa Epstein, "Caring for the Soul's House: The Jews of Russia and Health Care, 1860-1914" (Ph.D. Dissertation, Yale University, 1995).

[35] Herschberg, *Pinkes Bialistok*, 1, 331.

[36] Ibid., 332-34.

[37] *Spradzowanii Kalender b belostok* (St. Petersburg, 1913), 65.

[38] Concerning the rigid hierarchical organization of the *kehilla*, see Katz, *Tradition and Crisis*, 65-102.

[39] Herschberg, *Pinkes Bialistok 2*, 331-5.

[40] Lindenmeyr, *Poverty Is Not a Vice*, 116. Louise McReynolds and Cathy Popkin, "The Objective Eye and the Common Good," in *Constructing Russian Culture in the Age of Revolution, 1881-1940* (ed. Catriona Kelly and David Shepard; Oxford: Oxford University Press), 60.

[41] *Bakasha me-Linat Hatzedek*, 1901 (Bialystok: July 10, 1901), Jewish National Library, L331. David Sohn, ed., *Bialistoker bilder album:* (New York: Bialystok Historical Association, 1951), 96.

[42] "Hoda'at Linas Hatzedek, 1885," PL 331, Central Archives for the History of the Jewish People.

[43] Dovid Klementinovski, *Dr. yosef khazanovitsh: der idealist, natsionalist un folksmentsh* (New York, Bialystoker Historical Association, 1956).

[44] Ibid., 9.

[45] Ibid., 12-13.

[46] For more on the Haskalah movement that originated in Western Europe, see Michael Meyer's excellent overview in *Jewish Identity in the Modern World* (Seattle: University of Washington Press, 1990); David Sorkin, *The Transformation of German Jewry, 1780-1840* (Oxford: Oxford University Press, 1987). In Eastern Europe, the Haskalah followed different patterns. See Immanuel Etkes, ed., *ha-*

Dat veha-hayim: tenu'at ha-Haskalah ha-Yehudit be-Mizrach Eropah (Jerusalem: Merkaz Zalman Shazar, 1993); Shmuel Feiner, *Haskalah ve-Historyah: toldoteha shel hakarat-'avar Yehudit modernit* (Jerusalem: Merkaz Zalman Shazar, 1995); and Mordechai Zalkin, *Ba'a lot ha-shahar: ha-Hasklah ha-Yehudit ba-Imperyah ha-Rusit ba-me'ah ha-tesha'esreh* (Jerusalem: Y. L. Magnes, 2000). For more on the Haskalah in Western and Eastern Europe, see Shmuel Feiner and David Sorkin, eds. *New Perspectives on the Haskalah* (London: Littman Library of Jewish Civilization, 2000).

[47] Ibid., 15-16.

[48] Epstein, "Caring for the Soul's House."

[49] Nancy Mandelker Frieden, *Russian Physicians in an Era of Reform and Revolution, 1856-1905* (Princeton: Princeton University Press, 1981), 333, based on V. I. Grebenshchikov, "Opyt razrabotki rezul'tatov registratsii *vrach*ei v Rossii," *Spravochnaia kniga dlia vrachei*, 2 vols. (St. Petersburg, 1890), 1: 111-13. Even more remarkable, Jewish women represented twenty-four percent of Russia's female physicians. See Carole Balin, "The Call to Serve: Jewish Women Medical Students in Russia, 1872-1887," *Polin* 18 (forthcoming).

[50] Christine Johanson, *Women's Struggle for Higher Education in Russia, 1855-1900* (Kingston and Montreal, 1987), 77-78.

[51] G. Vol'tke, "Meditsinskiia professii po deistvuiushchemu russkomu zakonodatel'stvu," *Evreiskaia Entsiklopediia: Svod znanii o evreistve i ego kul'ture v proshlom i nastoiashchem* (St. Petersburg, 1906-1913) 10:780.

[52] Herschberg, *Pinkes Bialistok 2*, 432-42.

[53] "Hoda'at Linas Hatzedek, 1885," PL 331, Central Archives for the History of the Jewish People.

[54] Klementinovski, *Dr. yosef khazanovitsh*, 31.

[55] Wisniewski, "The *Linas Hatsedek* Charitable Fraternity," 124.

[56] Bialystok proverb quoted in Ibid., 121.

[57] Nahum Prylucki "Przemowienie na uroczystej akademii z okazji jubileuszu 50-lecia *Linas Hatsedek*," 6, quoted in Wisniewski, "The *Linas Hatsedek* Charitable Fraternity," 124.

[58] *Jewishabend Post* (June 28, 1900), 6.

[59] Ibid.

[60] Two discussions of the Great War's devastating impact on Russian civilian life, resulting from both warfare and tsarist authorities' efforts to confront the challenges of war particularly in western borderlands of the Russian Empire where Jews primarily resided, are Gattrell, *A Whole Empire Walking;* and Eric Lohr, *Nationalizing the Russian Empire: The Campaign against Enemy Aliens during World*

War I (Cambridge: Harvard University Press, 2003).

[61] The devastation of the war is chronicled in detail by several aid agencies active in the area. See the files of *Liga pomoshi golodaivshchim evreiam v zaniatykh nepriatelem mestnostiakh* [League to Aid Starving Jews in Enemy-Occupied Territories], founded in 1917, which established several soup kitchens and dispensed over 100,000 rubles in aid between 1917 and 1919; *Gosudarstvennyi arkhiv Rossiiskoi Federatsii* [GARF] (State Archives of the Russian Federation) f. 9529, op. 1, del. 5, 1 and f.9529, op. 1, del. 2, 6, 22. For a larger statistical overview of the impact of the war, see Yakov Bachrach, *Demografie fun der yidisher befelkerung in bialistok* (Bialystok: Kehila Farvaltung in Bialistok, 1937), 10; Piotr Wróbel, "Na równi pochyjej. Żydzi Biaegostoku w latach 1918-1939: demografia, ekonomika desintegracja, konflikty z Polakami," *Studia Podlaskie* (1989): 174-75

[62] The extensive anti-Jewish violence in the Ukraine, in which thousands of Jews lost their lives, was not replicated in Poland; however, the ferocious debates over minority rights after the establishment of the Second Polish Republic vividly illustrated that Jews in Poland were far from immune to the repercussions of East European ethnic nationalism. Ezra Mendelsohn, *The Jews of East Central Europe between the World Wars* (Bloomington: Indiana University Press, 1983), 73-74. See also Katarzyna Sztop-Rutkowska, "Konflikty polsko-żydowskie jako element kształtowania się ładu polityczno-społecznego w Białymstoku w latach 1919-1920 w świetle lokalnej prasy," *Studia Judaica* 5:2-6:1 (2002-2003): 131-50, for more details on the specific situation in *Bialystok*.

[63] M. Goldberg, "Bialystoker Textil Industria," *Unzer Lebn* (October 8, 1937), 8.

[64] Herschberg, *Pinkos Bialystok*, 292. Wróbel, "Na równi pochyłej," 177.

[65] Yosef Lipnick, "Dovid Sohn's rol in der landsmanshaft," in *Bialistoker yoyvelzamlbukh* (New York: Bialystok Historical Association, 1961), 12. Source for photograph of David Sohn is David Sohn, ed., *Bialistoker bilder album* (New York: Bialystok Historical Association, 1951), 82.

[66] Lipnick, "Dovid Sohn's rol in unzer landsmanschaft," 12-13.

[67] Ibid., 13.

[68] Ibid., 12. Source for photograph of Bialystoker Center, David Sohn, ed., *Bialistoker bilder album*, 210.

[69] Goldberg, "Bialistoker Textil Industria," 8.

[70] For more on the Grabski reforms, see Antony Polonsky, *Politics in Independent Poland, 1921-1939: The Crisis of Constitutional Government* (Oxford: Clarendon, 1972), 119-22; and Pavel Korzec, *Juifs in Pologne* (Paris: Presses de la Fondation nationale des sciences politiques, 1980), 142-50.

[71] Isaac Lewin, *A History of Polish Jewry During the Revival of Poland, 1918-1919*

(New York: Shengold,1990), 167-205.

[72] The *kehilla's* authority was based on the Minorities Rights' Treaty that required Poland to set up institutions to protect the rights of all minority groups living within its borders. Concerned after the pogroms of 1918 and 1919, the League of Nations required Poland to set up separate governing bodies and schools for non-Polish nationals in order to maintain its independence. Poland resented having to sign this treaty. For more on the Minorities Treaty (including a translation of the treaty itself), see Lewin, *A History of Polish Jewry, 1918-1919*, 167-205, 207-11.

[73] Ibid., 185. The *kehilla* marriage registry vividly illustrates the overwhelming influx of Jewish migrants between 1923 and 1924. Over sixty-five percent of the Jewish couples who registered to marry were not originally from Bialystok. See *Księga ślubów Rabinatu: Protokólarne Oświadczenie 1923-4*, Folder PL/5: Central Archives for the History of the Jewish People.

[74] Mordechai Babitsh, "A rizikalishe shlikhes in a kritisher tsayt," in *Bialystoker yoyvelzamlbukh*, 19.

[75] Ibid., 19-20.

[76] Source of photograph, *Bialystoker Stimme* 187 (April 1961), 21.

[77] Samuel Kassow, "Communal and Social Change in the Polish Shtetl: 1900-1939," in *Jewish Settlement and Community in the Modern Western World*, (ed. R. Dotterer, et al.; Selinsgrove, 1991), 56-84; Rachel Rojanski, "American Jewry's Influence upon the Establishment of the Jewish Welfare Apparatus in Poland, 1920-1929," *Gal-Ed* 11 (1989): 59-86.

[78] "Bericht fun bialistoker tsenter un bikur holim," *Bialystoker Stimme* 3 (March 1922), 23; "Bericht fun Bialistoker tsenter," *Bialystoker Stimme* 1 (November 1921), 18.

[79] Polonsky, *Politics in Independent Poland*, 108-09.

[80] For a full accounting of how these funds were allocated, see "Protokol 100: July 30, 1920," *Protokol-bukh fun bialistoker relif komite*, Folder A-18/3.2, Tel Aviv University Archives; Also see accounts of *Mayos Hitim Bialistok* in Folder A-18/138, Tel Aviv University Archives. See "Bericht fun bialistoker tsenter un bikur kholim," 23.

[81] Malka A. Interview with Rebecca Kobrin, March 1999, Kiryat Bialystok, Israel. Informant asked not to be identified.

[82] "Unzer eygene velt," *Bialystoker Stimme* 5 (October 1922), 10. Also see Sohn, *The Activities of the Bialystoker Community in America*, 17.

[83] *Bericht fun Payen Bank in Bialistok* (Bialystok, 1926); Sohn, "A Half Century of Bialystoker Activity in America," 5.

[84] It is fascinating to compare the financial report of Bialystok's *Ezras Yesoymim*

from the period before 1920 and the period following the intervention of the Bialystoker Relief Committee in Bialystok. See *Ezras Yesoymim, 1917-1920* (Bialystok, 1921), and *Report fun Ezras Yesoymin, 1923-1927* (Bialystok, 1928). Both these booklets can be found in Folder 17, Bund Archives/M-14, YIVO Institute for Jewish Research.

[85] Source for photograph, Folder A-18/151, Center for the Study of Diaspora Jewry.

[86] Shaul Stampfer, "Chasidic Yeshivot in interwar Poland," *Polin* 11 (1998): 20.

[87] Stampfer, "Chasidic Yeshivot in interwar Poland," 20-21.

[88] *Hoveret Likrat ha-'Asaphah Bes Medresh Bes Yosef* (Bialystok, 1937). Morris Sunshine Report to the Bialystoker Relief Committee, Folder A-18/3, Center for the Study of Diaspora Jewry.

[89] See reports of the Jewish hospital in Folder 17, Bund Archives/M-14, YIVO Institute for Jewish Research; For more on its overseas fundraising efforts, see *Australisher Yidishe News*, 7/12/1935, 8/16/1935, 8/30/1935, 9/6/1935, 12/13/1935.

[90] The issue of Polish-Jewish relations has long been a topic of scholarly inquiry. Some pioneering studies on the subject include Magdalena Opalski, *Poles and Jews: A Failed Brotherhood* (Hanover, 1992); Alina Cała, *Asymilacja Żydow w Krolestwie Polskim, 1864-1897* (Warsaw, 1989); Frank Golczewski, *Polnisch-Jüdische Beziehungen, 1881-1922: Eine Studie zur Geschichte des Anti-Semitismus in Osteuropa* (Wiesbaden, 1981); William W. Hagen, "Before the 'Final Solution:' Toward a Comparative Analysis of Anti-Semitism in Interwar Germany and Poland," *Journal of Modern History* 68 (1996): 351-81; Ezra Mendelsohn, "Interwar Poland: Good for the Jews or Bad for the Jews?," in *The Jews in Poland* (ed. Chimen Abramsky, et al.; Oxford, 1986), 130-39; Christopher Weber, "Towards Competitive Suffering: A Re-examination of the Historiography of Polish-Jewish Relations (M.A. thesis, University of Guelph, 1996), 1-40; Cała, *Asymilacja Żydow*; and Golczewski, *Polnisch-Jüdische Beziehungen*.

[91] *Golos Belostoka* (August 21, 1919), 2. See also Wróbel, "Na równi pochyłej," 193.

[92] Marian Fuks, "Prasa żydowska w Białymstoku, 1918-1939," *Biuletyn Żydowskiego Instytutu Historycznego w Polsce* 145-6 (1988): 145-50.

[93] Wróbel, "Na równi pochyłej," 195.

[94] Ibid., 196.

[95] *Dos naye lebn* (October 7, 1919), 2.

[96] *Dos naye lebn* (October 8, 1919), 2.

[97] Pesakh Kaplan, Bialystok, to David Sohn, New York, November 11, 1919.

Folder A-18/24, Center for the Study of Diaspora Jewry.

[98] There are dozens of letters to David Sohn from the editors of every newspaper published in interwar Bialystok. See Folder A-18/24, Center for the Study of Diaspora Jewry.

[99] Editorial Staff, *Naye bialistoker stime*, Bialystok, to David Sohn, New York, April 4, 1925. Folder A-18/24, Center for the Study of Diaspora Jewry.

[100] See the following letters of Pesach Kaplan to David Sohn, August 8, 1923, October 8, 1924, July 1, 1925. The letters sent by Kaplan to Sohn can be found among Sohn's personal papers, Folder A-18/38-18, Center for the Study of Diaspora Jewry.

[101] A column titled "Gelt fun amerike," which discussed the allocation of émigré funds, appeared daily between 1919 and 1922. Features titled "Vos hert zikh in bialistok" and "Vos hert zikh in amerike?" appeared several times a week during this period. See *Dos naye lebn* (August 24, 1919); *Dos naye lebn* (July 27, 1919).

[102] For an insightful discussion of the changes wrought by the Bund and Zionism, see Gitelman, *The Emergence of Modern Jewish Politics,* 12-19.

Enlightened Self-Interest:
The Men and Women Who Opened Schools for Jewish Girls in Late Imperial Russia

Eliyana R. Adler

Between 1831 and 1881 well over 100 private schools for Jewish girls opened in Tsarist Russia.[1] Unlike the government school system for Jewish boys, initiated in 1844, these schools were part of a grassroots effort, opened by enterprising educators across the Pale of Jewish Settlement. The burgeoning of interest in Jewish women's education was a result of changes internal to the Jewish community, including the growth of the Haskalah, or Jewish Enlightenment, but must also be seen in the context of Russia as a whole.

Throughout the nineteenth century, educational opportunities for Russian women, particularly of the upper classes, grew at a steady pace.[2] What began with a significant increase in the quantity and quality of secondary educational institutions led both to the availability of professional and higher educational options and to the substantive spread of elementary schools by the end of the century.[3] As Russian women expanded their educational horizons, they sought access to greater professional and educational opportunities and to further the spread of education in the empire.[4] Education was a major concern of the liberal Russian intelligentsia by the turn-of-the-century period.[5]

This concern for education would enter the Jewish community by two distinct but related paths. First, the most wealthy and assimilated Jewish families sought for their children the same level of culture and education as their Russian counterparts. If wealthy Russian girls could entertain their families and impress their suitors with their piano playing and refined French conversation, Jewish girls of the same class ought to be able to as well. Second, members of the Jewish intellectual elite read and were influenced by the writings of the Russian intelligentsia. The *maskilim* [followers of the Haskalah] advocated increasing educational opportunities not only for the benefits of the spread of knowledge, but also in an effort to russify the Jews and encourage their acculturation.[6]

At the same time as the *maskilim* were advocating greater educational access and wealthy Jewish families were hiring tutors to teach their daughters European languages and manners, more and more Jewish families of modest means were also becoming aware of the advantages of increased education for Jewish girls. Whereas the traditional *heder* curriculum for Jewish boys was well entrenched, there was far less antipathy toward changing education for Jewish girls. In a society where women were often expected to play an active role in commerce, the advantages of teaching girls basic literacy and numeracy was obvious. Additionally, the advent of state-sponsored schools for Jewish boys meant that founding modern private schools for Jewish boys was no longer encouraged by the government.

Thus, the Russian Jewish community was ripe for the development of schools for Jewish girls. But who was in a position to staff such schools? Individuals, whether responding to local interest, their own perception of the greater good for the Jewish community, economic opportunity, or some combination of all three, had to have certain knowledge and skills to open these schools. This paper is an exploration of the types of individuals who opened schools for Jewish girls and of the factors that led them to do so. The first section will seek to quantify these educators, in so far as possible. The second will look to qualitative data to illuminate the backgrounds and motivations of the principals of private schools for Jewish girls in Russia.

EDUCATORS: AGGREGATE

At this point I have isolated 146 educators who opened or ran private schools for Jewish girls up until the early 1880s. The information about them comes chiefly from correspondence with the government and secondarily from published lists of schools. The data that can be gleaned from such sources are obviously limited. It is not possible, for example, to trace the educational backgrounds of all of the founding principals. Although a few list themselves as the graduates of one or another formal institution, the vast majority only provide proof that they have the necessary certifications to teach.

Nonetheless some interesting facts emerge [See table]. Most of the 146 educators, not surprisingly, are Jewish. One hundred twenty-nine can be shown to be Jewish, while only ten are described as non-Jews. More surprising, however, is that all of the ten non-Jews were women. In fact, the preponderance of women in this study is quite notable. Over forty percent of the principals can be determined to be women. Among the forty-three women, thirty-three were Jewish.

Among the men, approximately half noted in their materials that they were employed by the state as either teachers in the government Jewish schools or as state rabbis. As this designation was undoubtedly a factor in their favor in applying to open a private school, it is safe to assume that most, if not all, of the remaining forty-seven Jewish men were not employed by the state. Beyond that, it is not possible to infer any other general information about the men.

The data thus allow for dividing the women by confession and the men by profession. In the following section we look at individual cases to shed greater light on the broad categories and in particular on what led them to open schools for Jewish girls.

EDUCATORS: MOTIVATION AND MEANS

It is, of course, neither possible nor advisable to outline the life stories and presumed motivations of close to 150 educators. This section will use case studies in each of the four major categories to highlight issues of importance before coming to some general conclusions.

I. Jewish Men Employed by the Russian Government in Jewish Communities

Yehuda Leib Gordon, later a renowned Hebrew writer, opened his first private school for Jewish girls soon after arriving in the Lithuanian town of Shavli in 1861. He was serving as a teacher in the government Jewish school there at the time. Not long after opening the girls' school, Gordon wrote to a friend of his hopes that it would improve his financial situation. His salary from the state was small, and he had a growing family to support.[7] However, it is not possible to reduce Gordon's calculations to the purely financial. In prose, poetry, and journalistic pieces, Gordon made abundantly clear his concern for the status of Jewish women. Undoubtedly, his most enduring statement on this subject was his epic poem, *Kotzo shel yud* [The Tip of the Yud], dedicated to the Hebrew writer Miriam Markel-Mosesohn.

In the following stanza Gordon laments the unenviable situation of the heroine, and through her all Jewish women, with textual references to both "The Woman of Valor" from the Book of Proverbs (31:10-31)

and the well-known rabbinic statement on women's education from the Mishna (Sota 3:4):

> What matter that you were gifted with a sensitive heart and beauty,
> That God apportioned you talent and intelligence?
> For you, of course, Torah is folly, beauty is fault,
> Any talent is for you deficiency, intelligence is flaw.[8]

Gordon did not limit his advocacy for women to the public sphere. He encouraged women writers in his private correspondence and also went to great lengths to assure that his own daughters received a proper education.[9]

Gordon thus provides a telling combination of financial need and genuine dedication to women's education. However, it was Gordon's latter-day fame that assured that his personal letters were saved. For most of the other principals of schools for Jewish girls, nowhere near as much documentation was preserved. There is no way of knowing if other educators wrote to friends about their financial woes, or how they educated their own daughters. Nonetheless, Gordon's case does illuminate some important issues.

Firstly, as a state employee, Gordon was well placed to open a private girls' school. Under Tsar Nicholas I, the Russian government, as part of its efforts to integrate the Jewish community more effectively, initiated two separate reforms that led to the employment of Jewish men. The state Jewish school system opened in 1844, and 1835 saw the creation of the state rabbinate.[10] Jewish men employed by the Russian government were in an excellent position to open private schools for Jewish girls for both practical and ideological reasons.

Both state teachers and rabbis had to know Russian in order to fulfill their roles. State school teachers had the additional advantage of having passed examinations more than equivalent to those required for private school teachers. In both cases, previous service to the state also increased the possibility that their schools would advance the goals of the government in seeking to transform the Jewish community. In their correspondence with the Ministry of Education regarding private schools for Jewish girls, these individuals often proudly stated their status and years of service.

In addition, these men, in choosing to serve as state teachers or rabbis, had already signaled their allegiances within the Jewish community. They were already seen as either dangerous elements or welcome harbingers of change. Despite the fact that the private schools for girls succeeded in enrolling students from a variety of social and economic groups, the schools were modern and new and also aroused suspicion and opposition at times. A state rabbi or teacher was not risking his communal standing by introducing formal education for Jewish girls into his community.

In fact, that very standing may have led some teachers and rabbis into girls' education. The more progressive members of a community would often seek out such individuals to tutor their children. The revolutionary Eva Broido, born in 1876 in the Lithuanian town of Sventsiani, described in her memoirs being tutored in Russian literature, along with two cousins, by a teacher in the local state Jewish school.[11] Ita Yellin's forward-looking yet rabbinic family had her tutored by a state rabbi in Jewish subjects while she attended a private Russian school in Mogilev.[12]

If enough local families looking for modern education for their daughters sought out teachers and rabbis, they may have decided to open schools to meet the demand. Gordon, during his first posting as a government school teacher in the town of Ponivezh, tutored local children as well as teaching in the school. It was not until his second posting in Shavli that his tutoring led to opening a school for Jewish girls.[13] He would do the same upon his arrival in Tel'she in 1865 on his third posting.[14] Gordon may not have been the only government employee to turn a thriving tutorial business into a more formal and stable arrangement.

Other Jews affiliated with the government may have had their first exposure to teaching girls through their colleagues or other teachers. When Bentsel' Podshkol'nik, a teacher of penmanship in the Rossieny (Kovno province) school, submitted his application to open a private girls' school, he proposed to teach religion and writing himself and to hire other teachers from the local government Jewish school for the remaining subjects.[15] Maria Siavtsillo, a non-Jew, planned to hire the local government rabbi to teach religion in the Jewish section of her girls' school in Kovno.[16] Although there is no extant record of whom they hired and what became of them, a parallel situation provides one possible outcome. When Gordon left Tel'she, his school passed into the hands of the state rabbi Khazanovich. It seems that Khazanovich was actually employed in the school during Gordon's tenure.[17] Thus Gordon hired the local state rabbi, thereby making him an ideal candidate for running the school after his own departure.

This example also points to the fluidity between the various roles. State rabbis, teachers in government Jewish schools, and principals of private Jewish girls' schools shared, at minimum, some knowledge of Russian and some level of commitment to the modernization of the Jewish community. Which hat an individual chose to wear may have depended as much on local circumstances as on a firm professional self-consciousness. A man by the name of Bank took the necessary teachers' examinations and taught for nine years in the government Jewish school in Kamenets-Podol'sk. When the school closed, he passed an additional set of examinations to become a state rabbi. After three years in that position, and with no future, in 1867 he requested permission to open a school for Jewish girls in Tul'chin, also in the Podolsk province.[18] Bank, as an educated and Russian-speaking Jew, had a number of options for employment in his community. Although teaching Jewish girls was clearly not his primary professional goal, it fit into a rubric of jobs dedicated to transforming the Jewish community from within.

In addition to their relationship and recognition from the state and their status within the Jewish community, state teachers and rabbis shared the difficulty of low wages. According to the draft legislation for the government Jewish school system, teachers were to be paid according to the number of hours they taught and the level of prestige of their subject. The highest paid teacher in the lower level school could expect 200 rubles per year.[19] Such a sum, although roughly commensurate with the salaries of other low-level employees of the Russian state, was not enough to support a family.[20]

State rabbis had even less access to adequate pay. Like the Orthodox clergy, state rabbis did not receive a regular salary. Rather, they were expected to work out terms of payment with their communities. These usually involved fee for service arrangements wherein rabbis charged local Jews to record their births, deaths, and marriages in the required metrical book. In many locales, this did not add up to a means of livelihood. It was not uncommon for state rabbis to hold other full-time positions, such as in pharmacy or medicine. These individuals may have been the men with the highest level of secular education in their towns, and they agreed to serve as rabbis as a service to the community. However, state rabbis without professional education had to look to other options to supplement their income.

Thus state teachers and rabbis shared financial need as well as professional and social proximity to teaching Jewish girls. In some cases, we can also see how the path from tutoring or part-time teaching led to becoming a principal. What is much harder to find evidence of is the ideological side of the equation. Gordon, of course, published extensively on his vision of the Haskalah, not only in his fiction but also in a constant stream of pieces to the Russian Jewish press.

In an 1866 article for the Russian-language supplement to the Hebrew periodical *ha-Karmel*, Gordon printed a speech he had delivered at the opening of his girls' school in Tel'she. In it he explained patiently and passionately why Russian Jews must learn Russian and how Jewish women were the key to this transformation.[21] Nonetheless, it is difficult to know how typical Gordon was. Shmuel Feiner has shown that even among convinced *maskilim* there were very real differences in the understanding of women's proper role and training.[22] Gordon was an outspoken advocate of women's rights. Although he was not the only government Jewish school teacher to submit articles on women's issues to the Jewish press of the time, he was one of a small number and was probably unusually committed to educating Jewish girls.

For state Jewish teachers and rabbis, the path toward women's education is fairly clear. Many tutored Jewish girls or taught in private schools run by their colleagues before opening their own schools. These men were also socially and ideologically allied with the forces of modernity. Finally, their very real financial concerns should not be ignored.

II. Jewish Men Not Employed by the State

The path is less straightforward for Jewish men not employed by the state. The only obvious trait they shared is level of education. No individual who had attended only the *heder* and yeshiva and sought no additional formal or informal educational avenues would have been in a position to open a legal private girls' school. The regulations for opening a private Jewish school required either certification of graduation from a Russian educational institution or of having passed examinations to serve as a private tutor. Thus, either through intensive private reading or tutoring or through a Russian education, these men had chosen to bypass or surpass the traditional Jewish men's curriculum and to learn Russian.

We can surmise that these men were among the most educated and russified members of their communities. Yet, if they were in fact fluent in Russian and interested in teaching, why not apply for the more stable jobs of state teachers or rabbis? One possible answer is that although these men could function in Russian at some level, they were not in a position to pass the examinations for either of those positions. Perhaps, they represent those Jewish men striving toward russification or enlightenment but hampered by their own education; men who would have liked to have gone to Russian schools themselves, but not having been able to do so, strive at least to make it possible for others to reach that level. Alternately, they might have felt that private education offered them greater financial or pedagogic opportunities. For the first twenty years of their existence, the state schools required non-Jewish principals, thus cutting Jews out of leadership roles. The curriculum and salaries were also not open to negotiation. Private schools offered at least the promise of greater leeway.

The case of the Germaize family in Vilna can be instructive. Levin Germaize opened a private school for Jewish boys in 1840.[23] His was not the first modern school for Jewish boys in Vilna, but joined several other successful schools. The 1844 legislation that created state sponsored schools for Jewish boys also essentially put the already existing modern private schools out of business. Private schools for Jewish boys, as competition to the new state schools, were no longer welcome. The principals of such schools had the option of handing their schools over to the non-Jewish principals and having them join the new system, or closing them down.

Germaize discovered yet another option, opting to turn his boys' school into an institution for Jewish girls.[24] He continued to run the school until passing it onto his son, Isak Germaize, in 1859.[25] The younger Germaize ran the school for girls successfully for nearly twenty years. However, in 1875, an inspector visiting the school found seventeen boys present, in addition to the properly registered girls. Germaize claimed at first that he thought he had permission to teach boys as well, and then later that his leg was hurting on that particular day and he found it impossible to go to the homes of all of his private students. To make a long story short, the school was closed in 1877, despite Germaize's repeated entreaties to the government.[26]

What emerges from this case is that neither Levin Germaize nor his son Isak was committed exclusively to the education of Jewish girls. Levin embraced the cause for pragmatic reasons, allowing him to continue making a living when his previous school was no longer viable. Isak took over the school for girls, but seems to have supplemented his income by teaching boys as well. The Germaizes devoted their lives to teaching Jews in a modern educational setting; however, whether it was boys or girls seems not to have been their primary concern.

The Germaize case raises another salient issue, that of family connection as a route to teaching. Isak essentially inherited the family business and continued to run it after the death of his father. The same is true of the state rabbi of the Bessarabian town of Khoton. Israel Tiutinman, already serving as the local state rabbi, became the principal of the private school for Jewish girls upon the death of his father, the founder, in 1865.[27]

Just as bakers' children were raised helping in the family business and learning its ins and outs, teachers' children similarly received informal training in the family business. A father who knew enough Russian to apply formally and teach in a Russian school, and who felt it was a priority to teach Jewish children Russian, undoubtedly gave his own children a proper Russian education. It was therefore no accident that both Germaize and Tiutinman had the skills to take over their fathers' schools. In fact, the younger Tiutinman's gravitation to the state rabbinate makes sense in light of his father's proclivities. Thus the sons were socialized towards teaching and the Russian language, and were able to fill their fathers' roles.

We can see a similar dynamic at work in the known cases of educators who were following in the parents' footsteps, even though not inheriting their actual schools. Sara Berman applied for, and received, permission to open a private school for Jewish girls in St. Petersburg in 1873.[28] Her school joined the twin private schools for poor Jewish boys and girls run respectively by her parents, Lazar and Anna Berman.[29] Before coming to the capital, Lazar had taught in a government Jewish school in Dubno (Kiev province) and run a private school for Jewish girls there.[30] Liuba Kenigsberg, who established a school for Jewish girls in Berdichev in 1872, was the daughter of a government Jewish school teacher.[31]

Family connections provided one route towards teaching girls for educated Jews. Indeed for the Jewish man with some level of knowledge of Russian and some level of commitment to changing the Jewish community, education was among the best options. Such men could not, however, obtain employment in non-Jewish schools, and the government sponsored Jewish schools were not for everyone. Teaching Jewish girls may not have been the first choice for these men, but it did advance their goals. In the end it is not possible to ascertain the degree to which ideology played a role in their decisions.

III. Jewish Women

Anna Iuzefovich opened her school for Jewish girls in Simferopol in 1862. Several months later, an official of the Odessa Educational circuit wrote to St. Petersburg requesting financial help for the fledgling school. Beyond stating that the school, based on his own inspection, was functioning well, the education official emphasized that Iuzefovich was married to a medical doctor and that both of them were directly involved in running the school.[32] Thus, despite the fact that Anna Iuzefovich had obtained the certifications and permissions to open her private school for Jewish girls, it was the status of her husband that convinced at least one official of the value of her school.

The situation was even more stark for the seven women listed as co-principals with their husbands. In these cases a couple filed a joint application to open a private girls' school. However, only the certifications and qualifications of the male member of the couple were listed on the documentation. The school plan of the Levin family in Minsk, for example, twice referred to Mendel's status as a teacher of Russian in the local government Jewish school as well as stating that he would teach all academic subjects. Mendel's wife Rakhel, although listed as co-principal, has no stated qualifications or role in the school.[33]

For these wives and co-principals, it is simply not possible to ascertain any information about educational background or motivations. Some may have been deeply devoted to the cause of women's education and may have married men who would help them achieve their goals. Others may simply have served as figureheads, obviating the potential improprieties of a man running a school for girls. Many of the male principals who did not list a wife as co-principal made sure to show that their schools would nonetheless include the perceived benefits of the feminine presence. Bentsel Podshkol'nik's plan for his school in Rossiene (Vilna province) in 1857 stated, "A special governess, with appropriate permission, will be [hired] for the ongoing supervision of the orderliness and manners of the pupils."[34]

Of the thirty-three Jewish women listed as principals, however, only seven were co-principals with their husbands. Fully twenty-six Jewish women opened schools for Jewish girls entirely on their own merits. For these women an unusually high educational level was a necessity. They had either to provide certification of their graduation from a gymnasium or to pass an examination. Unfortunately, in most cases little to no information appears in their files on how they obtained their educational level. Although a few letters contain more information—such as when the curator of the Vilna educational circuit informed the Ministry offices in St. Petersburg that the girls' school originally opened by Gordon and later passed onto Rabbi Khazanovich would now, following Khazanovich's death, be placed in the able hands of Lidia Rudian, a graduate of the Kovno women's gymnasium[35]—most of the paperwork simply states that the principals had the "proper certifications."

Simeon Kraiz, based on data collected by the Jewish Colonization Association from a slightly later period, has suggested that Jewish women who worked in modern educational institutions were more likely than their male counterparts to have themselves received a modern formal education, whereas Jewish men were more likely to have had a traditional Jewish education.[36] In her recent monograph on Jewish women and literacy in Eastern Europe, Iris Parush comes to a similar conclusion based primarily on literary sources.[37] It is not possible to confirm this picture based purely on the data on these educators. There were those Jewish women, like Anna Berman and Matil'da Rotshtein, who hired Jewish men to teach religion in their schools and themselves taught general subjects.[38] However there were also women like Maria Mitkovitser, who taught religion in her private school for Jewish girls.[39]

So what led these and other educated Jewish daughters to open schools for their coreligionists? One answer is a lack of other viable options. Teaching and tutoring were the only professional options open to female high school graduates in the Russian empire without further study. At various times, depending on the vagaries of officialdom, medicine, midwifery, pharmacy, and dentistry were open to female professionals, but even when the legal climate was favorable, pursuing higher education required funding and other sacrifices well beyond the means of most Jewish women.[40]

To be sure, Jewish women did actively pursue higher education and were in fact overrepresented in the women's courses outside, and especially inside, the Pale of Settlement.[41] Nonetheless, the actual numbers remained fairly small. Professional education required not only money for tuition, but often also a move to another location and thus added living expenses. Residency restrictions also severely limited the opportunities for study outside of the Pale. For most Jewish women, even those with a good secondary education, higher education was simply beyond their reach.

Puah Rakovski, after separating from her husband, sought to support herself and her children as a midwife. However, neither her husband nor her father approved, which meant that she had access to neither a valid passport nor to funds. In the end she was able to garner support for a second plan. Rakovski was to reside with her grandfather while she completed the necessary reading and tutorials to pass examinations to become a teacher. The process took seven months of intense work. In her memoirs, Rakovski describes all of the subjects she studied as well as the grueling oral examination and model classroom teaching. Rakovski gained permission to open her first school for Jewish girls in Lomzhe and later opened a popular Zionist school in Warsaw.[42]

Although slightly outside the perimeters of this study in terms of both geography and chronology, Puah Rakovski offers a useful example. Rakovski exemplifies both financial need and passionate commitment. She needed a way to support herself and her children, but it is also clear from her writings that Rakovski considered her school a holy mission. Both as a feminist and a Zionist she was committed to providing the best possible education to her pupils. In the following passage, Rakovski explained what was at stake:

> Who says a girl should be allowed to learn Hebrew! Why that is certainly heresy [*apikorsos*], because one who teachers his daughter Torah it is as if he taught her licentiousness [*tiflus*]. Our people paid dearly for this archaic attitude. If our grandfathers and fathers and rabbis, as spiritual leaders, had not held this to be true, but the opposite, that Torah education should know no gender differentiation, such that Jewish daughters, exactly like the sons, had to be brought up on our Torah, and our culture and doctrines, unknown thousands of Jewish mothers would have been saved from assimilation, from apostasy, and through them also their sons, whom we have lost due to the attitudes they inherited from their assimilated mothers.[43]

Like Gordon, Rakovski combined conviction and commitment with genuine need. Also like Gordon, Rakovski, as a memoirist and active Zionist, was unusual among her contemporaries. Most left no record of their hopes and dreams. Mathil'da Rotshtein applied to open a school for girls in Kiev in 1871. Her application highlighted her difficult financial situation with her husband unable to work for health reasons and three children in the home. She also stated that she herself would be able to teach German, Russian, and crafts and that she had graduated from a school, although she was no longer in possession of the documents and did not offer specifics.[44]

It seems clear that Rotshtein would not have turned to teaching at that particular moment in her life were it not for her husband's illness. Here then is a case where a Jewish woman turned to educating other Jewish women for purely utilitarian reasons. On the other hand, Rakovski's story began in a similar way. She too needed money for her family and turned to teaching only reluctantly. Yet she went on to embrace the possibilities of educating her sisters. No such records exist for Rotshtein. She was granted permission to open a school, but there is no way of knowing whether the school served primarily as a source of income or whether she also actively used it to broaden the horizons of her coreligionists.

IV. Non-Jewish Women

In June 1848, the Kurland native Miss Doroteia Ekert requested permission to open a private school for Jewish girls in Vilna. Ekert had the educational qualifications to teach Russian and other secular subjects, and stated in her school's academic plan that "for the teaching of religion and literacy in the Judeo-German language, a Jew will be chosen by the parents of the pupils and with the permission of the Government to teach."[45] Her school soon received approval and opened its doors. But what led this educated Christian woman to turn her talents and background to the education of Jewish girls?

The evidence suggests that rather than Ekert coming to the Jews, the Jews came to Ekert. From 1845 until 1848 Ekert had been running a women's school in Vilna, but, she was forced to close it for lack of students. The fact that within such a short time after closing her general women's school Ekert was able to make contact with and gain the support of local Jews, while not a Jew herself, suggests that she had some previous connection. It is most likely that some Jewish girls had attended her general women's school. When that school proved untenable, Ekert realized that a group of Jews desired to educate their daughters in a modern, Russian, upper-class setting. She was thus able to count upon the support and attendance of local Jews in opening her new school.

For Miss Ekert, then, the idea of educating Jewish girls was a response to the desires of the Jewish community. As a single woman with a good education, Ekert was well suited for the teaching profession. In fact, it was the only profession available to her without further study. But instead of serving as a governess or private tutor, she wanted to run a school and found that Jews wanted to send their daughters to her school.

Ekert's materials do not speak of motivations or goals. As a single woman, it would seem that she turned to teaching at least in part to make a living. That she taught girls was a given, that she taught Jews may well have developed out of the particular circumstances in Vilna at the time. Was she, as an educated woman, convinced of the great societal or individual import of teaching women? It is difficult to know. Perhaps the only hint that she enjoyed what she was doing, and felt it was important, is that she continued running the school after she married.[46]

In 1856 the principal of a boarding school for upper-class girls in Kovno, Maria Siavtsillo, requested permission to open a section of her school to Jewish girls. The Jewish pupils would be taught in a separate room and receive religious instruction from the government rabbi.[47] Although Siavtsillo does not say as much, her case appears to mirror Ekert's. Siavtsillo became aware that her school could expand by accepting Jewish girls. Perhaps local Jews had even approached her. Unlike Ekert, she chose to allow her original school to remain open, but to add a separate section for Jews.

For a single well-educated Russian woman in need of making a living, education was a good option. If not highly respected, it was at least respectable, and elementary education of girls was a growing endeavor. For many women in this position, there was a personal interest in seeing to it that other girls had the opportunities for self-improvement and self-fulfillment provided by education. But of course it would have been far more natural for these women to educate others of their own faith. Culturally and linguistically, Jews were different from their neighbors.

It would thus appear that the demands of the market were crucial in leading non-Jewish women into Jewish schools. Interestingly, all ten of the non-Jewish women who ran schools for Jewish girls did so in the northern provinces of the Pale of Settlement. In fact, it was in this area that most of the private schools for Jewish girls opened. It was here that Jewish families sought out a modern and formal education for their daughters first and continuously. It was also here, significantly, that a particularly well-educated group of non-Jewish women lived.

From the time of the annexation of the Baltic lands well into the nineteenth century, Baltic Germans held a privileged position in Tsarist Russia. The usefulness of a native elite for the purpose of administration, as well as dynastic ties, guaranteed their status. The Lutheran Church in Russia was thus able to oversee high-level educational institutions.[48] Among the various ethnicities listed in the 1897 census, the Baltic Germans, male and female, surpassed all others by several percentage points in terms of formal education beyond elementary school.[49] Some of the women who came through the Lutheran educational system in the Baltic provinces later turned to educating their Jewish neighbors.

To my knowledge, no personal writings of these women survive. Their correspondence with the Ministry of Education, of course, conforms to the styles and expectations of such writing. In requesting additional funds for her school for Jewish girls in 1878, Nadezhda Bel'skiia wrote plaintatively of the difficulty of obtaining the best teachers on limited funds and of the importance of helping these girls to complete their education. However, a request for funding must by definition use hyperbole to state the case as well as the importance of the institution.

It is thus difficult to get beyond the level of opportunism in understanding how and why non-Jewish women opened schools for Jewish girls. Certainly non-Jewish Russian women in the late nineteenth century did not set out to become teachers for Jewish girls. No matter how they came to be teachers, they turned to teaching Jewish girls in particular because Jewish families wanted to educate their daughters and were willing to use non-Jewish teachers and principals. What we cannot know is how this relationship impacted on both sides. Did it lead to greater understanding between the two communities? Did the non-Jewish women see for themselves some sort of mission in russifying the Jews? We cannot yet answer these questions.

CONCLUSION

Part of what makes these educators intriguing is that they were both products of the changes filtering into the Russian Jewish community and agents of its spread. The expansion of Jewish women's education during the second half of the nineteenth century was the result of many interrelated factors, including a growing interest in women's education in educated Russian society, the influx of Haskalah ideas from the west, russification in the Jewish community, and a grassroots recognition of the benefits of modern formal education for girls and for boys.

These forces joined to create a new professional opportunity for the Jews of Russia and for a selection of their neighbors as well. Over the course of the second half of the nineteenth century these 150 or so educators were able to provide thousands of Jewish girls across the Pale of Settlement with access to basic literacy in Russian and new conceptions of the Jewish religion. Some of these girls would themselves go on to teach. Tsitsilia Osipovna Shikman, a graduate of Shevel' Perel's school for Jewish girls in Vilna, went on to teach Russian in the girls' section of a Vilna grammar school and Flora Kagan, who also graduated from Perel's school, later taught French and Russian at another school for Jewish girls in Vilna.[50] Although it is not possible to trace the trajectories of all of the other students, they unquestionably influenced their environment.

The men and women and Jews and non-Jews who took upon themselves the task of educating the next generation of Jewish girls did not do so solely out of a conscious concern to change the face of the Jewish community. It appears, in fact, that some of these individuals turned to teaching Jewish girls for purely pragmatic reasons because that was the best job they could get. Others wrote passionately of their commitment and concerns. Of course, the norm lies somewhere in the middle. Most of those who opened private schools for Jewish girls did so out of a combination of enlightened concerns and pure self-interest.

Examining the available information about these educators helps us to understand not only their motivations, but also the paths that led to teaching Jewish girls. For Jewish men, serving in the state rabbinate or Jewish school system led to opening a school for girls in many cases. For Jewish men and women, family connections also led directly and indirectly to the choice of education as a profession. Women, of course, had far fewer professional options than men. Educated non-Jewish women residing in the Pale of Settlement had the unexpected option of teaching Jewish girls. It would appear that for many, if not most, of the principals surveyed here, opening a school for Jewish girls was more the result of communal interest than of an initial commitment. Nonetheless, they would go on to provide thousands of Jewish girls with a modern formal education.

Principals of Private Schools for Jewish Girls, 1831-1881*		
Jewish Men		93
	Teachers in state Jewish schools	38
	State Rabbis	7
	Other	48
Women		43
	Jewish: Sole Principal	26
	Jewish: Co-Principal	7
	Non-Jews	10
Unknown		10
	Male	3
	Jewish	3
	No Information	4
Total		**146**

*The information in this table is drawn from numerous individual files as well as published and unpublished lists of schools. In most cases it was possible to ascertain basic information about the principals from these sources. Lacking this, I have used the name and wording of documents to figure out the gender and religious affiliation of the individual. In some cases even this was not possible. The two Jewish men who served both as teachers in state Jewish schools and as state rabbis are counted among the teachers.

NOTES

[1] See my "Private Schools for Jewish Girls in Tsarist Russia" (Ph.D. diss., Brandeis University, 2003), especially chapter four and pages 279-83. This figure (and this study as a whole) does not include the Kingdom of Poland, where modern private schools began opening earlier and in different circumstances. On schools in the Polish areas see for example Sabina Levin, "Bati-ha-Sefer ha-elimentariim ha-rishonim l'yeladim bnei moshe be-Varsha, be-shanim 1818-1830," *Gal-Ed* 1(1973).

[2] For the most complete chronicle of this expansion, see Elena Likhasheva, *Materialy dlia istorii zhenskgo obrazovanii v Rossii, 1086-1856* (St. Petersburg, 1899); and *Materialy dlia istorii zhenskgo obrazovanii v Rossii*, 1856-1880 (St. Petersburg, 1901).

[3] Christine Johanson, *Women's Struggle for Higher Education in Russia, 1855-1900* (Kingston and Montreal: McGill-Queen's University Press, 1987), chapter 1.

[4] Richard Stites, *The Women's Liberation Movement in Russia: Feminism, Nihilism, and Bolshevism, 1860-1930* (Princeton: Princeton University Press, 1978), 166-78, 191-98.

[5] Patrick L. Alston, *Education and the State in Tsarist Russia* (Stanford: Stanford University Press, 1969), chapter 5.

[6] A great deal has been written about the Russian Jewish *maskilim* and their platform for the improvement of education for the Jews. For a recent and successful treatment of the issue, see Mordekhai Zalkin, *Ba-'alot ha-Shahar: ha-haskalah ha-Yehudit ba-Imperya ha-Rusit ba-me'ah ha-tesha' 'esreh* (Jerusalem: Hebrew University, 2000), chapter 1.

[7] Y. Y. Weisberg, *Igerot Yehudah Leib Gordon* (Warsaw, 1894) vol. 1, 69.

[8] From an unpublished translation by David S. Zinberg.

[9] See, for example, Weisberg, *Igerot*, 133, 163-64, and *ha-Olam* 38 (1936): 656. For more on Gordon's literary career and public and private life, see Michael Stanislawski, *For Whom Do I Toil?: Judah Leib Gordon and the Crisis of Russian Jewry* (New York: Oxford University Press, 1988).

[10] For more on these two important reforms, see Michael Stanislawski, *Tsar Nicholas I and The Jews: The Transformation of Jewish Society in Russia, 1825-1855* (Philadelphia: The Jewish Publication Society, 1982).

[11] Eva Broido, *Memoirs of a Revolutionary* (London: Oxford University Press, 1967), 4.

[12] Ita (Pines) Yellin, *Leze'eza'ai* (Jerusalem: Ha-ma'arav Printing House, 1928), 12.

[13] Stanislawski, *For Whom Do I Toil?*, 27, 40.

[14] Ibid., 68.

[15] *Rossiiskii gosudarstvennyi istoricheskii arkhiv* [hereafter RGIA], fond 733, opis 98, delo 214, list 2-2ob. The standard Russian archival notation will be used hereafter: f. (*fond*), op. (*opis*), g (*god*), d. dd. (*delo, dela*), l. ll. (*list, listy*), ob. (*oborot*).

[16] RGIA, f. 733, op. 98, d. 94, l. 1 #ob.

[17] RGIA, f. 733, op. 189, d. 437, l. 3.

[18] RGIA, f. 733, op. 189, d. 198, l. 1-1 ob.

[19] RGIA, f. 733, op. 97, d. 13, l. 189.
[20] Bruce W. Lincoln, "Daily Life of St. Petersburg Officials," *Oxford Slavonic Papers* n.s. 8 (1975): 97-98.
[21] L. Gordon, "Rech'," *ha-Karmel: Prilozhenie k evreiskomy zhurnalu gakarmeliu* 6:28 (1866): 121-22.
[22] Shmuel Feiner, "Ha-ishah ha-yehudit ha-modernit: mikrah-mivhan be-yahase ha-haskalah veha-moderna," *Zion* 58:4 (1993).
[23] L. M. Rozenthal, *Toldot hevrat marve Haskalah be-Yisrael be-erets Rusia* (St. Petersburg: 1885), 170.
[24] S. G. Lozinskii, *Opisanie del byvshego arkhiva Ministerstva narodnogo prosveshcheniia: Kazennyie evreiskie uchilishcha* (Petersburg: 1920), 297.
[25] RGIA, f. 733, op. 189, d. 570, l. 7.
[26] RGIA, f. 733, op. 189, d. 570, ll. 6-11.
[27] RGIA, f. 733, op. 189, d. 130.
[28] RGIA, f. 733, op. 189, d. 474, l. 1-1ob.
[29] RGIA, f. 733, op. 189, d. 170 [File on the schools of Lazar and Anna Berman].
[30] RGIA, f. 733, op. 98, d. 427.
[31] RGIA, f. 733, op. 189, d. 481, l. 1; Rozenthal, *Toldot hevrat marve Haskalah*, 110.
[32] RGIA, f. 733, op. 98, d. 794, l. 1.
[33] RGIA, f. 733, op. 97, d. 419, ll. 2-2 ob.
[34] RGIA, f. 733, op. 98, d. 214, l. 2 ob.
[35] RGIA, f. 733, op. 189, d. 437, l. 3.
[36] Simeon Kraiz, "Bate-sefer yehudiim be-sefa ha-rusit be-Rusia ha-zarit" (Ph.D. diss., Hebrew University of Jerusalem, 1994), 319-20.
[37] Iris Parush, *Nashim kor'ot: yitronah shel shuliyut ba-hevrah ha-Yehudit be-mizrah Eropah ba-me'ah ha-tesha'-esreh* (Tel Aviv: Am Oved, 2001).
[38] RGIA, f. 733, op. 189, d. 170, l. 40 ob; f. 733, op. 189, d. 428, l. 2 ob.
[39] RGIA, f. 733, op. 98, d. 300, l. 2.
[40] For more on the development of higher education for women in Russia, see Johanson, *Women's Struggle*.
[41] Ruth A. Dudgeon, "The Forgotten Minority: Women Students in Imperial Russia, 1872-1917," *Russian History/ Histoire Russe* 9:1 (1982): 16-17.
[42] Puah Rakowski, *Zikhroynes fun a yiddisher revolutsionerin* (Buenos Aires: Tsentral-Farband fun Poylishe Yidn in Argentina, 1954), 39-54. See also the recent translation, *My Life as a Radical Jewish Woman: Memoirs of a Zionism Feminist in Poland,* (ed. Paula E. Hyman; Bloomington: Indiana University Press,

2002).

[43] Rakowski, *Zikhroynes*, 19.

[44] RGIA, f. 733, op. 189, d. 428, l. 2b ob.

[45] RGIA, f. 733, op. 97, d. 288, l. 2-2 ob.

[46] See for example RGIA, f. 733, op. 97, d. 336, l. 4.

[47] RGIA, f. 733, op. 98, d. 94, ll. 1-1 ob.

[48] Edward C. Thaden, R*ussia's Western Borderlands* (Princeton: Princeton University Press, 1984), 98, 196-97.

[49] Henning Bauer, et al., *Die Nationalitaten des Russischen Reiches in der Volkszahlung von 1897* (Stuttgart: Franz Steiner Verlag, 1991), 93-95.

[50] YIVO Institute for Jewish Research, Record Group 24, file 141, pages 74, 17.

The Transformation of Zionist Religious Rhetoric as Seen Through Its Yiddish-Language Propaganda: The Case of Galicia

Joshua Shanes

Recent scholarship on Jewish nationalism has focused on the movement's appropriation of traditional Jewish symbols and language. Jewish nationalists hoped in this way to legitimate their movement in terms of traditional Jewish values and to attract traditional Jews to the Jewish national idea. Israel Bartal, for example, describes how "the new nationalism made extensive use of traditional symbols that had been consciously and sometimes unconsciously expropriated from their traditional society, who did not always discern the novelty hiding behind the seemingly familiar words."[1] Eli Lederhandler, in an important essay on the relationship between Zionism and messianism, writes similarly that messianic rhetoric among early Jewish nationalists should not be mistaken for a genuine eschatological vision, but rather constituted a cultural code, a "vocabulary that made it possible for nationalists to enhance their effectiveness and legitimacy by hitching their star to a transcendent purpose:"

> In their struggle to gain recognition and support, [early Zionists] brandished certain evocative words – *geula* [Redemption], *yeshu'ah* [salvation], *ye'ud* [destiny], *kibbuz galuyot* [the Ingathering of the Exiles], *hazon* [prophetic vision], *ziyon* [Zion], and *erez avoteinu* [the Land of our Fathers] – that they knew were central to religious meaning in Judaism. By using such terms they were declaring their intention to decipher and proclaim their contemporary significance. Previously the sign and scepter of rabbinic dominance, the invocation of such consecrated words was intended to carry political weight in Jewish society.[2]

Although both of these scholars focus on Russian Zionist thinkers, their analysis provides an extremely cogent framework for understanding the rhetoric of Galician Zionists as well, particularly in their Yiddish-language publications. Jewish nationalism in Galicia was initially a movement focused nearly exclusively on the secular intelligentsia, especially Polonized students. Its activities and publications were thus primarily Polish-language affairs. Nevertheless, Galician Zionists did make some effort towards Yiddish-language propaganda as well, increasingly so as the nineteenth century drew to a close. I want to look at four Yiddish-language brochures produced by Galician Zionists, two during the movement's infancy in 1890 and 1891, the two others published a decade later in 1903 and 1904. While both the earlier and later texts appropriated religious rhetoric along the lines suggested above, the nature of this appropriation was not static, but rather reflected an important transformation within the Zionist movement itself.

DER KANTCHIK

In 1890 and 1891, Galicia's flagship Zionist association *Zion* released its first, and virtually only Yiddish-language publications of that period. Although advertised as popular works written for the "people," these booklets' intended audience was not the traditional masses, but rather the growing, but still small class of young students who had been raised in a religious milieu, but were increasingly drawn toward the modern world.[3] *Zion*'s leadership wanted to ensure that these secularizing students would ultimately settle in the Jewish national camp.

The first booklet, *Der Kantchik* [The Whip], subtitled *Kinos for Tisha B'av* [Lamentations for the Ninth of Av], begins with a warning against assimilation and an attack on Jewish "do-gooders" who were encouraging Jews to abandon "their" language in favor of Polish. (Whether this meant Yiddish or Hebrew was left deliberately vague—the brochure frequently extols the virtues of "our holy Hebrew language"—but here seems to be referring to the former.) Assimilation, it explains, is both undesirable and impossible because it denied the Jew his essential identity:

> Is it possible, my dear Jews, that one fine day, one of you will think to yourself that you are unhappy with your father, your mother and your brothers and sisters, and you will get up and go to the market to find a new father, a new mother, and new sisters and brothers? You laugh—it is really comical. And yet it is just the same when a person wants to become a Pole. What is born with you, you cannot later change....[4]

The Transformation of Zionist Religious Rhetoric 287

Such rhetoric clearly makes sense among Jews already experiencing Polonization, not among traditional Jews not yet similarly tempted. In fact, as the work progresses, it evinces an outspoken contempt for religious Jews by mocking them for their insincere tisha b'av prayers for the return to Jerusalem:

> But you, real Jews, how dare you come yet into the synagogue to complain over the destruction of Jerusalem? How are you not ashamed before God to say such lies?....You can't [do anything about it]? You don't have any money? For rendezvous in Carlsbad and Franzensbad you can spend thousands, but have you yet once given something for the land of Israel? Maybe you throw here and there a penny in the *Erets Yisrael* charity can for old Jews who go there to die and make a cemetery out of the land of Israel. Why don't they go to live there? Why don't you send young, healthy people with strong hands to work the land, for which you pray morning and night? Your prayers are chatter without heart and feeling.[5]

Again we see a modern program designed to appeal to readers already dissatisfied with the religious establishment and searching for a new identity. Indeed, it argues that Zionism is the most authentic interpretation of Judaism and that those who oppose it are hypocritical, even irreligious. The book closes with a discussion of *Zion*'s political agenda, particularly the establishment of modern Jewish schools (an explicitly anti-religious program based on the Haskalah's campaign against the traditional *heder*), the elections, and the need for a Yiddish-language journal (a paper "for the people" written in a "simple Yiddish") to defend Jewish interests.

DER VEKER

One year later, *Zion* published a sequel to *Der Kantchik* titled *Der Veker* [The Alarm Clock].[6] (The group misleadingly labeled the booklet volumes two and three in the "*Folksbibliothek*" [people's library] series, despite no such designation appearing on its predecessor.) Like *Der Kantchik*, *Der Veker* reflects an agenda designed to influence religious Jews seeking enlightenment, and likely to offend those who opposed it. It tells the story of a brilliant Talmudic student, Moshe, who through exposure to a Hebrew translation of Graetz's *History of the Jews* is awakened to the hypocrisy and closemindedness of the religious world, in which neither

Hebrew language nor Jewish history are valued at all, and thus begins a search for a more authentic Jewish identity. When a German book is found in his possession, his community stipend is cut and he is forced to seek menial labor to support himself.[7] This experience awakens him to the bitter poverty most Jews suffered, a situation of which the religious elite was totally unaware and unsympathetic.[8] After his father writes from Argentina of the miserable lot of immigrant Jews there, he and a relative resolve to move to Palestine together.

For good measure, the booklet interweaves a second story of a Jewish "assimilationist" in Galicia, who, despite his university education, could not secure any employment as a result of increased anti-Semitism. Devastated, his sister teaches him Hebrew, and he finds a position as a teacher in the Jewish school. The entire story is framed in appeals by *Zion* to support the Russian refugees by contributing to the Zionist project in Palestine and to join and support the Galician Zionist movement.

The innovation of cloaking nationalist propaganda inside a fictional story, narrated in a simple Yiddish style that closely resembled traditional storybooks, is clearly an important development both in Galician Zionism and in the history of Yiddish literature.[9] Moreover, the story justifies the Zionist ideology through the appropriation of religious imperatives: How can one pray properly without understanding Hebrew? What does "Next Year in Jerusalem" mean if not supporting those who actually try to move to the land of Israel?[10] In others words, it presents the demands of the Zionist movement as natural conclusions of religious Judaism, despite the fact that this rhetoric had never carried the meaning assigned to it by Zionists. At the same time, however, *Der Veker* does not pretend to be a defender of Orthodoxy. On the contrary, its content clearly betrays the author's sharp anti-religious (or at least anti-clerical) sentiment. It ridicules the religious establishment as both religiously hypocritical and socially insensitive, and argues that Zionism constitutes a more authentic Jewish ideology. In short, like *Der Kantchik*, it sought to influence the secularizing religious youth, who shared many of these criticisms, in favor of Zionism and the Jewish Enlightenment.

These two booklets constituted virtually the only Yiddish-language propaganda published directly by the Galician Zionist organizations in their first two decades of existence, from 1883 until 1903. The reason for this is quite simple—the core of Zionist leadership consisted of Polonized intellectuals who focused their outreach on other Polonized Jews. Not only

The Transformation of Zionist Religious Rhetoric

was their party organ published in Polish, but the vast majority of their public events were conducted in Polish or German as well.[11] What, then, does one make of these texts? To be sure, these exceptional booklets do validate scholarly arguments about the secular transformation of religious rhetoric. However, their starkly anti-clerical message clearly belies any pretense of leadership among traditional Jews, whom they categorically deride.

An interesting development began to emerge in the last years of the nineteenth century. As the Jewish nationalist movement grew increasingly confident, many of its leaders, especially those who themselves came out of a traditional background, increasingly attempted to attract members from within the traditional community itself. Traveling lecturers increasingly gave speeches in Yiddish, for example, and they increasingly held their lectures in synagogues or study houses rather than in Zionist or municipal halls.

Indicative of the Zionists' increasing turn towards traditional Jews is a pair of Yiddish-language People's Books [*Folks-bikhlekh*] published by Cracow Zionists in 1903 and 1904. In length and style, the booklets recall *Zion*'s "*Folksbibliothek*," published by the Lemberg group in 1890-91. A closer look at their content, however, reveals an important transformation in the Zionist program over the course of the decade. The earlier books had attacked traditional religious authority together with the assimilationists, hoping thereby to attract to Zionism modernizing religious students who had similarly rejected strict orthodoxy. Now, ten years later, Zionists were increasingly attempting to reach not only modernizing religious students, but also members of the traditional community itself. Their propaganda, therefore, could not attack the religious establishment so easily, but rather had to highlight more respectfully the compatibility of Zionism with Judaism, as it was then understood.

HANUKAH

The first booklet, *Hanukah*, presents itself as a traditional telling of the Hanukah story based on Talmudic and Midrashic sources, which it conspicuously cites. The author explains that at the time of the Hanukah story three parties existed among the Jews: "The Chasidim, [who were] the fully religious [*ganz frume*], the Sadducees, those who held strong in the Jewish religion, and the Hellenists, those who wanted all Jews to become true Greeks."[12] This innovative, if not entirely accurate, version of history particularly in its subtle distinction between the Chasidim and the Sadducees set up a vitally important argument for the author when, halfway through the booklet, he turns to the question, "What do we learn from this history?" Predictably, the author attempts to draw direct parallels between the "parties" during the Hellenistic period and the Jews in contemporary Galicia.

Today's Hellenists were, of course, the "assimilationists," "mostly *gebildete*, doctors, civil servants, merchants, small bankers and other such wealthy people." These misguided people blame the Jews' incomplete assimilation for the rise in anti-Semitism, he writes, and therefore seek total assimilation. Notably, the crimes of the assimilationists that the author lists focus on their religious laxities (Reform Temples which look like churches, neglect of *kashrut*, Sabbath and Hanukah-lights, etc.), matters that would have most offended traditionalist Jews.[13]

The most important innovation of the book is its critique of the Chasidim, a name he inaccurately applies to the masses of "simple" Jews in Hasmonean times who were "too afraid" to oppose Greek rule. Today's Chasidim, he concludes, are the same. Unlike *Der Kantchik* and *Der Veker*, *Hanukah* does not accuse the religious masses of hypocrisy because, for example, they pray for redemption but do not support the Zionists. On the contrary, the author praises their sincerity at great length. The Chasidim, he writes, "are true, good Jews, who want with their whole heart that they and their children should remain Jews":

> They have not yet given up hope that Jews must one day be redeemed from exile. They have not removed from their prayer books the words "Zion" and "Jerusalem." They still pray three times a day and ask God to lead them to the land of Israel and renew them as a People, as a free and independent People in their own land, as God had promised them....We do not want to suspect any Jew that he means any differently in his heart as he prays in his mouth. We want to recognize that not only do the majority of religious Jews mean this with their whole heart, but that all of them, all religious and "genuine" Jews [are sincere]. Just one thing is difficult for us: what are they waiting for? And how exactly do they suppose that God will help...where one holds his hands in his pockets and does not want to do anything himself?[14]

Ultimately, the booklet, like its predecessors a decade earlier, argued

The Transformation of Zionist Religious Rhetoric

for actively speeding the redemption through human agency, something that clearly contradicted Jewish tradition, at least as it was interpreted by most religious authorities at the time.[15] Unlike its predecessors, however, *Hanukah* portrays the religious masses extremely sympathetically, suggesting that their resistance to Zionism is based on a mild misunderstanding of Torah; namely, the role of human agency in bringing the redemption. The Maccabees, of course, provide just the instance of religious Jews actively fighting to restore national sovereignty that the author needed to prove his religious credentials:[16]

> Haven't they learned anything from those "Chasidim" in the Hasmonean time, who hid themselves in the desert...while the "Hellenists" in Jerusalem turned the world upside-down, converting young and old, contaminating the Temple, until the Hasmoneans came and began to fight, to make war—even on the Sabbath, just to save the land from the enemy and to be able to live free, as God intended.

Finally, the author points to unnamed religious authorities who have seen the truth of Zionism and embraced the new movement. In other words, the booklet argues, religious Jews need not fear that they would be joining a heretical movement (as most religious leaders in fact argued).[17] "Many religious, great rabbis and sages have understood this as common sense," the booklet concludes, "that God only helps those who do something themselves, and He sends His blessings only where there is already something there." That is why they have joined the Zionists, "just as the 'chasidim' who joined the Hasmoneans."[18]

WHAT IS ZIONISM?

In 1904, Cracow Zionists produced a second *Folks-bikhlekh*, titled *What is Zionism?*[19] Although twice the length of its predecessor, and written mostly in Judeo-German (i.e., German in Hebrew characters) rather than in Yiddish, it too sought to reach out to the religious Chasidim who constituted the overwhelming majority of the Jewish population. The author begins with a brief history of the Zionist movement, describing the contribution of the "true Jewish sages" Moses Hess, Leon Pinsker (famous, readers are told, for quoting the Talmudic dictum, "If I am not for myself, then who will be for me"), and, of course, Theodor Herzl ("a great sage, welcomed in the courts of kings"). Clearly, the author hoped to convince religious Jews unfamiliar with these extremely secular thinkers that they were in fact Orthodox. Similarly, he calls the First Zionist Congress a gathering of "Jewish sages from around the world" who met to decide whether Herzl's plan was feasible: "Since the destruction of the Temple, since the Jews have been in exile, this was the first time that Jews were gathered from all four corners of the world to advise openly about the situation of the Jews, and to consider by what means to help the Jews."[20] Thus the Congress is portrayed as a sort of Sanhedrin that lent religious support to Herzl's plan, rather than an assembly of confirmed, mostly secular Zionists already committed to Herzl's leadership.[21]

Throughout the work, the author strives to prove the feasibility of Zionism. He writes, for example, that leading non-Jewish intellectuals were nearly universal in their positive assessment of the movement.[22] More disturbingly, he misrepresented foreign governments, particularly the Sultan of the Ottoman Empire, as being entirely favorable to the enterprise. The only problem, he writes, is that the Sultan feared that not enough Jews would come; he demanded proof that the Jews would all come. This is why the shekel, the annual dues owed by every Zionist, was set at one mark, one frank, etc. Beyond the funds it raised for organizational expenses, it gave a head count of committed Zionists.[23]

This much was actually quite true. The practice was another appropriation of Jewish tradition—the original shekel collection was God's preferred method of counting the Jews after the exodus from Egypt. The suggestion that Herzl constituted today's Moses or that the shekel counted not Zionists but Jews (i.e., genuine "Jewish" Jews) was absolutely deliberate. "What is Zionism?" goes so far as to calm those who doubt the feasibility of Herzl's plan by recalling the biblical passage in which Jews in Egypt doubted Moses's declaration that the time of their redemption had come.[24]

Ultimately, "What is Zionism?" concludes, much the same as its predecessor (*Hanukah*), by lavishing praise on the piety of Galician Jews while insisting that the Torah demands of Jews that they take action themselves in order to receive God's blessings. Only divine blessing brings our sustenance and healing, it proclaims, yet no one would sit idly by without working for food or going to doctors.[25] The same is true of the Jewish return to the land of Israel. At the same time, however, in an attempt to disarm Orthodox critics who still accused Zionism of false messianism, the booklet candidly admits, "In truth, Zionism will not bring redemption

The Transformation of Zionist Religious Rhetoric 293

for the Jews like the exodus from Egypt or the redemption from the Babylonian exile." Rather, it is an attempt to find a safe haven [*makom menucha*] for persecuted Jews throughout the world, who simply cannot go on suffering. "The true redemption will first be with the coming of the Messiah." Nevertheless, it concludes, if all the Jews will join together under the flag of the Zionists and everyone will give according to his ability, in this merit perhaps the promise of the prophets will be realized and the true redeemer will come.[26] Thus he manages to appropriate prophetic language even as he disavows this very messianism.

CONCLUSION

Recent scholarship has reminded scholars of the importance of reading Zionist rhetoric carefully in order to appreciate its sometimes more, sometimes less subtle transformation of traditional Jewish language. These four texts clearly highlight the extent to which this is the case. The very nature of the Yiddish language, with its easy integration of religious rhetoric and biblical verse, enabled Zionists to take advantage of such rhetoric and its religious connotations on behalf of an argument that was certainly untraditional.

At the same time, however, these texts also indicate the sophistication of their authors and the changing nature of their audience. While all four writers attempted to appropriate religious rhetoric in order to establish themselves as the new priesthood of the Jewish people, they carefully catered their publications to their intended readers. The earlier texts, as we have seen, present sharp anti-clerical polemics attractive to modernizing Jews anxious to justify their estrangement from religious Judaism while simultaneously affirming an alternative Jewish identity in Jewish nationalism. As Zionists increasingly attempted to reach out to traditional Jews potentially attracted to the idea of Jewish nationhood, such anti-religious rhetoric was dramatically curtailed, at least in the movement's Yiddish-language propaganda. While it could not avoid antagonizing "Orthodox" leaders appalled by the activist heresy of modern Zionism, it did succeed in attracting traditional Jews uncomfortable with outspoken secular attacks on the religious establishment, but willing to consider Zionist arguments that based themselves on religious rhetoric, despite their "heretical" program.

NOTES

[1] Israel Bartal, "Responses to Modernity: Haskalah, Orthodoxy, and Nationalism in Eastern Europe," in *Zionism and Religion* (ed. Shmuel Almog, et al.; Hanover: Brandeis University Press, 1998), 21.

[2] Eli Lederhandler, *Jewish Responses to Modernity: New Voices in America and Eastern Europe* (New York: New York University Press, 1994), 30.

[3] For a review of the first book, see *Selbst-Emanzipation*, October 3, 1890. According to Ehrenpreis, *Zion* issued the manifesto in Yiddish in order to counteract the spread of "assimilationism" among the Jewish urban masses, but it was primarily the more modern elements of Jewish society who were attracted to Polonization, not the traditional masses. Ehrenpreis, "Zionist Movement in Galicia," [Hebrew] *Hamagid* (November 15, 1894), 353.

[4] *Der Kantchik*, 7.

[5] Ibid., 17.

[6] Samual Gutman, *Der Veker* (Lemberg, 1891). *Zion* did not initially intend to publish a sequel; it did so only because *Der Kantchik* sold poorly and, according to Gershom Bader, because *Zion*'s attempt at a Yiddish newspaper (the *Yidishe Folkszeitung*) had folded. The booklet is printed anonymously by the association *Zion*, but *Hamagid*'s review (July 9, 1891), 215, indentifies the author. (Gutman later became rabbi at the progressive Temple in L'vov, ironically as a result of his ability to preach in Polish.) An original copy is available at the Jewish National Library, Jerusalem.

[7] Notably, the story has the religious establishment blame Moshe's "heresy" on the Orthodox political party *Machzike-Hadath* because of the rotten influence of their "newspaper," published (heretically) in Hebrew. The accusation was not merely that the "Chasidic" youth were being exposed to worldly knowledge, but that they were being exposed to the Hebrew language itself, which they had no business studying as a modern language (*Der Veker*, 21). This accusation was in fact raised against the party's chief Chasidic supporter, the Rebbe of Belz, by its chief Chasidic opponent, the Rebbe of Sadeger. In his memoirs, the paper's first editor Isaac Ewen commented that history vindicated the Rebbe of Sadeger, for the newspaper did in fact serve as a way station for young Chasidim to join the Haskalah and later the Zionists. For an English translation, see Lucy Dawidowicz, *The Golden Tradition: Jewish Life and Thought in Eastern Europe* (Boston, 1967), 199.

[8] A prospective match for him had been threatened when the bride's father discovered that Moshe's father was a simple worker. This awakened a deep

animosity in Moshe for the haughty contempt for manual labor by the religious elite; even the *heder* teacher, whose social position ranked very low in traditional Jewish society, scorned his father "because he is a manual laborer who earns his tiny piece of bread honestly, with his own hands" (*Der Veker*, 22).

[9] According to its review in *Hamagid*, *Der Veker* was deliberately written in a more colloquial Yiddish than its predecessor in order to be better understood "by the masses."

[10] This is the final sentence read at the Passover feast, a prayer for the coming of the Messiah and the ingathering of all Jews to the land of Israel. Despite its appropriation by the Zionists, the prayer did not demand that Jews move to Jerusalem or support those that do. As Eli Lederhandler put it, "'Next year in Jerusalem' is not a statement of geographic intent, but of spiritual aspiration" (*Jewish Responses to Modernity*, 26).

[11] Zionist groups directly published few Yiddish-language materials before the end of the century, but Jewish nationalists published a number of short-lived Yiddish-language newspapers independently throughout the 1890s. See my "Papers for the Folk: Jewish Nationalism and the Firth of the Yiddish Press in Galicia," *Polin* 16 (2003): 167-87. See also "Neither Germans nor Poles: Jewish Nationalism in Galicia before Herzl, 1883-1897," *Austrian History Yearbook* 34 (2003):191-214.

[12] M. Henes, *Chanukah* (Cracow, 1903), 6.

[13] Ibid., 12. Some "enlightened" houses even shame themselves with Christmas trees, adds the author for good measure.

[14] Ibid., 12.

[15] On Orthodox reactions to Zionist messianism, see Aviezer Ravitsky, *Messianism, Zionism, and Jewish Religious Radicalism* (Chicago: University of Chicago, 1996).

[16] Although ironically first sponsored by the integrationist society *Shomer Israel* in 1883, *Hanukah* celebrations (known as Maccabee festivals) had served as Galician Zionism's most important annual event since the beginning of the movement in the 1880s, quickly spreading throughout Central and Eastern Europe. On the centrality of *Hanukah* in the early Zionist movement, see Francois Guesnet, "Hanuka and its Function in the Invention of a Jewish-Heroic Tradition in Early Zionism, 1880-1900," in *Nationalism, Zionism, and Ethnic Mobilization* (ed. Michael Berkowitz; Leiden: Brill, 2004), 227-45.

[17] Ravitsky, *Messianism*, 40-78.

[18] Ibid., 13.

[19] Shmuel Goldberg, *What is Zionism?* (Cracow, 1904).

[20] Ibid., 9.

[21] Religious and secular Zionists alike struggled to obscure the Zionist Congress's

overtly secular orientation in presenting itself to traditional Jewry. On traditional Jewry's opposition to Herzlian Zionism, see Yosef Salmon, *Religion and Zionism: First Encounters* (Jerusalem, 2002), 279-306.

[22] Goldberg, *What is Zionism?*, 15.
[23] Ibid., 13.
[24] Ibid., 31.
[25] Ibid., 29.
[26] Ibid., 32.

Aristotle & the Ostjuden: Philosophical Thought Among the First Generations of Eastern European *Maskilim*

Abraham P. Socher

Amos Funkenstein posed the following historical puzzle about the intellectual character of the Jewish Enlightenment [Haskalah]:

> The Haskalah saw itself as part of the Enlightenment. Many of its basic tenets corresponded indeed to those of the "Aufklärer," "philosophes," and "illuministi." Yet its attitude towards the medieval tradition of Jewish philosophy was throughout different and positive: so much so that one can, without exaggeration, tie the beginning of the Haskalah to the renewed interest in medieval religious philosophy. The contrast with the European Enlightenment is blatant and calls for an explanation.[1]

It is a commonplace of Jewish historiography that the eighteenth century exponents of Haskalah regarded the movement of medieval Jewish rationalism as both precedent and example. This is famously typified in the well-known *maskilic* adaptation of the medieval slogan "from Moses to Moses no one arose like Moses." In the late middle ages, the statement had paired the biblical lawgiver with the great medieval philosopher and halakhist Moses Maimonides; it was now used to pair the latter with Moses Mendelssohn, the standard bearer of the Haskalah.[2] What is striking and productive about Funkenstein's question is that it points out just how anomalous such an identification was within the context of the European Enlightenment.

Before discussing Funkenstein's puzzle and the way in which it is bound up with the question of Eastern European Jewish participation in the first phases of the Haskalah, I want to connect it to another related question in Jewish intellectual history. This is the question of when the movement of Jewish Aristotelian rationalism, of which Maimonides was the greatest exponent, really ended. The consensus view among historians of Jewish philosophy is that this school of thought petered out in the sixteenth century and was thereafter at best a set of literary sources that were occasionally and eclectically taken up by later thinkers, including the *maskilim* [proponents of the Haskalah].

Alfred Ivry has concisely summed up this position in a discussion of Jewish Averroism, which was the most systematic and radical current in the medieval Jewish Aristotelian tradition. Ivry writes:

> Jewish philosophy thus remained, in varying degrees, indebted to Averroës and to Jewish Averroism for its continued vitality into the sixteenth century. When Jews began to philosophize again in the late eighteenth century, Averroës and Aristotle were no longer their guides to truth.[3]

In speaking of the Jewish return to philosophy, Ivry is clearly referring to Moses Mendelssohn, who, though he had read Maimonides with devotion and care, turned principally to Leibniz and Wolff rather than Aristotle and Averroës when he began to philosophize in the middle of the eighteenth century. In this picture, medieval rationalism and the heroic image of Maimonides provided an historical precedent for such a turn, but did not provide a theoretical vocabulary or a set of technical issues. If this is true, then Funkenstein's puzzle becomes a question of *maskilic* rhetoric rather than the more interesting historical anomaly of a genuinely backward-looking Enlightenment, in which there might have been a serious engagement with medieval Aristotelianism.

For present purposes, I simply stipulate that this general picture is true of Mendelssohn, his lifelong engagement with Maimonidean texts—he attributed his hunchback to an adolescence bent over the *Guide of the Perplexed*—notwithstanding.[4] It is certainly true of many though not all of the late eighteenth century Western European *maskilim* (for instance, Lazarus Ben David, Markus Herz, Saul Ascher, but not Isaac Euchel or Solomon Pappenheim). But it is demonstrably not true of Eastern European *maskilim*, such as Solomon Maimon, Isaac Satanov, and Mendel Lefin. In fact, late eighteenth century Jewish philosophy is precisely marked by a brief return to, and struggle over, a set of characteristic medieval Aristotelian and even Averroistic arguments, doctrines, and tropes.

II

As Funkenstein recognized, one of the main reasons for the eighteenth century anomaly he had pointed out was biographical. The first encounter most eighteenth century Hebrew readers had with any version of systematic philosophical rationalism had been through the work of Maimonides, his commentators, and opponents, which they read as young students of rabbinic literature. Such a reader could gain access to this tradition most readily through the philosophical sections of Maimonides' canonical halachic works, the *Commentary on the Mishnah* and his comprehensive code of Jewish law, the *Mishneh Torah*, which were a part of any complete rabbinic library. Further study sometimes led to Maimonides' *Guide of the Perplexed*, which had been republished, together with the commentary of three late medieval commentators, for the first time in almost two centuries in 1742 by the enterprising Wullfian Press, which published several other non-halakhic books.[5] Finally, the independent works of other medieval and early modern Jewish philosophers and scientists, and even of Aristotle and his great twelfth century Arabic commentator Averroës, still circulated in Hebrew manuscripts and a few rare early modern editions.

Such works had introduced the *maskilim* to the possibilities of a philosophical rationalism and science, which were, if not quite commensurate with current European thought, at least intelligibly related to it in a way that other genres of Hebrew literature, such as halachic responsa and codes, talmudic commentaries and novellae, biblical commentaries and sermons, were not.[6] In republishing and commenting upon Maimonides and others in the Jewish philosophical tradition, these early *maskilim* sought to influence others in an intellectual culture whose epistemic ideal was still the well-glossed text rather than empirical observation or mathematical demonstration. However, the question remains as to the nature of the relationship between such texts and the philosophical discourse of the Enlightenment, in the eyes of the *maskilim*.

In a formidable series of books and essays, David Sorkin has implicitly addressed Funkenstein's question by reframing the Haskalah in the context of the contemporary movements of the Protestant theological Enlightenment and Reform Catholicism as a third moderate, harmonizing attempt at internal religious reform in eighteenth century Germany.[7] Although this is suggestive and no doubt certain ideas were in the eighteenth century air, it is important to note the relatively small extent to which Sorkin traces demonstrable lines of horizontal influence from texts and figures in these movements to *maskilim*. More critically, his attempt fails to grapple with the radically anti-rabbinic tenor of many of the *maskilim*, who were nonetheless deeply engaged with medieval texts. Such medieval preoccupation simply did not imply religious moderation.[8]

His general claim that the Haskalah drew upon the moderate fideistic "Hispano-Jewish" tradition of thought, epitomized by a medieval figure like Judah Halevi, is important, but underestimates the importance of more medieval radical voices (including Maimonides).[9] More crucially, it underestimates the extent to which the radical and moderate voices were part of a single discourse that the *maskilim* were attempting to renew in radically changed social circumstances. In fact, *maskilim* engaged Maimonides and the medieval philosophical tradition in different ways and at varying levels of intensity. What they shared was a set of distinctive texts, arguments, and concepts—in short, a world of discourse—at the center of which stood Maimonides' medieval Aristotelianism.

In the pages that follow, I argue for this claim through a brief discussion of three linked episodes involving five eighteenth century Jewish intellectuals in the decade after Moses Mendelssohn's death in 1786. Each of the three episodes is related to the attempt to re-present central texts of Aristotle, Maimonides, and the Averroist tradition of commentary to an enlightened Jewish readership. The figures that I discuss are Solomon Maimon (1752-1800), Isaac Euchel (1756-1804), Isaac Satanov(1732-1804), Mendel Lefin (1749-1826), and Pinchas Eliyahu Hurwitz (1765-1821).[10]

III

Solomon Maimon (who cheekily renamed himself after the medieval master) was perhaps the most original of the *maskilim* mentioned above. In fact, he was so famously brilliant and idiosyncratic that he might be thought to be a kind of outlying case, so that even if it is granted that he was a kind of late Aristotelian Averroist, he will merely have been the exception that proved the rule. In fact, Maimon's life and thought can be understood only as a participant in a larger religious and philosophical discourse of the early Haskalah, that has been largely lost or occluded in later historical accounts.

Maimon's mature philosophical work has, until recently, been discussed mostly in the light of his theoretical commitments to, and revision of, Kantian Idealism and Kant's immediate predecessors, Leibniz and Wolff. However, he was decisively marked by his early encounter with Maimonides, his radical Aristotelian commentators, and their opponents.

Indeed, as I have argued at length elsewhere, his influential work as one of the first great post-Kantian Idealists is best understood as in large part growing out of this medieval philosophical tradition.[11]

I begin at the outset of Maimon's publishing career, with the publication of his post-Kantian commentary to the first part of Maimonides' *Guide of the Perplexed*, titled *Giva'at ha-Moreh* and edited by Isaac Euchel, who was also the editor of *Ha-Meassef*, the flagship journal of the Haskalah. One of the most interesting things about this project is the genuine enthusiasm that Euchel, who was arguably the most influential literary *maskil* of the period, showed for the re-publication and interpretive renovation of the most canonical work of medieval Jewish philosophy.[12] Needless to say, no lapsed Catholic *Aufklärer*, or even proponent of Catholic Reform, ever performed such services for Aquinas' *Summa*. In 1789, Euchel and an anonymous Maimon published a prospectus for the work in *Ha-Meassef* which promised to elucidate, correct, and supplement the Maimonidean "peripatetic philosophy...which follows Aristotle and those who followed him," in light of the author's deep and sustained study of modern philosophy.[13] They published his commentary together with the fourteenth century Averroist commentary of Moses of Narbonne (Narboni). Narboni had completed his *Beur* to the *Guide* in 1362, and, though it had been known by Maimonidean cogniscenti for centuries, the commentary had never been published.[14]

In exhorting the readers of *Ha-Meassef* to support the publication of *Giva'at ha-Moreh*, Euchel placed it squarely in the tradition of radical Maimonidean commentary, emphasizing that it elucidated not only the *Guide* but Narboni's commentary as well:

> *Maskilim*! You see the great value of these commentaries, the depth of the thought of the sage Narboni, and the lucid way in which he is explicated by the author of *Giva'at ha-Moreh*, who establishes each idea and enlightens with the lamp of his commentary...both the *Guide* and Narboni clearly. There is no need to speak further in their praise for you will judge their excellence and utility for us in this time.[15]

In short, Maimon's commentary promised to help re-motivate not merely a canonical work of Jewish philosophy, but also the world and vocabulary of medieval Jewish philosophical discourse.

It is worth noting, in this connection, the particular place that Narboni occupied in that world. In 1625, Joseph Solomon Delmedigo—a good candidate for the last Jewish radical Aristotelian on Ivry's periodization of Jewish philosophy—wrote to a student that the four leading commentators on the *Guide of the Perplexed* (he was familiar with eighteen) were like the "four sons" of the Passover Haggadah. One was wise, one wicked, one simple, and one did not know how to ask.[16] The three "good" sons were, respectively, Shem Tov ben Joseph ben Shem Tov, Asher ben Abraham Crescas, and Profiat Duran, whose commentaries had been included in the Rennaisance edition of the *Guide* and its 1741 reprint.[17] The wicked son was Narboni, whose comments often unpacked or radicalized (depending upon one's perspective) the esoteric philosophical doctrine of Maimonides' text in an Averroist key.[18] The remark was probably meant as a compliment by Delmedigo.[19]

Narboni's wickedness, and that of other Jewish Averroists, had been to find within Maimonides' *Guide* a set of radical Aristotelian theses regarding topics such as creation, God's knowledge of particulars, and the linked topics of human knowledge and the possibility of immortality.[20] In each case, such interpreters understood Maimonides' project to be one in which the received doctrines of biblical and rabbinic tradition were brought before the tribunal of medieval Aristotelian reason and reinterpreted, if necessary, in order to conform with it.

Perhaps most radical was their suggestion that, according to Maimonides, Jewish religious doctrine and practice were not so much constitutive of the good life as a means towards it. Thus, the beliefs and commandments of the Torah were understood to have been promulgated because they lead the adherent to human perfection, which, strictly speaking, lies beyond them. That perfection consists not in devout religious practice or belief, but rather in Aristotelian *theoria*: the contemplation of the universal truths of science and metaphysics and theology through union with the Active Intellect. On such a reading, Maimonides' *Guide* genuinely demonstrates the social utility of the apparent irrationalities and superfluities of Jewish religious doctrine and practice, but it also points beyond them to a knowledge whose universality is unmarked by the particularities of religion or indeed any particulars at all.

The appeal of this philosophical vision to proponents of the Haskalah such as Maimon and Euchel was that it provided a traditional (though always contested) basis for the sovereignty of universal reason over religion. Such a vision mirrored the social promise of the European Enlightenment that Jews might meet with their Christian counterparts as equals within the public sphere of discourse.[21] Moreover, it did so by using the biblical and rabbinic prooftexts and Hebrew theological idiom in which Maimon, Euchel, and their readers were schooled.

The danger of such a philosophy was in the antinomian possibilities of its instrumentalization of religion. If the commandments of the Torah were prescribed only as a first approximation of the philosophical life to which they ultimately point, why not dispense with them altogether?[22] The special resonance of Delmedigo's witticism about Narboni, and his attraction to Maimon and Euchel, should now be clear. The wicked son asks "What is this service to you?" from some standpoint outside the culture; in so doing, he removes himself from the community of believers.

Maimon began his commentary to Maimonides' *Guide* with the following programmatic statement:

> The *telos* [*tachlit*] of man's activities, in his aspect as a possessor of freewill and choice, is human excellence [*hatzlachat ha-enoshit*], and this human excellence necessarily follows upon the attainment of perfection [*shelemut*]. Here, then, is a topic worthy of research: what is the nature of this attainment of perfection, which we have mentioned? And what are the means through which it is possible to reach it? And we shall say: the perfection of any being consists in the passing over from the potential to the actual, as with the perfection of a tree, for example, which produces fruit. And the perfection of man is intellection [Haskalah].[23]

Although Maimon eventually goes on to develop this line of thought in some ways that can no longer be called "peripatetic," each of the key terms as well as the overall argument of this passage is thoroughly Aristotelian, and its conclusion that the *telos* of man, and the nature of human excellence, is simply a true cognition of the world is in keeping with the radical Maimonidean tradition.[24] Moreover, Maimon was entirely aware of this and expected his audience to be so as well.

Indeed, Maimon's precise choice of words to describe this true cognition is telling. He refers to it as "Haskalah." Here too, Maimon is employing medieval philosophical terminology with care, since the word is just the abstract noun form of the Hebrew word for intellect, *sekhel*, but it is also, the self-chosen name of the Jewish Enlightenment. Thus, Maimon can also be taken to be making the polemical claim that the ultimate purpose of man is conforming to the ideal of the Berlin Jewish Enlightenment or, perhaps more plausibly, to be staking out a version of the Haskalah that was closer to Aristotle and Averroës—or more precisely to Maimonides and Narboni—than that of Mendelssohn.

Maimon's punning polemic and its theoretical background did not go unnoticed. A few years later, in 1797, Pinhas Eliyahu Hurwitz, an eclectic traditionalist from Vilna who had also lived for a while in Berlin and was familiar with the participants of the Berlin Haskalah, objected. Hurwitz's book, *Sefer ha-Berit* ["The Book of the Covenant"], was exceedingly odd and occasionally brilliant. For our present purposes, it can be described simultaneously as a counter-Enlightenment primer of science and philosophy for the traditional Jewish reader and a commentary on the Kabbalistic system of the sixteenth century mystic, R Hayyim Vital. Remarkably, it combines a defense of traditional Judaism in post-Lurianic terms with a pre-Copernican account of natural science. The book was published anonymously in Brünn; before Hurwitz revealed his authorship, it was rumored to be the work of the great R. Eliyahu of Vilna or possibly even a posthumous work of Moses Mendelssohn. In an interesting passage, Hurwitz attacked Maimon for his Aristotelian arrogance. He wrote:

> And I saw the philosopher and author of the *Giva'at ha-Moreh*, in the Introduction to his commentary to the *Guide of the Perplexed*, boast that philosophy brings us to the final perfection in our times. And his words are not surprising, for in all of the previous generations, philosophers have spoken like this, in particular since Aristotle.[25]

Hurwitz was familiar with the terms of Maimon's argument and even inclined to agree with him that the Haskalah was simply another version of medieval radical Aristotelianism. However, he also held that the results of this philosophy could never be conclusively established and ultimately betrayed the particular terms of the Jewish covenant with God.[26] Hurwitz was very far from being a proponent of the Haskalah in any form, let alone the radical enlightenment supported by Maimon and Euchel. What is important for our purposes is that he understood the Aristotelian language in which they spoke and responded in kind.

IV

Isaac Satanov, who ambivalently stood in the space between a self-declared heretic like Maimon and a traditionalist like Hurwitz, also explicitly recognized the challenge of a kind of revived Averroism and attempted to fashion a more moderate philosophical Haskalah, which looked to Aristotle and Maimonides, but not to Averroës and Narboni. In 1789, at precisely the same time as Maimon and Euchel were planning their radical edition of the *Guide of the Perplexed*, Satanov re-published a late medieval Hebrew translation of Aristotle's *Nichomachean Ethics*, titled *Sefer ha-Middot* ["The Book of Virtues"], together with his own commentary. In this commentary (especially to *Ethics*, Book X), Satanov wrestled with the relationship between Aristotle's ideal of the contemplative life and the demands of Halachah, which do not seem to allow for the more or less solitary cultivation of the theoretical intellect.

As a work of philosophy, Satanov's commentary is eclectic and literary to a debilitating degree. Although he was a master of Hebrew style in all genres, Satanov simply did not possess the philosophical acuity of Maimon or Euchel. But its interest for us is elsewhere. What it demonstrates is the recognition on the part of a leading Eastern European Jewish intellectual of the continued relevance and potency of Aristotle and the Jewish Aristotelian tradition. In his *Haskama*, [rabbinic approbation] which prefaced the book, R. Tzvi Hirsch Levin, the moderate Chief Rabbi of Berlin, underlined precisely the contemporary need for a moderate, fideistic commentary to Aristotle.

Five years later, Satanov succeeded Maimon's collaborator Isaac Euchel as the head of the Berlin Haskalah's publishing house. Among his first projects was a new and complete edition of Maimonides' *Guide of the Perplexed*. As a savvy publisher, Satanov economized by using the plates of Maimon's *Giva'at HaMoreh* together with the *Biur* of Narboni for the first part of the *Guide*. However, he declined to use either commentary for the newly typeset second and third parts of the *Guide* (the remaining parts of Maimon's commentary were thus lost, and Narboni's *Biur* was not published in a complete edition until 1852). Instead, Satanov wrote his own more moderate commentary, in which he explicitly refrained from "correcting" the master, as had Maimon (and for that matter Narboni).

In this new, complete edition of the *Guide* (the first since the 1553 Sabionetta edition), Satanov included only his own commentary, which as he explicitly stated in the Introduction aimed neither to modernize nor to radicalize the teachings of Maimonides. Satanov promised his readers to explicate Maimonides' *Guide* in its proper context as one which more than any other work "since the Second Exile of Israel from its land...provides the Torah of God with a way and a path for the words of our sages of blessed memory," rather than updating or subtly undermining them.[27] In short, Satanov aimed to play the "good son" to Solomon Maimon's "wicked son," in the same way in which Shem Tov had attempted to moderate and blunt the sharp edge of Narboni's Averroist interpretation of Maimonides in the fifteenth century. To return to Alfred Ivry's thesis about the history of Jewish philosophy, Satanov returned to Aristotle but not to his great commentator Averroës or his successors.

Mendel Lefin, who like Isaac Satanov was from the city of Satanov, Podolia, held similar ambitions for the appropriation of Maimonides for a moderate religious Enlightenment. Lefin was a gifted translator and publicist who is perhaps best known for his ethical tract *Heshbon Ha-Nefesh*, which adapted Benjamin Franklin's plan for the cultivation of the virtues from his Autobiography.[28] In 1785, he began re-translating the *Guide*, paraphrasing Samuel Ibn Tibbon's difficult Hebrew into more mellifluous, if less philosophically precise, *maskilic* Hebrew.[29] In so doing, Lefin was attempting a project similar to that of Satanov through the medium of translation rather than commentary. Although he spent a considerable amount of time conceptualizing the project and even worried about Maimon and Euchel's rival project, he never finished it. It was published by two disciples posthumously in 1729.[30]

In a way, Lefin's little read translation of the Guide of the Perplexed marks the end of this brief revival of Aristotelianism among *maskilim*, especially those of Eastern European origin, which I have limned. It was conceived at a moment in the eighteenth century, when, improbable as it may now seem, the revival of and struggle over Aristotelian philosophy, especially as expressed by Maimonides, was a key item on the philosophical agenda of the Haskalah. By the time it was published a generation later, that moment had passed, and the perplexed were no longer in need of this particular Guide, or for that matter those provided by Aristotle or his great commentator Averroës.

V

In conclusion, I hope to have at least strongly suggested that the claim, common to the distinct historiographies of both Jewish Philosophy and the Jewish Enlightenment—that the influence of Aristotle and his great medieval commentator Averröes had waned with the waning of the middle ages—is not quite the case. There was an interesting and brief-lived efflourescence of Jewish Aristotelian thought at the end of the eighteenth century, which was led by Eastern European *maskilim* who had been schooled in the traditional rabbinic curriculum. A full demonstration of this proposition would require a systematic re-reading of the first generation of Haskalah writings, of which the works of Maimon, Euchel, Satanov, and Lefin are a significant part. Such a project is long overdue, and one may well wonder why this episode of late Aristotelian or Averroist thought has been so thoroughly obscured. Once such a re-reading has been undertaken, we can also re-examine the extent to which the rival schools of eighteenth century Eastern European Jewish thought, Chaisidism and the rabbinic movement of *mitnaggedim*, will show a similar employment of this system and the strain under which its vocabulary suffered to bear the required theological freight at the outset of modernity.

Maimon, Satanov, and others were able to return to, and contend over, the terms and claims of radical Aristotelianism because they had been preserved by a literary tradition of canonical texts, even if they had fallen in some desuetude for a period of time. For an eighteenth century intellectual whose primary context was in Hebrew letters, this was in fact a more radical, or dangerous option than the synthesis of Leibniz and Wolff propounded by Mendelssohn. Indeed, Maimon made a cogent argument that an updated version of this position could provide a better foundation for the Enlightenment than Kant's Critical Idealism. But the generation that succeeded them knew neither Aristotle nor the complex Hebrew literary tradition in which his work was embedded. Consequently, they overlooked key texts, misread medieval philosophical terms of art, and misconstrued the discourse of early Jewish Enlightenment.

NOTES

[1] Amos Funkenstein, *Perceptions of Jewish History* (Berkeley: University of California Press, 1993), 234-35; see also his earlier discussion in "Das Verhältrisder jüdischen Aufklärung zur mittelalterlichen jüdischen Philosophie," *Aufklärung und Haskala Wolfenbüttler Studien zur Aufklärung* 14 (1990): 13-21.

[2] See James H. Lehman, "Maimonides, Mendelssohn and the Me'asfim: Philosophy and the Biographical Imagination in the Early Haskalah," *Leo Baeck Institute Year Book* 20 (1975): 87-108.

[3] Alfred Ivry, "Jewish Averroism," in *The Columbia History of Western Philosophy* (ed. Richard Popkin; New York, 1999), 199-200. See also the famous peroration of Isaak Husik, *A History of Medieval Jewish Philosophy* (New York, 1916), 428-32, who views the sixteenth century as the end of Jewish Philosophy *tout court*. In this respect, Husik was really following the line set out by Solomon Munk, *Melanges de Philosophie Juive et Arabe* (Paris, 1859).

[4] Mendelssohn wrote a commentary to Maimonides' *Millot Ha-Higayyon*, which went through several editions. For his Maimonidean scholiosis, see the hagiography of Isaac Euchel, *Toledot Rabbenu haHakham Moshe Ben Menahem* (Lemberg, 1860), 23.

[5] The previous publication had been the Renaissance edition of Sabbioneta (Venice, 1553). See Jacob I. Dienstag, "Maimonides' *Guide of the Perplexed*: a bibliography of Editions and Translations," in *Occident and Orient: A Tribute to the Memory of Alexander Scheiber* (ed. Robert Dan; Leiden, 1988), 98-100. On this and other publications of the Wulffian Press in Jessnitz, see Alexander Altmann, "Moses Mendelssohn's Kindheit in Dessau," *Bulletin des Leo Baecks Instituts* 10 (1967): 237-75; and Azriel Shohat, *Im Hilufei Tekufot* (Jerusalem, 1960), 207-08.

[6] See also the opening characterization of eighteenth century *maskilim* in Harry Austryn Wolfson, "Solomon Pappenheim on Time and Space and his Relation to Locke and Kant," in *Studies in the History of Philosophy and Religion* (ed. Isadore Twersky and George Williams; Cambridge, 1977), 606-07. An analogous desire to find connections between Hebrew literary traditions and contemporary Enlightenment discourse also helps to explain the centrality of biblical literature to the Haskalah.

[7] David Sorkin first set out his case in "From Context to Comparison: the German Haskala and Reform Catholicism," *Tel Aviv Jahrbuch für deutsche Geschichte* 22 (1991): 23-58. He makes it most extensively in *The Berlin Haskalah and German Religious Thought: Orphans of Knowledge* (London, 2000), which builds on his earlier book on Mendelssohn, *Moses Mendelssohn and the Religious Enlightenment* (Berkeley: University of California Press, 1996). It should perhaps be mentioned that Sorkin was a student of Funkenstein's (as, a few years later, was I). For a brief, explicit confrontation with Funkenstein's puzzle, see David Sorkin "Emancipation, Haskalah, and Reform: the Contribution of Amos Funkenstein," *Jewish Social Studies* 6 (1999): esp. 105-06.

[8] Compare, for instance, Sorkin's mild characterization of Isaac Euchel (on whom, see below) in *The Berlin Haskalah*, 112-13, with that of the widely quoted impression of the (rather moderate) Rabbi of Berlin, Tzvi Hirsch Levin: "Truly it is a world turned upside down. Once pigs ate acorns [*Eichel*], and now Euchel

Aristotle & the Ostjuden

eats pig!," in Israel Zinberg, *A History of Jewish Literature* (trans. Bernard Martin; Cincinatti, 1976), 135, fn. 34.

[9] In a series of studies culminating in *The Jewish Enlightenment* (trans. Chaya Naor; Philadelphia: University of Pennsylvania Press, 2002), Shmuel Feiner has taken the measure of what he calls the "Early Haskalah," which included moderate traditionalists, like Judah Leib Margoliot, who advocated the pursuit of secular knowledge from within a pre-modern religious framework. This is true and important, but does not affect my argument about the importance of Aristotelian philosophy to later and more radical figures.

[10] The first four of these eighteenth century figures are in fact mentioned by Funkenstein. The fifth, Hurwitz, was not really a *maskil*, as will shortly become apparent. For present expository purposes, however, the texts I will discuss overlap only partially with those mentioned by Funkenstein.

[11] For an extensive biographical argument to this effect, see my book, *The Radical Enlightenment of Solomon Maimon: Judaism, Heresy and Philosophy* (Palo Alto: Stanford University Press, 2005).

[12] The press was established in 1784 as the publishing arm of the Free School of Berlin. See the classic study of Moritz Steinschneider, "Hebräische Drucke in Deutschland," *Zeitschrift für die Geschichte der Juden in Deutschland* 5 (1892): 154-86. On Euchel, see Shmuel Feiner, "Isaac Euchel, Entrepreneur of the Haskala in Germany," *Zion* 52 (1987): 427-69 [Hebrew].

[13] Solomon Maimon (Anon.) and Isaac Euchel, "Panim haMoreh," *Ha-Meassef* 5 (1789): 243-63.

[14] The manuscript used by Maimon and Euchel is now held at the Bodelian Library. Euchel notes the date of its purchase, in 1788, on the colophon.

[15] Maimon and Euchel, "Paim," 261-63. A list of more than two dozen prominent subscribers in nineteen cities followed.

[16] In Abraham Geiger, ed., *Melo Hofnayim* (Berlin, 1840), 18 [Hebrew section]. Earlier versions of Delmedigo's letter were published in Yehuda Leib Meises, *Qinat haEmet* (Vienna, 1828), 228-32, and originally in Delmedigo, *Sefer Elim*, where Maimon and Euchel might have encountered it. On the complicated and uncertain provenance of these differing versions, see the discussion of David Ruderman, *Jewish Thought and Scientific Discovery in Early Modern Europe* (New Haven: Yale University Press, 1995),146-52.

[17] Delmedigo's wise son is Shem Tov ben Joseph ben Shem Tov, the last great figure of the Shem Tov family, whose representatives were found among both the great defenders and opponents of philosophical rationalism in the fourteenth and fifteenth centuries. Many of Shem Tov's key comments may be read as responding

to and moderating Narboni's Aristotelian radicalism. For discussion of one such instance, see Bernard Septimus, "Shem Tov and Narboni on Martyrdom," in *Studies in Medieval Jewish Thought* (ed. Isadore Twersky and B. Septimus; Cambridge: Harvard University Press, 1987), 447-55 (on *Guide* III:34).

[18] Narboni, known in the Latin tradition as Maestro Vidal, has been the subject of several important studies over the last few decades. For recent overviews, see Colette Sirat, *A History of Medieval Jewish Philosophy* (Cambridge: Cambridge University Press 1985), 332-41, and the introductory essays in *Ma'amar al Shelemut ha-Nefesh* (ed. Alfred Ivry; Jerusalem, 1977); and Kalman Bland, trans. and ed., *Epistle on Conjunction With the Active Intellect* (New York: Jewish Theological Seminary of America, 1987), which is a Hebrew translation of, and supercommentary to, Averroës' Middle Commentary on Aristotle's *De Anima*.

[19] For a conspectus of Delmedigo's works, see Isaac Eisenstein-Barzilay, *Yoseph Shlomo Delmedigo (Yashar of Candia)* (Leiden: Brill, 1974); the material ought to be revisited in light of criticism such as that of Ruderman, *Jewish and Scientific Discovery.* Sirat places Delmedigo at the very end of her survey of medieval Jewish philosophy, (*Medieval Jewish Philosophy,* 411), though one might also place him among the first of the figures of early Jewish modernity (he was familiar with Galileo). He is not to be confused with his more famous ancestor, Elijah Delmedigo (1460-93), author of *Behinat haDat* and translator of Averroës and others for Pico della Mirandola.

[20] It should be noted that, unlike the so-called "Latin Averroists" at the University of Paris in the thirteenth century, the Averroism of these Jewish writers was much more straightforward: they translated, commented upon, and applied the works of Ibn Rushd, some of which survive only in the Hebrew translation. For the classic nineteenth century studies of these figures, see Moritz Steinschneider, *Die hebräischen Übersetzungen des Mittlealters und die Juden als Dolmetscher* (Berlin, 1893); and Ernst Renan, *Les Ecrivains Juifs Francais du XIVe siecle* (Paris, 1893).

[21] I adopt here the language of Jürgen Habermas, *The Structural Transformation of the Public Sphere: an Inquiry into a Category of Bourgeois Society*, (trans. Thomas Burger; Cambridge, M.I.T. Press, 1989). See also Jacob Katz's classic discussion of the "semi-neutral society" in *Out of the Ghetto* (New York: Schocken, 1978).

[22] Indeed, late medieval Jewish critics of philosophy repeatedly blamed the apostasy of much of Spanish Jewry on the religious disloyalty bred by such a philosophy. An early instance of this is Joseph ben Shem Tov's unfavorable comparison of Spanish *conversos* with the Ashkenazi martyrs at the time of the crusades, in *Kevod Elohim* (Ferrara, 1556), 27 a-b. The accusation and accompanying unfavorable comparison with unphilosophical Ashkenazi Jewry became a topos. It was

revived as a partial historical explanation by Yitzhak Baer, who was also implicitly comparing Spanish Jewry of the fourteenth and fifteenth centuries to the modern enlightened German Jewry, of which he was a product, in his *History of the Jews in Christian Spain* (Philadelphia: Jewish Publication Society, 1966).

[23] Maimon, *Giva'at ha-Moreh*, 1.

[24] I have translated *hatzlachat ha-enoshit* literally as "human excellence." It is another Hebrew Aristotelian term of art and plays the same role as *summum bonum* does in parallel Latin discussions.

[25] Pinhas Eliyahu Hurwitz, *Sefer Ha-Brit* (Jerusalem, 1990), 189, and see 362-63. For an account of Hurwitz's career, see Israel Zinberg, *A History of Jewish Literature* (Cincinnatti, 1973), vol. 6, 260-72. On the book, see Ira Robinson, "Kabbala and Science in *Sefer Ha-Berit*: A Modernization Strategy for Orthodox Jews," *Modern Judaism* 9 (1989): 275-88, although I am not in agreement with all of his conclusions, in particular his characterization of Hurwitz as a *maskil*. This is simply a failure to recognize that there was a relatively sophisticated counter Enlightenment among European Jews as well.

[26] In this passage, Hurwitz actually goes on to invoke Kant, in rather naive counter-Enlightenment fashion, as having shown the impossibility of establishing metaphysical proofs on the basis of reason, thus making room for kabbalistic faith.

[27] Isaac Satanov, *Moreh ha-Nevuchim* (Berlin, 1794), unpaginated Introduction to Second Part.

[28] See Nancy Sinkoff, "Tradition and Transition: Mendel Lefin of Satanow and the Beginnings of Jewish Enlightenment in Eastern Europe, 1749-1826" (Ph.D. diss., Columbia University, 1996).

[29] As far as I know, among *maskilim* only Isaac Euchel, who had studied Arabic at Königsberg, actually had the linguistic wherewithal to read Maimonides' Judeo-Arabic. See his sample translation of Avicenna's *Book of Healing*, *Ha-Meassef* 7 (1795), 92-95.

[30] *Moreh haNevuchim* (Zolkiew, 1729). For the somewhat complicated publication details, see Sinkoff, "Tradition and Transition," 197.

Searching for "Catholic Israel" in Focsani: Solomon Schechter's Childhood in Romania

Howard Lupovitch

> It follows that the center of authority is actually removed from the Bible and placed in some living body....This living body, however, is not represented by any section of the nation...but by the collective conscience of Catholic Israel as embodied in the Universal Synagogue....This synagogue, the only true witness to the past, and forming in all ages the sublimest expressions of Israel's religious life, must also retain its authority as the sole guide for the present and the future....It is neither Scripture not primitive Judaism but general custom which forms the real rule of practice....The norm as well as the sanction of Judaism is the practice actually in vogue.[1]

For over a century, biographers of Solomon Schechter and historians of the Conservative Movement have pondered what Schechter meant by the phrase "Catholic Israel." To date, three explanations are most prevalent: that "Catholic Israel" is an English rendering of *Klal Yisrael*, the all-inclusive notion that Jews comprise a single great community; that the term represents the sum total of the collective consciousness of the Jewish people, past and present; and that the term refers more exclusively to committed, religiously observant Jews.[2] At one time or another, each explanation has been championed by one or more towering figures within the Conservative Movement, leaving Schechter's intended meaning still a mystery to contemporary readers.

A key to unraveling Schechter's seemingly cryptic meaning lies in looking beyond the conflicting permutations that scholars have ascribed to this term and considering instead a common thread among these permutations: the notion that the world of traditional Judaism is fluid enough to embrace a broad and diverse spectrum of religious and cultural expressions. In order to flesh out this notion of diversity, it is necessary to explore Schechter's notion of Catholic Israel from a novel direction. In general, scholars have presumed this notion to be the end product of Schechter's intellectual odyssey across the sea of western enlightenment, an amalgam that combined the idealism of Positive Historical Judaism with the pragmatism of Anglo-American Judaism. Thus, scholars have pored over Schechter's voluminous scholarship in search of his intended meaning. As such, scholars have overlooked a concrete example of Catholic Israel—the world in which Schechter lived for the first thirteen years in his life. Schechter's childhood home in Focsani, Romania, was a living example of what the adult Schechter conceptualized and idealized as "Catholic Israel."

The Jewish community of Focsani, though typically Ashkenazic, encountered the world of the nineteenth century in a manner that differed from other Eastern European Jewish communities. This community was situated at the crossroads of the Ashkenazic world of Eastern Europe and the Sephardic world of the Ottoman Empire, the two main centers of traditional Judaism during the nineteenth century. Situated on the border between Moldavia and Wallachia, the Jews of Focsani were influenced by both the typically Ashkenazic community of Iasi, the capital of Moldavia, and Bucharest, the hybrid Ashkenazic-Sephardic capital of Wallachia. Iasi had a Jewish community that was typically Polish in its size and communal organization and overwhelmingly Chasidic in its outlook. Wallachia and its capital city of Bucharest, while comprised largely of Ashkenazic immigrants from Russia and Galicia, had a prominent Sephardic presence into the twentieth century, owing to the its proximity to the neighboring Ottoman Empire. It was thus affected by the religious mentality and cultural outlook of Sephardic Jews more so than other communities in Eastern Europe.[3]

The relative influence of Iasi and Bucharest on Jews in Focsani ebbed and flow during the nineteenth century along with larger political and cultural currents. In general, the Jews of Focsani were influenced by the growing presence of European powers in Wallachia and Moldavia after 1829. Until 1859, this influence emanated principally from Iasi, leading Jews in Focsani along a typically Eastern European path—entrenched religious tradition, concerted resistance to acculturation and religious innovation, and the pressures of a rising tide of anti-Semitism. Until 1859, Focsani Jews had been governed on two levels—imperially by the Ottoman government, and locally from Iasi, the capital of Moldavia. After

1859, Bucharest became the capital of united Moldavia and Wallachia; as a result, Jews in Moldavia were governed from Bucharest and no longer from Iasi. This meant greater influence of Bucharest Sephardim and of western powers.[4]

As Bucharest replaced Iasi as the center of Romanian Jewry in a unified Romania, the Sephardic outlook of Bucharest's Jewish elite and the influence of Western European powers in Bucharest altered the course of development followed by the Jews of Focsani. This paper will consider, in an admittedly preliminary fashion, several ways in which the leadership of Bucharest altered the typically Ashkenazic path of Focsani Jews after 1859: first, the willingness of Jews in Focsani, following the lead of Sephardic Jews in Bucharest, to embrace Romanian culture and nationalism; second, the role of Western European philanthropy, channeled through Bucharest, in diffusing ideological opposition to innovations such as improving communal education; and finally, cultivating support for early Zionist initiatives such as the *Hibbat Zion* movement.

Schechter's childhood roots in Romania are virtually absent not only in considering the origins of Catholic Israel, but more generally in biographies of Schechter. The latter begin in earnest with Schechter's departure from Romania. Like a latter-day Solomon Maimon, Schechter's life is typically presented as a story of migration from east to west; that is, as the story of a teenager in the backwoods of Eastern Europe who abandons the world of Chasidic and Talmudic darkness.[5] Like Maimon, Schechter discovers during the course of his life the ever greener pastures of enlightenment as he moves westward, first to Lemberg, then to *bet midrash* in Vienna, then to the *Hochshule* in Berlin, then to England, and finally to America. The further west Schechter traveled, the more boldly he appeared on the radar screen of Jewish historiography; his years in Romania barely register.

Typical in this regard is Herbert Parzen, who telescoped Schechter's early years into three sentences without mentioning his hometown at all: "Solomon Schechter was born in Romania in 1848 and received the customary Yeshivah education. Like hosts of other talmudic students in Eastern Europe, western thought intrigued him. So, at the age of 25, he moved to Vienna."[6] More serious biographers such as Meir Ben-Horin were only slightly less negligent: "Schechter was born in Focsani, Romania. His father, a Habad Hasid, was a ritual slaughterer. In his teens he studied with the rabbinic author Joseph Saul Nathanson in Lemberg. From about 1875 to 1879 he attended the Vienna *bet ha-midrash*."[7]

The omission of Schechter's Romanian roots, it should be noted, reflects a larger tendency in historical works on origins of the Conservative Movement and, more generally, on the history of the Ashkenazic world. The former emphasize the German-Jewish roots of Conservative Judaism, presenting the Conservative Movement as the American progeny of Positive Historical Judaism, thus resolving the conflict of interests between more progressive and more traditional advocates of Reform Judaism. There is much truth to this conception, yet it reflects neither the constituency nor the founders of Conservative Judaism. The constituency of the Conservative Movement was, almost from the outset, predominantly of Eastern European origin. The movement was born in late nineteenth century America, when American Jewry was itself being transformed into a Eastern European born Jewish community. Several of the founders of the movement, while having ties to Zacharias Frankel's Positive-Historical Seminary in Breslau, had roots outside of German Jewry. Aside from the Romanian-born Schechter, Sabato Morais was the product of Italian Jewry; Alexander Kohut was Hungarian.[8]

That neither the constituency nor several key founders of Conservative Judaism were of German-Jewish origin takes on greater significance when one considers that the central aim of the movement was to find a usable middle ground between religious tradition and innovation. Positive Historical Judaism, to be sure, offered one model for such a middle ground, a distinctly German-Jewish model. Like other German-Jewish movements, Positive Historical Judaism had a dual aim: to prove Jews worthy of emancipation in the eyes of German intellectuals and statesmen by demonstrating the rational and moral elements of Judaism, and to provide disaffected Jews with an alternative to Reform Judaism, religious indifference, or outright conversion. The manner in which Positive Historical Judaism set out to accomplish this dual aim differed from Reform and Neo-Orthodoxy, but all three movements shared the same larger goal.[9]

Positive Historical Judaism, however, was not the only European Jewish movement that propounded and designed a balance between tradition and innovation. Within every Jewry, in fact, there were Jews who discovered a middle ground alternative between tradition and change. Because the constituencies advocating tradition and innovation varied from Jewry to Jewry, the middle ground between them also varied. Alexander Kohut, for example, came to Conservative Judaism by the way of the Status Quo Movement in Hungary, a movement that, by rejecting the centrality of religious ideology, differed fundamentally from Positive Historical Judaism.[10] Morais' Italian forbears had attained a usable balance between tradition and innovation centuries before such an endeavor was carried out by Ashkenazic Jews.[11] The foundational role of Kohut, Morais, and Schechter suggests that Conservative Judaism, the latest in the series of attempts to adjoin tradition and progress within a particular social and political climate, combined elements of multiple middle ground movements.

This omission of Schechter's Romanian roots is no less indicative of a larger trend in Jewish historiography that presents the Ashkenazic experience largely as an amalgam of German-Jewish History, on the one hand, and Polish or Russian Jewish History, on the other. The history of Ashkenazic Jews in the Baltics, the Netherlands, the Danube basin, and the Balkans, to the extent that these Jews are mentioned at all, is presented largely as an extension of one of these larger narratives. Romanian Jewry, in this regard, is no exception. The most widely discussed aspects of Romanian Jewish History are the triumph of Chasidism in Romania—an extension of the rise and triumph of Chasidism in Poland—and widespread anti-Semitism in nineteenth century Romania, which is viewed as an extension of Russian-style anti-Semitism.

These are important elements, to be sure; even in tandem, though, they ignore a key aspect of Romanian Jewry History. Romanian Jewry was the only large Ashkenazic population that lived under Ottoman rule for an extended period of time.[12]

During the years that Schechter lived in Focsani, the state now known as Romania had not yet been created. Until 1859, the two provinces that eventually comprised Romania, Moldavia and Wallachia, were separate provinces in the Ottoman Empire. The two provinces were amalgamated in 1859 to form Romania, a single Ottoman province. Romania was formally recognized as an independent state by the Treaty of Berlin in 1878.[13] Moldavia, the northern of the two provinces, abutted the traditional Jewish world of Eastern Europe, bordering Russia to the northeast, Galicia to the northwest, and Transylvania, then part of Hungary, to the west. Wallachia bordered the Jewish communities of the Balkans, which were predominantly Sephardic.

Focsani is located on the Milcov River, the natural border between Moldavia and Wallachia. Most of the town belonged to Moldavia, but the southern quarter was part of Wallachia.

Until the beginning of the nineteenth century, the Jewish community of Focsani never numbered more than a few hundred. The earliest reference to a Jewish community in Focsani was provided by Nathan of Hanover, the author of *Even Mezulla*, who was rabbi there in 1683. By 1690, there was a Jewish cemetery in the Moldavian half of the town. In 1695 the Jews of Focsani contributed to the Sultan's military campaign, and, in 1698, several Jews paid income tax to the imperial treasury. In 1796, the Jews received permission from the crown to admit an additional sixteen families. The first synagogue was built until 1797. As late as 1820, there were only twenty Jewish taxpayers.[14]

The small Jewish community was made up of a majority of Ashkenazic Jews from Galicia, Russia, and neighboring parts of Moldavia; a minority were Sephardic Jews from Wallachia, the Balkans, and other parts of the Ottoman Empire. The coexistence of Ashekenazic and Sephardic Jews was a frequent occurrence in Southeastern Europe, which dates back at least to the seventeenth century, if not earlier; yet, the synergy between Ashkenazic and Sephardic Jews in towns like Focsani is a largely unexplored feature of European and Ottoman Jewish History. An early participant in and eyewitness to this encounter was Ephraim Cohen of Vilna, better known perhaps as the great-grandfather of eighteenth century controversialist Jacob Emden. Cohen left Vilna in 1648 and, after stops in Prague and Moravia, became the rabbi of the Ashkenazic community of Buda during the late 1660s.

Once in Buda, he was in frequent contact with the Sephardic world, frst and foremost with the Sephardic community of Buda. He sent his son to study in Salonika and was consulted in legal matters by Sephardic Jews in Sophia.[15] In one responsum, he was asked whether an Ashkenazic Jew can fulfill the mitzvah of prayer while praying in a Sephardic synagogue. Cohen answered succinctly, "Ashkenazic Jews can pray in Sephardic synagogues according to the Sephardic ritual; Sephardic Jews can pray in Ashkenazic synagogues according to Ashkenazic ritual."[16]

The fluid interchange between Sephardic and Ashkenazic Jews continued in Ottoman occupied Europe throughout the eighteenth century, facilitated by the underdeveloped character of Jewish communal life. In minuscule communities like Focsani, neither Sephardic nor Ashkenazic Jews could sustain even the most rudimentary communal institutions without the other. Until the end of the eighteenth century, most communities in either province lacked even the most rudimentary trappings of communal life—schools, rabbis, and synagogues. They shared a school and a cemetery. In most communities, to the extent that there was any leadership at all, leadership defaulted to the burial society. Until 1810, Ashkenazic and Sephardic Jews shared a cemetery and burial society.[17]

The minuscule size of the Jewish communities like Focsani, moreover, fostered stable relations between Jews and Christians. Most Jews in Focsani were wine growers and wine merchants, but some were artisans, who benefited from Focsani's market fairs, which facilitated a major exchange of goods between Moldavia and Wallachia. Jews and non-Jews from both directions brought raw materials to the markets, which the Jewish artisans manufactured into finished products. Like other artisans, Jewish artisans participated in the unspoken division of occupations between the various ethnic groups. Only gypsies were locksmiths, only Germans and Hungarian were wagonmakers, only Moldavians and Wallachians were furriers, only Serbs were carpenters and masons, and only Jews were tailors, cabinetmakers, tinsmiths, and glaziers. Jews dominated their specialties no less than other ethnic groups dominated theirs. As one early nineteenth century observer noted:

> Sometimes it delights ones eyes to see Jews sitting in a store next to their Christian neighbors in fellowship and harmony....There are many artisans among Jews and it is amazing that the Jews choose specific crafts such that there is not a single Jewish blacksmith, carpenter, in these parts, and no cobblers, but only tailors, woodcutters, painters and glaziers. All the roofs of the houses and domes of the churches were made by Jewish glaziers.[18]

Another observer noted more cynically: "Jews choose only those crafts that yield less discomfort and danger, and more profit."[19]

From the 1820s on, circumstances eroded this seemingly idyllic coexistence of Jews and their non-Jewish neighbors. In 1821, a devastating fire consumed much of the town. The same year, as Jews and Christians began to rebuild the town, the Greek revolt against the Ottoman government precipitated a breakdown of law and order throughout Moldavia and Wallachia, amidst which there were attacks on Jews and Jewish property. The focal points of this violence were Iasi and Bucharest. Violence in smaller towns such as Focsani was sporadic and less concerted by comparison. At the end of the 1820s, the situation in Focsani was strained but largely unchanged.

Neither the fire nor the escalating violence disrupted the stability of Jewish-Christian relations in the town as much as a sudden change in the size and character of the Jewish community. The latter resulted in no small part from the Treaty of Adrianople. This treaty between the Russian and Ottoman Empires, among other things, gave increased influence over the internal affairs of Moldavia and Wallachia to European powers. Russian and Habsburg influence was more pronounced in Moldavia, which abutted the two empires, leading to a rapid influx of Jews into Moldavia from neighboring Bessarabia and Galicia.[20] In Focsani, the Jewish community increased steadily and at an accelerating pace after 1829, reaching 287 in 1831, 736 in 1838, and 1,855 in 1859.[21] The vast majority of these settlers were Ashkenazic Jews.

In Focsani, as in much of Moldavia and Wallachia, these new Jewish settlers comprised a conspicuous and, from the vantage point of local observers, distinctly foreign element. Increasingly after 1829, the Jewish community of Facsani was indistinguishable from Jewish communities in Galicia or Russia. Like other Moldavian Jews, most Jews in Focsani by 1859 were Chasidic Jews who earned their living as innkeepers and were increasingly despised by the local populace.[22] The growing presence Jewish foreigners eventually prompted hostility from the non-Jewish elements in the town. When King Carol I visited Foscani in 1851, he noted: "As I encounter the particularistic customs of the Jews, in Moldavia, I begin to understand the antipathy of the people toward this foreign race." Such antipathy culminated with a blood libel accusation against Jews in Focsani in 1859.[23]

Remarkably, the blood libel did not deter Jews from settling in Focsani; on the contrary, after 1859, the Jewish population increased at an accelerating pace, more than tripling between 1859 and 1899, when it reached 5,954. The Jews constituted twenty percent of the town population in 1859 and over twenty-five percent by 1899. This increase was due, in no small part, to the fact that, while hostilities against Jews continued, after 1859 the Jews of Focsani gravitated toward Bucharest Jewry and away from Iasi in their attitude toward the modern world and, in particular, in their support for Romanian nationalism. As a result, conditions for the Jews in Focsani improved from those endured by Jews in Moldavia to the less harsh conditions faced by Jews in Wallachia.

In Wallachia, as in Moldavia, a steady stream of Jewish immigrants from Russia and Galicia increased the Jewish population substantially after 1829. The impact of this influx in Wallachia, however, was less deleterious as it had been in Moldavia. The Treaty of Adrianople, in addition to giving foreign powers greater influence in Ottoman Affairs, allowed Jewish merchants in the Balkans to travel and trade freely along the Danube River, thus increasing the presence of Sephardic Jews in Wallachia from neighboring parts of the Balkans.[24] Ties between Jews in Wallachia and other parts of the Balkans were further encouraged by the superior travel conditions in Wallachia as opposed to Moldavia.[25]

The diverging character of Jewish life in Moldavia and Wallachia was exemplified by the growing differences between the Jewish communities of Iasi and Bucharest after 1829. As in Iasi, the Jewish community of Bucharest consisted largely of Jewish immigrants from the Russian and Habsburg Monarchies. The latter had been a wellspring of Jewish immigrants since 1718, when the Treaty of Passarovics had given all Habsburg subjects the right to settle and trade in the Ottoman Empire. From this point on, the majority of Jews in Bucharest, as in Iasi, were Ashkenazic.[26]

Unlike Iasi, however, the overwhelmingly Ashkenazic community of Bucharest was overshadowed by a Sephardic Jewish elite. In 1740, Constantin Mavrocordat, the governor of Wallachia, invited a Jewish banker from Kushta to Bucharest as his financial advisor, a title that passed to his son and grandson and then to a family friend during the 1790s. In exchange for services rendered, the governor and his successor awarded the advisor and his entourage special privileges. Such protection was, at times, critical. During the 1790s, the prince protected all Jews in Wallachia from pending riots.[27]

The preeminent status of Sephardic Jews in Bucharest reached an apogee in 1851, when Hillel Manoach was named imperial court banker by the Sultan and appointed to the Bucharest city council at the Sultan's behest. In general, the Sephardic community of Bucharest was better organized and more affluent. By 1820, this community owned twelve community buildings; the rent from these buildings provided one-fourth of the community's annual revenue.[28]

The influx of Ashkenazic Jews during the 1820s prompted this enclave of Sephardic Jews to spearhead a local campaign to limit the number of Ashkenazic immigrants. In 1820, Sephardic leaders asked the governor to ban Moldavian Jews from settling in Bucharest. In 1840, when the governor banned Jews from villages in Moldavia from settling in Bucharest, he asked Sephardic leaders to help enforce this statute. Despite these measures, the Ashkenazic community continued to increase, prompting the Sephardic commuity to distance itself from its Ashkenazic counterpart. In 1830, the Sephardic Jews formally separated from the rapidly growing Ashkenazic community.[29]

The Sephardic Jews of Bucharest were a far less conspicuous element than were Ashkenazic Jews. The generation that migrated to Bucharest from elsewhere in the Ottoman Empire was largely acculturated to Ottoman norms, dressing in Turkish style. As one observer noted in 1858:

> Their eastern demeanor is recognizable in all their actions, particularly in their spiritual preparations. Cleanliness and purity dominate their homes and the way they dress and they negotiate/intercourse is calm and quiet....They rarely mix with their Ashkenazic brothers. And it is a rare thing if they marry one. And everywhere they live they have separate synagogues and communal institutions. They also have separate headstones... and after they lay the dead to rest women sit in circles and sing choral dirges with eastern melodies....Their wedding ceremonies, too, have distinct, strange, eastern characteristics. The betrothal is regarded almost like the nuptials itself, and although they give their brides larger dowries, nonetheless divorce is virtually unheard of among them, and this is all the more amazing since it has become so commonplace among Christians and Ashkenazic Polish Jews.[30]

Other observers noted a similar difference between Ashkenazic and Sephardic women: "In home life, the sephardim recalls oriental life, and although the woman does live in a harem like a muslim woman, she is willing to remain at home and her husband to bring home what she needs....She is treated like a queen (this breeds apathy and laziness)."[31]

By the 1850s, though, Sephardic Jews had begun to acculturate and dress in European fashion, while Ashkenazic Jews continued to dress in a traditional Jewish fashion. As one observer noted: "By and large, in Wallachia, women, especially Sephardic women, tend to stay home and learn French, while, in Moldavia, women have a larger role in commerce."[32] The affinity among Sephardic Jews for western culture was indicative of a Sephardic brand of traditional Judaism that was more conducive to the nascent demands of a Romanian nationalism that embraced westernization.

Western influence was more pronounced in Wallachia, spurred by the openness of Sephardic Jews, and in particular the Bucharest Sephardic elite, to western culture:

> After the Peace of Adrianople a powerful arm, a protectorate, appeared from the north upon the hand of the supreme Turkish rule in Moldavia and Wallachia....Day by day the signs of northern rule appeared improving these lands. From this point on the order of inhabitants changed completely, and the situation of Jews, too, for the better. It is almost unbelievable the changes that took place in Wallachia and, to a lesser extent, in Moldavia, in ten short years—changes in dress, education, manners, and general outlook. These are the rays of enlightenment [Haskalah] that first appeared in these lands from the sun that dwells in the north....The French language drove out Greek as the language of educated people.[33]

The affinity of Sephardic Jews in Bucharest for Western culture diffused some of the antagonism toward Jews in Wallachia. By mid-century, one observer noted that Wallachians and Moldavians regarded Jews quite differently and attributed the difference to the increasingly Polish character of Moldavian Jews:

> In Moldavia Jews are called Jidani [Jew] and in Wallachia they are called Evreul [Hebrew]. This shows that Jews are hated much more in Moldavia than in Wallachia. Indeed Moldavians see Jews the ways Poles did in the past....These common people lack the sense and ability to look to the real essence of something, and when they see a Jew standing next to him dressed in a strange and foreign way, they think this is a Jew who lived eighteen hundred years ago.[34]

The widening disparity between Moldavia and Wallachia was reflected in the attitudes of Romanian nationalists toward Jews. In general, Romanian nationalism was at best ambivalent toward Jews and other ethnic minorities. At times, Romanian nationalism leaned in a liberal direction, invoking an image of Romania as a haven for minorities: "Romania has always been a land tolerant of immigrants and a land that welcomes guests." This view found a more receptive audience in Wallachia than in Moldavia, where Romanian nationalist crystallized by the 1860s into riots and other virulent forms of anti-Semitism. There was little doubt as to the source of this hostility: "They [Jews] made themselves conspicuous in their dress, from the other inhabitants of the land, and this aroused much hatred in the hearts of the population, for it is natural that if a small group of people lives among a large people and is distinct in every way, they will be seen as foreign and despised."[35]

In response to this violence, state officials banned Jews in Iasi from wearing Polish clothing, forbade them from coming to court in Polish garb, and ordered them to wear European garb, "so there is no animosity between Jews and other peoples." The same official added: "In Wallachia, most Jews already dress in European garb."[36] In other instances, though, the presumption that Moldavian Jews were largely Polish worked to the Jews' advantage. Shortly after the two provinces were united by the Peace of Paris, the new joint government issued a decree forbidding Wallachian Jews from settling in villages and evicting those who were there. This decree was not extended to Moldavia, ironically, because of the large presence of Jewish innkeepers in the rural economy. As one government minister noted:

> In Moldavia the situation cannot be repaired because leaseholders, vineyard-growers have business ties with Jews, and if we did this it would harm the entire population. But not so in Wallachia! Here we can evict Jews from villages with little opposition from the local population, so let us do so.[37]

Yet, while helping Jews materially, it nonetheless fueled the notion that Jews in Moldavia were a conspicuous element of the population.

For Jews in Moldavia, the growing hostility toward Jews in response to a growing Jewish population and lingering perception that Jews were foreigners was much like the situation facing Russian Jews. The rapprochement between Jews and non-Jews in Wallachia, as compared to the antagonism between Jews and non-Jews in Moldavia, measured the ability of a Westernized, Sephardic elite in Bucharest to diminish the level of anti-Jewish sentiment confronting Jews in Moldavia and Wallachia. Such rapprochement was complimented by a willingness of Sephardic Jews in Bucharest to adapt to the changing world of the nineteenth century. In this regard, the openness of Sephardic Jews to the outside world was further encouraged by the presence of Jewish organizations from Western Europe in Bucharest, notably the Alliance Israelite Francaise and B'nai B'rith.[38] A useful measure of the success of Bucharest Jews in channeling the influence of these organizations to the communities of Moldavia and Wallachia is the efforts to reform Jewish communal education in Focsani.

The debate over Jewish education in Focsani began in 1866, when local Jews sought to open a progressive school under the sponsorship of the Alliance. When local Orthodox Jews objected, the school closed. In 1874, a second attempt was made to open a progressive school under the auspices of B'nai Brith. When the local Orthodox objected, B'nai B'rith leaders overruled them by appealing to Bucharest, and the school remained open. By 1887, the school had 274 students; by 1888, 300 students; and by 1891, 370 students.[39]

In a way, the ability of B'nai B'rith to maintain a Western-style school in Focsani over the objections of local Orthodox Jews measured the disparate influence of such organizations in Moldavia and Wallachia. In Iasi, the Alliance failed to overrule local Orthodox objections to school reform, and, after nearly ten years, the director of the Alliance office finally gave up. In sharp contrast, in Bucharest the support of western organizations like the Alliance was instrumental in thwarting the campaign of local Orthodox Jews, even though the latter was led by a prestigious Orthodox leader, the Malbim.[40] The success of the progressive school in Focsani thus delineated the scope of Jews from Bucharest and their western European Jewish supporters in Romania. Such influence extended beyond Focsani into Moldavia only with difficulty and with limited success.

More successful were initiatives by Jews in Bucharest and Western European Jews to cultivate support for programs to settle Romanian Jews in the land of Israel and, eventually, to find widespread support for early Zionist initiatives. Indicative of this success was the first statewide assembly of individual *Hibbat Zion* chapters, which took place in Focsani in 1882. Thirty-two chapters sent representatives to this meeting, nineteen from Jewish communities in Wallachia and thirteen from Jewish communities in Moldavia. The latter is striking given the Orthodox aversion to such Zionist initiatives. Moreover, the rabbi of Focsani, an avowed traditionalist, presided over the meeting and endorsed the aims of *Hibbat Zion*.[41]

By 1882, Solomon Schechter had long since left Focsani for Poland, en route eventually to the New World. Yet even before he left Focsani in 1861, the interplay between the traditional worlds of Eastern Europe and the Ottoman Empire, between Bucharest and Iasi, and between Ashkenazic and Sephardic Jews had left a notable imprint on the Jews of Focsani. These Jews, most of whom had been reared only in the traditional world of Russia or Galicia, had benefited from the efforts of the Bucharest Jewish elite to improve their living conditions and help them embrace the potential benefits of modern life. The influence of the Sephardic mentality in Bucharest softened the choice between tradition and change Jews in Foscani and, more generally, in Wallachia had to face. They would eventually have to make this decision, but it would be far less of an either/or proposition than the choice faced by their coreligionists elsewhere in Eastern Europe. Jews in Focsani found a way to integrate old and new ideas—patriotism, education reform, religious commitment, and even practical Zionism—in a comparatively seamless fashion. A generation later, Solomon Schechter would present this seamless collection of ideas as a pillar of Conservative Judaism.

NOTES

[1] Solomon Schechter, *Studies in Judaism* (Philadelphia: Jewish Publication Society of America, 1896), xvii-xix.

[2] David J. Fine, "The Meaning of Catholic Israel," *Conservative Judaism* 50:4 (1998): 29-30.

[3] Theodor Lavi, ed., *Pinkas ha-Kehilla: Rumaniya* 1 (Jerusalem, 1970), 204.

[4] Ibid., 205.

[5] On Maimon's encounter with Haskalah, see Shmuel Feiner, "Solomon Maimon and the Haskalah," *Aschkenas* 10:2 (2000): 337-59.

[6] Typical of this omission is H. Parzen, *Architects of Conservative Judaism* (New York: Jonathan David, 1964), 29.

[7] Meir Ben-Horin, "Solomon Schechter," *Encyclopedia Judaica* 14, 948.

[8] Jack Wertheimer, "Pillars of the Conservative Movement: Reports from the Field by Graduates of 'Schechter's Seminary,'" *Conservative Judaism* 47:3 (1995): 55-57.

[9] Michael Meyer, *Response to Modernity: A History of the Reform Movement in Judaism* (Detroit: Wayne State University Press, 1998), 84ff.

[10] Howard Lupovitch, "Between Orthodox and Neolog: the Origins of the Status Quo Movement," *Jewish Social Studies* 9:2 (2003):117.

[11] Salo W. Baron, "Italian and Dutch Haskalah," in *Social and Religious History of the Jews II* (Philadelphia: Jewish Publication Society of America, 1937), 127-40.

[12] A more detailed and thorough analysis of this historiographical tendency is a desideratum. For a preliminary analysis, see my review of Raphael Patai, "The

Jews of Hungary," *AJS Review* 3:2 (1998).

[13] V. Cristian, "La Roumanie et les Traités de Paix de SAn Stefano et de Berlin," *Revue Roumaine d'Historie* 17:1 (1978): 55-56.

[14] Lavi, *Pinkas ha-Kehillot*, 42.

[15] Jacob Emden, *Megillat Sefer* (Jerusalem, 1979), 9-10.

[16] Ephraim ha-Cohen, *Sha'ar Ephraim* (Lemberg, 1886) #11, 31:b.

[17] Abraham Lachower, "Jewish Burial Associations in Moldavia in the 18th and the Beginning of the 19th Centuries," *YIVO Annual of Jewish Studies* 10 (1955): 305.

[18] Ya'akov Geller, *The Sephardic Jews in Romania: the Rise and Decline of the Sephardic Community in Bucharest* [Hebrew] (Jerusalem, 1983), 32-33.

[19] Ibid., 47.

[20] Emil Virtosu, "Les Relations de la Moldavie et de la Valachie avec L' empire Ottoman, Reflectess Pa le Sceau de Prince Regnant," *Revue des Etudes Sud-Est Européennes* 4:1-2 (1966): 199-200.

[21] Lavi, *Pinkas ha-Kehillot:* (Hebrew section), 19, 23; English section, 203.

[22] Lavi, *Pinkas ha-Kehillot* (Iasi).

[23] Ibid., 43.

[24] Geller, *The Sephardic Jews in Romania*, 63.

[25] Ecaterina Negruti, "The Role of Jews in founding Towns in Moldavia during the first half of the Nineteenth Century," *Acta Historia Iudaeorum Romaniae* (1996):116.

[26] Geller, *The Sephardic Jews in Romania*, 40.

[27] Ibid., 17.

[28] Ibid., 49.

[29] Ibid., 52.

[30] *Ha-Magid* (Lyck) 1:3 (January 22, 1856), 11.

[31] Ibid., 11-12.

[32] "Juden und Judenthum in Wallachie und Moldavie," *Ben Chananya* 6 (1863): 112.

[33] *Ha-Magid* 5:5 (February 7, 1860), 20.

[34] Ibid., (March 9, 1860), 35-36.

[35] Ibid., 5:14 (April 6, 1859), 54.

[36] Ibid., 3:30 (August 3, 1858), 118.

[37] Ibid., 6:9 (February 27, 1861), 57.

[38] Aron Rodrigue, "Jewish Society and Schooling in a Thracian Town: the Alliance Israelite Universelle in Demotica, 1897-1924," *Jewish Social Studies* 45:3-4 (Old Series) 1983: 265-68.

[39] Lavi, *Pinkas ha-Kehillot*, 195-96.

[40] David Berger, "Malbin's Secular Knowledge and his Relationship to the Spirit of the Haskalah," *Yavneh Review* 5 (1996): 28.
[41] Lavi, *Pinkas ha-Kehilla*, 205-06.

Language Violence: Auschwitz Convent Controversy

Zev Garber

"Language is a reciprocal tool: it reveals and at the same time it is revealing. That is, not only do we use language to explain the things that define our world, but, by the same token, the same way we use language also necessarily discloses how we explain and define ourselves within that world."[1] We normally do not think much about language as an instrument to do good or to execute evil nor do we understand the working of its medium (words and syntax) in expressing how we think, feel, perceive or desire. Understanding the constraints of language on what we can and cannot do was the focus of my initial study into Shoah or Holocaust.

At an international conference, "Remembering for the Future: The Impact of the Holocaust on the Contemporary World," Bruce Zuckerman and I called into question the validity of the label "Holocaust" to describe the extermination of European Jews during World War II.[2] We pointed to the shocking use of a specific religious term for the genocide, making the Nazi murderers priestly officiants of divine propitiation. We challenged Elie Wiesel's attempt to make the (aborted) sacrifice of Isaac in Genesis the biblical analogy for the "Final Solution." Going far beyond questions of terminological propriety, we discerned basic psychological attitudes in the conventional Jewish view of the Shoah; namely, that the event is limited to Jewish victims of the Nazis and a fulfillment of the Jews' traditional role as God's people, chosen to suffer for the redemption of humankind. We decry all this as theological gerrymandering and see the Shoah as the tragic of "Thou shall not murder," in which both murderers and victims are ordinary people in an extraordinary situation, a secular event without saints or demons.

We fear that attitudes behind the continual use of the term "The Holocaust" may lead to the view that Jews are Christ-like sacrificial "lambs of God" or to extreme chauvinism. Still, on some profound level of meaningfulness, the *Shoah* (biblical Hebrew meaning "destruction, ruin," and suggesting no religious or sacrificial overtones) must be taken as emblematic. If Shoah is to remain the paradigmatic genocide, then it must be a paradigm that shows true horror; i.e., what all people are capable of doing and what all people are capable of suffering; its message of survival must be shared with all who have suffered and will suffer.

At "Remembering for the Future II", Zuckerman and I probed the language of Shoah disputation, and we pointed out the many complications and difficulties that accompanied the Auschwitz Convent controversy.[3] More than a text of faith and facts on the ground, the conflict is circumscribed by religious and cultural differences expressed in language predisposed by certain choices of interpretation. We are suggesting that people who speak different languages cannot share the same conceptual framework; conversely, different conceptual forms cannot be expressed in the same language.

For communication to occur, some prior agreement must exist between speaker/sender and hearer/receiver. But if our need to communicate arises out of our social nature, then our group identity determines a significant part of what we perceive to be moral goodness or blameworthiness, along with our obligation to do right, be good, and damn evil. This may well explain why controversy and not communication prevailed at the Auschwitz convent.

The assumption is that antagonists in a dispute must move beyond thought control and herd mentality. We must rediscover—and, in many cases, discover—the meaning of Auschwitz. Since meanings are not given independently of language, we must come up with a suitable hermeneutic that honors the dead and does not abuse the memory of the living. The cry of "Never Again" must never become the subtext, "Never Again for Us."

Loyalists of covenant and of convent alike have created a virtual wall of words at Auschwitz, but we must believe that the wall is permeable. And by exploring the inside and outside of the language of bias, we can confront the cycle of contempt and move from strife to Shalom. Applying our theory to reality, we now ask: What happens when dialogue breaks down? When language recedes from cordiality to hostility? And what do we do about seemingly unending tensions released by the Auschwitz Convent controversy?

These are the basic elements of this controversy: the placing of a large 26-foot cross (so-called "Papal Cross") used by John Paul II at a mass conducted in the garden of the Carmelite Convent at Birkenau in

1979, a site where Nazis killed 152 Poles; it faces Auschwitz proper, where thousands of Polish people, mostly intellectuals, were murdered by the Nazis in 1940, and where an estimated 1,500,000 Jews were eradicated in furnaces of death; the rise of the Polish voice in determining "whose Auschwitz?"; the agreement between the Roman Catholic Church and several Jewish organizations reached at Geneva in 1987 that the convent be moved to another place and the collapse of the Geneva Agreement among Polish ecclesiastics; the slow-paced intervention by the Vatican, suggesting that the Polish-born Pope John Paul II sees the controversy as a local affair; the flip-flop statements from the Primate of Poland, Cardinal Jozef Glemp, who said preceding the convent closure (June 20, 1993), "Auschwitz shall never again be a place of controversy," and his homily in defense of the "Papal Cross" (Summer 1998): "The cross has stood and will stand at Auschwitz. Many people have not liked and do not like the Eiffel Tower, but that is no reason to move or reconstruct it. In the same way, the cross at Auschwitz must not be a subject of bargaining, for it is among believers, for whom the cross is salvation;"[4] the appeal from the Social Committee in Defense of the Oswiecim Cross (established in 1998) to deck the whole convent area with crosses; the considerable opposition, in particular, the nationalistic, anti-Semitic "Association of Poles—Victims of World War II," to any Jewish say at Auschwitz, and so forth. Connect the pieces and you get not dialogue but disputation, not conformity but perplexity.

The aspect of all this puzzlement that gets the most news coverage—the debate over the convent's location—is the least of all worries. After all, the Church has abandoned the convent at Auschwitz,[5] and the municipality of Oswiecim has terminated the lease with the Carmelite order. The nuns have moved either to new quarters across the road or to another convent altogether. Indeed, in place of the convent, there is now, off the grounds of Auschwitz, the Center of Information, Meetings, Dialogue, Education, and Prayer (and an adjacent new Carmelite convent). Construction began on February 19, 1990. At the time the Archbishop of Cracow, Francisek Machurski, and Minister Jacek Ambroziak broke ground in a symbolic ceremony, which was graced with Cardinal Machurski's greeting: "May justice, peace, and love radiate from this place. May people draw the strength here to overcome everything that divides them, for the sake of that good which is for us second only to God himself, the good of man."[6] The Center opened its doors on February 28, 1992. The Center and the convent are now operating under the jurisdiction of the private Auschwitz

Foundation based in Cracow, directed by a German priest, Father Manfred Deselers, and supported by the Cracow Archdiocese.[7] Finally, in 1999, an act of the Polish parliament removed the small crosses from the disputed area, but made the "Papal Cross" permanent.

Alas, by hoc signo on the gravel pit behind the covenant overlooking the "Valley of Ashes," the Führer's ghost lingers over Catholic and Jewish victims. The Poles claim that Auschwitz is located in their sovereign land: the "Papal Cross" is found just outside Auschwitz I, where three-quarters of those killed were Polish Catholics, and two miles from Auschwitz II (Birkenau), where most Jews were murdered. Further, the "Papal Cross" was blessed by Pope John Paul II at a memorial mass for the Polish priest Maximilian Kolbe, imprisoned in Auschwitz for his political and religious views, who voluntarily took the place of a Polish workingman selected to die by the Germans in reprisal for a successful prison break by an individual in Kolbe's block.[8] The Jews counterclaim that in Auschwitz-Birkenau, symbol of Hitler's inferno, nearly 1,500,000 Jews were murdered. In addition, Poland had agreed to put Auschwitz on the UNESCO list of World Heritage sites (1979). This acknowledged, and the Geneva Agreement (1986-87) confirmed, that there should be no religious symbols at the camp. Though individual Poles risked their lives and property to save Jews, much of the Polish population, was indifferent to the murder of Jews on their soil, and this continues to be a problem today.[9]

What of the future? Would the presence of the "Papal Cross" overlooking Auschwitz destroy this shared memory in Polish-Jewish and Catholic-Jewish relations? We think not, and we maintain that Jew and Pole can sustain their emotive feelings in a cultural milieu dedicated to the belief that divergent views of history are to be respected. However, how do we placate the Auschwitz memory between Jew (Judaism) and Pole (Catholicism) without the problems of politics, politeness, and paternalism? We advise self-criticism, interpersonal dialogue, and the need to study and observe the totality of a group's behavior—and not through doctrinal teaching or popular and journalistic readings.

Learning the complexity of the historical, religious, cultural, psychological, and political factors of Polish nationalism and religion is imperative for Jews. For the Poles, the "Papal Cross" symbolizes Catholic *heilsgeschichte* theology and loyalty to Polish nationalism. Jews need to be reminded that 3,000,000 Polish nationals died during the Nazi occupation, of whom nearly 100,000 were killed at Auschwitz, and that the "Papal

Cross" with the *Corpus Christi* is the symbol of a nation's loss. Nonetheless, the authority of the Polish Nation and Church needs to understand the Jewish complaint that the crosses are morally offensive because they are seen as the upshot of Christian imperialism and laden with Christian replacement theology.

In other words, the crosses at Auschwitz do not represent the Cross at Cavalry.[10] It needs to be repeatedly emphasized that Jesus did not teach what was to become the Church's understanding of his mission and teaching (i.e., anti-Judaism along with anti-Semitism), that the traditional negative teachings about the Jews have been used to justify the great acts of evil against them, and that Jesus points to God not the State-Church ("Christendom"), in whose power Jews were at different times forcibly converted, placed in ghettos, expelled from the land, and murdered. Centrifugal to this radical Christ and Caesar symbiosis is the "teaching of contempt" born at Cavalry, nursed by the Church Fathers (post-Apostolic and medieval), advanced in the eras of the Crusades, Inquisition, and Reformation, and pontificated by well-known and not so well-known papal edicts and councils, which circuitously sustained the advocates of the Endlösung. For Jan Karski, the Polish Catholic who brought information about the Shoah to the West, the crosses at Auschwitz are seen as an affront to the true intent, mission, and purpose of Christ's Cross.[11]

In conclusion, to deflect the cross, messages of ill intent, and serious controversy between the claimants of Auschwitz-Birkenau, we suggest that the infamous death camp be kept in history; let it be ugly, ignoble, and punctuated by the screams of those who found themselves in mortal peril. To convert the genocide of millions into symbols of sacrifice, royalty, and resurrection makes the Shoah a "biblical" event rather than an event of our time, a myth rather than a reality. Also, let us reimagine the religiosity of the event. That is to say, stay with the Cross of Christianity not Christendom (which helped provide the seedbed for the Shoah) so that never again may church teaching contribute to a crooked cross of the future. Also, understand "Love your neighbor as yourself"[12] as "respect your neighbor for s/he is like you." Seen in this way, proper memory without anti-Semitism and anti-Polonism is honored.

APPENDIX

In the beginning was the canard of word disorder. The Auschwitz Convent controversy became an international crisis in August 1989, when Pope John Paul II made a remark at his weekly general audience (August 2) about the infidelity of the Jews to the word of God and his prophets, who proclaimed "through Christ's redemptive sacrifice and through the power of the Holy Spirit...a new and everlasting covenant;"[13] and Jozef Cardinal Glemp concluded his remarks of a homily on Wisdom as the foundation of order at Czestochowa (August 26):

> We have feelings toward the Jews, but today I would like to say, dear Jews, do not talk with us from a position of a people raised above all others, and do not dictate conditions that are impossible to fulfill. The Carmelite sisters living next to the camp at Oswiecim wanted and want to be a sign of solidarity among peoples that embrace both the living and dead. Do you, esteemed Jews, not see that your pronouncements against the nuns offend the feelings of all Poles, and our sovereignty, which has been achieved with such difficulty? Your power lies in the mass media that are easily at your disposal in many countries. Let them not serve to spread anti-Polish feeling. Recently, a squad of seven Jews from New York launched attacks on the convent at Oswiecim. In fact, it did not happen that the sisters were killed or the convent destroyed, because they were apprehended. But do not call the attackers heroes. Let us maintain the level of civilization on which we live. Let us be able to distinguish certain things that are simplified and confused. Let us distinguish Oswiecim-Auschwitz, where mostly Poles and other peoples perished from Brzezinka-Birkenau, lying at a distance of some kilometers, and where mostly Jews perished. Let us distinguish next the civil plane from the theological plane. Do not permit a new doctrine about the presence or absence of God on the place of sacrifice, justified and understood by all people who believe in God, to become a political instrument in the hands of people, more particularly non-believers.[14]

The above selection is part of Cardinal Glemp's sermon on the eve of the fiftieth anniversary of the outbreak of the Second World War and in celebrations to mark the feast of the Most Holy Mary at the Polish shrine of Our Lady of Czestochowa. In its entirety, the section "Dialogue with the Jews", conveys a balanced, though debatable, view of Polish attitudes toward Jews: positive ("For many Jews, Poland was their Fatherland not only because of citizenship but also because of their authentic love for it"), negative (Jewish elitism, international media power, propensity to kill), and revisionist (Polish Oswiecim-Auschwitz; anti-Polinism is the cause of Polish anti-Semitism).

Furthermore, in an interview with the Italian journal, *La Republica*, on September 2, Cardinal Glemp suggested that the 1987 Geneva Agreement[15] be renegotiated since the Catholic signatories represented a "group of people lacking competence," who did not understand the position and feelings of the Polish people. In this interview, in the Czestochowa homily, and in a later interview and address,[16] he explains his position in this way: (1) The Jews are represented by a highly structured ethnic group and the Catholics by an informal religious group of outsiders who do not truly understand the situation of Polish ethnic-national-religious feelings; (2) the convent represents the basic human rights of the Carmelite sisters, and it is accepted and respected by the Polish people as part of the efforts of the Fatherland—of the Church and of the Nation—on its path to peace in a post-Communist Poland; and (3) the Geneva document is not an agreement but a declaration of intent hurriedly prepared; it cannot be legally implemented, since the Polish side was underrepresented and then unfairly burdened with its implementation.

Cardinal Glemp's position was criticized within Poland by the Solidarity leadership and outside Poland by American and European Cardinals, including the Jewish-born Cardinal Jean-Marie Lustiger (Paris), whose parents were murdered at Auschwitz. Yehudah Bauer, Israel's leading historian on the Shoah, remarked, "Rather than have the Auschwitz complex remain a universal, international monument to suffering, one which Jews can accept because they are free to relate it to the overwhelming disaster brought upon the Jewish people, and upon them primarily, he [Glemp] appropriates Auschwitz for the Polish nation, by self-definition a Catholic nation."[17] Nobel Laureate and Holocaust survivor Elie Wiesel observed that Glemp's insensitive language encourages anti-Semitism and violence, which in turn makes Jews "once more into objects of religious terror, reminding us of what happened fifty years ago."[18]

Eventually, Cardinal Glemp rescinded his position, and his later preaching and teaching are in accordance with the Vatican's position on the removal of the convent from within Auschwitz proper.[19]

NOTES

[1] Cited in a discussion of the term "Holocaust" and the psychology behind its popular usage. See Zev Garber and Bruce Zuckerman, "Why Do We Call the Holocaust 'The Holocaust'? An Inquiry into the Psychology of Labels," *Modern Judaism 9.2* (1989): 197-211. Updated and reprinted in Z. Garber and Bruce Zuckerman, *Double Takes: Thinking and Rethinking Issues of Modern Judaism in Ancient Contexts* (Lanham: University Press of America, 2004), chapter 1.

[2] Ibid.

[3] See Zev Garber and Bruce Zuckerman, "The Führer/Furor Over the Auschwitz Convent: The Inside and Outside of the Language of Bias," in M. Berenbaum and B. R. Rubenstein with H. R. Feibel and S. and Z. Garber, eds., *What Kind of God? Essays in Honor of Richard L. Rubenstein* (Lanham, MD: University Press of America, 1995), 95-109; and C. J. Colijn and M. S. Littell, eds., *From Prejudice to Destruction: Western Civilization in the Shadow of Auschwitz* (Münster: LIT Verlag, 1995),167-79. Updated and reprinted in Z. Garber and B. Zuckerman, *Double Takes*, chapter 3.

[4] Excerpted from the *World Jewish Congress Policy Dispatch*, August 1998.

[5] See "Letter of Pope John Paul II to the Carmelite Sisters" (9 April 1993), in *The Carmelite Convent to the Crosses at Auschwitz* (ed. A. L. Berger, et al.; Binghamton: Global Publications, SUNY-Binghamton, 2002).

[6] The words echo Jesus' great commandment, love of God and love of neighbor, found in Matt 22: 37-39, Mark 12: 29-31, and Luke 10:27. For the original wording and difference in the *Shema* commandment, see Deut 6:4-5; on brotherly love, see Lev 19:18.

[7] Private communication from Fr. John T. Pawlikowski (16 October 2002).

[8] Father Maximilian Kolbe was beatified in 1971 and proclaimed a saint of the Roman Catholic Church in 1982. Kolbe's admirable act of self-sacrifice, however, is marred by his private and public anti-Semitic views. A case in point is his widely circulated homage to the hideous *Protocols of the Elders of Zion* (1894) and his argument for the exclusion of the Jews from the Polish economy.

[9] For example, Jozef Cardinal Glemp's public refusal to accept Polish responsibility in the murder of 1600 men, women, and children in Jedwabne, Poland, in July 1941. On crimes committed by Poles against Jews in Jedwabne and other places in northeastern Poland following the German invasion of the Soviet Union in 1941, see the two-volume report issued by Poland's Institute of National Remembrance, http://ipn.gov.pl/summary_1.pdf (vol.1) and http://www.ipn.gov.pl/summary_2.pdf (vol.2).

[10] See remarks by Zev Garber on James Carroll, *Constantine's Sword: The Church and the Jews* (Boston and New York: Houghton Mifflin, 2001), in *Religious Education* 87:2 (Spring 2002): 184-97.

[11] The crosses "have nothing to do with faith or religion. They are an expression of conceit, contempt, and desire to humble our 'older brothers' in our joint faith in God. These feelings and actions are contrary to true Catholicism and they bring painful, acute shame because the use of religion and its symbols for political purposes is sacrilege." See "Statement of Jan Karski," in Berger, *Carmelite Convent*, 316ff.

[12] Lev 19:18 (see footnote 6).

[13] See Carrol Rittner and John K. Roth, eds., *Memory Offended: The Auschwitz Convent Controversy* (New York: Praeger, 1991), 245.

[14] Excerpt from the New York Times (29 August 1989). For the complete text of Cardinal Glemp's homily, see *Memory Offended*, 220-25.

[15] An agreement reached by Catholic and Jewish leaders to remember and never to forget the atrocities carried out by Nazi Germany during World War II generally and at Auschwitz-Birkenau in particular. The official Catholic-Jewish agreement called for the removal of the Auschwitz Convent and was signed by a number of Catholic Polish leaders, including the Archbishop of Cracow, Cardinal Machurski, and a few European cardinals of the Church.

[16] Interview conducted by Professor Jacek Wozniakowski and published in the weekly Catholic newspaper, *Tygodnik Powszechny* (17 September 1989). The address was delivered at the Sixth Congress of Polish Theologians meeting at the Catholic University of Lublin on September 12, 1989. Interview and lecture are published in *Memory Offended*, 228-32 and 233-34 respectively.

[17] Yehudah Bauer, "Auschwitz: The Degrees of Distortion," *Jerusalem Post* (international edition, 30 September 1989). This article is critical of Polish and Jewish views "of what Auschwitz was and what really happened there." This article is reprinted in *Memory Offended*, 251-53.

[18] The full text of Elie Wiesel's reaction to Cardinal Glemp's remarks is found in the *Jewish Journal of Greater Los Angeles*, week of September 22-28, 1989, and other Anglo-Jewish newspapers nationwide.

[19] On remembering the Jedwabne massacre, however, Cardinal Glemp's quid pro quo apologetics is again exhibited. On the one hand, he recognizes that Poles had contributed to the killing of Jews at Jedwabne and elsewhere, and, on the other hand, he wonders about the Jewish silence regarding the Jewish Bolsheviks, who persecuted Poles after the war. His May 15, 2001, interview with the Catholic Information Agency insinuates that Jewish anti-Polonism is a factor. For an

assessment of the Polish-Catholic view on Jedwabne, see K. Gebert, "Parallel Monologues: Catholics, Jews and Jedwabne," in *Jews and Christians in Conversation* (ed. E. Kessler, et al.; Cambridge: Orchard Academic, 2002), 143-67.

Coming into Their Inheritance: Jewish-American Autobiographers Encounter Eastern Europe

Steven Weiland

For many Jewish immigrants to the United States in the last decades of the nineteenth century and the first decades of the twentieth, and for their children, the homelands of Eastern Europe were best forgotten. Even Irving Howe was pessimistic about the fate of memory: *The World of Our Fathers* was a tribute and a valedictory.[1] True enough, we are living in a revival of interest in Yiddish, and every sizeable city seems now to have its own professional Klezmer band. But what interest Jewish-American writers and readers show in the past is largely personal. Autobiography appears to be our most popular genre. So it is in the book world generally.

According to Vivian Gornick,[2] herself the author of a widely admired memoir about Jewish-American generations, *Fierce Attraction*, the question being asked in exemplary texts in this genre is simply, "Who am I?" For Jewish-American autobiographers that means reflecting on or agonizing over their Jewish and American identities. The latter is typically made in New York, or Cleveland, or even a small town in the South—a place the Jews came to. However, probing the Jewish element of personal identity for many of our most compelling writers means reflecting on where the Jews came from. Who would argue that the Jews are not at home in America? But who would say that the homelands of Eastern Europe do not still have a place in the minds of Jewish-Americans, at least those anxious about the making and meanings of their own stories?

CONTEMPLATING THE "OLD COUNTRY"
Two recent Jewish-American autobiographies offer very different attitudes, the first of disdain for the "Old Country," the second of longing for it. In his account of the life of Abe Trillin, *Messages from My Father*,[3] the famed *New Yorker* writer Calvin Trillin says that his "immediate family would not have struck any one as foreigners." But his grandparents and

father had emigrated from Ukraine in the first decade of the twentieth century. Arriving at the port of Galveston, Texas they settled eventually in Missouri, first St. Joseph and then Kansas City. And while Trillin's friends, and those of his parents, might not have seen them as immigrants, "the Old Country—untalked about, basically unexperienced by anyone in our immediate family—was a constant in our lives."[4] Even so, one reason Trillin is so devoted to his father and his memory is that he had none of the "old shtetl outlook;"[5] that is, pessimism, fearfulness, and mistrust of non-Jews. Trillin's family nostalgia extends only to Kansas City in the 1930s.

For contrast, consider Dorothy Gallagher's *How I Came into My Inheritance*.[6] Invited to accompany her mother on a trip to Ukraine, also the homeland in this family, she declines. But after her parents' death she reflects: "Of course I could have gone. Why didn't I? And why did I never ask her a simple question? What was it like where you were born, mama? Was the countryside beautiful? Did you see mountains? Hills? A river? Was the snow very deep in winter? Did you pick berries in the spring?"[7] A few years later, Gallagher was in Romania with a friend. "We saw breathtaking things," she says. "We saw time immemorial. We saw landscapes as beautiful as a fairy tale."[8] They see pain and suffering too, particularly in the faces of Jews from the United States trying to find traces of families lost in Romania's Holocaust.

So too does Gallagher now feel like a seeker, thinking of her familys origins and her parents' last difficult years in the United States: "I stood at the edge of the Tisza River looking across at Ukraine. I wasn't quite there, but I was as close as I was ever going to get. And now, in this odd and wracked corner of the world...grief slipped away."[9] Having struggled with her aged parents over money she thought herself entitled to, she finds an inheritance of a different kind. Trillin has no interest in returning to the Eastern European scenes of his Jewish ancestry; Gallagher feels a strong impulse to do so. Her expressive affiliation with her family's past registers her reconciliation with them.

Between indifference and romance there are the experiences of Jewish-American autobiographers for whom Eastern Europe is both a place of origins and of endings. As children of Holocaust survivors, they know well the scenes of deportation and death. But in such places there is also to be found an "inheritance." Polish émigré Eva Hoffman has made explicit what was implicit in her influential account of coming to North America (*Lost in Translation: A Life in a New Language* [1990]): "History has often seemed thicker, more pressing, and oppressive in Eastern Europe: few lives have been disconnected from it, or unaffected by it."[10] Three accounts of Eastern European inheritance follow, each highlighting a different feature of what such a journey can mean to those who make them—and to us.

"WE HAD OUR FAMILY MYTHOLOGY"

Julie Salamon,[11] who now writes about media and culture for the *New York Times*, was for many years the film critic for the *Wall Street Journal*. That is how she came to know Steven Spielberg and to be invited to observe some of the filming of *Schindler's List*. Her mother and stepfather decide to accompany her, making the trip an inquiry also into the problems of personal history. "Like every family," Salamon says, "we had our own mythology, and I accepted it, more or less." Her parents had survived the death camps, and her mother had often told her two daughters how lucky she was and "how happy we were." But Salamon's father died when she was still young. His death "cracked the notion that my parents were infallible, having been tested in the cruelest of history's laboratories. I came to realize how little I knew of what they had been before, when they had been unlucky and unhappy."[12]

Salamon's situation is unusual. A few years after coming to the United States, her parents settled in a small town in southeastern Ohio, where her father was the only physician. They were the only Jews in town, and the second half of her memoir, *The Net of Dreams*, tells the story of what it was like to be a family with such a past in such a place.

Salamon is candid about her knowledge of Eastern Europe before she goes, confessing, for example, to not being able to find the Carpathian Mountains on a map. But she asks too whether she was "avoiding" what she did know, or her version of Calvin Trillin's problem, "That my family was part of the East (uneducated, impoverished, uncultured), not the West. That my family had lived among *shtetl* Jews, or awfully close to them."[13]

In Ohio they had proudly identified themselves as Czech, but the map Salamon studies to prepare for her trip shows that whatever the political boundaries were when her mother was born in 1922, their destination is now "awfully close to the Russian Pale." Mindful of enduring cultural differences, or at least generational ideas about them, she says, "This wasn't the Czechoslovakia of Bohemia or Moravia with its comparatively noble history. This is the land of the *shtetl*—and of Gypsies, Slovaks, Hungarians and Ukranians—an ignorant backwater."[14]

The set of *Shindler's List* and an afternoon at Auschwitz have their revelations, but these turn out to be less important than a visit to Huszt, now in Ukraine and less than 100 kilometers from the borders of the Slovak Republic, Hungary, and Romania. It is where her mother was born and grew up; and from there she was deported to Aushwitz in 1944. "I had always thought of Huszt as my mother's city, not my father's,"[15] but her Eastern European encounter reverses her perspective.

Returning after so many years, her mother is at first disoriented. But after a few hours she finds fragments of the Huszt she knew. There are only a few Jews there now, but among them is a ninety-year old woman who knew Lili Salamon as a child and who calls her now by her Czech name "as though five years, not fifty, had passed since they'd seen each other."[16] Mrs. Klein's son Pityu, a retired lawyer who lives with her, had played a key role in a critical incident in the life of Salamon's father, "his final trip to his past."

Her father had gone to Huzst from Vienna just a few weeks after the War ended, desperate to know what had happened to his first wife and young daughter. From that time on he was a haunted man, his American-born daughter says, who was told by everyone he questioned in Huzst that they were sent away on one of the Nazi transports and almost certainly were murdered when they arrived at Auschwitz. Pityu Klein, then seventeen and well known to Salamon's father as the son of one of the town's other doctors, had helped guide him to this conclusion. Pityu and his parents had survived the war in hiding.

Julie Salamon's encounter in Huzst is filled with drama that is apparent to her even though she cannot speak Czech: "I didn't know it, but Pityu Klein was recounting the day my father had come back to Huszt after the war and taken Pityu with him to find what he could."[17] They found nothing that meant anything to him. His wife and daughter were dead, as were his parents, his three sisters and their husbands, and virtually all of his nieces and nephews. It is only a return to Huszt with her mother that opens up to Salomon her father's most intimate history, for "the anger stayed inside him like a dangerous chemical whose corrosive effects were erratic and largely unknown."[18] With her own losses in the War and the Holocaust, the wish to forget, and signals from her husband after they had settled in the United States, Salomon's mother had never more than barely acknowledged his story, leaving the children to guess at the source of the dark moods that sometimes interrupted their father's otherwise even domestic and professional temperament.

Thus, the story Salamon had always wanted to tell of an isolated but happy Jewish family life in rural Ohio must now be told against the backdrop of her time, brief as it was, in Eastern Europe. The difference that now matters is not between the cultured and the uncultured versions of Eastern Europe that Jewish-American autobiographers recognize ruefully as inherited signs of status, but between forms of memory. Distance—geographical and temporal—had supported family myths. Now an account of the family can be written that is closer to history and experience.

"NO ONE WANTS A MARTYROLOGY INSTEAD OF A HISTORY"

In the fall of 1996, Helen Epstein[19] traveled to Vienna to help celebrate the one hundredth birthday of her mother's cousin. While the family attended the opera and dined at luxurious restaurants, Epstein found herself "acting out." She wore t-shirts and jogging shoes in the elegant hotel dining room and otherwise showed her contempt for where she was. "I was fighting for distance," she says, "the farther removed anyone was from Europe, the better."

At the time of her visit to Austria, she had already completed a history of her mother's family across three generations, which was to be published to great acclaim the following year. In her research she had found a reason for her attitude, the barrier to understanding or admiring her grandfather. As she put it in *Where She Came From*: "I dislike what I perceive as the Vienna in him, his snobbery, his entitlement and self-centeredness."[20]

The truth was, thinking about Central and Eastern Europe had preoccupied Epstein for many years as she reconstructed from a few documents the tragic story of her great grandmother Therese's unhappy marriage and suicide, and then the lives of her grandmother and mother. It is not primarily a Viennese story, but a Czech one, and Epstein reveals in the difference how she came to be so devoted to that nation's history and culture, or the "home" she found in it.

Epstein knows well the autobiographer's situation. "In most families," she says:

> there are multiple versions of the family story: the larger the family, the more various the versions. In my family, as in many families of Holocaust survivors, it is difficult to construct even one. There are too few relatives. They possess few documents.

Disaster has dispersed them. Moreover, each has designed his or her own strategy for coping with the destruction of the world into which they were born. One forgets, the other attenuates, another denies key parts of the narrative."[21]

For Epstein, the part of her own story that matters the most is origins. In her brief time in Eastern Europe, Julie Salamon was satisfied to learn of the circumstances of her parents' marriage. Epstein wants to find the source of the peculiar qualities of the Jewish women in her family who preceded her and how they were able, or not, to make modern roles for themselves in Eastern Europe. Her mother had died in 1989, and within a few months Epstein began what turned out to be a creative journey in family and social history.

Hers is in part a Holocaust story. But she says that "No one wants a martyrology instead of a history,"[22] and, based on a brief account of the family her mother had provided, she was determined to take the story far enough back in time so that she could explain her great grandmother's suicide. Epstein had been a journalism professor at New York University for many years, so she knew something about research. But like many family historians it was difficult for her to find her way to what records or documents remained. Persistence and luck finally took her to an area southeast of Prague. By this time, it was more than genealogy that mattered. It was where her family had come from and what the locations meant for their experience and prospects in the world. By the time she had finished her work, Epstein had been to Czechoslovakia many times. But it was the impact of a very early visit that I want to focus on here.

Starting out in Jilhala, where Epstein's mother thought that her grandmother had lived, proves unsatisfying, not only because there are no useful records there but because this town is so unappealing, dominated by its post-War Communist period architecture and a history of being inhospitable to Jews. But Epstein is transformed by her next stop. Driving through a landscape with the gentle and appealing look of the "pre-industrial world," she stops in Brtnice. It is the kind of village, she observes instantly, in which a Grimm fairy tale might be set. But it is the one in which her narrative actually begins: "The town is surrounded by gentle hills planted with barley and rye, the fields edged by small woods. Smoke rises from cottage chimneys; an occasional wooden cart stands near the road. The scale is child size; small houses, tiny gardens." There was a synagogue once in Brtnice, but there is little sign now that Jews ever lived

Coming into Their Inheritance 345

there. Even so, Epstein writes, "Once I turned off the motor of [the] car, the only sounds were birdsong and the rustle of the wind. I felt a powerful sense of familiarity, as comfortable here as I had been uncomfortable in Jihlava."[23]

It is in Brtnice that Epstein finds the evidence she needs to feel certain that it is where her grandmother's story began. "For the first time," she says, "I began to have a sense of Therese's world. It was not the poor, dusty, Eastern European *shtetl* nor the desperately overcrowded German *Judengasse* but something more moderate and more integrated into Christian life."[24] Jews persecuted in nearby places were welcome in Brtnice. And Jews sought refuge there during the Holocaust. "Anyone who came here," Epstein told herself, "would be drawn to the calm beauty of the town. But another voice inside me was insistent: it said I belonged here."[25] By then she knew something of Czech history, particularly the positioning of Moravian Jewish communities midway on the religious spectrum, "not as secular as the Berliners but not as observant as the *shtetl* Jews either."

In searching for Therese, Epstein had found something in herself she had long suspected was there but could not reach except in the activity of family history, travel, and autobiography. It is summarized in this sentence: "Who would not wish to belong to the people among whom [Therese] lived in a place as lovely as Brtnice?"[26]

But Therese ultimately left for a larger nearby town and then Vienna, where her independent will clashed with the social and domestic conventions of her time. The stories Epstein then tells of Therese's daughter (her grandmother Pepi) and of her own mother derive from this historical condition as it was challenged and modified in Czecholovakia between the Wars. This was the time of the Czech Republic and the heroic liberal leadership of Thomas Masaryk (1850-1937), the philosophy professor who became an internationally respected political leader and was elected in 1920 as the first President of Czecholslovakia. Re-elected twice before he retired in 1935, Masaryk was an antagonist of anti-Semitism in Czech nationalism and promoted a liberal internationalist vision for the newly independent country. As a child, from the talk of her parents, Epstein had come to think of it as a kind of utopia or Camelot. Whether it was or not does not matter. As she searches for signs of generational continuity in Brtnice and elsewhere, Epstein admits that she "did not wish to discover that my sense of connection was imagined or a longing for something that could not be retrieved." Her ambitious narrative makes her origins vividly present in the image of Brtnice and in the activity of family and cultural memory.

"IT'S MY STORY AND THAT MAKES ALL THE DIFFERENCE"

"For many years I forgot Budapest," Harvard French Professor Susan Rubin Suleiman[27] says early in her *Budapest Diary*. And it is easy to see why. She was born in Budapest in 1939, six weeks before the start of the War. In March of 1944, when the Germans invaded Hungary, she was sent away to live with a farm family while her parents considered their fate. They survived the war, and, in 1949 all left the country illegally, leaving everything they had behind. Suleiman remembers it this way:

> For me a big adventure was starting again, like the last year of the war—but this time I was older, aware of the loss involved. When we walked out of our apartment on a hot August day, taking a few belongings as if we were leaving on a brief vacation, I told myself I might never again see that house, that street, that city.[28]

When she did return for the first time, in 1984, it was with her two sons (then age 7 and 14): "I told myself I expected no great revelations from Budapest; but I desired to see again, and let my boys see, the city of my childhood, which had suddenly become for me, now that she was dying, the city of my mother's youth."[29]

There is little romance in Suleiman's memories of her parents. And she is candid about her own often unsatisfying private life:

> This is the story: survival, adaptation, luck. And never—almost never—looking back. What this has cost me, I am only now beginning to tally: abandoned friendships, lost loves, walls build around a solitude so deep that even motherhood cannot fully breach it. To others my life may look like a glittering palace. To me it sometimes feels like a bombed out house, with only the walls still standing.[30]

With such a wartime image, Suleiman directs us to the longtime effects of her earliest experiences. But these rise in her public voice only when she spends the winter and spring of 1993 on academic leave at a new Hungarian institute for advanced study. Having made a life as a successful teacher and scholar in the humanities, Suleiman knows well the situation of "postmodern identities," particularly in a region full of shifting borders and changing names for its towns and cities. "It's unsettling," she says, "like shedding your skin or acquiring false papers."[31] Like other Jewish-American travelers to eastern Europe, Suleiman wants authentic documentation of her family's experience. Hungarians refer to their records in a term she translates as the "Motherbook," an image that appeals of course to Suleiman's metaphoric habits of mind.

Her experience in Budapest was "euphoric." Over the course of the half year she begins to feel at home:

> It's not my real home, found again at last. I'm too much of a foreigner for that, even if I do speak Hungarian. Yet it is one more home....The process of displacement/replacement, which I've thought of as the pattern of my life—each new home displacing the one before it—no longer holds: Budapest doesn't displace or replace any other home but is added to them. When I leave here, the door will not slam behind me.[32]

Unlike most other travelers to Eastern Europe, Suleiman is not very interested in finding distant relatives. She takes her experience in the present to be the essence of her time in Budapest, rather than reaching for what once was. Accordingly, much of *Budapest Diary* is devoted to her interest in literature, theater, and films, and the new friends these yield as she makes her way into the intellectual and artistic life of Budapest. She sees signs of an apparent revival of anti-Semitism in right-wing journalism, but more in the context of Hungarian intellectual life than as an actual threat to the Jewish community (Eastern Europe's largest).

Her search for birth and marriage certificates succeeds in part, but she admits to uneasiness about the activity of tracking down the past: "I have the feeling of living an exciting detective story, and yet when you think about it objectively, it's a poor little story of nothing at all. But it's mine, and that makes all the difference."[33] So, when she hastily plans a trip to Poland to find evidence of her father's life in Gorlice, she does not anticipate its impact. It turns out that city hall has no records at all of its Jewish population. The Nazis had destroyed everything. And no Jews live there now. But by chance she learns that a Jewish refugee from Gorlice, now living in Australia, is just then visiting his birthplace to settle a property claim. He is the guest of an elderly non-Jewish Pole who is writing a history of Jewish life in the area.

An intense few hours of conversation, including uncertain but suggestive memories by her new Polish friends of her father's family and its

Jewish circle, revives Suleiman's spirits. She appears "reborn" to her travel companion from Budapest. And in her reflections on her unexpected mood she reflects the weaving of historical witness, Jewish affiliation, and the wish to document the ties of generations in autobiographical encounters with Eastern Europe:

> Why feel happy, in this city where not a single Jew was still living, where even the paper traces of the Jews had been so thoroughly obliterated that my father, as far as documents were concerned, had never been born? Was it because I had met a living Jew after all, who had walked these streets as a young man and remembered his youth as beautiful? Was it because I had met extraordinary Poles who had helped Jews at their own expense and were continuing to help them? Or was it simply because I had carried out my once vague plan, visited the city of my father's birth and found some small trace of his family?[34]

Whatever the primary source of her fresh mood and new perspective on her experience, we know that being in Poland and Hungary is indispensable, particularly to someone like Suleiman struggling for an expressive turn in her life that will make her a different scholar and person: "We drove back through the high mountains as the sun was setting, lighting the horizon in pale reds and pinks and etching the far off peaks in deep purplish blue."[35]

There are signs that Suleiman's own horizon, the prospects she has for integrating her past and present, is similarly rich and meaningful. But she is a realist too about her experience and skeptical about the durability of Eastern European encounters for American Jews. In an interview that followed publication of *Budapest Diary*, she says:

> Going there wasn't like trying to recreate [my mother's] whole life, but it was a connection that could only be established by the experience of looking. It's not so much what you find, because you usually don't find much. It's the experience of walking and trying to find something; taking the train and getting off the train and finding the city hall and trying to see whether you could even find the house where she was born. Does it still exist? The experience of the search was what was interesting or compelling or irresistible or necessary, rather than what you actually found when you got there.[36]

So it is for Suleiman. But, as I hope is evident, I do not think she can speak for autobiographers like Epstein and Salomon, who found in Eastern Europe reasons and resources essential to their mature Jewish-American identities.

CONCLUSION: NARRATING NOSTALGIA

Can we choose an inheritance? Biology says no, but history and culture say yes, or at least maybe. In the Jewish historical dramas of diaspora and assimilation, profoundly disturbed by the Holocaust and then resumed in the United States, there are innumerable variations of inheritance according to geography. They seek reconciliation of painful and productive memories. These might be classified as forms of nostalgia as they have been defined by the Russian émigré cultural theorist Svetlana Boym.[37] "Restorative nostalgia" wants reconstruction of the emblems and rituals of a homeland. "Reflective nostalgia" signifies the gap between personal identity and what is sought and found in the past. According to Boym, "This defamiliarization and a sense of distance drives [reflective nostalgics] to tell their story, to narrate the relationship between past, present, and future."

Our three Jewish-American autobiographers are reflective in spirit, but still differ in their narrative nostalgia. Julie Salamon's is an instrumental encounter with Eastern Europe, fruitful in the revision of family myth and in her relationship with her long dead father. Helen Epstein's Eastern European commitment is historical, a deep and durable resource for her Jewish identity. The benefits of Susan Rubin Suleiman's time in Hungary and Poland are mainly professional, for her intellectual identity is stronger at this time in her life than what is Hungarian or Jewish in her make-up.

Following their return to Czernowitz with her parents, Marianne Hirsch and Leo Spitzer wrote that "Children of refugees inherit their parents' knowledge of the fragility of place, their suspicion of the notion of home."[38] And so, what Jewish-Americans make of an Eastern European inheritance—that "old *shtetl* outlook" or otherwise—is a sign of how memory and experience can interact on behalf of a more benevolent view. For our best autobiographers the ratio between the two is adjustable and representable, precisely because they have made the trip home.

NOTES

[1] Irving Howe, *World of Our Fathers* (New York: Simon & Schuster, 1976).
[2] Vivian Bornick, *The Situation and the Story: The Art of Personal Narrative* (New York: Farrar, Straus, and Giroux, 2002).
[3] Abraham Trillin, *Messages from My Father* (New York: Farrar, Straus, and Giroux, 1996).
[4] Ibid., 48.
[5] Ibid., 57.
[6] Dorothy Gallagher, *How I Came into My Inheritance: And Other True Stories* (New York: Random House, 2001).
[7] Ibid., 184-85.
[8] Ibid., 186.
[9] Ibid., 187.
[10] Eva Hoffman, *Exit into History: A Journey Through the New Eastern Europe* (New York: Viking, 1993).
[11] Julie Salamon, *The Net of Dreams: A Family's Search for a Rightful Place* (New York: Random House, 1996), 7.
[12] Ibid., 7.
[13] Ibid., 13.
[14] Ibid., 13.
[15] Ibid., 186.
[16] Ibid., 188.
[17] Ibid., 189.
[18] Ibid., 190.
[19] Helen Epstein, *Where She Came From: A Daughter's Search for Her Mother's History* (Boston: Little Brown, 1997).
[20] Ibid., 143.
[21] Ibid., 13.
[22] Ibid., 24.
[23] Ibid., 38.
[24] Ibid., 40.
[25] Ibid., 45.
[26] Ibid., 60.
[27] Susan Rubin Suleiman, *Budapest Diary: In Search of the Motherbook* (Lincoln: University of Nebraska Press, 1996).
[28] Ibid., 8.
[29] Ibid., 11.

30 Ibid., 225.
31 Ibid., 106.
32 Ibid., 171.
33 Ibid., 167.
34 Ibid., 211.
35 Ibid., 211.
36 Marjorie Agosin, *Uncertain Travelers: Conversations with Jewish Women Immigrants to America* (ed. Mary G. Berg; Hanover: Brandeis University Press, 1999), 150.
37 Svetlana Boym, *The Future of Nostalgia* (New York: Basic Book, 2001).
38 Marianne Hirsch and Leo Spitzer, "We Would Not Have Come Without You: Generations of Nostalgia," *American Imago* 59:3 (2002): 253-76.

Other volumes in the
Studies of Jewish Civilization Series
distributed by Nebraska University Press:

2001 - Volume 11   "A Land Flowing with Milk and Honey"
                    Visions of Israel from Biblical to
                    Modern Times

2002 - Volume 12   Millennialism from the Hebrew Bible to
                    the Present

2003 - Volume 13   Spiritual Dimensions of Judaism

2003 - Volume 14   Women and Judaism

2005 - Volume 15   Food & Judaism